James Harvey Sanders

Horse-Breeding

Being the general principles of heredity applied to the business of breeding horses

James Harvey Sanders

Horse-Breeding

Being the general principles of heredity applied to the business of breeding horses

ISBN/EAN: 9783337149345

Printed in Europe, USA, Canada, Australia, Japan

Cover: Foto ©Andreas Hilbeck / pixelio.de

More available books at **www.hansebooks.com**

HORSE-BREEDING;

BEING THE

GENERAL PRINCIPLES OF HEREDITY

APPLIED TO

The Business of Breeding Horses,

WITH

INSTRUCTIONS FOR THE MANAGEMENT

OF

STALLIONS, BROOD MARES AND YOUNG FOALS,

AND

SELECTION OF BREEDING STOCK.

BY

J. H. SANDERS,

Founder of "The Breeder's Gazette," "Breeders' Trotting Stud Book," "Percheron Stud Book," Honorary member of the Chicago Eclectic Medical Society, and of the Illinois Veterinary Medical Association, etc.

CHICAGO:
J. H. SANDERS PUB. CO.
1893.

TABLE OF CONTENTS.

PREFACE 5
PREFACE TO THE REVISED AND ILLUSTRATED EDITION 9

CHAPTER I.

GENERAL PRINCIPLES OF BREEDING.—General Laws of Heredity—Causes of Variation from Original Types—Modifications from Changed Conditions of Life—Accidental Variations or "Sports"—Extent of Hereditary Influence—The Formation of Breeds—In-Breeding and Crossing—Value of Pedigree—Relative Size of Sire and Dam—Influence of First Impregnation—Effect of Imagination on Color of Progeny—Effect of Change of Climate on the Generative Organs—Controlling the Sex.. 11

CHAPTER II.

STALLIONS, BROOD MARES AND FOALS.—Selection of Breeding-Stock—General Management of the Stallion—Controlling the Stallion When in Use—When Mares Should be Tried—The Number of Mares to be Served—Effect of Age on the Fertility of the Stallion—Effect of Age on the Quality of the Get—Percentage of Foals to Mares Served—Management of the Stallion After the Season Closes—Effects of Castration on Stallions—Fighting Between Stallions—The Brood Mare—Causes of Barrenness in Brood Mares—The Productive Period in Brood Mares—Time of Foaling and Period of Gestation—General Suggestions as to Food and Nursing—Feeding the Young Foal—Weaning the Foal—Effect of Exercise on Development—Breaking the Foal—Views of Dr. Reynolds, of Liverpool, on Horses..................................... 88

CHAPTER III.

BREEDS OF HORSES.—General Features—Thoroughbreds—Trotters, Roadsters, Pacers and Saddle Horses—Orloffs or Russian Trotters—French Coach Horses—Cleveland Bays—Hackneys—Shire or Cart Horses—Clydesdales—Percherons—Boulonnais—Other French Draft Breeds—The Suffolk Punch—Other Breeds. 184

CHAPTER IV.

DISEASES PECULIAR TO BREEDING-STOCK.—Hygiene of the Eye—The Eye as Affected by the Teeth—Umbilical Hernia in Young Foals—Scours, or Diarrhœa, in Colts—Strangles, or Distemper.——THE STALLION.—External Injuries—Inflammation of the Penis—Inflammation of the Testicles—Cancer of the Penis and Sheath—Prolapse, or Paralysis of the Penis—Scrotal Hernia—Waterbag, So-Called—Excessive Venery—Non-emission of Semen, or Proudness, So-Called—Sexual Sluggishness—Spermatorrhœa—Vesicular Eruptions on the Penis—Foul Sheath—Masturbation—Cryptorchids (Ridgelings, So-Called).——THE BROOD MARE.—Barrenness—Nymphomania—Tumors Within the Vagina and Uterus—Leucorrhœa, or So-Called Whites—Colt-Founder, So-Called—Œdema During Pregnancy—Superimpregnation—Heat During Pregnancy—Laceration of the Rectum—Abortion—Difficult Parturition—Laceration of the Perinæum—Mange—Lice on Colts..293

CHAPTER V.

DISEASES OF THE GENERATIVE ORGANS.—Congestion and Inflammation of the Testicles (Orchitis)—Sarcocele—Hydrocele—Dropsy of the Scrotum—Varicocele—Abnormal Number of Testicles—Degeneration of the Testicles—Warts on the Penis—Degeneration of Penis (Papilloma, Epithelioma)—Extravasation of Blood in the Penis—Paralysis of the Penis—Self-Abuse (Masturbation)—Mal du Coit (Dourine)—Castration of Stallions—Conditions Favorable to Successful Castration—Castration of Cryptorchids (Ridgelings)—Pain After Castration—Bleeding After Castration—Strangulated Spermatic Cord—Swelling of the Sheath, Penis, and Abdomen—Phymosis and Paraphymosis—Tumors on the Spermatic Cord—Castration of the Mare—Sterility—Indications of Pregnancy—Duration of Pregnancy—Hygiene of the Pregnant Mare—Extra-Uterine Gestation—Moles (Anidian Monsters)—Cystic Disease of the Walls of the Womb (Vesicular Mole)—Dropsy of the Womb—Dropsy of the Amnios—Dropsy of the Limbs, Perinæum, and Abdomen—Cramps of the Hind Limbs—Constipation—Paralysis—Prolonged Retention of the Fœtus (Foal)—Abortion—Symptoms of Parturition—Natural Presentation—Difficult Parturition—Premature Labor Pains—Difficult Parturition From Narrow Pelvis—Fractured Hip-Bones—Tumors in the Vagina and Pelvis—Hernia of the Womb—Twisting of the Neck of the Womb—Effusion of Blood

CONTENTS.

in the Vaginal Walls—Calculus (Stone) and Tumor in the Bladder—Impaction of the Rectum with Fæces—Spasm of the Neck of the Womb—Fibrous Bands Constricting or Crossing the Neck of the Womb—Fibrous Constriction of Vagina or Vulva—Fœtus Adherent to the Walls of the Womb—Excessive Size of the Fœtus—Constriction of a Member by the Navel String—Water in the Head (Hydrocephalus) of the Foal—General Dropsy of the Fœtus—Swelling of the Fœtus With Gas—Emphysema—Contractions of Muscles—Dropsy of the Abdomen in the Foal (Ascites)—Tumors of the Fœtus (Inclosed Ovum)—Monstrosities—Entrance of Twins Into the Passage at Once—Table of Wrong Presentations—Fore Limbs Incompletely Extended—One Fore Limb Crossed Over the Back of the Neck—Fore Limb Bent at the Knee—Fore Limb Turned Back From the Shoulder—Head Bent Down Between the Fore Limbs—Head Turned Back on the Shoulder—Head Turned Upward on the Back—Hind Feet Engaged in the Pelvis—Anterior Presentation With Back Turned to One Side—Back of the Foal Turned to the Floor of the Pelvis—Hind Presentation With Leg Bent at Hock—Hind Presentation With Legs Bent Forward From the Hip—Hind Presentations With the Back Turned Sideways or Downward—Presentation of the Back—Presentation of Breast and Abdomen—Embryotomy—Flooding (Bleeding From the Womb)—Eversion of the Womb—Rupture or Laceration of the Womb—Ruptures of the Vagina- Inflammation of the Womb and Peritoneum—Leucorrhœa—Laminitis, or Founder, Following Parturition—Diseases of the Udder and Teats (Congestion and Inflammation of the Udder)—Tumors of the Udder—Sore Teats, Scabs, Cracks, Warts.............335

CHAPTER VI.

DENTITION OF HORSES.—Incisors of Foal at Birth—Incisors of Foal at Birth—Incisors of Foal at Two Months—Incisors of Foal at Six Months—Incisors of Foal at One Year—Molar Teeth of Foal at One Year—Molars of Foal at Two Years—Incisors of Cart Filly at Two Years—Incisors of Horse at Three Years—Incisors of Horse at Four Years—Incisors of Horse at Five Years—Incisors of Horse at Six Years—Incisors of Horse at Seven Years—Mclars of Horse at Two Years and Seven Months—Molars of Horse at Three Years and Eight Months—Incisors of Mare (Solace) at Ten Years—Incisors of Horse (Peep-o'-Day Boy) at Eight Years—Incisors of Horse (Lothario) at Twelve Years.................404

PREFACE.

A very large proportion of the matter contained in this volume was prepared for publication several years ago when I had more leisure to study and write upon the topics herein considered, and when I was fresher from the field of practical experience than now. Much of it has since been printed in fragments at various times, some of it in the form of editorial articles for the monthly journal that was so long under my management, some in essays or addresses at meetings and conventions of breeders of live stock, and still other portions of it in the weekly stock-breeders' paper that for more than three years past has occupied my almost constant attention. A little more than four years ago I thought myself about ready to gather up the fragments that were already prepared and give them to the public in book form; but other and more pressing duties intervened, and it is only within a few months past, having been relieved from official duties that had for three years claimed all the time that I could possibly spare from the management of *The Breeder's Gazette*, that I have found leisure to look over and arrange the matter which has been gradually accumulating for so long a period. I give it now to the public, realizing that, in common with all human effort, it must needs be far from perfect, but with a feeling of satisfaction in knowing that the work has at least been conscientiously done; and that such parts of it as are not derived from a knowledge bought with my own personal experiences have, for their foundation, the teachings of others who are regarded as eminent authorities in the specialties upon which I have quoted them. To the introductory chapters, wherein the general principles of breeding are discussed, I have given much thought; and I am confident they may be studied with profit, not only by horse-breeders, but by all who are disposed to investigate the laws which govern the transmission of hereditary qualities from parent to offspring, whether it be in the human species or in the lower orders of animal life. In the descriptions of breeds I have endeavored to be judicially candid and fair; to "nothing extenuate nor set down aught in malice"; and where controverted points have been touched upon, while I have endeavored to state my views plainly, and to sustain them by such arguments and facts as to my mind are conclusive, yet I have tried to do so in a manner that would not prove offensive to those whose opinions and conclusions may differ from my own.

Aside from the introductory chapters on the general principles of breeding, which are applicable alike to all breeds and all varieties of live stock, I have endeavored to make the work a practical guide to the management of the breeding stud—a book which any farmer or farmer's boy, or any novice in the business of horse-breeding, may read and study with profit. In the course of my long experience as editor of a live-stock paper, covering a period of about sixteen years, the constantly recurring questions that have been sent in for answer have served to direct my attention especially to the points upon which information is most frequently sought, and these points I have endeavored to most fully answer in the pages which follow.

While I have not intended that this book should in any sense be regarded as a veterinary work, yet I have thought I might add greatly to its practical usefulness by incorporating with it the material portions of several articles, prepared at my request by Prof. James Law, of Cornell University, N. Y., and previously published under my direction, wherein he treats of some of the diseases to which stallions, brood mares and young foals are especially subject. And I have also added a number of pages of matter of a similar nature, prepared especially for this work by N. H. Paaren, M. D., State Veterinarian of Illinois, whose high scientific attainments and many years of extensive practice have especially fitted him to give valuable counsel upon such topics.

In the belief that the book will be found interesting to all students of the science and art of breeding, and especially helpful to those who have the care and management of breeding studs, whether on a large or small scale, it is given to the public with a full consciousness of the fact that it does not contain a tithe of what might profitably be written or said upon the subject.

J. H. SANDERS.

CHICAGO, Feb. 1, 1885.

PREFACE TO THE REVISED AND ILLUSTRATED EDITION.

A little over eight years have elapsed since this volume was first given to the public, and so favorable has been the reception accorded it that edition after edition has been called for, and many thousand copies have been printed and sold, both in this country and in Europe, it having been translated and republished in Germany under the especial supervision and patronage of Herman Von Nathusius. From time to time since the first edition was published many minor changes have been made in the text and a considerable amount of new matter has been furnished as an appendix. But the demand for the work has continued so active that I have thought it but justice to the public as well as to myself that I should now thoroughly revise the work and incorporate therein such additional matter as the experience of the past eight years has suggested, to bring it more fully up to the requirements of the present day. Accordingly the entire work has been carefully gone over, some portions relating to matters that were in controversy at the time the work was written have been eliminated and much new matter, especially in relation to the various breeds, has been added. The original chapter concerning the breeding of trotting horses treated at considerable length of what was then a matter of earnest controversy; and the correctness of the principles of breeding therein laid down has been so thoroughly demonstrated by the experience of the world since then, and so generally adopted, that I have felt constrained to leave that portion of the work substantially as it was originally written, although to the young breeder of to-day it may appear strange that so much space should be devoted to what ought to have been obvious to all intelligent men without waiting for the confirmation which the experience of the past ten years has furnished.

The chapter by Prof. Law on "Diseases of the Generative Organs," taken by permission from the recent Government publication on the "Diseases of Horses," more especially that portion devoted to difficult parturition, will, I am sure, be found a most valuable addition to the work.

In the illustrations of the various breeds I have not attempted to give, in any case, a picture of *the model horse* of the breed, but rather to present an illustration that should in each case be *typical and characteristic* of the breed represented; and in this the artist has been in most cases reasonably successful.

Feeling certain that with the changes made and the matter now for the first time incorporated in the work the book will prove vastly more valuable to the practical breeder than the previous editions, it is respectfully submitted to the public.

J. H. SANDERS.

CHICAGO, September, 1893.

CHAPTER I.

GENERAL PRINCIPLES OF BREEDING.

It is stated in Holy Writ that "God made man a little lower than the angels," and by common consent the horse is usually placed next highest in the scale of living things. It will not be inappropriate then, in a treatise mainly devoted to the breeding of this, the noblest of the brute creation, to discuss some of the general principles which govern the transmission of hereditary qualities from parent to offspring, and which are beyond a question substantially the same throughout all animal life. Through the practical application of these laws to the business of breeding domestic animals, which for many years past has so largely occupied the attention of intelligent men in Europe and America, the great mass of our agricultural population have become familiar with their inexorable power and force; and with a knowledge of the immutability of these laws has come a realization of the stern fact that the human species furnishes no exception to their operation.

The passage in the Decalogue, which declares that the iniquities of the fathers are visited upon the children unto the third and fourth generations, is clothed with a new and startling significance since it has come to be generally understood that this declaration is a concise statement of the operations of a physiological law, from which there is absolutely no escape. That the physical as well as the mental and moral infirmities and peculiarities of the father and mother are visited upon the children, even *beyond* the third and fourth generations, is as true of the human family as it is of cattle, horses, sheep, and swine.

It is not my purpose to attempt to controvert the principle that "all men are born free and equal," which stands as the corner-stone of our political system. Undoubtedly this is true when applied to "rights under the law," but that all men are born physically, morally, and intellectually equal will scarcely be claimed by the most ardent admirer of our democratic institutions. There is a solid foundation, in physiological fact, for the admiration with which the "first families of Virginia" have been regarded, and the same may be said of many of the families of New England and other parts of our country. Dr. Oliver Wendell Holmes makes his "Autocrat of the Breakfast Table" give utterance to his belief in this great truth and his faith in the value of pedigree in the human family when he says: "I go always, other things being equal, for the man who inherits family traditions and the cumulative humanities of at least four or five generations." To know that a man or woman is descended from an old family whose record has been honorable, beyond reproach and without taint, is the very best possible evidence, next to his own individual record, that he also is worthy of confidence and respect; and a taint in the blood of an opposite character should certainly be regarded with as much distrust as a similar taint in the blood of any of our domestic animals, *and for the same reasons.* What is "bred in the bone" will be transmitted. Beauty of form and feature, strength and force of intellect, elegance and grace of motion, integrity and honesty of character, susceptibility of culture and refinement, or boorish stupidity, as well as all the virtues and vices, are as clearly transmissible and inheritable qualities in man as are the color of the hair and the shape of the body in horses and cattle.

A subject of such vital importance, involving as it does so much of weal or woe to the human race, and which places in the hands of intelligent persons such power over the animal kingdom, may well command the attention of thinking men, aside from its practical value as an aid to the reproduction of desirable forms and qualities in our domestic animals. It has been said of Bakewell, one of the first great improvers of live stock in Great Britain, that he regarded the animals upon his farm as wax in his hands, out of which in good time he could mould any form that he desired to create. In fact, all our domestic animals have been, to a great degree, moulded and fashioned by the hand of man. The same uniformity that now characterizes the bison, the elk and the deer probably belonged to the horse, the cow, the sheep and the swine, in a state of nature. The ponderous English Cart horse and the diminutive Shetland pony, are all believed to have descended from an original as uniform in its characteristics as are the members of a herd of bison upon our western prairies. The Shorthorn, the Hereford, the Devon, the Jersey, and all of the various breeds into which our cattle are now divided, are descended, it is believed, from the same original type.

CAUSES OF VARIATION FROM ORIGINAL TYPES.

That the changed conditions of life to which animals have been subjected by domestication—the variety of uses to which they have been put, the food upon which they have subsisted, the climate in which they have been reared, and selection for special uses—have produced the varieties which are now so apparent, is generally admitted. Very much of this divergence is due to climatic influences, which alone are sufficiently powerful, in the changes of food and of habit which necessarily follow, to account for nearly all the varieties which have been produced. A warm climate and a bountiful supply of nutritious food from birth to maturity promotes growth and development, while a scanty supply of nutrition and a rigorous climate have a positive tendency in the opposite direction. A knowledge of the effect of heat and cold upon growth and development has been taken advantage of by breeders for the purpose of producing dwarf specimens. The breeder of Bantam fowls is careful to have his chicks hatched late in the season, so that the early approach of cold weather may arrest development. The bleak, barren and tempestuous islands (lying in the high latitude of 59 and 60 deg.) north of Scotland, with their scanty subsistence and long winters, have dwarfed the horse of that country until he appears as the diminutive Shetland pony, while, from probaably the same original, the rich herbage, nutritious grains and mild climate 10 deg. further south, on the European coast, have given us the immense draft horses of ancient Normandy and Flanders.

But while climate and the necessarily accompanying influences have done much to cause the divergence which now exists in races that were once uniform, selection by the hand of man has also been actively at work, in some cases co-operating with the influences of climate, thereby accelerating the transformation, and in others counteracting its effect. We have an illustration of this in the horses of Canada. It is quite evident that the causes that have given us the tough, shaggy pony of Lower Canada, if continued without interruption for a succession of generations, and accelerated by the efforts of breeders in selecting animals for the purpose of reproduction, with the same object constantly in view, would in course of time give us a race as diminutive as the ponies of the Himalaya Mountains or of the Shetland Islands. But this climatic influence has been retarded and counteracted by Canadian breeders, who have rejected the smaller specimens for breeding purposes, and have constantly drawn upon the large draft breeds of Europe for fresh crosses. To such an extent has this infusion of fresh blood been carried, especially in Upper Canada, or Ontario, that the influences of climate have been overpowered and the progression during the last twenty-five years has been decidedly in the opposite direction. The efforts of Canadian breeders in this direction have been aided materially by the improved condition of agriculture in the Dominion, which has led to a more liberal system of feeding and more thorough protection from the rigor of the climate. And thus the forces and influences of nature, in some cases aided and in others counteracted by the efforts of man, have constantly been at work, breaking up the uniformity which originally characterized all our domestic animals, until divergence from the original type has become, in many instances, truly wonderful.

The influences of selection, in creating divergence from a type singularly uniform, finds a most striking illustration in the case of the domestic pigeon, of which there are now nearly 300 known varieties, more or less distinct, and all probably descended from the common wild rock pigeon. Among these varieties the divergence is remarkable, not only in the color of the plumage, which in the original is uniform, but in the shape and markings of the various parts. Who would believe, at first thought, that the pouters, the carriers, the runts, the barbs, the fantails, the owls, the tumblers, the frill-backs, the jacobins, the trumpeters, etc., and all their sub-varieties, with differences so strongly marked, are descended from one common parent stock! Yet that this is true, and that all the varieties from the original type have resulted from changed conditions of life, climatic influences and artificial selection and crossing, is generally admitted by naturalists.

It is one of the principles of heredity, that when there is a great uniformity in a species divergences from the usual type in the offspring are slight and rare; but when this uniformity, from no matter what cause, has been broken up, divergences in the offspring are frequent and great, although there is always present a tendency, more or less powerful, to revert to the original type. This tendency is most frequently manifested when breeds or races, widely differing in their present forms, are crossed upon each other. In such cases, or violent crosses as they are called, it frequently happens that the progeny resembles neither parent, but shows strong marks of the type from which both of its ancestors originally sprung. Darwin gives numerous illustrations of this tendency to reversion in his experiments with pigeons of various breeds and colors, one of which I quote, as follows:

I paired a mongrel female barb-fantail with a mongrel male barb-spot, neither of which mongrels had the least blue about them. Let it be remembered that blue barbs are excessively rare; that spots, as has been already stated, were perfectly characterized in the year 1676, and breed perfectly true; this likewise is the case with white fantails, so much so that I have never heard of white fantails throwing any other color. Nevertheless, the offspring from the above two mongrels were of exactly the same blue tint as that of the wild rock pigeon, from the Shetland Islands, over

GENERAL PRINCIPLES OF BREEDING. 19

the whole back and wings; the double black wing bars were equally conspicuous; the tail was exactly alike in all its characters, and the croup was pure white; the head, however, was tinted with a shade of red, evidently derived from the spot, and was of a paler blue than in the rock pigeon, as was the stomach. So that two black barbs, a red spot and a white fantail, as the four purely-bred grandparents, produced a bird of the same general blue color, together with every characteristic mark, as in the wild *Columba livia*, or rock pigeon.*

This tendency to reversion in different breeds of domestic animals when crossed accounts for many of the disappointments which breeders experience in their efforts to improve their stock, and serves greatly to complicate the breeding problem.

MODIFICATIONS PRODUCED BY CHANGED CONDITIONS OF LIFE.

It is quite certain, from what we know of the effect of climate and of changed habits upon animals in a state of domestication, that if two branches of the same tribe or species, essentially alike in every feature, should, by some chance, become separated and compelled to subsist under widely different conditions of life, being left entirely to themselves and the operation of natural laws, in course of time a

---

*Those who have a desire to investigate this subject, as illustrated by the breeding of pigeons, will find a very full history of the various breeds, their processes of formation, and the effects of selection and crossing of breeds, in Darwin's "Variations of Animals and Plants under Domestication," Vol. I, pp. 163 to 272.

very marked difference would occur in their structure or habits. There is a tendency in all animal life to adapt itself to the conditions under which it must exist; but the change may be so abrupt and complete as to overcome this tendency; and, under such a condition, the race would speedily become extinct, or gradually die out with a few generations of sickly and enfeebled descendants; but, under circumstances less abrupt and unfavorable, a few might survive, being those individuals that, from some peculiarity of organization, suffered least from the change. These animals, in their turn, would reproduce the peculiarities of their race, modified to some extent by the new conditions which environed them; and these again would produce animals still better adapted to the new order, until, in course of time, we should have a race widely differing from the original type, created or evolved by a survival of those best fitted to exist under the new order of things, and remoulded and refashioned by the changed conditions of life.

If we accept the commonly-received doctrine of the origin of the human race—that is, that all mankind are descended from a common parentage—we are driven to the conclusion that all the differences which are so apparent in the human family at the present day are the result of the operation of the law of adaptation to changed conditions and of climatic influences, to which I have just referred. And yet there is as great a divergence from a uniform type in the human race as in any of the lower orders of animals that are recognized as belonging to a single species.

In the practical business of breeding domestic animals it is important that due prominence be given to the operation of the laws to which I have alluded, for it follows that a race or breed most perfectly adapted to a certain locality, a certain mode of life, conditions of climate, and character of subsistence, may, in time, when transported to a distant clime, or even when subjected to changed conditions of life in the same locality, lose all its distinguishing characteristics and become practically worthless. On the other hand, a race of but little value in its native state may be so modified by a change in climatic conditions, or by the character, quality and quantity of the aliment furnished, as to become of the highest value to the breeder; and these modifications, although frequently so slow as to be almost imperceptible in a single generation, are accelerated by the power of inheritance under a continuation of the conditions which inaugurated them. A high or low temperature, and abundant or scanty nutrition, will, as before stated, affect physical development either favorably or unfavorably. Elevated plains, low marshes, and mountain ranges are each adapted to support a species of animal life in some respects distinct from the others; and hence a knowledge of the effect of the various climatic conditions, and of the different kinds of food, becomes of the utmost importance to the breeder in determining the kinds of domesticated animals that he can produce with profit.

There is perhaps no variety of animals that has been domesticated by man in which the effects of climate and nutrition are more apparent than in horses. Temperate regions, grassy plains, and, consequently, abundant nutrition, produce increased size and strength; mountain ranges, with bleak, cold climate and scanty subsistence, dwarf the frame and produce the hardy, diminutive pony. The fertile plains of Germany and Flanders, with their salubrious climate and abundant herbage, have been the home, from the very earliest period of history, of the ponderous draft horses which still distinguish that region, and have been the sources from which all the countries of the world have drawn the foundation for their draft breeds. The bleak and barren Shetland Islands, and the mountainous tract which lies between the plains of India and the crest of the great Himalaya range, are the homes of races of diminutive ponies, rough, shaggy and hardy. The highest inhabited land of Asia, which forms the source of the Ganges, the Indus and the Bramapootra—a country as rugged and bleak as can well be conceived—contains immense numbers of small, sinewy and agile horses. The extreme regions bounded by the mountains of Siberia on the north, the Sea of Okhotsk on the east, and the Little Altaic Mountains on the west—the home of the Kalmucks—abound in a tough and hardy race of ponies.

I have not been able to find an exception to this law of nature in the history of the world. Wherever the horse has existed for centuries on rich, fertile plains, and in a temperate climate, we find him distinguished for size and strength; wherever he has been the inhabitant of inhospitable, mountainous regions he becomes diminutive and hardy. Of course these results have obtained where the horse is left largely to take care of himself. Man may do much by supplying warm stables and abundant food, and by selection, to counteract the influence of climate, but in spite of his utmost care the tendency will constantly be as Nature has pointed out. Mountainous regions and a rigorous climate will produce the smallest, toughest, hardiest horses (as we have seen in the New England Morgans and the Canadian ponies of our own country), while our rich and fertile prairies and luxuriant valleys are adapted by nature to be the home of the ponderous draft horse.

Prof. Low in his great work, "The Domesticated Animals of the British Islands," has a very interesting chapter on the effect of climatic influences upon animal life, from which I quote the following:

The effect of heat is everywhere observed, as it modifies the secretions which give color to the skin, and the degree of covering provided for the protection of the body, whether wool or hair. In the case of the human species the effects of temperature on the color of the skin, and, with this, on the color of the eyes and hair, are sufficiently known. We cannot pass from the colder parts of Europe to the warmer without marking the progressive diversities of color, from the light complexion of the northern nations to the swarthy tinge of the Spaniards, Italians, and Greeks, and when we have crossed the Mediterranean into Africa the dark color, which is proper to all the warmer regions of the globe, everywhere meets the eye. The Jews, naturally as fair as the other inhabitants of Syria, become gradually darker as they have been for a longer or shorter time acclimated in the warmer countries; and on the plains of the Ganges they are as dark as Hindoos. The Portuguese who have been naturalized in the African colonies of their nation have become entirely black. If we suppose, indeed, the great races of mankind to have been called into existence in different regions we must suppose that they were born with the color, as well as with the other attributes, suited to the climates of the countries which they were to inhabit. It accords with this supposition that the Negro remains always black, even in the highest latitudes to which he has been carried; and that the black races of the Eastern Islands retain the color proper to them in the mild temperature of Van Diemen's Land. The Mongolian, even in the coldest regions of Northern Asia, retains the hue distinctive of his family, but with a continually deepening shade as he approaches to the inter-tropical countries. The native of China, of a dull yellow tint at Pekin, is at Canton nearly as dark as a Lascar The American Indian retains his distinctive copper hue amid the snows of Labrador, but on the shores of the Caribbean Sea becomes nearly as black as an African.

Temperature likewise affects the size and form of the body. The members of the Caucasian group towards the Arctic Circle are of far inferior bulk of body to the natives of temperate countries. The Central Asiatics, in elevated plains, are sturdy and short, the result of an expansion of the chest; the Hindoos are of slender form and low physical powers, so that they have almost always yielded to the superior force of the northern nations from the first invasion of the Macedonians to the ultimate establishment of European power in the Peninsula. The Negro, on the other hand, in the hottest and most pestilential regions of the habitable earth, where the Caucasian either perishes or becomes as slender as a stripling, is of a strength and stature which would be deemed great in any class of men—affording a strong presumption in favor of the opinion of the distinctness of his race and its special adaptation to the region in which it has been placed.

In quadrupeds the effects of temperature are everywhere observable in the covering provided for their bodies, whether wool or hair, and which in the same species is always more abundant in the colder than in the warmer countries. In all quadrupeds there is a growth of down or wool underneath the hair, and more or less mixed with it. In warm countries this wool is little if at all developed; but in the colder it frequently becomes the principal covering of the skin, forming along with the hair a thick fur. In the warmest regions the domestic sheep produces scarcely any wool; in temperate countries he has a fleece properly so called, and in the coldest of all his wool is mixed with long hair which covers it externally. The wool, an imperfect conductor of heat, preserves the natural temperature of the body, and thus protects the animal from cold, while the long hair is fitted to throw off the water which falls upon the body in rain or snow. But in the warm season the wool, which would be incommodious, falls off, to be renewed before winter, while the hair always remains. The dog, too, has a coat of wool which he loses in countries of great heat, but which in colder countries grows so as to form along with the hair a thick fur, so that in certain cold countries there have been formed breeds of dogs to produce wool for clothing. The dogs of Europe conveyed to warm countries frequently lose even their hair and become as naked as elephants, and in every country their fur is suited to the nature of the climate.

Similar to the effects of temperature is that of humidity, the hair becoming longer and more oily in the moister countries. Even within the limits of our own islands, the ox of the western coasts, exposed to the humid vapors of the Atlantic, has longer hair than the ox of the eastern districts. Even the effects of continued exposure to winds and storms may modify parts of the animal form. There are certain breeds of gallinaceous fowls which are destitute of the rump, so called. Most of the common fowls of the Isle of Arran, on the coast of Scotland, have this peculiarity. This little island consists of high hills, on which scarcely a bush exists to shelter the animals which inhabit it from the continued gales of the Atlantic. The feathers of a long tail might incommode the animals, and therefore, we may suppose, they disappear; and were peacocks to be reared under similar circumstances it is probable that, in the course of successive generations, they would lose the beautiful appendage which they bring from their native jungles.

The effects, likewise, of altitude are to be numbered among those which modify the characters of animals. In general the animals of mountains are smaller and more agile than those of the same species inhabiting plains. In man the pulse increases in frequency as he ascends into the atmosphere, so that, while at the level of the sea the number of beats is 70 in a minute, at the height of 4,000 feet the number exceeds 100. The air being rarer a greater quantity of it must be drawn into the lungs to afford the oxygen

GENERAL PRINCIPLES OF BREEDING. 27

necessary to carry off the excess of carbon in the system. But gradually, as man and other animals become naturalized in an elevated country, the digestive and respiratory organs, and with these the capacity of the chest and abdomen, become suited to their new relations. Humboldt remarks on the extraordinary development of the chest in the inhabitants of the Andes, producing even deformity; and he justly observes that this is a consequence of the rarity of the air, which demands an extension of the lungs.

The effects have been referred to of use or exercise in modifying certain parts of the animal form. The limbs of many animals inured or compelled to speed become extended in length, as of the dogs employed in the chase of the swifter animals. The limbs of an animal deprived of the means of motion become feeble and small, as the wings of domesticated birds. In the natural state the cow has a small udder, yet sufficient to contain the milk which her young requires; in the domesticated state, by milking her, the organ becomes enlarged so as to contain a quantity of milk beyond what the wants of her own offspring demand. Nor are the characteristics thus acquired confined to the individuals on which they have been impressed, but may be transmitted to their posterity.

The lessons taught by these illustrations are obvious. None of our improved breeds are adapted to *all climates* and *all conditions* of life. To be at their best they must each be kept, as nearly as possible, under the same conditions of food and climate as those under which they have attained their excellence. Any material change in either of these conditions is liable ultimately to make a material change in the character of the breed. These changes are usually unfavorable ones, although not necessarily so. Change of itself, when in the direction of better care, more generous feeding and more genial climate, will tend to produce greater size, a more graceful form, and greater excellence. At the same time improvement in these particulars is quite likely to be at the expense of what is termed hardiness, or ability to withstand exposure and rough usage.

ACCIDENTAL VARIATIONS OR "SPORTS."

When animals in a state of nature are not disturbed in the enjoyment of the conditions under which they have existed for ages, as the American bison or buffalo, the elk, the deer, the wolf, etc., the uniformity which prevails among all the individuals of the race is remarkable; and all the peculiarities of structure, color and character are transmitted from generation to generation with almost unerring certainty; and here the maxim of the breeder, that "like produces like," scarcely ever meets with an exception. Such animals are, in the truest sense of the word, *thoroughbred*, or purely bred. There has been no commingling of blood or crossing of various strains to give the race a composite character, and hence when we have seen the sire and dam we can tell with certainty what the progeny will be. Were any of our domesticated animals purely bred, in the sense that the bison, the elk or deer are purely bred, the breeding problem would be a simple one, and like would invariably produce like so long as the conditions of life remained the same. The same principle holds true in the reproduction of vegetable life. An absolutely pure seed reproduces its kind, but when cross-fertilization has once taken place the result is uncertain. If the flower of the Baldwin apple tree be fertilized by the pollen of a Winesap the seed from this union will produce neither the one nor the other. It will be an apple because both of its parents were apples; but as they were of different varieties, or forms, or characters, so the produce will have a character of its own, differing from both of its ancestors. And even if the stigma of the Baldwin be fertilized by pollen of its own kind the result is uncertain, because the parent is itself the result of cross-fertilization. The application of this principle to the crossing of different races of domestic animals is evident, and I shall have occasion to refer to it hereafter.

But, notwithstanding the uniformity of which I have spoken, in the produce of absolutely pure or unmixed races there arises occasionally what is termed an accidental variation from the established type—a *sport*, as it is frequently called. The color of the American deer is of a fixed type, and a departure from uniformity in this particular is very rare—yet a white deer is occasionally found—and so of other animals in which the color is an equally well-established characteristic. Man has five fingers on each hand and five toes on each foot, and in this particular the race is uniform; yet a "sport" is occasionally found where the number of fingers or toes is increased to six. When these accidental variations once occur they are liable, under favorable conditions, to be transmitted by inheritance; but under the ordinary operations of Nature's laws, when the conditions of life remain unchanged, these anomalies usually disappear within one or two generations and the normal and characteristic type of the race is resumed. A well-authenticated instance of the transmission of accidental variations is found in the oft-quoted case of Edward Lambert, whose whole body, with the exception of the face, the soles of the feet and the palms of the hands, was covered with a sort of horny excrescence, which was periodically molted. His six sons all inherited the same peculiarity, and the only one of the six that survived transmitted it, in turn, to all his sons. This abnormal characteristic was transmitted through the male line for six generations, and then disappeared.[*] It is a very remarkable illustration of the peculiarities of heredity that the females of this family should have failed to inherit this pecu-

---

[*] "Philosophical Transactions," Vol. XVII, p. 23.

liarity. Another very remarkable case of this nature that came under my own observation was that of a family residing in Iowa, where the mother and three daughters were entirely destitute of hair, but the sons all had quite as much as the average of men. We have also several well-authenticated cases of the transmission, for a few generations, of an abnormal number of fingers or toes, as in the case of the Colburn family, where each of the members had a supernumerary toe and finger, which anomaly was transmitted, although irregularly, for four generations before it entirely disappeared. The writer is personally cognizant of a case in which the second and third toe of each foot were united, and which anomaly has been transmitted for three generations to one only out of an average of eight descendants in each family. But, as before remarked, when the conditions of life remain unchanged these anomalies almost invariably disappear, and the descendants ultimately resume the typical character of the race.

From the fact that these accidental variations have shown themselves to be, in a limited degree, transmissible by heredity, we may infer that if selections were made with a view to their perpetuation they might ultimately become fixed characteristics. Indeed, there is a considerable weight of evidence tending to show that even variations produced by mutilation, or by other artificial means, are sometimes transmitted, especially when the mutilation has been intimately connected with the nervous system. Dr. Prosper Lucas gives numerous well-authenticated instances of this character, and is decidedly of opinion that variations or mutilations that are the result of disease are transmissible. That eminent scientist, Dr. Brown-Sequard, gives an interesting account of some experiments with guinea pigs. By an operation upon a certain nerve he produced epileptic convulsions; and the produce of the animals upon which this operation was performed manifested the same symptoms.* But, notwithstanding the numerous instances given by the eminent authorities above quoted, I am of the opinion that the cases of the transmission of these artificially produced variations are so rare as to be practically of no account in the calculations of the breeder.

The law which governs the transmission of these accidental variations, whether they be the result of a "sport" or of external influences, appears to be that when such variations from the common type are in antagonism to the conditions of life to which the individual is

---

*"Proceedings of the Royal Society of Great Britain," Vol. X, p. 297.

GENERAL PRINCIPLES OF BREEDING. 33

subjected the variations are not perpetuated; while, on the other hand, if they are in conformity to the existing wants or conditions, thereby better fitting the individual to succeed in the struggle for existence, natural selection and a survival of the fittest will tend to perpetuate them.

It is evident, therefore, that the laws of heredity tend to reproduce in the progeny the character of the ancestors, and that when the ancestry is of a fixed and uniform type the maxim that "like produces like" admits of few exceptions. Yet there are exceptions even here, as we have seen in the case of sports; and the modifications produced by changed conditions of life, adaptation to new uses and new modes of subsistence, tend to vary what, under the operation of the unrestricted laws of heredity, would fix a given type and leave the breeder's art powerless to effect change or improvement.

Heredity, which makes of every individual the sum, or aggregation, of that which has lived before him, is essentially a conservative force, and opposes all changes, all progress, all improvement; but evolution, which compels heredity to give way to internal and external causes, and modifies both the physical and mental organism, places in the breeder's hands the means of effecting wonderful changes.

EXTENT OF HEREDITARY INFLUENCE.

I have spoken of two forces that, in their effects, appear to be diametrically opposed to each other—heredity, which makes of every individual the sum, or aggregation, of that which has preceded it, and evolution or spontaneity, which constantly tends to give to animal life new forms and to each individual peculiarities which belong to it alone. Of these heredity is unquestionably the stronger force, because, as I have before remarked, when uniformity has once been established the general principle that like produces like finds very rarely an exception. In fact the influence of heredity is *always* present, and in the reproduction of animal life never fails to assert itself in a greater or less degree. Every living thing brings forth young after its own kind—in some cases the exact counterpart of the parent, and in others slightly modified; but always showing more or less of the parent type. Men do not gather grapes of thorns nor figs of thistles, neither do Short-horn cows bring forth buffalo calves nor draft mares produce thoroughbred race horses. Hence, although we may frequently meet with very striking differences between the parents and the progeny, yet a moment's reflection will show us that the points of resemblance are always very much greater than those of difference.

GENERAL PRINCIPLES OF BREEDING. 35

We are so accustomed to look at the operation of this law in its *details* that we overlook the aggregate of results. We mate a purely-bred black Essex sow and boar, and look upon it as a matter of course that the pigs produced will all be black and possess the general characteristics of the Essex breed; but if, having selected our breeding pair with a view to the transmission of a peculiar form of the head or shape of the ear we find in the produce that few, and possibly none, possess the peculiarity which we have sought to perpetuate, we are apt to lose faith in the power of heredity. And yet it would be an argument *against* the uniform operation of this law were the produce all to possess the peculiarity which distinguished the sire and dam, for this was in them an exceptional feature; and the fact that the pigs possessed, in lieu of this peculiar mark, the character that belonged to their ancestors in general is rather a testimony to the inherent power of heredity than otherwise. Were our pair of pure Essex swine to produce Poland-China or Berkshire or Yorkshire pigs there would be room for suspicion or for complaint that the laws of heredity had been violated; but such a transgression of Nature's law so rarely occurs that when it does take place we may properly call the result a "sport." Hence, the failure of an individual to reproduce features that are peculiar to itself, or of a pair of individuals distinguished for the same peculiarity, to transmit it to the offspring should excite no surprise in the mind of the breeder. Let it be remembered *always* that *heredity transmits with certainty, only what has become a fixed characteristic in the race.* Sports, accidental variations and individual peculiarities only occur in opposition to this law, and their transmission is at best uncertain. Heredity may be depended on to govern the general characteristics which determine the species and the less general ones which distinguish the breed, but when we come to individual characteristics, which have never acquired a general character in the ancestry, it frequently fails. In short, *the transmission of the greater share of all the characteristics is a thing of universal occurrence, but their transmission in toto is an ideal conception that is never realized;* and only in proportion as the ancestry has assumed a fixed and unvarying type do we find this ideal of the effect of heredity approximated.

That peculiarity called atavism, or reversion, so often noticed in our domesticated animals, and which has so frequently set at naught the calculations of the breeder, has often been quoted as an illustration of the failure of the law of heredity; but it is in fact only a tribute to its power. By selection, change of climate or of nutrition, or by crossing, or by all of these means combined, we may succeed in obliterating certain well-defined characteristics, and in modifying a given type, until the new form or character that we have created will, in its turn, be transmitted with reasonable certainty; but suddenly the germ that has lain dormant for so many generations asserts itself, and, greatly to our surprise, the characteristics of the original stock will reappear. As I have before remarked, these cases of reversion most frequently occur when cross-breeding is resorted to. The counter currents of hereditary influence, which are, by this means, brought into contact, having a common origin, appear to awaken into being a germ which has for generations been a silent factor in each of the newly-created breeds, and enables it to again assume control of the organism.

In addition to the general and well-defined operation of the laws of heredity to which I have alluded, its operations in the transmission of individual characteristics, although not clearly defined, and never to be depended upon, are often wonderful. The son is frequently, in some respects, the exact duplicate of the father, and the daughter of the mother. Sometimes a peculiarity which belonged to the grandsire lies dormant in the son, but crops out as strong as ever in the second or third generation. Again, we find peculiarities transmitted from father to daughter, and from mother to son, and even especial sexual characteristics transmitted by the father through a daughter to a grandson, or by the mother through a son to a granddaughter; but it is worthy of remark that in no case are all the peculiarities of any one individual transmitted. Indeed, it would be strange were it otherwise, because each individual is the joint product of two other individuals, each endowed with peculiarities of its own; and that each should be transmitted as an entirety is absolutely impossible. Rarely do we find in the offspring a blending of the peculiarities of the parents in exact proportion—as one might theoretically argue would be the result were the parents of equally well-established types—but rather that in some respects the offspring resembles the father, in others the mother, in some forming a partial or exact mean between the two; and in still others the produce being utterly unlike either, but possessing an individuality or character peculiarly its own. I might illustrate this by instances from the experience of every breeder, but it is not necessary. The effect has been observed by all who have given any attention whatever to the subject of breeding.

THE FORMATION OF BREEDS.

I have spoken of the uniformity which characterizes animals of a given species in a state of nature, and of the various causes that serve to disturb this uniformity in our domesticated animals when subjected to changed conditions of climate or nutrition. I have also treated of the effect of heredity, which makes of the offspring the sum or aggregation of the qualities that existed in its progenitors, and of the opposing law of evolution or spontaneity which tends to give to each animal a character of its own. I now propose to consider how these known laws and forces may be utilized in the formation of breeds; and, at the threshold of this division of my subject, it is necessary that we should understand what is meant by the terms used.

The animal kingdom is divided by naturalists into four great branches—*Radiata, Mollusca, Articulata,* and *Vertebrata.* These branches are again divided into classes. The *Vertebrata*, to which branch all our domesticated animals belong, are divided into eight classes, the last of which are the *Mammalia,* embracing all animals that give suck to their young. These classes are divided into genera, and these again into species. For example: we have the genus *Equus,* of which the horse, the ass, the zebra and the quagga are species; and these different species are again divided, with reference to certain peculiarities, into breeds. A breed, therefore, is a classification by which we distinguish a group of animals possessing qualities which are not common to all animals of the same species, and which peculiarities have become so firmly established that they are uniformly transmitted by heredity. Thus, we have the Shetland ponies, a breed of horses possessing all the general characteristics of the species to which they belong, but especially distinguished from other breeds by their diminutive size; and the Devons, a breed of cattle uniformly of a deep red color, and possessing other distinctive features that are not uniformly found in any other breed of cattle.

It will be observed that these divisions, from first to last, are more or less arbitrary; and, as it is impossible to define exactly the point where the mineral kingdom leaves off and the vegetable kingdom begins, or to distinguish positively the line of demarcation between vegetable and animal life, so throughout the entire animal kingdom the various divisions or classes approach each other by almost imperceptible gradations, until in many cases it is impossible to locate the dividing line. This is especially true of breeds. We may assume any standard that our fancy may dictate, as the color or texture of the hair; the shape or size of any particular part of the body, as the head or the ear; any particular function, as the quantity or quality of the milk in cattle; peculiarities of locomotion, as the trot or pace in the horse; of habit or instinct, as exemplified in the Setter or in the Shepherd dog, etc.; and classifying with reference to the possession of any one of these assumed peculiarities we may divide a species into breeds. Theoretically there is no limit to the extent to which this division into breeds may be carried; but practically it is confined to marked differences in *appearance, function, use, disposition* or *quality*. And whenever we have, by any means, produced *a group or family of animals possessing and transmitting uniformity in any particular, in which there is a lack of uniformity in the species to which they belong*, they are fairly entitled to be classed as a breed.

Taking advantage of the almost numberless shades of divergence from the original type to be found among the different species of domesticated animals, the laws of heredity and spontaneity enable man to work wonderful transformations and improvements by selecting such individuals as most nearly approximate to his ideal and which manifest a tendency to assume the desired form. By coupling such individuals there is a probability that the quality for which they were selected will be reproduced in the offspring, and that it will be even more prominent than in the parents. I say there is a *probability* that this will be the result, but it is by no means certain; for, as I have remarked, only the general and firmly-fixed characteristics which distinguish the species are transmitted with absolute certainty, and the transmission of accidental qualities or especial excellence in any given particular, while always possible, can never be depended upon with certainty. If, however, we select parents both distinguished for the same accidental variation or accidental excellence the chances that this will be transmitted to the offspring are, theoretically, twice as great as when only one of the parents is in possession of the desired quality; and if in the produce from this coupling we see manifestations of the desired tendency we may unite the animals so bred with an increased probability that they, in turn, will transmit it to their offspring. It is mainly by this process of selection and coupling, with a view to the attainment of certain desirable qualities, persevered in for many generations, that all noted breeders have succeeded in moulding the forms or establishing the breeds that have given them celebrity.

It must be borne in mind that the very processes of Nature which make it possible for man to effect improvement in any species of domesticated animals conspire to make the work of creating a new type of heterogeneous materials extremely difficult. In making selections with a view to the perpetuation of any variation from an established type we must always begin with such individuals as have manifested a tendency to assume the desired form and transmit it to their offspring. With a mixed and heterogeneous ancestry, representing various shades of divergence from the original type of the species, progress in any given direction by selection will, under the most favorable circumstances, be slow, and the results will frequently be anything but satisfactory. There is always a tendency in the offspring of a mixed or improved race to revert to the original form of the species from which it is derived. This tendency, as I have shown, is most frequently manifested where animals of a widely different character are coupled, as in the case of cross-breeding with distinct varieties or breeds; and this, although not without its compensating advantages in many cases, introduces new elements of divergence. Hence the breeder will often find failure where he had most expected success. The force of heredity is usually exerted to compel the progeny to adhere to the character which has become fixed in the species, rather than to follow a variation from the established type that was accidental or spontaneous in the immediate ancestry; but when, through selection of both parents with reference to this particular for several generations, the influence of heredity has once been enlisted in the transmission of an accidental variation, it lends its powerful aid in favor of the perpetuation of the improved form. Spontaneity may occasionally interpose a new feature, or atavism turn us back toward the original; but by continuing to select from the families which have been bred with reference to the desired form we shall eventually succeed in fixing the new type so firmly that its transmission will be the rule and failure the exception; and *when this point has been reached we have succeeded in forming what may justly be called a breed.*

IN-BREEDING AND CROSSING.

It has been claimed by many that success in establishing desired forms or qualities may be obtained with the greatest certainty, and in the least possible time, when selection is confined to the same family. Thus, we find a certain male that manifests an unusual degree of excellence in some particular, and which, it has been found, he usually transmits to his offspring. We select a female manifesting the same tendency, and the two are coupled. Possibly the offspring may not show a trace of the unusual excellence we have sought to perpetuate. We reject this, and couple the same sire and dam a second time, and perhaps we are rewarded by offspring possessing the desired quality. This produce, if a female, when of proper age is coupled with her own sire, and this produce again, if a female, is bred to the same male, that was her sire as well as her grandsire. This process is sometimes resorted to for three or four successive generations, with a view of intensifying or perpetuating a quality for which the sire is especially noted, and which it is found he transmits with certainty; for it is a well-known, although inexplicable fact, that of two animals bred precisely alike, and manifesting the same spontaneous variation, one will transmit the peculiarity with considerable certainty, while not a trace of it will appear in the produce of the other. The same principle often finds its application in coupling the son with his own dam, and then, if the produce be a female, using upon her the same male, that is at once her brother and her sire. This process of coupling near relatives, which is generally termed breeding in-and-in, is unquestionably very effectual, and is frequently the only available source from which breeding-stock can be obtained that possess and transmit the desired quality. But there is always danger that such a course of breeding will result in a loss of constitutional vigor and fertility in the produce, and it should be practiced with great caution. Should any constitutional defect or weakness be noticed as the result of breeding in-and-in an infusion of fresh blood must be obtained by resorting to a male or female not closely related, but possessing as nearly as may be the desired quality. It should be borne in mind that defects are quite as liable to be transmitted as good qualities; and while we are fixing a type of superior excellence in one particular, we should be careful that we are not, with equal certainty, perpetuating and intensifying a serious defect.

It is believed by many that breeding in-and-in has a refining tendency—that its effect is in the direction of fineness of texture, lightness of bone, smoothness, evenness and polish, at the expense of robustness, strength, vigor and power; hence, it is one of the most potent of agents in the production of dwarf breeds, and the main reliance of breeders of Bantam fowls and other diminutive races. It is certainly a powerful and invaluable agent in the hands of an intelligent person in the formation or modification of a breed, but can never be successfully followed by general farmers, who must produce hardy, prolific and vigorous animals.

The great number of intermarriages which took place in the royal family of Egypt during the reign of the Ptolemys has occasionally been referred to by the advocates of close in-breeding; and the magnificent personal appearance of these rulers, their close resemblance in form

GENERAL PRINCIPLES OF BREEDING. 47

and feature, and especially the widely-famed beauty of countenance and form, as well as the mental vigor displayed by Cleopatra, the last of the line, have often been quoted as a strong argument against the theory that breeding in-and-in necessarily produces physical deterioration; but a close examination of the line of descent leaves the balance of the argument rather on the other side. Galton, in his "Hereditary Genius," in speaking of this family, says:

> This race of Ptolemys is at first sight exceedingly interesting, on account of the extraordinary number of their close intermarriages. They were matched in-and-in like prize cattle; but these near marriages were unprolific—the inheritance mostly passed through other wives. Indicating the Ptolemys by numbers, according to the order of their succession, II married his niece, and afterward his sister; IV his sister; VI and VII were brothers, and they both consecutively married the same sister—VII also subsequently married his niece; VIII married two of his own sisters consecutively; XII and XIII were brothers, and both consecutively married their sister, the famous Cleopatra. Thus there are no less than nine cases of close intermarriages distributed among the thirteen Ptolemys. However, when we put them into the form of a genealogical tree we shall clearly see that the main line of descent was untouched by these intermarriages, except in the two cases of III and VIII. The personal beauty and vigor of Cleopatra, the last of the race, cannot therefore be justly quoted in disproof of the evil effects of close breeding. On the contrary, the result of Ptolemaic experience was distinctly to show that intermarriages are followed by sterility.

Galton then proceeds to show that nearly all of these incestuous marriages were unfruitful, the only exceptions being that of Ptolemy II with his niece, from which was produced Ptolemy III, and Ptolemy VII with his niece, the produce being Ptolemy VIII, the grandfather of Cleopatra, the descent in all other cases passing through wives that were not nearly related to this family.*

The testimony of experienced naturalists and of intelligent and careful observers among practical breeders is uniformly in favor of the proposition that a cross in the blood gives increased size and vigor to the produce. It is an equally well-established fact that cross-breeding, or the pairing of animals of distinct varieties, usually results in increased fertility; but it is rather singular that, while this result usually attends the pairing of distinct varieties of the same species, yet if cross-breeding be carried so far as to unite distinct species, although increased size and vigor are still attained, fertility is almost entirely lost. A familiar illustration is seen in the produce of the horse and the ass. The mule, resulting from such a union, is often larger than either parent, and is noted for his hardiness and powers of endurance, but the power of reproduction is in nearly all cases totally wanting. The same is true of most other hybrids. It is a singular fact that a loss of fertility is also one among the very first bad

---
* "Hereditary Genius," by Francis Galton, p. 152.

results manifested from long-continued breeding in-and-in—which is the very opposite of violent out-crossing; and yet all experience proves this to be true.

The space that can be devoted to a discussion of this branch of the subject will not admit of an elaborate investigation of the principles of genesis by which this apparent contradiction is explained. The majority of my readers are more concerned with *facts* and *results* than with *theories* and philosophical abstractions. But, at the risk of giving more of theory than will be relished, I will venture to state that, in order to produce a sexual union which shall be fruitful, and call into life a new organism, according to the opinion of most scientists, it is essential that the sperm-cell and the germ-cell, which, united, form the source of life to the new being, shall each proceed from a different organism; and that breeding in-and-in, as usually practiced—being the selection of individuals of as nearly as may be a similar organization, with the avowed purpose of creating uniformity of character—will, in the course of time if not counteracted by opposing influences, produce such a unity of organism in the members of a given family as will result in a loss of that differentiation which appears to be necessary to insure the fusion of the sperm-cell of the one with the germ-cell of the other.

In commenting upon this aspect of genesis, Herbert Spencer says:

Remembering the fact that among the higher classes of organisms fertilization is always effected by combining the sperm-cell of one individual with the germ-cell of another, and joining with it the fact that among hermaphrodite organisms the germ-cells developed in any individual are usually not fertilized by sperm-cells developed in the same individual, we see reason for thinking that the essential thing in fertilization is the union of specially-fitted portions of *different* organisms. If fertilization depended on the peculiar properties of sperm-cell and germ-cell, as such, then in hermaphrodite organisms it would be a matter of indifference whether the united sperm-cells and germ-cells were those of the same individual or those of different individuals. But the circumstance that there exist in such organisms elaborate appliances for mutual fertilization shows that unlikeness of derivation in the united reproductive centers is the desideratum.*

After explaining at some length the apparent contradiction of this theory which is found in plants that are self-fertilizing, Mr. Spencer further remarks:

There is reason to believe that self-fertilization, which at the best is comparatively inefficient, loses all efficiency in course of time. After giving an account of the provisions for an occasional, or a frequent, or a constant crossing between flowers, and after quoting Prof Huxley to the effect that among hermaphrodite animals there is no case in which "the occasional influence of a distinct individual can be shown to be physically impossible," Mr. Darwin writes: "From these several considerations, and from the many special facts which I have collected, but which I am not here able to give, I am strongly inclined to suspect that,

---

* "Principles of Biology," Vol. I, p. 279.

both in the vegetable and animal kingdoms, an occasional intercross with a distinct individual is a law of Nature. * * * In none, as I suspect, can self-fertilization go on for perpetuity." This conclusion, based wholly on observed facts, is just the conclusion to which the foregoing argument points. * * * If, then, in a self-fertilizing organism, and its self-fertilizing descendants, such contrasts as originally existed among the physiological units are progressively obliterated—if, consequently, there can no longer be a segregation of different physiological units in different sperm-cells and germ-cells, self-fertilization will become impossible; step by step the fertility will diminish, and the series will finally die out.*

A similar view of this subject is presented by Mr. Darwin in a letter published in the London *Agricultural Gazette* of May, 1878, from which I extract the following:

I will venture to add a few remarks on the general question of close interbreeding. Sexual reproduction is so essentially the same in plants and animals that I think we may fairly apply conclusions drawn from the one kingdom to the other. From a long series of experiments on plants, given in my book "On the Effects of Cross and Self-Fertilization," the conclusion seems clear that there is no mysterious evil in the mere fact of the nearest relations breeding together; but that evil follows (independently of inherited disease or weakness) from the circumstances of near relations generally possessing a closely similar constitution. However little we may be able to explain the cause, the facts detailed by me show that the male and female sexual elements must be differentiated to a certain degree in order to unite properly and to give birth to a vigorous progeny. Such differentiation of the sexual elements follows from the parents and their ancestors having lived during some generations under different conditions of life.

---

* "Principles of Biology," Vol. I, pp. 281, 282.

The closest interbreeding does not seem to induce variability, or a departure from the typical form of the race or family, but it causes loss of size, of constitutional vigor in resisting unfavorable influences, and often of fertility. On the other hand, a cross between plants of the same sub-variety, which have been grown during some generations under different conditions, increases to an extraordinary degree the size and vigor of the offspring.

Some kinds of plants bear self-fertilization much better than others; nevertheless it has been proved that these profit greatly by a cross with a fresh stock. So it appears to be with animals, for Short-horn cattle—perhaps all cattle—can withstand close interbreeding with very little injury; but if they could be crossed with a distinct stock without any loss of their excellent qualities it would be a most surprising fact if the offspring did not also profit in a very high degree in constitutional vigor. If, therefore, any one chose to risk breeding from an animal which suffered from some inheritable disease or weakness, he would act wisely to look out not merely for a perfectly sound animal of the other sex, but for one belonging to another strain, which had been bred during several generations at a distant place, under as different conditions, as to soil, climate, etc., as possible, for in this case he might hope that the offspring, by having gained in constitutional vigor, would be enabled to throw off the taint in their blood.

The view of the case presented by Darwin and Herbert Spencer in the foregoing extracts affords an explanation of many apparent contradictions which result from breeding in-and-in. The farmer who *permits* his stock to pair miscellaneously, without infusing fresh blood for many generations—as is the case with some —must necessarily practice breeding in-and-in; but, as in such cases the stock is almost invariably, at the beginning, of a heterogeneous character, it will require a much greater period of time before breeding in-and-in shall have produced a sufficient degree of unity of organism to interfere with fertility or to cause a loss of vitality than in cases where the stock, to begin with, is of a uniform type, or "purely bred." In such cases, also, there is no effort on the part of the farmer to produce uniformity by selection of individuals for coupling. If there be any selection at all the standard by which it is made is a capricious one, changing from year to year; and it is a well-known fact that in such hands uniformity of type is never reached, neither have any bad effects usually been observed from in-breeding in such cases.

If the theory above advanced be correct no bad results will necessarily follow from breeding in-and-in until uniformity of type, which implies unity of organism, is attained, and this, as we have seen when breeding from a mixed stock, is a very slow process.

Upon this aspect of the case Herbert Spencer remarks:

Relations must, on the average of cases, be individuals whose physiological units are more nearly alike than usual. Animals of different varieties must be those whose physiological units are more unlike than usual. In the one case the unlikeness of the units may frequently be insufficient to produce fertilization; or if sufficient to produce fertilization not sufficient to produce that active molecular change required for vigorous development. In the other case both fertilization and vigorous development will be made probable.

Nor are we without a cause for the irregular manifestation of these general tendencies. The mixed physiological units composing any organism being, as we have seen, more or less segregated in the reproductive centers it throws off, there may arise various results, according to the degrees of difference among the units and the degrees in which the units are segregated. Of two cousins who have married the common grandparents may have had either similar or dissimilar constitutions; and if their constitutions were dissimilar the probability that their married grandchildren will have offspring will be greater than if their constitutions were similar. Or the brothers and sisters from whom these cousins descended, instead of severally inheriting the constitutions of their parents in tolerably equal degrees, may have severally inherited them in very different degrees; in which last case intermarriages among the grandchildren will be less likely to prove infertile. Or the brothers and sisters from whom these cousins descended may severally have married persons very like or very unlike themselves, and from this cause there may have resulted either an undue likeness or a due unlikeness between the married cousins. These several causes, conspiring and conflicting in endless ways and degrees, will work multiform effects. * * * Hence it may happen that among offspring of nearly-related parents there may be some in which the want of vigor is not marked, and others in which there is decided want of vigor. So that we are alike shown why in-and-in breeding tends to diminish both fertility and vigor, and why the effect can not be a uniform effect, but only an average effect.*

It follows, then, as a practical deduction from the foregoing, that the more purely bred and uniform in type our stock becomes the greater is the danger from breeding in-and-in. That while, as before remarked, it is a powerful

---

* "Principles of Biology," Vol. I, pp. 283 and 284.

agent in the hands of a skillful and intelligent person in the formation of a breed, it must be used with the greatest of caution with animals of a uniform type, and that with miscellaneously-bred stock its evil effects are comparatively slow in showing themselves.

Many who have given the subject of breeding *as a science* only a casual investigation—who have studied only the methods of a Bakewell, a Colling, a Booth, or a Bates, without taking into account the *circumstances under which these methods were practiced*—have hastily adopted the conclusion that what was successful in such hands as theirs must still be correct in practice; that because Bakewell and Colling bred in-and-in to fix a desired type, and by continuing that process for a time succeeded in effecting substantial improvement in their cattle and sheep, it must necessarily follow that the surest method of preserving the excellence attained by them is to continue in precisely the same road. Or, to put it rather more mildly, because in the *formation of a breed* these men experienced little if any damage from the practice of breeding in-and-in to the extent to which they carried it, modern breeders of purely-bred animals can continue to breed in-and-in with impunity!

There is no one point upon which practical breeders, as well as scientists, are more perfectly agreed than that the ultimate tendency of breeding in-and-in is injurious—that when carried to *excess* it will always result in a loss of constitutional vigor in the produce; that while its tendency may be in the direction of fineness of texture, lightness of bone, smoothness, evenness and polish, it is invariably at the expense of robustness, strength, vigor and power. On the other hand, scientists as well as practical breeders, with perhaps equal unanimity, concur in the belief that a cross in the blood usually gives increased size and vigor to the produce, and that cross-breeding, or the pairing of animals of distinct varieties, usually results in increased fertility.

The belief has largely obtained among practical farmers and feeders that all purely-bred races or breeds are lacking in hardiness and stamina; and that when breeding for the dairy, the shambles, or for practical use on the farm, the greatest measure of success is attained through the medium of cross-breeding. The first of these assumptions is not necessarily true. When the breeding and management of purely-bred races have been in accordance with Nature's laws there is no foundation for the assertion that they are deficient in hardiness; and the widespread belief to the contrary has resulted mainly from the bad effects which inevitably follow long-continued incestuous or in-

and-in breeding. That with certain kinds of purely-bred stock this course of breeding has been so extensively practiced as to very greatly impair the vitality of the animals so bred no intelligent, careful observer will deny; while in others, where selection has constantly been made with reference to hardiness, strength and endurance—where close in-breeding has been avoided, and where there has been no unnatural forcing and pampering, the pure races or breeds have no peers in these valuable qualities. The lack of hardiness complained of in purely-bred stock where it exists is due to a peculiar course of breeding not justly chargeable to the fact that the animal is a purely-bred one, and not necessarily following the course of breeding essential to the creation of a breed. The thoroughbred race horse, or "blood horse," the purest and best established of all our breeds of domesticated animals, is a pointed illustration of this fact; and the reason is obvious. With the breeder of the race horse vitality has always been a paramount consideration, as upon this depends the ability of the horse to last in a long and closely-contested race; hence, a course of breeding that had a tendency to impair the vital forces has never found favor with breeders of these horses. None of the practices that have combined to impair the strength and vigor of purely-bred cattle, sheep, or swine, have been resorted to by them. In-breeding and pampering have both been frowned upon. Selection of the stoutest and best specimens of the breed has been the touchstone of their success. Once in and twice out has been as near an approach to in-breeding as has ever found favor among them; hence we find the thoroughbred horse of to-day the superior of all the other representatives of the equine race in speed and endurance.

It appears evident that if the laws of heredity are as I have here stated—that is: that the tendency of in-breeding with established races or breeds is to weaken the vital forces, and that cross-breeding gives increased vigor and vitality—we have an explanation of why the general farmer finds it most profitable to raise grade or cross-bred stock for the dairy or for feeding purposes. The purely-bred races or breeds, as a rule, have been perfected to a wonderful degree in certain qualities; and when the general farmer, desiring to improve his flocks and herds in any of these particulars, procures a purely-bred male to use as a sire, even though such animal may be suffering some of the bad effects of in-breeding himself, the excellence that characterizes the breed to which he belongs, reinforced and reinvigorated by contact with the current of fresh blood that

GENERAL PRINCIPLES OF BREEDING. 59

he meets in the farmer's mixed stock, gives a produce of greatly increased value for everything *except the purposes of reproduction.* All intelligent breeders agree in condemning *close* in-breeding; but they are not agreed as to what *constitutes* close in-breeding. May we not, upon the theory herein advanced, base a rule which will safely govern our practice? With purely-bred stock, or well-established breeds, keep as far from in-breeding as is compatible with uniformity of type and purity of blood; but in the formation of a breed from heterogeneous materials, use it as the most potent of all agents, without fear of bad results, provided the parents are healthy, vigorous, and well formed, until a considerable degree of uniformity has been reached; bearing in mind the cardinal fact that in proportion as unity of form and organism is attained, constitutional vigor and fertility is endangered by such a course of breeding. May we not, also, find in this theory an explanation of the well-known fact that in-bred animals which are barren when coupled with each other frequently prove fruitful when united with individuals of a different breed?

THE VALUE OF PEDIGREE.

A pedigree is the genealogy of an animal. As usually understood it consists of the names of the ancestors for a greater or less number of generations. Its value consists, not so much in the number of generations through which the ancestry can be traced to some distinguished progenitor, as in the *quality* or *character* of the ancestry; and in proportion as we approach the "top" of a pedigree—that is, the immediate progenitors of a given animal—the more important does the character of the ancestry become.

As has been clearly shown in the preceding pages, it is a well-settled fact in breeding that, as a rule, the longer the line of descent in unbroken succession through ancestors uniformly distinguished for unusual excellence the greater is the probability that that peculiar excellence will be transmitted. Hence the true test of the value of a pedigree is not so much in its length as in the merits of the individuals that compose it. Four or five "top crosses" with animals of rare individual merit make a pedigree of much greater value to the practical breeder than ten, twenty or as many more as you like of animals of no special excellence. The farther back this genealogy of good animals extends, and the more uniform the quality of the ancestry, the better; but the more immediate the ancestry in any given case the more important does its quality become. Each immediate parent contributes one-half of the blood or pedigree inheritance of the individual, while each great-grandam or sire contributes one-eighth only; and the farther the removal the more unimportant does any given factor or cross become for good or evil in a pedigree. However desirable it may be to have a record connecting our horses with Flying Childers, Eclipse or Messenger, and our cattle with Hubback or Favorite, at a distance of ten to twenty generations, it is manifestly of far greater importance to know that our own cattle and horses are good, and that their ancestors for the last four or five generations were of surpassing excellence. If our own animals are good, and the top crosses have been uniformly of the same character, we may reasonably expect the progeny to be satisfactory; while, on the contrary, if there be no special merit in the sire and dam, or their immediate ancestors, we may show as many lines as we like to some great ancestor ten or fifteen generations removed and it will not wipe out the stain of the defective recent crosses.

No pedigree can be a good one that does not usually produce good animals; no pedigree should be prized above other pedigrees unless it usually produces better animals. If, tried by this test, any pedigree fails, no matter how much it may have been idolized, its value is fictitious and its effect is hurtful rather than beneficial. The only true aristocracy of blood is one that brings superior merit; without this it is a delusion and a snare. No matter what it *may have been* eight or ten generations ago, if from a wrong system of breeding, if from a lack of care in selection, or from any other cause, any particular strain has ceased to be uniformly superior, in itself, it has lost its patent of nobility. Let all young breeders, and old ones, too, for that matter, try "pedigrees," and "families," and "strains" by this test, without being dazed by some imaginary halo that attaches to a name handed down from the misty traditions of the past, and it will be the better for them, no matter what particular line of breeding they may be engaged in.

RELATIVE SIZE OF SIRE AND DAM.

The relative size of sire and dam is a subject upon which much has been written, and upon which I am satisfied there has been much wrong teaching. It is true that nearly all writers upon the subject have laid down the rule that, in coupling, the male should be smaller than the female; but it is also true that very many persons write dogmatically upon subjects which they know very little about; and it is further true that writers upon heredity, for years and years past, have done but little more than to repeat each other, accepting what has been said by others as true without question, not knowing or caring to know anything about the facts in the case. I imbibed the doctrine that the male should be smaller than the female from my early reading upon the subject, and began writing from the same standpoint; but very early in my career as a writer upon stock-breeding my esteemed friend, the late Judge T. C. Jones, of Ohio, from whom I have taken many valuable lessons, called my attention to the manifest unsoundness of this theory, and said that he was fully convinced that the teaching of the books upon this subject was all wrong, and that, while he did not advocate great disparity in the size of parents, he was satisfied that when there was a difference it should be the reverse of what the books taught—that the male should, as a rule, be larger than the female. It was a startling proposition to me, but it set me to thinking and watching the subject closely; and now, looking back over more than a quarter of a century of experience, I say emphatically that Nature's plan, as exemplified in all mammalia, is that the male parent should be the larger of the two. In all animals, from the horse down to the hog, wild as well as tame, the male, as a rule, is larger than the female of the same breed. No observant man can have failed to notice this. What pure breed or race of animals, in any country, can be named as an exception to this rule? And is this not also true of the human race? How many of my readers are there who can call to mind numerous instances of handsome, well-formed and robust children the offspring of a large father and a small mother! The same result has been observed in hundreds of other cases where large draft horses have been coupled with small or medium-sized mares. In fact, it is the almost universal testimony of those who have watched closely the result of the cross of the imported draft stallions brought to this country from France and Great Britain, that the very best results have been obtained, not from large, coarse, and loosely-made mares, as theorists would have us suppose would be the case, but from those of medium size, compactly made and highly bred.

The excellent results obtained by crossing bulls of the large breeds upon our small native cows; also, the health, vigor, and fine form of the lambs got by large Cotswold rams out of small ewes of the Merino breed, all go to prove that this supposed law of Nature is no law at all. In fact, if we study Nature, we shall be compelled to admit that her law is just the reverse of what has been claimed. It is, therefore, safe to assume that the results are more likely to be satisfactory where large males and small females are coupled for breeding purposes than where the reverse is the method practiced.

GENERAL PRINCIPLES OF BREEDING. 65

I would not recommend, neither does it follow as a legitimate deduction from this general law, that *great* extremes of size should be coupled. In fact, Nature has herself interposed many obstacles to prevent such a course of breeding.

There is not, as has often been alleged, any increased danger in parturition from the use of sires larger than the dams. It is the dam that determines the size and growth of the fœtus, and not the sire. Wrong presentations, faulty construction of some parts of the organs of generation or of the pelvic bones of the female, an emaciated or too plethoric condition of the dam at the time of parturition, an unnatural or deformed fœtus, are the usual causes of difficult parturition, and these conditions are brought about independent of the relative size of sire and dam.

It goes for nothing to say that improvement in any breed has resulted from the use of males of a smaller breed upon females of a larger. If one desires to bring about improvement in any direction he must select with a view to that quality, independent of other considerations. Were I desirous of improving the butter-producing quality of the Holstein cow I should use a Jersey bull, notwithstanding the male might be smaller that the female. I would couple large, coarse-wooled ewes with a Merino ram if I desired to increase the density of the fleece; and I would breed large draft mares to thoroughbred or trotting sires if I desired to procure fine style, better action and greater powers of endurance. But all of this is independent of, and does not conflict with, the general law of relative size, and does not disprove the proposition that it is Nature's plan that the male should be the larger of the two parents.

INFLUENCE OF FIRST IMPREGNATION.

One of the most interesting as well as one of the most stoutly-disputed questions connected with the business of stock-breeding is this: Does the first impregnation of a female have any influence over the character of the produce from subsequent impregnations? Experienced practical breeders have been arrayed on opposing sides in discussing this question, and each has been ready to maintain his position by illustrations from his own observation. Prof. James Law, of Cornell University, who is one of the most learned and eminent of living veterinarians, and whose reputation as a patient, conscientious, painstaking investigator of problems of this nature is second to that of no other man in the world, was requested by me some years ago to prepare an exhaustive article upon this subject. He complied with this request, and the article, which was published at the time in a monthly journal then under my charge, I herewith reproduce as the most thorough treatise upon this interesting subject I have yet seen:

Physiologists and breeders have long noticed that the influence of the sire is not always confined to his immediate offspring, but that the subsequent progeny of the same female by other males often reproduce in a remarkable manner the personal traits of the first sire and his produce. All quadrupeds show this tendency in a greater or less degree.

We find the statement made by the immortal Haller: that where a mare had borne a mule by an ass and afterward a foal by a horse, the foal exhibited traces of the ass. The same thing has been noticed by Becker, Haussman, Low and others. Lord Moreton bred a hybrid between a young chestnut mare (seven-eighths Arabian) and a quagga. The hybrid had the bristly mane, striped body and large head of its sire. One or two years later this mare was covered by a black Arabian horse, and the resulting foal had the erect, short, bristly mane, the dun color, and stripes on neck, body and limbs of the quagga. A third foal, produced two years later, got by the same Arabian horse, still showed the same marks of the quagga. This case is all the more striking in that the mane of the Arab is especially soft and silky and lies flat on the side of the neck, and that the Arabian horse has never been known to show a striped marking of the body. A case entirely similar is recorded by Harvey: A mare of Sir Gore Ouseley's was bred to a zebra, producing a hybrid, and in the two succeeding years was put to two thoroughbred horses, but the foals in both cases were striped and partook of the character of the zebra. In the Royal Stud at Hampton Court a number of mares were bred to the horse Colonel, and the following year to the horse Acteon, but the progeny of the last horse bore unequivocal marks of the horse Colonel, the sire of their half-brothers and sisters. Again, a colt belonging to Earl Suffield, got by Laurel, strongly resembled the horse Camel by which his dam had had a foal the preceding year.

McGillivray records the following cases: A polled Angus heifer bore her first calf to a Short-horn bull, and was then served by a black polled Angus bull; but the calf resulting from the last connection approached the Short-horn bull in color and shape, and grew horns. Another polled Angus cow was served by a cross-bred bull (one-fourth polled Angus, three-fourths Short-horn) and bore a cross. Next year, though served by a pure black polled Angus bull, the result was still a cross, as shown by shape and color.

Dr Wells, of Grenada, put a flock of white ewes to a chocolate-colored, hairy ram, and the following year to a white ram of their own breed, and yet the lambs got by the last had the fleece more or less of a chocolate hue and largely mixed with hair. Mr. Shaw, of Leochel Cushnie, Aberdeen, divided his flock of black-faced Highland ewes, and had one part served by a Leicester ram and the other by a Southdown. The next year he had all served by a ram of their own race, but the lambs showed the persistent influence of the English rams in their hornless heads and brownish faces. Again, in the following year, they were served by a pure black-faced ram, and there still resulted two hornless lambs, two dun-faced, with very small horns, and three white-faced, with horns quite rudimentary.

Mr. Giles put a black-and-white Essex sow to a wild boar of a deep chestnut color, and obtained a crossed litter, with the color of the wild boar predominating in several. After the wild boar had been dead some time this sow was put to a black-and-white boar of her own breed and produced a litter of pigs, some of which were distinctly marked with chestnut. A second litter, by a boar of her own breed, again showed the chestnut markings, which had hitherto been unknown in the pure Essex.

Among dog-fanciers it is a matter of notoriety that an entire litter of pure-bred puppies cannot be expected from a thoroughbred bitch which has once been lined by a dog of another breed. This was noted by the French poet Jacques Savery as early as the middle of the seventeenth century, and is confirmed by writers on dogs generally. I will quote but one example from Harvey: A pure Skye terrier, of a dark brown color, with red legs, bore two litters of puppies to a mongrel cur, all of which were colored like the sire—black, with red legs and white feet. On the third occasion she was lined by a pure Skye terrier, of a grey color; and, to avoid accidents, was locked up with this dog during the whole continuance of the heat. The issue was two puppies closely resembling the mongrel cur in color, shape and general appearance. Instances of the same kind have fallen under the observation of almost every dog-fancier.

Many have sought to explain the phenomenon as a simple result of the strong impression made upon the mind of the dam by the sire of her earlier offspring; and, doubtless, this may sometimes co-operate, but is altogether inadequate to account for the frequency of the occurrence. The imagination affects the progeny of a very limited number of females, whereas the phenomenon we are considering—among the domestic quadrupeds—is the rule rather than the exception, so that a more satisfactory cause must be sought for.

McGillivray advances the theory that the elements from the blood of the fœtus, absorbed into that of the mother, *contaminate* her blood, and reduce her to a *cross*, thus rendering her forever after incapable of producing a pure-bred offspring. Not that he supposes the blood of the fœtus, as such, to circulate within the veins of the mother, but that fine particles from the blood of the offspring pass through the intervening layers of cells, and thus reach the maternal blood and reproduce themselves there. But the whole theory is an assumption. We know that the placenta, or after-birth, by which the fœtus is connected to the mother, serves the purposes of both stomach and lungs. From the glands in the walls of the womb a milk-like liquid is constantly secreted, which, being absorbed by the fœtal vessels branching in the placenta, is carried into the blood of the young animal and serves to nourish it, just as the milk from the udder does after birth. Again, from the blood of the offspring circulating in the placenta carbonic acid is given off and taken into the maternal blood, while oxygen supplied by the blood of the dam is taken up by the blood of the fœtus. So far these membranes fulfill the functions of stomach and lungs to the young animal. But we have no proof of living particles from the blood of the fœtus entering into the circulation of the mother, unless we accept as such the very phenomenon we are endeavoring to find an explanation for; and this would only be admissible if no other or more reasonable explanation could be found.

A slight modification of McGillivray's theory is that of Darwin, advanced in his doctrine of *pangenesis*. He teaches that throughout the blood and system of every animal there are living particles, infinitesimally minute, but with certain plastic or formative powers, by virtue of which they can build up particular forms or produce peculiar characteristics in the animal economy. That such particles may remain dormant for months or years, or even for a number of successive generations of animals, being, meanwhile, transmitted from parent to offspring through the microscopic ovum and spermatozoon, and will only be roused to activity and growth and build up the forms and beings, like those from which they were derived, when there occurs a change of circumstances favorable to their development. By this means he explains many cases of apparent "sports," or variations from the type of the known ancestors; many sudden advances in excellence, and retrogressions.

As applied to the phenomenon under consideration it is taught that these infinitesimal particles (gemmules), passing through the membranes from the blood of the fœtus into that of the mother, circulate with it, affecting the ovarium of the female, so that the ovules and offspring subsequently produced by her when impregnated by other males are plainly affected and hybridized by the first male.

It will be readily conceded that such particles circulating in the blood of the mother will be much less likely to affect her own system, already matured, insusceptible and undergoing the changes of nutrition only, than the growing elements of the ovum or the tissues of the embryo in active process of growth, and with a power of development equal in some cases to the reproduction of an organ accidentally lost. Much, indeed, might be said in favor of the theory; yet, as in its less elaborate form propounded by McGillivray, it is founded on pure assumption and supported by no clear proof. The gradual extinction of the influence of the first male in successive pregnancies by other males is what would scarcely be expected if the blood was charged with gemmules from the first capable of reproducing themselves and especially prone to rapid increase and development in connection with the development of offspring. Again, similar elements must be introduced into the maternal blood when the vital fluid has been transfused into her veins from those of another person or of a beast, and the ovules then in course of development in her ovaries must be "affected and hybridized" if such blood is not exactly identical in composition with her own. But though transfusion of blood into the female system is not uncommon, and though that blood has been rereatedly taken from a person of a widely different race, no complaint has ever been made that the children have been thereby affected.

A more satisfactory explanation is that advanced by the present writer, in a paper read in 1875 before the American Public Health Association: "It is a well-known pathological fact that adjacent cells tend to engraft their plastic or formative powers upon each other. I prick my skin with a needle; immediately the injured cells and nuclei undergo a rapid increase in size and numbers. But the effect does not end there; those adjacent take on a similar action, and the extent of the resulting inflammation is only limited by that of the injury and the susceptibility of the parts. Again, in placing a slice of scarf skin in the middle of a raw sore we inoculate the cells of the adjoining granulations and empower them to develop scarf skin. How, then, can we avoid the conclusion that the impregnated ovum impresses its own characters on the mass of the decidua, and through this on the maternal mucous membrane, and that this in its turn impresses its characters on the membrane and embryo of the next succeeding conception?"

It has been opposed to the theory of *contamination of the mother's blood*, that in the case of woman the father of the first child rarely affects the appearance of those by other fathers. Mr. Allen has known instances in which white women had their first children by negroes, and afterward marrying white men had children as purely white as those of their neighbors. Instances in which an opposite result has ensued he attributes to the effect of imagination. Now, the theory I offer will perfectly explain the infrequency of the occurrence in the human subject, as compared with the lower animals. In the mare the connection of the afterbirth with the womb takes place over the entire surface of the latter. The points of intimate attachment, therefore, in successive pregnancies, are the same. In the cow and ewe the womb is studded with button-like processes, to the number of fifty or sixty, containing the uterine gland, and forming the points of attachment for the fœtal membranes in all pregnancies alike. In the sow the fœtal membranes of each pig are attached to the whole adjacent uterine mucous membrane as in the mare. Lastly, in the bitch each fœtal membrane has a broad, circular, villous belt embracing almost its entire surface, and connecting it to the mucous membrane of the womb. In all of these animals the fœtal membranes are connected with the same parts of the uterus in each successive pregnancy, so that the ingrafting or inoculation between membranes and womb, and between womb and membranes and fœtus, cannot fail to take place. It must be borne in mind that these membranes are outgrowths from the ovum or embryo, and thus, through the male and female generative elements, partake of the nature of both sire and dam. In other words, like the young animal, the product of conceptions of which they are a dependency, the membranes have been produced by the union of the male and female elements; and where they lie in direct contact with the womb, separated only by a thin layer of cells in part produced by the womb and in part by the membrane, an inoculating, engrafting or modifying action is effected by the one on the other. In woman the arrangement of the fœtal membranes is altogether different. Their intimate connection with the walls of the womb is confined to one circumscribed portion of the surface of each; and as the point of attachment can hardly fail to be different in successive pregnancies the chances of a former child influencing the characters of

GENERAL PRINCIPLES OF BREEDING. 73

the next are correspondingly reduced. Yet it is evident that this may occur, and, as a matter of fact, we find cases in which the bearing of a mulatto by a white woman has affected the appearance of some of her later children by a white man. But such a result is very exceptional in the human family, and this is precisely what is to be expected if our explanation of its cause is the right one.

It has been objected that a similar phenomenon has been observed in pigeons, and that in them this law of cell-inoculation could not take place. But this is, manifestly, a mistake. The eggs of birds are impregnated even as high up as the ovary. Says Owen: "In *coitu* spermatozoa enter the cloaca and penetrate the oviduct, ascending to the ovarium." The impregnated egg goes on enlarging by subdivision of its cells in the ovary and upper end of the oviduct, and, being as yet destitute of shell, its cellular structure is in direct contact with the maternal tissues. There is, therefore, a similar opportunity for cell-inoculation as in the mammal, although more limited in duration.

But our manner of viewing this subject is still further supported by a series of phenomena observed in hybridized flowers. Darwin quotes instances from Wiegmann, Gartner, Berkley, and others, to show that where the flowers of the white pea had been fertilized by pollen of the blue pea the resulting pods contained a mixture of blue and white peas. And this coloration was not confined to the cotyledons of the seed (the true embryo), but extended to the skin as well. More remarkable still: Mr. Laxton, of Stamford, "fertilized the tall sugar pea, which bears very thin, green pods, becoming purplish-brown when dry, with pollen of the purple-podded pea, which, as its name expresses, has dark, purple pods with thick skin, becoming pale, reddish-purple when dry."

Mr. Laxton has "cultivated the tall sugar pea during twenty years, and has never seen or heard of its producing a purple pod; nevertheless, a flower fertilized by pollen from the purple pod yielded a pod clouded with purplish red, which Mr. Laxton kindly gave to me. A space of about two inches in length, near the extremity of the pod, and a smaller space near the stalk were thus colored. On comparing the color with that of the purple pod, both pods having been first dried and then soaked with water, it was found to be identically the same; and in both the color was confined to the skin lying immediately beneath the outer skin of the pod."

Some of the peas were also clouded with purple, whereas the tall sugar pea is a pale, greenish brown—never purple. Darwin collects a number of other instances in which the fruit or seed capsule was affected by fertilization with strange pollen, in the case of stocks, palms, oranges, lemons, cucumbers, maize, daffodils, rhododendrons, cress and apples. Perhaps the latter furnish the most important examples. The fruit here consists of the lower part of the calyx and the upper part of the flower-peduncle in a metamorphosed condition, so that the effort of the foreign pollen has extended even beyond the limits of the ovarium. Cases of apples thus affected were recorded by Bradley in the early part of the last century; and other cases are given in old volumes of the "Philosophical Transactions." In one of these a russeting apple and an adjoining kind mutually affected each other's fruits; and in another case a smooth apple affected a rough-coated kind. Another instance has been given of two very different apple trees growing close to each other, which bore fruit resembling each other, but only on the adjoining branches. It is, however, almost superfluous to adduce these or other cases after that of the St. Valery apple, which from the abortion of the stamens, does not produce pollen, but, being annually fertilized by the girls of the neighborhood with pollen of many kinds, bears fruit differing from each other in size, flavor and color, but resembling in character the hermaphrodite kinds by which they have been fertilized.

Mr. Darwin evidently sees that his system would demand that the gemmules from the strange pollen should serve to fertilize or modify each other and distant flowers and buds then being formed on the same tree, for he remarks: "There is not the least reason to believe that a branch which has borne seed or fruit directly modified by foreign pollen is itself affected so as subsequently to produce modified buds;

GENERAL PRINCIPLES OF BREEDING. 75

such an occurrence, from the temporary connection of the flower with the stem, would be hardly possible."

Yet, if the gemmules were given off by the pollen it would be quite reasonable to expect such to be carried on with the descending sap, and to modify the buds then in process of formation, as they are represented to do the ovules in the female ovary. But, as in the case of the blood, so in that of the vegetable sap—we have no evidence that it contains particles possessed of plastic powers equal to the development of tissue. This is affected only by the nuclei or cells present in the substance of the tissues themselves; and as these nuclei communicate or are continuous with each other through minute branching processes, they easily affect those immediately adjacent, but have comparatively no influence upon those that are somewhat remote. The modification, therefore, of the fruit capsule, pod, fleshy drupe and fruit stalk surrounding the seed, is only what is to be expected from the contact of the male pollen with the cells of the female flower, and of these in their turn with those adjacent, while all other parts of the plant are entirely unaffected by the act. In the animal the process is identical in every respect; the continuous cells—maternal and fœtal—rendered continuous or placed in direct opposition with each other through their minute branching processes mutually influence the vital processes and formative powers of each other; and thus it comes that the nuclei of the womb, but one step removed from its contained embryo, acquire certain new characters from it, and in due time transmit these to later progeny. The efficiency of this new inoculating process will, of course, be greatest where the vascular connection is the most intimate; and, as we have seen, the effect on the progeny is most patent when these points of intimate vascular connection between mother and offspring are the same in successive pregnancies.

A correct view of this subject is of more practical importance than may at first sight appear, for, although the animal modified by the influence of the sire of an elder half-brother is necessarily a cross, whatever the mode of exerting such influence, an important question may arise regarding the purity of other offspring that bear no evidence of having been subjected to such modifying cause. If Mr. Darwin's theory is correct, that the whole blood of the mother is charged with gemmules from the embryo, which gemmules pass into all future ova, then all future offspring are essentially crosses, as will appear in their progeny, even if they themselves show no sign of modification. But, on the other hand, if the result is only due to the mutual influence of adjacent cells in the womb and fœtal membranes, as vegetable as well as animal physiology seem to imply, then the general system of the dam is unaffected, and her progeny, which have personally escaped such influence and show none of the modified characters, may be held to be of pure lineage, and may be bred from without fear of degraded offspring.

While there are many instances in history which go to confirm this theory, as presented by Prof. Law, yet I am inclined to the opinion, from long years of close observation, that the cases wherein the first impregnation of mammals affects the subsequent progeny are so rare as to make it practically of but little account in the calculation of the breeder. Indeed the cases wherein such resemblances are noticed in horses, cattle, sheep, and swine are so few and obscure as to lead me rather to the conclusion that they are accidental, or owing to an inherited similarity in the remote ancestry, rather than to some occult influence exercised by a first impregnation. The case of Lord Moreton's mare and the quagga foal has been pressed into service by every man who has written upon this subject within the last half century, and yet it proves nothing. The black stripe is a distinguishing mark that belonged to the feral dun horses in general, and which to this day occasionally crops out in *all* breeds of horses. And if the influence were as potent as some writers have claimed, especially when applied to the breeding of horses, it is time some more modern case might be cited. Hundreds upon hundreds of excellent mares, many of them thoroughbreds, in Kentucky and Tennessee, have produced their first foals to a jack and have afterward produced beautiful offspring from highly-bred sires. I can recall many illustrations upon this point that have come under my own observation. In fact the whole theory of gestation, the manner in which the fœtus is attached to and nourished by the womb of the female, seems to make the commingling of the blood of the latter with that of the former an impossibility. In the case of the bitch there is a marked difference from all other domestic animals in the manner in which the placenta is attached to the womb—as is very clearly shown by Prof. Law in the foregoing article—and here alone, among domestic animals, do we find any considerable number of results which tend to confirm the theory that a first impregnation affects subsequent ones. It is noticed so frequently, however, here, that dog-fanciers almost universally recognize it as a rule, and exercise the greatest possible care lest a bitch should first be lined by a mongrel or a dog of some other breed. But aside from this single exception I do not think the cases are sufficiently well authenticated or sufficiently numerous to justify the practical breeder in paying any especial attention to it, especially when to do so would require a departure from plans that would otherwise be followed.

EFFECT OF IMAGINATION UPON THE COLOR OF PROGENY.

The question has frequently been asked, Does a sudden fright, or any peculiarity of association in a pregnant animal, have any effect upon the color or markings of the progeny? and the answer given has sometimes been "yes," and sometimes "no." In fact *both* sides of the question have been stoutly maintained by intelligent gentlemen, who have claimed to speak from extensive personal observation and experience. Ever since the day when Moses wrote the account of the method employed by Jacob to over-reach his father-in-law in the division of his cattle (see Genesis, chap. XXX), there have been those who believed it possible, through a strong mental impression, to affect the color and otherwise mark the offspring; and ever since the day when I, then in my early boyhood, first read the account of Jacob's success in breeding cattle that were "ring-streaked, speckled and spotted," I have been on the lookout for evidence bearing upon the old patriarch's theory.

The result of these observations has been to confirm me in the belief that while color, as well as all other peculiarities, *usually* follows the ordinary laws of heredity, it is nevertheless true that strong mental impressions do *sometimes* set aside the ordinary laws of Nature and produce surprising results. One very clearly-defined case came under my observation when a lad on my father's farm. A flock of sheep had been bred on this farm, without any infusion of fresh blood, for many years. Not a black sheep, nor one with a black spot or mottled face, had ever been known among them. On one occasion, after most of the ewes had been bred, a black ram was turned into a small lot with them. Had a strange dog, a wolf, or any other wild animal, been suddenly let down among them they could not have been more terribly frightened. They circled round and round the lot, and made the most frantic efforts to escape from the supposed monster, while he kept turning round and round in the center of the circle, in vain trying to approach the ewes, that seemed almost ready to die with fright. This was kept up until from sheer exhaustion the ewes began to slacken their pace; but it was not a long time before the flock became reconciled to the presence of the stranger. Now what was the result? *Every ewe that was pregnant at the time of this fright dropped offspring more or less marked with black*, while *some* of those that were served by this ram a few weeks later, after they had become accustomed to his presence, dropped lambs that were pure white. The case attracted much attention in the neighborhood at the time, and has often been referred to since as a convincing illustration of the effects of color-marking from severe fright.

Other instances have come under my observation; none of them so convincing as the one above narrated, but showing unmistakably the effect of imagination or association. A grey mare owned by a friend of mine was bred to a grey Percheron horse for four years in succession, and produced four foals. During her first impregnation she had for a stable companion and working mate a bay mare, and the foal was a bay. The next year her mate was a chestnut and the foal was a chestnut. Afterwards she was worked and kept with several different animals, of various colors, and her foals were all greys, like herself and the sire.

These cases, with many others of a similar character, that have come under my own observation, as well as hundreds that have been noted by others and reported to me, have, as before stated, confirmed me in the belief that "markings" do *sometimes* occur from strong mental impressions; but the precise conditions under which this phenomenon takes place are unknown. The effect is so uncertain that, practically, it may be entirely ignored by the breeder with impunity, until some modern Jacob shall arise who can tell us just how and when to use the "peeled rods."

EFFECT OF CHANGE OF CLIMATE ON THE GENERATIVE ORGANS.

It has often been remarked that a change of climate appears at times to have a serious effect upon the organs of reproduction, especially those of the male. A well-informed writer in an English journal not long since stated that experience had taught him that no water-fowl will breed the same year that its home is changed, referring, I presume by the context, to a material change as to distance or climatic conditions. I have noticed the same result with quadrupeds, more especially with horses imported from France, England and Scotland. Several horses that, within my knowledge, have totally or partially failed to get foals for a year or two after importation, have, after becoming thoroughly acclimated, proved themselves very sure foal-getters. I have also had many cases of a similar nature reported to me concerning bulls of the various breeds, and a still greater number, perhaps, of rams and boars.

It is quite reasonable to suppose that a material change in climate, or even in the mode of feeding, may so derange the organs of reproduction as to cause partial or total loss of sexual power. We know that a change in climate, or even in food, or water, often completely upsets a race horse; and that they are never considered fit to do themselves credit upon the turf when taken from this country to England, and *vice versa*, short of a year's acclimatization. It is not strange, therefore, that the effect should be equally as marked upon the generative organs as upon the motor apparatus; and upon cattle, sheep, and swine as upon horses. And breeders should not be in too great haste to declare an animal a non-breeder under such circumstances. Ample time should be given for thorough acclimatization in all cases of this nature.

CONTROLLING THE SEX.

It has been said that there is nothing new under the sun, and that each succeeding generation spends most of its time in shoveling over the same earth that has been examined in vain by its predecessors in search of hidden treasures. Theories that have been advanced, investigated and abandoned come up again year after year to be discussed, investigated, and again cast aside as unreliable. They appear periodically; and the lapse of a decade is sufficient to pass in review, through the agricultural press, the whole brood upon any given subject bearing upon agriculture. That of controlling the sex of offspring has, ever since the days of Aristotle, been one of the most fruitful topics of discussion, and the various theories that have been advanced appear and reappear with perennial vigor. These theories may be briefly summarized as follows:

1st. A strong mental impression on the part of the parents, but especially of the mother, at the time of conception, will determine the offspring.

2d. The concentration of the attention of the dam on her peculiarly feminine qualities, at the time of sexual union, will secure female progeny.

3d. If the amorous desires of the male are stronger than those of the female the progeny will be a female, and *vice versa*.

4th. The development of the fœtus in the right side (horn) of the womb will secure a male, and in the left side a female.

5th. The point of origin of the artery of the testicle from the main abdominal trunk (aorta) will determine the sex of the majority of the offspring, the male sex predominating in proportion as the origin is more anterior.

6th. The male germ is supplied by the right testicle or ovary, and the female by the left.

7th. The excitation of one side or the other of the system of the male at the time of coition will determine the sex of the young.

8th. The persistent selection for breeding purposes of females which yield one sex mainly, and of males from females of the same kind, will finally secure a race producing a great excess of the sex in question.

9th. In uniparous animals every successive ovum that reaches maturation is of the opposite sex from that which immediately preceded it. Hence, by serving on the second occurrence of heat we may secure the same sex as in the last fœtus.

10th. The stage of development attained by the ovum at the period of impregnation determines the sex of the product of fecundation, the less developed proving females, the more mature males.

11th. The personal preponderance in strength and vigor of the one parent will determine an excess of its own sex in the progeny.

12th. The nature of the food of the parents, and particularly of the mother before conception, will influence the production of the different sexes.

The theory that just now appears to be more generally believed in than any other is the 9th in the foregoing list. This is based upon the belief that, naturally, animals which usually bring forth but one at a birth will produce the sexes alternately—that if the first ovum produces a male, the next ovum, if impregnated, will produce a female; consequently, if a cow or a mare, after having produced a female, is impregnated at the first period of heat thereafter, the produce will be a male. If female produce only is desired, one period of heat should elapse after the birth of a female before the dam is again served by the male. This is what is known as the Stuyvesant theory, and many cattle-breeders of my acquaintance firmly believe that it can be relied upon in a majority of cases.

GENERAL PRINCIPLES OF BREEDING. 85

Several other theories have been advanced, but the foregoing are among the principal ones. It may be that several of these causes have some influence in determining the sex, but it is quite certain that some of them, notably the 4th, 6th, and 7th, can have no influence whatever, and that none of them can be depended upon. Nature has wisely provided, in order to preserve an equilibrium in the sexes, that their determination should be placed beyond the control of any single cause. It is known that some males get a large preponderance of one sex or the other, and that some females will produce one sex only; sometimes, for a series of years, the observations of one man will tend to confirm a certain theory of sex production, while in other hands the same theory will utterly fail. Taking up at random Part I of Vol. V of the English Short-horn Herd Book I find not less than thirteen cows that have produced five calves or over, the entire produce being of one sex. In two of these cases three different bulls were used, in eight cases four different bulls, and in two instances six different bulls. Some very remarkable cases were noted: The cow Ann by Abraham (2905) dropped nine bull calves in succession, the last two by Belshazzar (1703), and then her tenth calf, also by Belshazzar, was a heifer. Dorothy by Fisby (1040) dropped six bull calves in succession by four different sires, the fourth and sixth being by Roman (2561), but the seventh, by the same bull, was a heifer. Her eighth calf was also a heifer. Down Horn by Budget (1759) began with a heifer; her next was a bull by the same sire as the first, and then she dropped five more bull calves in succession by as many different sires. Fair Helen by Young Albion (15) began with a bull calf, and then went on with five cow calves in succession by four different bulls. Florence by Lindrick (1170) began with a heifer, then a bull, then six heifers by six different sires, and then two bulls, also by different sires.

With mares the same law doubtless applies. Turning to the Stud Book I find that the thoroughbred mare Rosemary produced two males from two different sires; next she produced three females, two of them by the same horse that got the males, then another male, and then eleven females in succession from nine different sires. Scythia produced six females, and no males, from three different sires. Another mare by Scythian, recorded on the same page, produced four males in successive years from as many different sires; and still another on that same page, also by Scythian, produced four females by as many different sires. Ærolite produced six males to successive covers of imp. Australian; while Dolly Carter, bred to the same horse, produced nothing but females.

GENERAL PRINCIPLES OF BREEDING. 87

Mary Lewis began with two male foals, the second being by Glencoe; her next foal, also by Glencoe, was a filly, and all her foals after that (six more), by four other sires, were females. Olivia produced seven males in succession from four different sires before she dropped her first filly. Neither Jack Malone, Muggins, John Morgan nor Bonnie Scotland could get anything but fillies out of Lantana. Mollie Hambleton produced six fillies in succession, three of them by Planet, and then she faced about and threw two male foals to Planet. In short, the pages of the stud and herd books furnish a complete refutation to any rule that has yet been formulated upon this subject.

It may be that we shall ultimately discover the circumstances under which these various causes operate upon each other, so that we shall be able, in many cases, to produce a given sex at will, but at present we know but little if any more upon the subject than was known by our grandfathers.

CHAPTER II.

STALLIONS, BROOD MARES AND FOALS.

If the reader has given any thought to the general principles which govern stock-breeding as elucidated in the preceding pages he must be well aware of the fact that he cannot gather grapes from thorns nor figs from thistles. The general rule that "like produces like" is true throughout all animal and vegetable life. Everything brings forth after its kind. We sow pure seed and expect the produce to be of the same kind. Wheat does not produce rye, neither will oats produce barley. The rule is just as true in animal life. The great principle that each begotten creature is but the essence of what has preceded it admits of very few exceptions. We have only to apply this general principle, with a knowledge of the special characteristics of the various breeds and families of horses, as portrayed in this volume, and the business of breeding horses of any given type becomes greatly simplified. No man would breed to a Shetland pony with the expectation of producing a draft horse, nor to the ponderous Shire or Clydesdale with the hope of the produce turning out a winner on the race course. The general characteristics of the breed to which the parents belong will be transmitted to the progeny; and in proportion as the breed is firmly established and uniform in its characteristics so will the produce be uniform in its character. Whatever has been "bred in the bone" will be transmitted. A pair of Shetland ponies will produce a Shetland pony with unerring certainty; because in all the characteristics which distinguish the ponies from other breeds of the horse kind they are uniform; but we cannot count with certainty upon the color of the hair or the individual peculiarities in many minute details, because in these minor points uniformity in the race has never been established. But whatever has been firmly fixed as a characteristic of the breed, whether it be peculiarity of gait, form, color, size, disposition, or speed, will be transmitted with a certainty in proportion to the degree of uniformity which has been attained in that particular in the ancestry.

The horses of the United States are of a heterogeneous character—a conglomeration of every breed and type of the horse kind in the known world. Until within a comparatively recent period no intelligent effort was made to keep any of the breeds pure except the thoroughbred. We have crossed in and out "without rhyme or reason" until, with the single exception of our thoroughbred horses, it is scarcely possible to trace the pedigree of any given American-bred horse four generations back without finding an admixture of all the various breeds and types that have ever been known. With such an ancestry it is not to be wondered at that disappointments meet the novice on every hand. He selects a fine-looking bay mare that will weigh nearly 1,500 lbs., in moderate flesh, clean-limbed and strong, and he looks about for a stallion possessing the same characteristics that he may couple the two together to produce a first-class draft horse. He has been told that "like produces like" so often that he believes it, and this theory leads him, very properly, to think that from such a pair his hopes of producing good draft horses will be realized. But he is disappointed; the produce is not like either of the parents; and he pronounces breeding a lottery, and the doctrine of the transmission of the peculiarities of the parents to the progeny a humbug. He forgets that heredity transmits with certainty only what has been firmly fixed in the ancestry; and he loses sight of the fact that his large, fine bay mare was herself the produce of a mixed ancestry—perhaps of a bay Clydesdale stallion and a little sorrel mare of unknown blood, and that his stallion was probably got by a half-blood French draft horse out of a dun pacing mare, whose dam in turn was a Mexican Mustang. The possession of the desired qualities in the sire and dam selected was an accidental circumstance; and intelligent breeders, with a knowledge of this fact, would not expect that these accidental qualities would be transmitted with certainty.

SELECTION OF BREEDING STOCK.

In the application of the general laws which govern the transmission of hereditary qualities to the business of breeding horses the first step is for the breeder to decide, in his own mind, what sort of horse he wishes to produce. If his fancy or interest leads him to breed horses for the race course he must keep constantly in mind the fact that for this purpose, whether for running or trotting, speed and endurance of the very highest order are indispensable; and here the least unsoundness will prove fatal. In order to live through the severe ordeal of training, and the still more trying one of the bruising campaign, which taxes the utmost powers of the horse day after day, there must be no weak spots in his composition. There must be no soft, spongy bones and joints; no brittle or contracted feet; no tendency to curbs, spavins or ringbones: no weak tendons nor feeble lungs in the horse that is to prove a profitable campaigner. No matter how much of mere speed the get of any stallion may have shown, if, as a rule, they have proven seriously defective in any part of their machinery, he should be avoided as a sire by those who are breeding for speed, whether runners or trotters; for the race course will quickly search out and bring to light the least taint of unsoundness or weakness in any part of the organization. Feet and legs, and bones and tendons, and joints and muscles, and heart and lungs, and brain and eye, must each do its part thoroughly in the great race horse. There must be that nice adaptation of the machinery, and that firmness and fineness of texture in the material of which the machine is built, which shall enable it to withstand the tremendous strain that is put upon it, and which distinguished great campaigners, like Lady Suffolk, Flora Temple, Goldsmith Maid, English Eclipse, and his American namesake, from the flashy ones that blaze out for a single season, like a brilliant meteor, and then sink into obscurity.

It is this perfection of organism which enables the horse to stand up, under preparation and training, year after year, profiting by his education and improving with age, that makes the really valuable race horse. It is a quality more valuable than speed, because whatever measure of speed it possesses can be depended upon and improved. In short, it is the quality which distinguishes the thoroughbred from the dunghill; the great race horse that, like a Goldsmith Maid or a Lexington, will always be in condition to struggle for a man's life, from those band-box race horses and newspaper trotters that are never heard from outside of private trials and breeders' catalogues.

These are the considerations that should influence breeders of horses for the turf; and no blind devotion to a fashionable pedigree, nor promise of mere speed in the youngsters got by any stallion, should induce us to overlook a prevailing tendency to any unsoundness or lack of endurance in his get. The number of heats and races won, and the number of successful years upon the turf, are more reliable lamps by which the breeder may guide his footsteps than the record of colt stakes and mere speed tests.

The ordeal of the race course, and more especially the trotting course, is very trying upon the legs and feet; and here soundness and quality of the highest order is essential. The turf horse that is always troubled with "a leg" is a nuisance. Curbs, spavins, ringbones, weakened or sprained tendons, "bucked" knees and stiffened joints are some of the troubles that affect the legs of the horse and greatly impair his usefulness.

The indications of a good leg are firmness, hardness and smoothness to the touch, showing an entire absence of adipose tissue; large, well-defined joints, entirely free from abnormal appendages; firm, but elastic, cords; a short pastern, short from knee and hock to pastern-joint. The shape of the bone should be broad and flat, and the legs should stand squarely and firmly under the horse, the toes turning neither in nor out. The bone should be of good size just below the knee, and flat: and large-sized cannon-bones, with strong, clean back sinews and suspensory ligaments are of great importance. "Curby hocks," "cow hocks," "bowed legs," "calf knees," and "over on the knees" are indications that are always unfavorable.

All these points are to be examined mainly when the horse is not in motion; and when fully satisfied in these particulars it is very essential to see that, having four good legs, the horse has the ability to use them properly; that he steps with a firm, free, elastic tread; that the legs and feet do not get in the way of each other when he is in motion, but move freely, without interference, and yet without any paddling or straddling motion. Stiffness of the joints may be most readily detected by causing the horse to step backward, and by seeing him in motion when first taken from the stall, before he has been warmed up.

The feet are, of course, a very important appendage to the legs. In shape, a medium between a flat foot and a mule-shaped one is to be preferred; and it should always be of good size, with a large degree of concavity in the bottom. The frog should be full and lively, free from thrush or canker; and the hoof must be hard and elastic, without cracks, and free from brittleness.

If all these details were looked after by breeders in selecting brood mares, as well as stallions, we should soon note a marked improvement in the legs and feet of our horses; for there is not a single good point or defect among those above enumerated that is not liable to be transmitted to the offspring. It is too often the case that mares especially, after having broken down through some inherent defect in the feet or legs, so that they can no longer be profitably used, are relegated to the breeding stud to transmit again to their progeny the malformation that made them worthless. Like does not always beget like in every feature and detail, but in general terms the saying is a true one, and defects are just as likely to be transmitted as good qualities. Mares or stallions disabled or crippled by accident, and not from constitutional tendency or weakness in any particular, may be safely used for breeding purposes; but those that have given way through weakness or defects in any part of the animal machinery should always be rejected. Breeders of trotting horses have been especially neglectful of these sound principles, and thousands of mares with some speed, but with legs and feet so unsound as to cause them to break down under very slight training, have been used for breeding purposes.

And so with any other form or type of horse that may be mentioned. If draft horses are desired select breeding stock from some of the best-established draft breeds. The distinguishing characteristics of weight and strength—which are the chief essentials in a cart or draft horse—are quite firmly fixed in the Clydesdale, the English Cart horse, the Suffolk Punch, the Percheron, and the Boulonnais, imported to this country from Europe, however much they may differ in other particulars; and they all may be relied upon, with a good degree of certainty, to reproduce their kind when judiciously coupled. But to this must be added docility, soundness and endurance. Given all these qualities, and then the more of action and style the animal possesses the better. He may be in possession of all these characteristics except the first, but being deficient in that he is not a good draft horse. On the other hand, he may weigh a ton, but if he be ill-tempered, unsound, or lacking in endurance his value is materially lessened. He may possess all the good points above enumerated, and yet be so deficient in energy and so heavy and sluggish in his movements as to come very far short of a perfect draft horse. Each of these qualities being desirable, it follows that the horse possessing all of them in the highest degree is the most desirable one. I do not propose to enter into a discussion as to the comparative merits of the various draft breeds. All have crossed kindly with our native mares, and all have marked substantial improvement, at least in the *size* of our draft stock, and some of the very best results in the production of work horses have been attained by a commingling of the blood of two or more of these imported strains.

I do not believe it is possible that a horse can be bred which will combine all the desirable qualities; the horse-of-all work is a myth; that cannot be realized. The general farmer needs a horse that combines a good degree of both action and weight, but the horse that suits *him* is not the heavy draft horse that is required in the trucks and drays of our cities. On the other hand, there has always been, and always will be, an active demand for road horses, with speed, style, docility and endurance as the qualities principally sought after, but too light for general farm work. Each of these types it will pay to breed, just as it pays to raise the various kinds of grain; but if all the resources of our country were directed toward producing wheat to the neglect of other grains we should very soon find the market overstocked and the business unprofitable. And so, when everybody catches the draft-horse fever we have, after a while, an oversupply of heavy horses and prices go down. There is room for all, and a steady demand at good prices for good specimens of each type of horses; and breeders of the best of any breed need have no fears of a serious decline in prices for such animals.

There are several styles of horses that sell well at present; and, in the breeding of any of these, farmers may, under favorable circumstances, engage, with a fair prospect of finding the business profitable. First, and highest-priced, are the very fast trotters and runners; but these very fast ones are not produced with certainty by even the most experienced breeders, with the best of breeding stock to work upon and the best of trainers to develop them; and it must be borne in mind, likewise, that it is only the fastest among the fast ones that bring exceptional prices. But there is a fascination about it which attracts many gentlemen of wealth and leisure to the business, the question of profit and loss being with them a secondary consideration. It affords them enjoyment and recreation, and it is indulged in mainly to that end; and into such hands the breeding of horses for speed alone, whether runners or trotters, may largely be left.

The next class, in the scale of prices, is the large, stylish, high-stepping carriage or coach horse. Such horses may be bred with a good degree of certainty, with the proper stock to breed from, and there is but little expense attending the breaking and training. Such as prove rather deficient in size, style, and action may make very serviceable farm horses, but to command the best price for the carriage or coupé there must be rather more of spirit, and they must be rather more "rangy" and possess higher knee action than is desirable for farm work. Such horses may be produced by coupling large, stout mares with a good-sized, highly-bred, stylish, high-stepping trotting stallion, or a stylish, large thoroughbred. The latter is the course of breeding by which the coach-horse breeds of England, France, and Germany were produced; and as these have already been extensively introduced into the United States they will no doubt be used to a very considerable extent here by breeders of coach and carriage horses. I would recommend, however, that good judgment and discriminating intelligence be made use of in selecting sires from among these imported horses, for some of them are but sorry mongrels in point of blood. Only those which show unmistakable evidence of high breeding and quality should be patronized, for here, as in all other cases, the mere fact of importation alone should not commend a horse to popular favor.

Another class of horses for which the demand is almost unlimited is the blocky, compact, low but quick-stepping and active draft horse. For use on our farms and for ordinary work they are wanted of from 1,100 to 1,300 lbs. weight. For our omnibuses and express wagons the demand is for the same style of horse, but heavier, weighing 1,300 to 1,500 lbs., while for carts and for heavy freighting they can scarcely be too large, provided they are sound, hardy, and active. The great trouble with horses of this class is a lack of endurance. Too many of them have broad, flat, brittle hoofs, or the opposite extreme of contracted, narrow heels; both are to be avoided. Many of them have unsound joints, especially at the hocks; and the bone is round, beefy, and of a coarse, porous nature. In selecting breeding stock to produce this class of horses especial regard should be had to these points. The hoof should be full and of good size—neither flat nor contracted at the heel. The legs should be clean and flat; the joints firmly corded, free from curbs, spavins, and beefiness. The flank should be full and low, for that indicates a good feeder. The chest should be wide and the girth large, for that indicates lung-power and what is termed "constitution." The fore legs should be set *under* the horse, and not be stuck on the outside, "like a pin in a log." He should be short on the back, slightly arched at the coupling, well ribbed up, full in the quarters, heavy-boned, short-legged, compact, blocky, gentle, good-tempered, active, wide-awake, but not nervous or restless. In motion he should travel free, level, and true, with feet and legs carried well under the body. Such a horse will *sell*, and sell *readily* at all times and at a good price, no matter what his color may be; and his price will increase in proportion to his size, from 1,100 up to 1,700 lbs.

The general farmer cannot afford to breed for racing speed; he must leave that to gentlemen of means, who, with the choicest brood mares as well as sires, and with every appliance for successful training, can engage in the lottery of breeding for exceptional speed, because they can afford to take the chances, and because they find a considerable portion of their reward in the relaxation from other cares which this business affords. But the general farmer must raise horses that he can sell or use. He must do the work of the farm mainly with mares that, while performing their labor satisfactorily, will each year produce colts which at four or five years old will be salable horses. He must keep such brood mares as, when coupled with good stallions, will usually produce horses that will meet the demands of commerce. And right here it may be well to say that while the demands of commerce are liable to a considerable degree of change from year to year, yet the breeder who produces a really first-class horse of any kind, will always find a ready market for it at a remunerative price.

Many people imagine that there is some great mystery—some occult science--involved in the selection and management of horses for breeding purposes, but there is nothing of the kind about it. It is only the application of good, common sense and perfect familiarity with the points of a horse, joined to a thorough knowledge of the best methods of feeding and managing horses in general; because the rules that apply in the selection of a foal that is designed to be used for breeding purposes, so far as the appearance of the animal is concerned, are precisely the same as if it were to be selected for other uses; and the general rules for the feeding, breaking and training for other purposes apply here as well.

I will presume that the breeder has definitely decided in his own mind what breed or strain or family he proposes to select from. He ought then to try to find a colt that has the longest possible ancestral line uniformly distinguished for the quality upon which he bases his selection, and then he should look carefully to see that no constitutional infirmities have been inherited. If there has been blindness—not the result of accidental injury—in the near ancestry, even though the colt himself may be apparently free from any defects in his organs of vision, this fact must be regarded as a point against him. And so of any other constitutional defect, weakness, or infirmity, whether of form, structure or disposition. Infirmities of temper are especially liable to be transmitted. It is very desirable that the breeder should know, as fully as possible, the character of the ancestry on both the paternal and maternal sides; and the farther back they can be shown to be free from constitutional defects of any kind the better. The colt himself may be free from any serious defects, but if they are known to have existed in his near ancestry there is always more or less danger that he will transmit them to his progeny. Every observant horseman of experience can call to mind numerous instances confirming the truth of this position. The writer once owned a grey stallion that was got by a grey stallion out of a grey mare. When placed in the breeding stud it was found that he occasionally got dun colts, even out of grey mares. Investigation into the ancestry of this horse developed the fact that his second dam was a dun mare. Here we had the inherited quality of color lying dormant through two generations, and reappearing under the most unexpected circumstances in the third.

But while all these points are important it may not be out of place to remind the reader that the man who expects to find all the good qualities and perfect immunity from fault of any kind, in any one animal, will look a long time in vain. This ideal can only be approximated, never reached, in any race or breed.

GENERAL MANAGEMENT OF THE STALLION.

The most frequent mistake made by inexperienced persons, and even by many who ought to know better, is the endeavor to have the stallion in fine show condition by the time the season opens. To this end various drugs, nostrums and roots are recommended; the horse is kept carefully housed and closely blanketed; he is loaded with fat; his muscles become soft and flabby for want of exercise, and although he may come out in the show-yard at the opening of the season looking "as sleek as a mole," and apparently in the very pink of condition, he is in reality not nearly so well fitted for service in the stud as he would have been had this fitting-up process been entirely dispensed with.

It may be laid down as a general rule, that a healthy horse needs no medicine whatever to put him in condition for the stud. The whole secret of successful preparation lies in a few words. Let him be well and regularly fed on healthy, nutritious food, with plenty of exercise every day, to keep his muscles firm and hard, and let him be well groomed, so that his coat may present a fine appearance. The skin should be kept thoroughly clean by occasional washing and frequent brushing and rubbing. The mane and tail should be especially looked after, with reference to cleanliness of the skin. If very dirty, soap may be freely used in the cleansing process; and when this is faithfully attended to there will be but little danger of having a fine tail or mane ruined by rubbing.

The food should mainly be good, sound oats —nothing is better; but this should be varied by an occasional ration of corn or barley; for horses, like men, are fond of variety in their food, and an occasional change of diet is conducive to health. Wheat bran is an invaluable adjunct to the grain ration, and can never be dispensed with. It is the cheapest, safest and best of all regulators for the bowels, and it is especially rich in some of the most important elements of nutrition. No specific directions as to the quantity of food can be given. Some horses will require nearly twice as much as others; and the quantity that may be safely given will depend somewhat upon the amount of exercise in any given case. Some horsemen recommend feeding three and others four times a day; but in either case no more should ever be given than will be promptly eaten up clean. If any food should be left in the box it should be at once removed and the quantity at the next time of feeding should be reduced accordingly. As a rule, it will be safe to feed as much as the horse will eat with apparent relish; and then, with plenty of exercise, he will not become overloaded with fat. The hay, as well as the grain feed, should be sound and free from mould and dust, and the stall should be kept clean, well lighted and perfectly ventilated.

The amount of exercise to be given will vary somewhat with the condition and habit of the horse. If he be thin in flesh, and it is thought best to fatten him up, the exercise should be lighter than it otherwise would be; and, on the other hand, if there is a tendency to become too fat this may be corrected by increasing the amount of exercise that is given. Draft horses should rarely be led or driven faster than a walk in taking their exercise, and they will require much less of it than the roadster or the running horse—a moderate "jog" daily will benefit them. I am clearly of the opinion that in no one particular is there more faulty management on the part of lazy grooms and stable hands than in the matter of exercising stallions while doing service in the stud. They should not be walked nor jogged so long that they will become jaded or wearied, but they should certainly have enough of it daily to keep the muscles hard and firm, the appetite good and to prevent them from laying on an undue amount of fat. No draft horse, under ordinary circumstances, should have less exercise than five miles a day, and the roadster and running horse may safely have six miles, which in some cases should be increased to eight or even ten.

The point to be aimed at in the stable management of the stallion is so to feed, groom and exercise as to keep the horse up to the very highest possible pitch of strength and vigor. The idea which prevails among many stable grooms that feeding this or that nostrum will increase the ability of a horse to get foals is sheer nonsense. Anything that adds to the health, strength and vigor of the horse will increase his virility or sexual power, simply because the sexual organs will partake of the general tone of the system; and, on the contrary, whatever tends to impair the health and vigor of the general system will have a deleterious effect upon the sexual organs. A healthy horse needs nothing but good food, pure air, plenty of exercise, with due attention to cleanliness and regularity in feeding and watering;

and when all these things are attended to properly the drugs and nostrums that stable lore prescribes as "good for a horse" would better be thrown to the dogs.

For the use of the stallion I like a box stall not less than twelve by eighteen feet, without any manger or rack whatever for the hay, and with a box snugly fitted in the corner for the grain. Many prefer that the feed boxes should be entirely detached from the stall, to be removed as soon as the horse is done eating. The hay is put on the floor in one corner of the stall, and thus there is nothing—no projections, boxes, racks, mangers, sharp angles, etc.—upon which a spirited, restless horse may injure himself. If, in addition to these precautions, the sides of the stall be lined all around—doors and all—with stout boards, standing out at the bottom about one foot from the wall, and sloping upward and toward the wall for a height of three and a half feet, you will have a stall in which it will be well-nigh impossible for a horse to injure his mane or tail by rubbing. In such a box the horse need not be kept haltered, and the owner may feel assured that the liability to injury is reduced to a minimum.

One of the most pernicious and dangerous of all practices, especially among breeders of draft horses, is that of overfeeding in order to produce great weight. Draft horses are not exactly bought and sold by the pound, like hogs and steers; yet frequently the first thing one of these draft-horse breeders will speak of is the weight of his horse. "That stallion weighs 1,900." "This filly weighed 1,400 at two years old," and similar remarks are specimens of the "horse talk" most common among breeders of draft horses; and they feed to produce *weight*, just as the man does who is feeding hogs or cattle for pork or beef. It is an easy matter to add 200 lbs. weight to a fair-sized horse when in ordinary flesh; and a draft horse that has less than two inches of adipose tissue on his ribs is not fit to show anywhere—at least so the fashion runs.

It is not strange that horses so overfed and loaded down with fat should be unable to work in warm weather, or that their reputation for endurance should suffer. A good roadster weighing 900 lbs. when in condition for work will make his mile in 2:30 or go for hours at the rate of ten miles per hour; but load the same horse with fat, until his weight is 1,200— which can easily be done—and you can "break his heart" in three minutes on the road. Goldsmith Maid was a marvelous trotter, and her easy, cat-like strides carried her to the front in 2:14 when she was in good condition to trot; but if she had been made as fat as a show-yard Clydesdale she would have waddled like a duck and a "four-minute horse" could have beaten her. Both endurance and procreative power are largely matters of *condition*, and draft-horse breeders seldom have their horses in that condition which is favorable to great excellence in either. For the reputation which has, to some extent, attached to them as soft and unable to stand up under hard work, and as being rather uncertain foal-getters, the breeders of these horses have only to thank their own pernicious system of extravagantly high feeding; and unless they abandon or considerably modify their practice in this regard the reputation of all our draft breeds is likely to suffer still further. Liberal, and even generous feeding, with plenty of exercise, is essential to perfect development; but feeding horses as we do hogs or steers, merely with a view to adding so many pounds to their weight, is a pernicious custom and should be condemned.

A well-informed writer in the *North British Agriculturist* some years ago animadverted very severely upon this pernicious system of overfeeding, which prevails in Great Britain to even a greater extent than in this country; and his remarks are so pertinent that I quote from the article as follows:

The number of useful horses sacrificed to forcing and feeding for show and sale appears to be on the increase alike in England and Scotland. Old Citadel, and other frequent prize-winners among thoroughbreds, hunters, and cobs stand the wear and tear of show-yard preparation better than most of the agricultural horses. A considerable number of promising young cart horses and mares at the Royal Meeting at Bristol were overlaid with beef and fat to the detriment of usefulness and soundness Abundant illustration of the evil is seen at every large show. Several of the Bristol contingent were sadly gummy and itchy about their legs; several were puffed and full in their hocks, looking as if they had been strained, and had got both bog spavins and thoroughpins; from the same senseless high feeding several had early developed sidebones. Yet, even with these notable defects—doubtless regarded by the judges as temporary, and not hereditary—several horses at Bristol managed to gain the coveted rosettes. Can judges and stewards at important meetings do nothing to carry into effect the sensible rules generally laid down in their printed programme as to overfeeding, but systematically ignored? Cannot symmetry, style, and usefulness be fairly estimated without dangerously overloading the animal with beef and fat? Should it be essential to the successful exhibition of a good horse or bull that for months he should drink, as many do, two or three gallons of cow's milk daily? This artificial treatment greatly improves the looks of plain, flat-sided, weak-loined subjects; but it cannot give the essential shape, style, and action; and besides the ailments already mentioned it engenders in horses, as in other animals, liability to anthrax or blood poisoning, of which quarter evil and splenic apoplexy in cattle are the most familiar examples. Many gross, overfed horses suffer from similar conditions; they take what at first appears to be a simple cold; the throat becomes very sore, congestion, rapidly followed by extravasation of blood, occurs throughout the lining membrane of the air passages; treatment in such gross, overfed subjects is singularly unsuccessful, and in fifteen or twenty hours the patient dies, suffocated from pulmonary apoplexy. Among the young horses got up for town sale, as well as those sacrificed to showing, it is wonderful to observe the amount of fat laid on, not only externally, but around the internal organs. The omentum of a four-year-old cart horse is sometimes overlaid with four or five inches of firm fat. Heart, kidneys, and other organs are proportionally loaded. Amidst the fibres of the heart and other muscles the enfeebling fat is also laid down, interfering with muscular capability. Woe betide the unfortunate animal which, in such a state of obesity, is put to severe exertion. Sudden death may result from the giving way of some organ or vessel weakened by the fatty degeneration, or dangerous disease of the air passages or laminitis is established; whilst eight or ten months of careful feeding and regulated exercise are required before such an overfed horse is fit for really hard work. Surely the reprehensible fashion of forcing and overfeeding animals intended for work or for breeding should be held somewhat in check by the consideration of the dangers of such a practice and by its serious interference with successful breeding!

It has been noticed that draft stallions imported to this country are frequently troubled with what appears to be chronic grease, or scratches, which causes ugly, itching sores on the legs; and, so far as my observation goes, the horses thus attacked have almost universally been such as have been kept in very high flesh, with but little exercise. From this fact I several years ago adopted the theory that this diseased condition was usually the result of the course of feeding and management pursued, and that no treatment would avail to cure the disease so long as the cause remained.

Acting on this theory I undertook the treatment of a stallion that was affected as above described. Commencing soon after the close of the season, he was turned out in a small pasture lot, which was so securely fenced that there was no possibility of his breaking out. From this time on, so long as the grass remained good, no other food was given him. His stable door opened into this pasture, and it was at all times left open, so that he could go in and out at his pleasure. When the grass began to fail, on the approach of winter, he was given each day as much corn-fodder as he would eat, but no grain whatever; always giving him the run of the pasture. This treatment was kept up until the 1st of February, the horse being confined to his stable only during the night, and not then except in extremely cold or stormy weather. He was thus kept about four months without any grain whatever, but with all the corn-fodder he would eat after the grass failed. As a result of this treatment, without the administration of medicines of any kind, he was completely renovated and cured, and no symptoms of the disease ever appeared afterward.

Another case, which affords a striking practical illustration of the effects of overfeeding and lack of exercise in the stallion, is that of an imported Percheron stallion, owned for many years by the late Hon. Z. T. Chandler, of Michigan. In July, 1876, the man in charge of Mr. Chandler's stables wrote me concerning the horse as follows:

This horse was imported to Baltimore in 1868. Two years after he was purchased by Mr. Chandler and sent to this farm, where he has ever since been. But he was put under very bad management—kept in his stall, with very little exercise, sometimes for months not stepping out of his stall, not even to be watered, loaded with fat—and of course he became a very uncertain foal-getter. He came into my charge late in the spring of 1873 in this condition. That season he only got seven colts, three of which died from premature birth. After the season was over, not believing in that way of treating a stock horse, I put him into the team, worked him steadily, fed sparingly, got his flesh off from him, brought him to the next season in spare flesh, hard as a plow-horse, required his groom to give him at least twelve miles of good active motion a day, and he produced that season a very fair proportion of colts. I have continued to handle him in the same way, and he is now about to close his season, having booked a hundred mares, very few of which have been returned to him. His flesh is as hard as that of a plow-horse; indeed, he is able, if I chose to put him to it, to go into the plow, and, to all appearances, do the best day's work of his life.

CONTROLLING THE STALLION WHEN IN USE.

Although the temper and disposition of the stallion are largely matters of inheritance, yet much depends upon the breaking and management. It is easier to spoil a horse than it is to cure him of bad habits after they are once formed If there is any manifestation of a disposition to be "headstrong" and unruly he should never be led out except by a bridle that will enable the groom to exercise the most perfect control over him. The one that I have found most effectual is made by taking an ordinary "snaffle" bit, with rings of moderate size, and with the head-piece made in the usual way; get a blacksmith to attach a well-polished, round iron bar to the right-hand ring by means of a small link connecting the bar and the ring; to the other end of the bar attach the usual sliding rein used on stallion bridles (see Fig. 1). Put the bridle on the horse in the usual way, and then, with the right hand on the bar and the left on the bridle-ring next to you, press the bar back and the ring forward until the bar will pass through the ring in the left hand. This bar should be made just as long as will admit of its being passed into the other ring in this manner; that is, it should be about equal in length to the bit and rings when stretched out straight, and the bit and rings should be so adapted to the size of the mouth and under jaw that when a little pressure is brought to bear upon the rein attached to the end of the lever formed by this iron bar the rings of the bit will be brought within an inch of touching each other (see Fig. 2). The leverage given by this appliance, when well fitted, will enable any one to hold the most unruly and headstrong horse in check. It is not necessarily severe when the horse behaves himself, and when he is not disposed to do this he can very suddenly be brought back on his haunches by a moderate touch on the rein. When the bar is not needed the rein to which it is attached may be passed over the head and down through the ring on the near side, as shown in Fig. 3, instead of under the jaw, as in Fig. 1.

It requires some skill and a good deal of patience to teach a stallion how to behave himself properly when brought out to serve a mare. He should never be allowed to go onto her with a rush; but he should be led up on the near side of the mare to within about ten to fifteen feet of her, and made to stand with his head toward the mare, about opposite her head; and when he is ready he should be led toward her and made to commence the mount when by her side instead of going for a rod or so with his fore feet sawing the air, as is often the case. By observing these directions there will be but little danger of injury to the stallion by a kick from the mare when he is mounting, especially if a good man is at her head to prevent her from wheeling toward the horse when he approaches. The danger to the horse is always greatest when he is coming off, because many mares will kick then that will stand perfectly still when he is mounting. To obviate this the groom who holds the horse should seize the mare by the bits with his left hand at this moment and bring her head around toward him by a sudden jerk as the horse is coming off.

But in most cases, indeed in *all* cases where there is not an absolute certainty that the mare will stand perfectly quiet, the hobbles

STALLIONS, BROOD MARES AND FOALS. 117

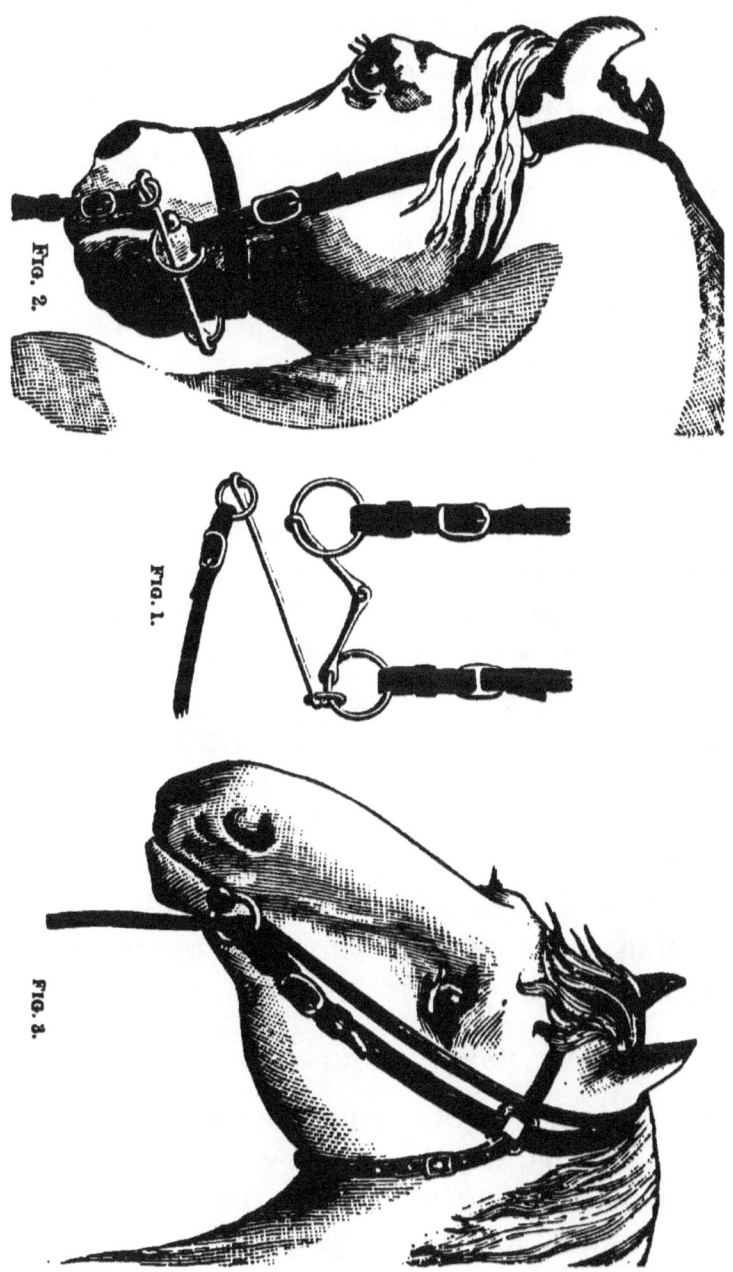

should be used, and then there can be no danger. To make these, prepare two straps of very strong but soft harness leather two inches in width and long enough to buckle comfortably around the mare's hind pasterns. The buckles must be strong and well made, and in each of these straps there should be sewed a strong, flattened ring. Next prepare a collar-piece of two-inch leather, and about as large as an ordinary horse-collar, so that the mare's head will readily pass through it; to this collar fasten securely two stout straps each an inch and a half wide and just long enough to pass down between the fore legs and reach the straps on the hind legs; attach stout buckles near the ends of the straps, but far enough from the ends to leave room to adjust them to different-sized mares; buckle these straps to the rings in the straps that are fastened to the hind legs, and buckle up short enough to effectually prevent the mare from kicking, if she should be disposed to do so. All this can be adjusted in a moment's time and by its use all danger from kicking is avoided.

WHEN MARES SHOULD BE TRIED.

A point upon which there is great diversity of opinion is when and how often a mare should be tried after she has been served by the stallion. A mare will almost invariably be "in heat" on the ninth day after foaling if she is healthy and has received no injury in giving birth to her foal; and most horse-breeders think it is best that she should receive the horse at that time if it is desired that she should be kept for breeding purposes. I can remember when it was the almost universal custom to try mares every week after they had been served, but that is not the present practice of experienced horsemen. The rule that now receives the most general sanction is not to try the mare again after service before the lapse of two weeks. I have taken a great deal of pains during the past few years to ascertain the views of prominent, intelligent and experienced breeders upon this point, and I find them, with very great unanimity, agreeing that after the ninth day from foaling there is no regular period for the return of heat (although some breeders think the twenty-seventh day is almost as certain a period as the ninth, and better for many reasons, while still others prefer the eighteenth day), neither is the period uniform in duration. Some mares will appear to be in heat nearly all the time, while with others it recurs but rarely and lasts but a very short time; consequently if the mare, after service, goes out of heat within a few days she should be served when she comes in again, even if that should be within nine days; but should the period not pass off she should not be served again under eighteen days. As a rule it is best to try the mare again within from two weeks to eighteen days after service, and then if she refuses the horse she should be tried every week for some four weeks; and if she fails to come in within that time it will be reasonably certain that she is in foal. She ought to be closely watched, however, for some weeks afterward, because in some cases mares will pass over a period of one or two months, or even longer, without any appearance of heat, and yet not be pregnant. Again, there are other mares—and they are more numerous than one would suppose—that will appear to be in heat and will freely receive the horse when they are in foal, and even almost up to the time of foaling.

For convenience in trying mares it is best to erect the barrier parallel to and about four feet distant from a solid fence or wall, so that the mare will be compelled when behind it to stand with her left side toward the horse: and the barrier should be so substantially built that it cannot be kicked or pushed down. In many cases the only barrier used is a strong pole fixed about three and a half feet from the ground; but it is much safer and better to build up the space to that height close and solid, with strong material of some kind, so as to lessen the danger from kicking and striking. This may be conveniently done by setting three posts firmly in the ground, about four feet apart, and nailing strong oak or other hardwood boards to these posts, on both sides, from the ground up to the required height, and then capping them over with a board of the same material. When trying the mare keep the horse well in hand, by the use of the bit previously described if necessary, and do not let him get his nose further back than to the mare's flank. If the stallion is a valuable one and is expected to do much service it will be best to have another horse of but little value for a teaser, but when the service required is but light it will work no injury to the horse to let him do his own teasing. Occasionally a horse will be found to have a peculiar aversion to a certain mare to such an extent that he will refuse to serve her. In such a case it is well to bring into the same inclosure another mare that is in heat, and when his amorous desire is aroused by her presence he can usually be made to serve the one that he had formerly refused.

THE NUMBER OF MARES TO BE SERVED.

The number of mares that a stallion may safely be permitted to serve during a season has long been a subject of discussion among horse-breeders. It is generally held that the two-year-old stallion will be all the better for not serving any mares at all, that a three-year-old should be limited to fifteen or twenty services, and that a four-year-old should not go beyond twenty or thirty. There can be no question that the use of the procreative powers by the unmatured horse tends to retard his physical development, and as a general rule it may be stated that there is no horse but would be the better for absolute continence until he is fully matured.

But while this position is unquestionably based upon sound physiological law, and the true theory of perfect physical development in the male, there are advantages attending the earlier use of the stallion to a moderate extent that perhaps more than compensate for all the damage that may result from it. It is very desirable at the earliest possible stage in the life of a stallion to ascertain what his qualities as a foal-getter are likely to be, and with this object mainly in view I consider it wise to let the two-year-old serve a few choice mares, merely enough to show the character of his get. I should, with the same object in view, permit him as a three-year-old to serve a rather larger number, which may thereafter be increased with each succeeding year until he is fully matured, when if properly taken care of with reference to food and exercise one hundred mares may be safely served during the season. With the young stallion that is to serve but a few mares I should prefer that these should all be served within the space of a few weeks—say two or three a week until his limit for the season has been reached—and then let him be withdrawn entirely from the breeding stud. He will soon forget all about it—will cease to fret after mares, and will have nothing to do but to *grow* until the next season. But when it comes to doing *business* with the stallion he should rarely be permitted to serve more than twice a day; and even this should not be kept up for any great length of time. One a day during the season is better; but the groom cannot always do as his judgment dictates in this matter. If the horse has had a period of comparative abstinence he may, if convenience demands it, serve three times in one day for a few days in succession; but this should not be kept up long, and a season of comparative rest for recuperation should follow this extraordinary demand. In the great breeding studs of Germany, under government direction, it was long held that from fifteen to twenty mares was enough for a stallion during the season; but the number has gradually been increased without perceptible detriment, until now the number frequently exceeds one hundred.

The number of mares that a horse serves during a season appears to have but little effect upon the percentage of foals begotten. We have no official statistics bearing upon this subject in this country, but such as we have from the books of private keepers of stallions abundantly prove this position. The condition of the stallion appears to be the controlling consideration, and so long as he is strong and vigorous his powers of reproduction continue. There may come a time, however, when from overtaxing this power partial or entire loss of virility may ensue. The books of service of Rysdyk's Hambletonian show the following result:

Years.	Age. Years.	Mares covered.	Per cent of foals.	Foals dropped.
1851	2	4	Not re	ported.
1852	3	17	76	13
1853	4	101	78	78
1854	5	88	70	62
1855	6	89	72	64
1856	7	87	73	64
1857	8	87	72	63
1858	9	72	75	54
1859	10	95	70	66
1860	11	106	68	72
1861	12	98	69	68
1862	13	158	70	111
1863	14	150	61	92
1864	15	217	67	148
1865	16	193	67	128
1866	17	105	71	75
1867	18	72	58	42
1868	19	None.	..	..
1869	20	22	81	18
1870	21	22	72	16
1871	22	30	80	26
1872	23	30	80	24
1873	24	31	65	20
1874	25	32	75	24
1875	26	24	8	2

This table makes the remarkable showing of 1,331 foals begotten by a single horse out of

1,930 mares served—an average of 69 per. cent of foals to mares served. His average of mares served from the time he was three years old up to the year of his death (not including 1868, when he did nothing) was about 83 per year.

The statistics of horse-breeding in Saxony, from 1856 to 1862, inclusive (seven years), also confirm the position advanced on the preceding page, viz., that the procreative power of the stallion depends mainly upon his strength and vigor. The returns for 1856 show that the stallions that served 90 to 100 mares each produced a greater percentage of live foals than those that served any other number, except those that served from 30 to 40. In 1857 those that served over 110 mares each produced 25 per cent more foals than those that served a less number. In 1858 those that served 60 to 70 mares got a larger percentage of foals than any other, except one that served less than 10. In 1859 the highest percentage belonged to those that served 50 to 60 mares. In 1860 the highest belonged to those that served over 90 mares; while those bred to 10 or less stood lowest. In 1861 those that served 80 to 90 mares lead, while those below 20 show the smallest percentage of foals. In 1862 60 to 70 were the most productive, while those below 10 were the lowest in the percentage of foals produced. From this data, as well as those derived from the statistics of horse-breeding in France and the general results attained in this country, so far as we can approximate them, it is safe to conclude that the number of mares served has no influence on the percentage of foals got, and that a horse properly treated may serve from 80 to 110 mares in a season with as large an average percentage of foals as one limited to less than half that number.

EFFECT OF AGE UPON THE FERTILITY OF A STALLION.

Another point upon which there has been much discussion is the effect which age has upon the fertility of a stallion; and here again we are left without any official statistics of horse-breeding in our own country, and will resort to those of Saxony. For the years above quoted, 1856 to 1862, inclusive, we find the returns disclosing the following state of facts: In 1856 the average get of the stallions aged six, nineteen, twelve, eighteen, and fourteen, respectively, and in the order named, was the highest, while those aged eight, nine, seventeen, sixteen, five, and seven were the lowest. In 1857 those aged four, twenty, fourteen, seven, and eight got the largest percentage, in the order named, while those aged five, nine, eighteen, seventeen, and six were the lowest; and those aged twenty-one and twenty-two got a greater per cent of foals than those aged five, six, nine, ten, seventeen, and eighteen. In 1858 the highest average was produced by stallions aged nine, ten, five, six, eight, fourteen, seventeen, twenty, and twenty-two years, and the lowest by those aged eighteen, nineteen, four, three, thirteen, and seven, in the order named. In 1859 the percentage was nearly uniform for all ages. In 1860 those aged seventeen, eighteen, and nineteen led the columns, while those aged four, twelve, and nine were last. In 1861 the percentage was quite uniform regardless of age. In 1860 a stallion aged twenty begot twice as large a percentage as one aged four; one aged ten stood the highest, while sixteen, six, and four stood at the bottom of the list. The table of the get of Rysdyk's Hambletonian, on page 124, also shows that in his case age apparently had nothing to do with his fertility. Hence we conclude that, as in the number of mares served, so in the matter of age, the reproductive powers of the stallion appear to be almost entirely a matter of condition.

EFFECT OF AGE UPON THE QUALITY OF THE GET.

There has also been much speculation as to the comparative value of the foals got by a given stallion at different periods of life. The statistics of European horse-breeding throw but little light upon this subject, but our own trotting statistics furnish us with abundant evidence to prove that here also age has no effect.

128   A TREATISE ON HORSE-BREEDING.

To illustrate this point I give the following list of celebrated running and trotting horses, among the most distinguished, either as sires or performers, that have ever been produced in America, with the age of sire and dam. The age of the sire is given at the time of copulation, and that of the dam at birth of foal. The list is taken at random from names that suggested themselves to me on account of their reputation as sires or performers, and without reference to what the figures might show:

Name of horse.	Age sire.	Age dam.	Name of horse.	Age sire.	Age dam.
Sir Archy	27	9	Parole	18	11
American Eclipse	9	12	Harry Bassett	17	8
Lexington	16	14	Longfellow	13	12
Boston	18	19	Preakness	16	14
Fashion	7	10	McWhirter	6	9
Duroc	28	6	Bramble	21	8
Wagner	17	7	Fellowcraft	11	9
Grey Eagle	6	11 or 12	Sensation	23	9
Tom Bowling	19	13	Iroquois	24	11
Ten Broeck	6	10	Huntress	9	12
Aristides	18	5	Voltaire	4	12
Foxhall	5	7	Prospero	3	7
Rarus	13	10	Dame Trot	4	8
St. Julien	14	8	Elaine	8	12
Goldsmith Maid	4	8 or 9	Walkill Chief	15	7
Alexander's Abdallah	2	..	Orange Girl	21	13
Volunteer	4	4	Indianapolis	4	12
Dexter	8	10	Woodford Mambrino	18	8
Nutwood	5	5	Wedgewood	5	16
Maud S	9	9	Rysdyk's Hamblet'n	23	..
Mambrino Gift	6	7	Mambrino Chief	18	..
Scotland	15	10	Darby	10	6
Trinket	4	10	Piedmont	6	11
Lula	14	9	Edwin Thorne	7	11
Clingstone	9	6	George Wilkes	6	8
Daniel Lambert	9	11	Dictator	13	14
Jay-eye-see	14	13	Nancy Hanks	22	8
Olitipa	18	10	Allerton	7	5
Spendthrift	17	5	Stamboul	8	14
Duke of Magenta	24	8			

Of the foregoing Prospero, Dame Trot, and Elaine have the same sire and dam; Nutwood and Maud S. are half-brother and sister; Mambrino Gift and Scotland are both out of Waterwitch—the former by a six-year-old trotting sire and the latter by a fifteen-year-old thoroughbred. Woodbine at eight years old produced Woodford Mambrino by a horse of eighteen, and when herself sixteen she produced Wedgewood by a five-year-old stallion. Hambletonian got Dexter, his best son, at eight years old; Nettie, his next fastest by the record, when he was sixteen, and Orange Girl, who comes next, when he was twenty-one. Volunteer got St. Julien ($2:11\frac{1}{4}$) at twelve years, Gloster (2:17) at nine, and Huntress ($2:20\frac{3}{4}$) at seven. Electioneer's three fastest by the record—Sunol, $2:08\frac{1}{4}$; Palo Alto, $2:08\frac{3}{4}$, and Arion, $2:10\frac{3}{4}$—were begotten when he was seventeen, thirteen, and twenty-one years old, respectively. Happy Medium got Nancy Hanks, 2:04, when he was twenty-two, and Maxey Cobb, his next fastest by the record, when he was only eleven. Of Blue Bull's four fastest the first and fourth were begotten when he was sixteen and the second and third when he was twenty-two.

PERCENTAGE OF FOALS TO MARES SERVED.

Still another question of great interest to horse-breeders is this: What is the actual average percentage of live foals that a given stallion will get under average circumstances? In other words: What percentage of foals must a stallion get to entitle him to be classed as a reasonably sure foal-getter? And upon this there is often much loose assertion without any real array of facts to back it up. It is to the interest of stallion-keepers to make the largest possible showing in this respect; hence they often talk at random, and not unfrequently pervert facts. Perhaps in most cases actual falsehoods are not stated; but the parties do not care to *know* the exact truth lest they may be led by self-interest to state an untruth. Hence they find it convenient never to know the exact truth, and content themselves by saying: "Oh, he got nearly everything with foal." Now, from a very extensive correspondence with reliable breeders who keep accurate accounts of results, as well as from my own observation, based upon an experience of thirty years with many different horses, I am decidedly of opinion that the average indicated in the table of the get of Rysdyk's Hambletonian is considerably above the general average of stallions in this country.

But this question is removed beyond the realms of conjecture by the recorded results in the government breeding studs of Germany. I give herewith a table which was compiled by myself a few years ago from the statistics of horse-breeding in the government studs of Germany, as given by the late Hon. J. H. Klippart in his report to the Ohio State Board of Agriculture. These statistics run back to 1859, and include all the intervening years up to 1874 (except 1869), in which are shown the results at eleven different points. The first column under each locality named shows the number of stallions employed for that year; the second gives the average number of mares served by each horse, expressed in whole numbers and decimals; the third gives the percentage of mares served that proved in foal, and the fourth gives the percentage of mares served that produced live foals. The table is full of interest and may be studied by horse-breeders with profit. It will be observed that the percentage of mares that proved in foal, as well as the percentage of live foals dropped, varies considerably in the different establishments. The highest percentage of mares in foal was at the great Trakehnen establishment, in 1860, when the average was 80.2; and here we also find the highest average throughout the entire series of years. But we find the average running as low as 40 per cent in 1874, at Wickrath, with only 33.3 per cent of live foals, while several localities report as high as 62.6 of live foals. It would be interesting to know the causes which produced the great differences in these averages and why it is that the stallions in the Trakehnen establishment were so much surer, or else a smaller percentage of the mares barren, than at Wickrath and some others. But the average result obtained from this great number of stallions and mares for so long a period may safely be accepted as establishing a general law or rule that can be depended upon under like circumstances. (The tables above referred to will be found on the two following pages.)

Taking the statistics of all the establishments reported from 1859 down to 1874, with an average of over 1,000 stallions and 42,000 mares per year, as above stated, we find the results as follows:

Average percentage of mares in foal..................... 67.7
Average percentage of live foals dropped................ 53.3
Average percentage of mares aborted or miscarried....... 4.8
Average percentage of mares dying or not accounted for.. 9.6

If the results as ascertained from the foregoing statistics may be accepted as the general rule it follows that the average stallion will make as much money for his owner by standing at $10 the season as he will at $14.75 to insure a mare with foal, or $18.75 to insure a living foal; and that a horse that can show 53 living foals to 100 mares served is an average foal-getter. Whether these figures will apply exactly to horse-breeding as managed in this country or

STALLIONS, BROOD MARES AND FOALS.

TABLE.—SHOWING THE PERCENTAGE OF MARES GOT IN FOAL, OF LIVE FOALS DROPPED, AND OF MARES THAT ABORTED OR MISCARRIED, IN ABOUT 1,000 STALLIONS AND ABOUT 42,000 MARES, PER ANNUM, FOR FIFTEEN YEARS.

		1859	1860	1861	1862	1863	1864	1865	1866	1867	1868	1869	1870	1871	1872	1873	1874
Trakehnen. *Insterburg.*	Av. percentage of live foals	55.5	56.8	54.6	56.4	62.6	59.5	56.5	56	50							60
	Av. percentage in foal	71.5	80.2	77.2	77.1	75.4	74	75	74	74	69.5	80	73.4	80	81	80	
	Av. No. of mares to each stallion	41.4	49.6	55.8	55.8	57.5	52.2	44.8	43.8	47.1						62.3	
	No. of stallions	307	314	316	314	324	328	319	302	297	295	298	291	302	313	327	
Marienwerder. *Prussia.*	Av. percentage of live foals	52.4	56.4	55.8	55.8	58.8	58.8	57.1	54.7	52.4	52.7	50.9	58.7	53.8	50.7	51.5	54.9
	Av. percentage in foal	62.2	67.8	67.8	68	69.1	69.8	68	69	71	71	66	67	67	63	64	66
	Av. No. of mares to each stallion	38.8	41.9	42.6	46.6	48.6	45.1	43.4	37.8	30.4	37.4	43.8	42.6	43.8	49.5	52	51
	No. of stallions	90	90	90	100	105	105	105	105	103	105	105	105	105	100	116	
Lindenau. *Mark Brandenburg.*	Av. percentage of live foals	51.6	47.1	49.6	50.2	50.4	50.9	50.9	50.7	50.9	51.8	51.1	53.3	50.9	50.8		
	Av. percentage in foal	62.2	64.5	64.1	65.5	66.3	66	68	67	68	71	70	65	65	65		
	Av. No. of mares to each stallion	38.5	42.0	42.1	26.2	46.4	42.6	38.7	33.9	32.4	33.4	36.2	37.9	40.9	59	49	
	No. of stallions	137	131	136	133	134	136	138	140	159	157	152	144	146	145	153	
Zirka. *Province of Posen.*	Av. percentage of live foals	55.1	56.8	58.3	60.5	60.2	62.2	62.6	62.8	62.3	55.3	51.9	54.6	50.8	50.9	53.8	
	Av. percentage in foal	71.2	70.2	70.3	72.8	71.8	73	73	73	73	64	65.9	71	66	68	64	66.8
	Av. No. of mares to each stallion	33.2	37.8	42	45.1	45.3	42.6	41.3	40.7	36.1	70.7	43.9	40.1	47	58	39	
	No. of stallions	198	128	135	142	143	140	144	145	143	163	174	180	204	225		
Lebus. *Silesia.*	Av. percentage of live foals	46.3	48.9	47.6	40.4	48.3	49.1	49.7	49.1	48.7	49.2	49.6	44.6	54.8	52.8	53.8	
	Av. percentage in foal	59.2	59	58.7	60.7	57.8	60	58	58	58	61	65	66	62	64		
	Av. No. of mares to each stallion	48.1	53.9	54	63.8	60.4	54.5	50.9	44.6	42.9	47	48.9	51.8	63.2	70	52	
	No. of stallions	149	141	143	139	150	150	152	152	156	157	163	159	160	167	176	

TABLE—SHOWING THE PERCENTAGE OF MARES GOT IN FOAL, OF LIVE FOALS DROPPED, AND OF MARES THAT ABORTED OR MISCARRIED, IN ABOUT 1,000 STALLIONS AND ABOUT 42,000 MARES, PER ANNUM, FOR FIFTEEN YEARS.—*Continued.*

Year	Repitz & Dohlen, Saxony				Wabendorf, Westphalia				Wickrath, Rhine Provinces				Polen, Schleswig-Hols'n				Celle, Hanover				Dillenberg, Hesse-Nassau			
	Av. percentage of live foals	Av. percentage in foal	Av. No. of mares to each stallion	No. of stallions	Av. percentage of live foals	Av. percentage in foal	Av. No. of mares to each stallion	No. of stallions	Av. percentage of live foals	Av. percentage in foal	Av. No. of mares to each stallion	No. of stallions	Av. percentage of live foals	Av. percentage in foal	Av. No. of mares to each stallion	No. of stallions	Av. percentage of live foals	Av. percentage in foal	Av. No. of mares to each stallion	No. of stallions	Av. percentage of live foals	Av. percentage in foal	Av. No. of mares to each stallion	No. of stallions
1859	43.9	58.4	97.1	115	45.2	59.2	91.1	75	49.6	57.6	35.4	50												
1860	48.7	57.3	38.5	107	46.6	59.9	33.9	77	50.1	58.7	43.1	50												
1861	47.5	63	37.6	105	46.4	59.4	50.2	79	49.8	56.9	50.7	50												
1862	50.2	61.5	33.5	100	46.2	60.7	34.6	80	52.3	59.9	36.5	51												
1863	51.1	64.2	44	105	47.1	59	34.8	81	52.9	58.6	34.9	55												
1864	52.9	65.5	41.9	100	47.8	60.3	30.6	77	53	60	28	51												
1865	51.3	52.9	42.6	99	51.6	63	25.1	74	52.1	52	23.2	48												
1866	51	66	40.1	97	47.8	64	24.8	78	48	60	21.9	66	46.2	61	26.6	15	55.5	65	43.6	216	39.9	48	45.6	82
1867	48.9	68	37.6	90	43.8	59	27.1	68	42.9	58	26	65	55.5	62	20.9	17	52.6	62	35.7	203	38.3	42	45.1	80
1868	49.3	63	33.4	84	46.7	60	29	68	43.8	53	39.9	52	53.9	61	27.2	24	53.8	63	37.9	190	45.2	48	36.9	83
1870	49.1	64	34	82	47.8	65	28.5	68	39.1	57	18.4	43	50.4	65	45.2	31	53.9	65	49.3	184	40.3	42	28.5	102
1871	49.1	62	36.2	72	51.5	68	29.7	64	45.2	56	15.7	41	56.2	63	46.8	35	56.5	66	39.7	172	46.2	50	33.4	91
1872	45.1	65	38.4	72	48.5	62	41.6	67	44	50	30.9	47	51.2	62	56	43	60	66	57.8	179	46.3	48	48.2	85
1873	50.9	59	48.3	79	50	64	54	73	39	40	48	41	49.3	59	73	51	58.8	68	68	191	46.3	53	54	109
1874	42.8	59	49	83	46.8	58	47	81	33.3	40	46	47	51.6	62	62	64	59.3	68	59	217	46	53	52	108

not is of course not definitely known; but they are so nearly in accord with the results of my own experience and observation that I have no hesitation in accepting them as substantially correct. It appears to be true throughout all animal life that the very large breeds of any species are not so prolific as the medium or average sized ones; and this fact should not be ignored in considering this question with reference to horses.

MANAGEMENT OF THE STALLION AFTER THE SEASON CLOSES.

The condition of the stallion for the next season's business will depend largely upon the manner in which he is kept from the close of the present one until the next season commences. In most cases the period from the 1st of October to the 1st of March is one in which the stallion is not called upon to do duty in the stud, and usually but little is done after July 1. It is a period of rest, of recuperation from the drain upon the functions of the sexual organs which service in the stud has required; but it should not be a season of pampered and overfed indolence, as is too often the case. When it is convenient to do so, the very best possible treatment that can be resorted to during this period is to use the stallion at light work. If a draft horse that has been (as they all ought to be) broken to work, let him be driven moderately by the side of a quiet mare or gelding, worked regularly up to the 1st of February, and fed enough grain to keep him strong and healthy, but not fat. Oats will be much better food for him than corn; but if it is found that he is becoming too thin, or if the work is comparatively heavy, corn may be used part of the time with good results. If the stallion is a trotter or a roadster by all means drive him on the road. If you can use him regularly as a business horse so much the better; and, as in the case of the draft stallion, feed him enough to keep him strong and hearty, and work him right along, as though you intended that he should earn his living. This I am satisfied from experience is the best treatment for stallions of any breed, and will result not only in bringing the horses to the beginning of the next season in better condition than any other, but the probabilities are that a horse so treated will get more and better foals than one that is not worked during this period.

But in very many cases, and especially in large breeding establishments, and with thoroughbred stallions, the course recommended above is practically out of the question. The next best thing, then, if the horse must perforce remain in comparative idleness during the period mentioned, is to provide him with a large paddock—the larger the better always—and let him have the run of it at all times during pleasant weather, stabling him only at night and during storms; and when kept under these conditions it will be best to dispense almost entirely with grain food of all kinds. A run to grass during the late fall, if it can possibly be provided, will be one of the very best things that can be had; but this will rarely be practicable in such cases. The main reliance for food under these circumstances must be good hay; but I very greatly prefer corn-fodder when it can be had, as it furnishes a complete change of diet from what the horse has been accustomed to—a change that will prove highly beneficial to the general health of the horse. It reconstructs him, as it were, and makes a new horse of him after a few months of such treatment, and is certainly the next best thing to the run at grass, before recommended. But while he is kept on this food due attention must be paid to his bowels lest he should become constipated—a condition that can usually be prevented or remedied, should it occur, by the occasional use of a bran mash.

The necessity for this change in diet from grain to coarse and bulky food, like hay or corn-fodder, is increased in proportion to the degree of confinement to which the horse must be subjected. There is nothing that will so soon destroy the health and vigor of the horse, and especially of his genital organs, as close confinement and high feeding; and the man who endeavors to keep his horse in show condition the year round will find that he has undertaken a difficult, not to say dangerous undertaking. It will work in some cases for a year or two; but, like constant indulgence in intoxicating liquors in man, it will in the end sap the strongest constitution. A strong, vigorous horse may be able to withstand the deleterious influence for a few years, but it is only a question of time with the best.

EFFECT OF CASTRATION ON STALLIONS.

It may be proper to supplement what I have written upon the management of the stallion by a few remarks concerning the effect of castration and the time at which it should be performed. It frequently happens that it is found desirable to castrate a stallion after he has performed several seasons of service in the breeding stud, but many owners are deterred from doing so from mistaken notions as to the danger of the operation and its probable effect upon the temperament of the horse. So far as the danger is concerned it is very slight with any horse in good health and not enfeebled by age if performed in pleasant weather and by one competent to do the work properly; and the idea that castrating a stallion after he has arrived at mature years will make him dull, sluggish, and lazy, is altogether erroneous. Such displays of animation as are caused purely by his sexual desires will of course be wanting, but aside from these little change in his temperament will be noticed. Most horses that are kept closely stabled and given but little exercise, as is usually the case with stallions, will, when brought out, show a playful disposition; but when put at regular work much of this will disappear. Very few horses are gelded on the European continent, and yet the stallions that are used for work are found to be as tractable and quiet as geldings would be under similar circumstances.

Stallions are usually greatly superior to mares and geldings in courage. It is a rare thing to find a stallion that is "skittish" or easily scared. In this particular castration produces a great change in most horses. The horse that, as a stallion, was not afraid of anything, could not be frightened, and was never known to shy or run away from any object, often becomes a timid, flighty creature when gelded. The stallion in a herd of wild horses appears to consider himself the protector of the herd, and, instead of flying at the approach of danger, is rather disposed to stand his ground, and in many cases even to act on the aggressive, and never deigns to fly until the females of his herd are in motion. This same cool indifference to danger appears to attach to the domesticated stallion, and makes him much less liable than a mare or gelding to take fright and shy or run away.

It is the opinion of most experienced breeders that keeping a horse entire has a tendency to develop his shoulders; and it certainly does increase the size of the neck. It also gives a different expression to the head, so that the experienced horseman can usually distinguish between a stallion and gelding, simply by seeing the heads, almost as readily as a cattle-dealer can tell a steer from a bull by the head and horns. It is also thought by most breeders that this unusual development of the neck and shoulders in the stallion is at the expense of development of the hind quarters.

It is the usual custom to castrate at two years old, but if the colt appears to be timid and skittish a greater degree of courage will be developed by leaving him entire for a longer period. If he is inclined to be vicious the earlier the operation is performed the better; and horses that as stallions are so vicious as to be positively dangerous usually become docile and obedient after having been castrated. But the stallion that is timid and "flighty" will become so much more so when castrated that his usefulness for any business purpose will be practically destroyed; and in such instances the operation should never be performed unless there be some imperative reason for it.

FIGHTING BETWEEN STALLIONS.

When several stallions are kept on the same farm or in the same stable great care should be taken to prevent them from breaking loose and doing serious injury to one another by fighting; but in spite of all the usual precautions such accidents are liable to occur. I recently read an account of a combat of this nature where various means of separating the horses were tried in vain, when it was resolved to try the lasso. At the first cast one of the stallions was securely caught, but it was only after three unsuccessful attempts that the other one was secured. With a few men at each rope the infuriated beasts were easily choked down and separated. I have seen several conflicts of this nature, and know by experience something of the difficulty and danger of attempting to separate the combatants; but this is the first instance in which I have heard of the use of the lasso, and it occurs to me that it may frequently be found to be the very best possible means of accomplishing the difficult and dangerous task. The horses must be fearlessly approached, however, to succeed even with the lasso; for while the fight is progressing they are usually on their knees attempting to bite each other on the legs. The noise which attends such a combat is positively terrific, and usually paralyzes the spectators with terror. The horses rush at each other with a roar, and when about to come in contact they usually wheel about and receive the shock on their haunches. After a few seconds of contact at this point, when the roaring is usually most terrible, they again wheel about, endeavoring to grasp each other's fore legs with their teeth. To ward off this mode of attack each stallion usually sinks to his knees, and then the battle begins in earnest.

When a jack attacks a stallion he almost invariably makes for the throat of his antagonist; and when once his teeth are closed with a firm grasp there is no means of releasing his hold except to lay the infuriated beast senseless by a blow upon the head; and even then mechanical appliances often have to be used to unlock the clenched jaws. Such a contest as the one last described usually results in the death of the stallion; and when both stallions and jacks are kept in the same stable the greatest care should be taken to avoid the possibility of a combat between them.

THE BROOD MARE.

The influence of the dam in the transmission of hereditary qualities is, in my opinion, usually very much underestimated, and it is frequently ignored entirely by horse-breeders. Instead of classifying the various "families" of horses with reference to the female ancestry, as is the usual custom with cattle-breeders, the female element in the pedigree of a horse is almost entirely lost sight of, while to the male is given especial prominence. This cannot be other than a serious mistake; and the man who keep a worthless animal in the breeding stud simply because he cannot sell her will not be able to compete with his neighbor who reserves the very best mares of his raising for breeding purposes, even though they both patronize the same stallion. The mare certainly exercises as potent an influence upon the progeny as the stallion; and while in exceptional cases a very inferior one may produce a good foal, yet if we examine the records of the trotting turf we shall find that in nine cases out of ten, even when the pedigree of the dam is unknown, she was "a great road mare." In fact the more closely I observe the workings of heredity in the human family, as well as in our domesticated animals, the more thoroughly do I become impressed with the overmastering influence of the ancestry in the maternal line. So far as my personal knowledge extends all of our really great men have descended from mothers that possessed more than ordinary mental power; and a writer of fiction who has within a few years past attained a considerable degree of prominence asserts that the world has not yet produced a single exception to this rule. Greatness springs from greatness and every living thing brings forth young after its kind. And especially in the matter of soundness do I insist that the mare which is selected for the breeding stud should be unobjectionable. There is scarcely an ill to which horseflesh is heir that is not transmissible by inheritance. The precise disease itself may not be inherited, but the constitutional weakness that makes this or that organ peculiarly susceptible to disease is clearly a transmissible quality. No one will pretend to say that flatulent colic is an inherited disease; but we have the very best of evidence that some horses are more subject to this disease than others and that they transmit this tendency to their offspring. Acute laminitis may not be a constitutional infirmity, but the peculiar formation of joint that falls an easy prey to this disease is as clearly transmissible as are color and form.

CAUSES OF BARRENNESS IN BROOD MARES.

I have spoken at considerable length elsewhere of the dangers to stallions from overfeeding. All that was there said concerning the harmfulness of this practice as applied to stallions might well be repeated here with increased emphasis. It is undoubtedly one of the most frequent causes of barrenness and the dangers attending parturition are more than trebled in cases of excessively fat animals. Deaths from parturient fever, or milk fever, are almost unknown in mares that are kept actively at work and are in only moderate flesh at the time of foaling. A case well illustrating this point came under my own notice recently of a farmer who had four mares that dropped foals in one season. The mares were all very fat and had been kept in high show condition for a year or more. One of the mares died of parturient fever and he lost three out of the four foals.

I have had occasion heretofore to quote from that most excellent authority, Prof. Law, of Cornell University. A few years ago he prepared, at my request, for publication in a journal which was then under my control, an article on the causes of difficult impregnation and barrenness, and from this article I quote so much as relates to brood mares:

> Females that are not put to the male until long after they have reached maturity are often difficult to impregnate for the first time. This is frequently noticed in mares that have spent a good part of a lifetime at hard work: and in these cases it may often happen that the long inactivity of the generative organs has produced an inaptitude for procrea-

tion. As a rule the disused generative organs fail to acquire that permanent development which attends on habitual impregnation; and even after a single conception a long period of non-breeding leads to a striking diminution of the womb and passages.

But difficulty is often experienced in securing the impregnation of heifers that have reached full maturity but are neither old nor hard-worked, and the same difficulty is met with in comparatively young and idle mares. In such cases the trouble may often depend on undue sexual excitement, which leads to a spasmodic and rigid closure of the neck of the womb during copulation or to excessive expulsive contractions of that organ and the vagina and the rejection of the semen before impregnation has been effected.

Another occasional cause of sterility in such cases is the degeneration of the fallopian tubes, which have become blocked by the abnormal fatty product and no longer allow of the descent and impregnation of the ovum.

The obvious preventive of these conditions is to maintain the functional activity of the organs from the time of full maturity onward. It is a fundamental law of organic nature that structures and functions are developed in ratio with their use, so long as this is kept within natural bounds, and the generative system is no exception to this law. The cow or mare that is bred every year is a more certain breeder than the one which is allowed to skip three or four years between successive conceptions. The faulty conditions resulting from this deferred or irregular breeding will be individually considered below.

There is not a Scylla but has its Charybdis. We should keep this in mind in avoiding the danger just mentioned, and not be driven to the opposite extreme of breeding from very young females, whose development and stamina will be impaired by the constant drain upon it for the nourishment of the coming progeny. It is notorious that females who breed too early fail to attain the full size and development of their family. * * * Females should not be put to the male until they are at least verging on maturity. Above all, the system of breeding from very immature animals should not

STALLIONS, BROOD MARES AND FOALS. 147

be continued in the same line from generation to generation, as that can only tend to accumulate and intensify the evil. In the exceptional case of a very forward animal, where an early conception is especially desirable, and where the young dam is either not allowed to suckle her offspring or is allowed to skip the following year without breeding, the course may sometimes be profitable; but, as a rule, breeding from immature animals should be avoided, for the reasons above mentioned.

An excess of rich and stimulating food, and consequent plethora, is a common cause of non-breeding. In some such cases there is an accumulation of fat, as referred to above; but this condition is seen also in rapidly induced plethora, and where no time has been allowed for the development of fatty degeneration. Among others, the following conditions will serve to explain these: With an extra tension of the liquid inside the blood-vessels the tendency is to secretion rather than absorption; the rich and stimulating quality of the circulating blood maintains an unusual activity in the glands of the womb, and the result of these combined causes is an excessive production of uterine mucus, among which the semen is expelled before impregnation can be effected. The rich blood is, further, a stimulant to the muscular walls of the womb and vagina, and leads to their contraction under slight exciting causes, so that here again we have an effectual cause of the rejection of the semen and its failure to impregnate.

The correction for this state of things is to reduce the richness and stimulating qualities of the blood. Many accomplish this by bleeding the plethoric animal before putting her to the male. This often succeeds, for it promptly reduces the pressure of the blood within the vessels, and, by determining the absorption of liquid from all available sources, dilutes that fluid and renders it less stimulating. There is one objection to this course—that a moderate abstraction of blood from a system full of constitutional vigor acts as a stimulus to a still more rapid formation of blood for the purpose of supplying the waste, and thus the present success may be gained at the expense of a still greater and perhaps dangerous plethora in the near future.

A preferable course is to place the animal on a spare diet for some weeks before she is to be put to the male and to further deplete the system by the administration of one or two doses of laxative medicine. For the mare, four or five drachms of Barbadoes aloes; but care should be taken that the laxative be given early enough to avoid having it still operating when the animal is put to the male.

In certain animals and breeds there is a responsive activity of the generative organs, independently of plethora or other diseased condition, and in animals of this kind impregnation often fails to take place because of the ready rejection of the semen. Such excitement is, of course, greatest during the most active stage of *heat*, and lessens as the period approaches its end. Animals of this kind may often be got to breed if put to the male when the *heat* is passing off, and when they will only just receive him, though it would have proved a failure had they been served while at the height of the sexual passion.

Closure of the mouth of the womb may often happen from the unnatural excitability just referred to, the muscle which closes the neck of the womb being so rigidly contracted that it is impossible for the semen to enter. This may be easily corrected in the large animals by steady pressure with the fingers and thumb, drawn into the form of a cone, until the tension gives way and the hand passes freely into the womb. Just before putting to the male let the oiled hand be introduced into the vagina until it reaches the round, projecting, puckered prominence—the neck of the womb—at the farther end of the canal. In the center of this projection will be felt the depression leading into the opening. Into this it may be only possible at first to introduce one finger; this is to be followed by two, three, and finally by the four fingers and thumb, brought together into a point so as to form a cone. When the passage has been sufficiently dilated the animal should be at once served by the male, as delay may allow the relaxed muscle to recover its tone and close the opening as at first. The same end may be attained by introducing an instrument with smooth, rounded blades, fashioned after the manner of a glove-stretcher, and gradually dilating the passage. It is an easy process in the mare, on account of the shortness and dilatability of the mouth of the womb.

Acute disease of the ovaries may prevent conception in two different ways: 1st. It may prevent the development of the ovum or germ of the future animal; and, 2d, it may cause such sympathetic excitement and contractions in the womb that the ovum cannot be fertilized and retained.

1st. *The failure to develop ova* is met with when the whole of both ovaries are involved in certain diseases. When, for example, these organs have undergone complete fatty degeneration, or when they are the seat of extensive cysts, tuberculous deposits or cancer. The fatty change is extremely common in the improved breeds of cattle, sheep and swine. The tuberculous and cancerous taints run in certain families, and are to be mainly obviated by rejecting from breeding such as are strongly predisposed. To prevent *fatty degeneration* we should avoid excess of all foods that are especially rich in oil or that tend greatly to the production of fat. Among these may be named Indian corn, linseed cake, sorghum and beet. The females should further have a full allowance of exercise to keep the lungs in full activity and favor the oxidation of the fat-producing elements of the food. Absolute rest in hot, close buildings is to be especially avoided.

2d. *Sympathetic Excitement of the Womb.*—When one ovary, or only a portion of an ovary, is affected, the ovum may still be produced; but such is the sympathetic excitement of the womb that the fertilizing semen or the impregnated ovum is invariably rejected. Cases of this kind usually come in *heat* at irregular intervals, and in some instances sexual excitement is almost continuous so that the subject will neither breed nor fatten. They can usually be recognized by their history and by the examination of the ovaries by the hand introduced through the straight gut (*rectum*). Unless in the case of slight congestions, or other removable disorder, such ovarian disease can only be treated by the removal of the diseased ovary, and if both are affected the animal is necessarily rendered barren. The operation does not differ from ordinary *spaying* of a healthy animal.

The tortuous tubes through which the ovum passes from the ovary to the womb are frequently the seat of fatty degeneration, so that they become at once blocked by the morbid product and incapable of their normal contractions and the ovum fails to reach the matrix. When remediable at all, which is only in the earlier stages and slighter forms of the change, this is to be met by the measures advised for fatty degeneration of the ovaries.

Nearly all active diseases of the womb unfit it for retaining the product of conception. Tumors, inflammations and catarrhs, or mucopurulent discharges, usually lead to the destruction or expulsion of the semen or the product of conception, so that in all alike the restoration of a healthy condition of the womb is a prerequisite to breeding. We cannot enter further into this subject at present than to say that in simple catarrhal inflammation benefit may be derived from a daily injection of one-half drachm of sulphate of zinc, one-half drachmn of carbolic acid, one ounce of glycerine and one quart of water—to be used tepid.

Certain kinds of food prevent conception, or, what is equivalent, lead to an early abortion. Among these may be named ergoted grasses, smutty wheat and corn, musty grain, and aliments which produce scouring, indigestion, colic and diseases of the urinary organs. In the same category may be included the free drinking of iced waters when thirsty.

It has been frequently noticed that the persistent breeding of near relations has resulted in a sexual incompatibility which rendered a male and female of the same family incapable of breeding together, though each was perfectly fertile with strangers. When we must breed close this should be guarded against by having two or more branches of the same family kept in a different locality and climate, the influence of which may thus be obtained without changing the blood.

THE PRODUCTIVE PERIOD IN BROOD MARES.

The most fertile period in the mare's life is usually at from five to fifteen years of age. They may in exceptional cases be put to breeding as early as at two years old, but I do not recommend such a course as it seriously interferes with a symmetrical development. If from any cause a two-year-old filly has been served by the stallion and become pregnant it will be every way better to let her pass over her third year without breeding, so that she will not produce her second foal until she is five years old; but a well-developed three-year-old may be safely put to the horse, and she may then be kept at breeding without intermission so long as she remains fertile. At about twelve years the reproductive powers of some mares will begin to wane, but a large proportion of them are quite as reliable breeders up to about fifteen years of age as at any earlier period, especially if they have been kept at breeding from their maturity. Above this age they usually become more uncertain; and regular breeders well up in "the teens" are comparatively rare. There have been, however, well-authenticated instances of mares up to twenty-six years of age producing healthy, living foals. Old Fanny Cook, the dam of the noted trotting stallions Daniel Lambert and Woodward's

Ethan Allen, produced fifteen foals and dropped twins (one of which is still living) when she was twenty-two years old. The great English race mare Pocahontas lived to be thirty-three years of age and produced fifteen foals; her last, Auracaria, being dropped when she was twenty-five years old, and, contrary to what might have been expected, this daughter of old age herself became a great brood mare, producing, among others, the grand race horses Chamant and Rayon d'Or. Many other very remarkable cases have been reported to me—one by Mr. G. W. Henry, of Burlington, Ia., of a mare, still living at the date of his letter (July, 1882), which then, at twenty-six years of age, had produced nineteen foals and was supposed to be again in foal.* Several other cases have come under my observation where mares have produced from fourteen to eighteen foals. But these are exceptional cases and no breeder can safely base his calculations upon them.

I think most experienced breeders will agree that a sufficient amount of exercise and work or training to thoroughly develop the physical powers of both sire and dam is desirable; and, having this point in view, I would not recommend that a filly be relegated to the breeding stud until she has been trained and raced for a year or two, if race horses are desired. With

---

* *The Breeder's Gazette*, Vol. II, p. 71.

ordinary road horses and farm horses the young mares may be used sufficiently to effect the same object while they are being bred. I am a firm believer in the tendency of animal life to adapt itself to its surroundings and conditions; consequently, I believe in working the sires and dams that are to get and produce work horses and in trotting or running those that are to produce trotters and runners. It is a law of nature which cannot safely be ignored. The famous old pacing mare Pocahontas paced some of the hardest races of her life in the winter of 1853-54, and her great son Tom Rolfe was foaled a few months afterward. Blink Bonny, the dam of Blair Athol, ran many races in her younger days. The same is true of Seclusion, the dam of Hermit, and of Marigold, the dam of Doncaster, and of Little Lady, the dam of Camballo, and of Pocahontas, the dam of Stockwell, Rataplan, King Tom, etc. But it is needless to specify further; the history of the turf furnishes incontestable evidence of the correctness of the propositions announced at the beginning of this paragraph; and so emphatically has the experience of trotting-horse breeders within the past ten years confirmed it that the practice of breeding from other than sires in which speed has been developed as well as inherited has almost become obsolete among intelligent breeders.

On the other hand, I would expect but little, as a brood mare, from one that had been kept continuously on the turf or at hard, wearing labor, without breeding until past the prime of life. The sexual powers must necessarily become dwarfed, if not entirely lost, from long-continued disuse after having reached maturity; and mares so treated have usually proven barren, although some notable exceptions to this rule may be named. But exceptions are not safe guides for the breeder to follow. It is the general average of results that marks the road to success in any given line of business.

TIME OF FOALING AND PERIOD OF GESTATION.

When the time of foaling approaches the mare should be turned loose in a large and strongly-made box-stall, or if the weather is mild in a lot or paddock. Everything should be removed from the stall that would be likely to entangle or injure the colt in its struggles to get on its feet. There should be no openings under the manger or elsewhere into which, in its struggles, it might chance to force itself; many dead colts are taken every year from such traps as these. If the weather is warm it is decidedly better to give the mare the run of a good-sized lot, for it is noticeable that when parturition approaches they usually have a decided aversion to confinement. If confined in a stall or small paddock the inclosure should be so secure as to prevent any attempts at breaking out, as these would be liable to result in injury to the mare, and possibly to the foal. The writer recalls one occasion in his own experience where a favorite mare, that was thought to be near the time of foaling, was brought from her accustomed pasture and placed in the stable for the night on account of a probable storm. The mare was left, as was supposed, securely fastened in her box-stall, but to my surprise the next morning she was found in her accustomed pasture with a foal by her side. Although usually quiet—never before known to jump a fence—she had broken open the door of her stall and jumped two good fences to get back to her accustomed haunts before dropping her foal.

The average period of gestation in the mare is popularly placed at eleven months, but a careful comparison of statistics gathered from the books of several extensive horse-breeders of my acquaintance, whom I know to be accurate and painstaking in their methods, places the average period at about 340 days. It is a popular belief that male foals are carried longer than females, but the statistics do not bear out this conclusion. The observations of Dr. W. H. Winter, of Princeton, Ill., covering seventy-two cases, make the average period for males about 341 days, and for females 338 days, the longest being 370 and the shortest 317 days. Mr. M. A. Brown, from thirty foals in one year, found the average to be slightly greater for males than females, while in the following year, from thirty-two foals, the females were carried longest. He also reports a perfectly well-authenticated case where a two-year-old half-blood Percheron filly was bred to an imported Percheron stallion and produced a strong, healthy horse foal at just 300 days.* Mr. Brown has no doubt of the accuracy of this statement, the filly having been served but once. This is the shortest well-authenticated period of which I have any knowledge, although immature foals at shorter periods have been reported. Veterinary writers generally place the extremes at from 300 to 400 days, but the longest period that has been reported to me was by a correspondent at Chatham, O., who states that a mare belonging to him was served May 7, and did not drop her foal until May 17 of the following year, being a period of one year and ten days.†

In view of the indefiniteness of the period of gestation the mare should be closely watched, as there are certain signs of the near approach of parturition which rarely fail. The udder frequently becomes greatly distended sometime

---

* *The Breeder's Gazette*, Vol. V, p. 556. † *Ibid.*, Vol. I, p. 735.

before foaling, but the "teats" seldom fill out full and plump to the end more than a day or two before the foal is dropped. Another sign, which rarely precedes the dropping of the foal more than a week or ten days, is a marked shrinking or falling away of the muscular parts on the top of the buttocks back of the hips. In some cases, however, the foal may be dropped without any of these premonitory signs. I remember a case on my father's farm, where a roan mare that had been purchased, and was not supposed to be in foal, was worked hard at the plow up to about the middle of May. She was fed and turned out to pasture one evening, as was the custom, after having been worked hard all day, and nothing unusual was noticed in her appearance. The udder was not noticeably larger than usual, but next morning we found her with a good strong foal by her side. She was a sorry nurse, however, and the foal lived only a few weeks, dying from "scours" brought on, I believe, by careless feeding of the mare.

When the mare is a valuable one, and the prospective foal is looked for with a good deal of interest, it is quite well to watch her closely, as many valuable animals have been lost which by a little attention at the right moment might have been saved.

Moderate work is not only harmless but

positively beneficial to mares in foal, provided proper care be taken not to overload them. It is certainly better than keeping them tied up in the stable or permitting them to run at large in the yards or fields with many other horses. In the former case they suffer from want of exercise, and in the latter they are exposed to numberless accidents resulting from racing, playing or fighting with each other. In my own experience in horse-breeding more abortions have resulted from mares being kicked or otherwise injured by other horses when in the pastures than from all other causes combined. Exercise is essential to good health; and when moderate work is given—care being taken to avoid overloading and proper attention being paid to the shoeing so that there shall be no danger of strains from slipping—the mare will get plenty of exercise without the exposure consequent upon running at large with other horses. If proper care be taken the mare can safely be used in the ordinary work of the farm up to the very hour of foaling; but as this time approaches it is important that the weight be not heavy nor the pace rapid. After the foal is dropped the mare ought to have at least three or four days of rest and quiet, although many farmers who are hurried with their work and cannot very well dispense with the services of the mare in the field find no evil results following from working the mare moderately from the day after the foal is dropped. This practice, however, is not to be commended.

GENERAL SUGGESTIONS AS TO FOOD AND NURSING.

Many mares are at best but poor nurses. Under the head of "Feeding the Young Foal" will be found some suggestions as to the best food to be used in case the milk of the dam is not sufficient, but the food of the dam may be made to greatly influence her yield of milk. The foods that have been found useful in increasing the flow of milk in the cow will have the same effect upon the milk of the mare. Wheat bran is especially valuable for this purpose if mixed with some other and more nutritious foods. It may be made into a sort of slop and fed with ground oats or rye, mixed with cut hay or sheaf oats. Plenty of good fresh grass is one of the very best of aids to healthy and abundant nutrition for both mare and foal. Whatever grain ration is used I would recommend that it be ground and fed wet, mixed with cut straw or hay.

When mares are worked while suckling it is better that the foal should be left in the stable and that the mare be taken to the foal for it to suck at least three times during the day, ample time being given for her to cool out thoroughly before the foal has access to her, otherwise a gorge of the overheated milk may produce serious disturbances in the digestive organs of the foal. Many farmers, however, find little inconvenience from permitting the foals, especially when quite young, to accompany the dams to the field and follow them while at their work. This gives them an opportunity to empty the udder of the mare as often as it may be deemed desirable and obviates all danger from overgorging that arises when the mare and foal are separated.

FEEDING THE YOUNG FOAL.

It sometimes happens that the milk of the dam is quite insufficient to promote healthy, vigorous growth in the young foal, and occasionally it becomes necessary to raise a foal entirely independent of the dam. In such cases the best possible adjunct or substitute for the milk of the dam is cow's milk. It should be sweetened at first, as the milk of the mare is sweeter than that of the cow. A little patient effort will soon result in teaching the colt to drink milk readily, but be careful not to give him too much at a time. A half-pint is quite sufficient for a colt two or three days old; but the ration should be repeated often—not less than six times a day—the idea being to give the colt really all it will drink, but to feed so often that it will not require very much at a time. As the colt grows older the amount should be increased, and grass, with oats, should be added as soon as the colt is old enough to eat. No ration is better for a colt than cow's milk with these adjuncts. After the colt is two months old skimmed milk should be substituted for the fresh cow's milk. Should there be any trouble from constipation it will be well to add about one pint of oil-meal per day to the ration; in fact I would recommend the use of oil-meal in all cases, as it furnishes a large proportion of muscle and bone-forming food. If the oil-meal is not obtainable flaxseed may be used. A half-pint of flaxseed boiled with two quarts of bran will make two good feeds for a colt, and this ration may profitably be alternated with the other food. Indeed, it will be well in all cases where, from lack of an abundance of milk of the dam, or from scanty nutrition of any kind, the foal is low in flesh, to early supply the deficiency with a good allowance of cow's milk in addition to what it gets from the dam. The effect of such a ration upon the growth and condition is wonderful, and in all cases where the foal is likely otherwise to enter winter low in flesh I can not too highly recommend its use. A quart of milk morning and evening, in addition to the grain ration, will be sufficient; and if it be sweetened a little at first the colt will take to it all the more readily.

WEANING THE FOAL.

When the colt is to be taken from the dam it should be tied in an adjoining stall, with the partition so open that they can easily see each other, and the food of the mare should be reduced to a very small ration of dry oats and hay. When her udder becomes so full as to cause her uneasiness a part of the milk should be drawn off, but she should not be milked dry. The first milking may be done by the colt itself, but afterwards it should be done by hand, as the milk in the drying-off process soon becomes unfit for the colt; and, besides, the drying off will be more speedily accomplished than when the colt is occasionally permitted to suck. After the milk has entirely dried up the mare and her foal may be separated and she may safely be turned out to grass.

Skimmed milk may still be given to the colt, especially if it is not in good condition to enter the winter; but clean, sound oats, ground or unground, constitute the best of all grain foods for the colt. I prefer to have them ground; and as cold weather approaches about one-fourth in weight of corn-meal may profitably be added, as it helps to lay on fat and keeps up the animal heat. A little oil-meal—say a pint a day—may also profitably be given with the oats for some time after weaning. Don't be afraid of feeding too liberally. More colts are injured the first six months after weaning by a too scanty supply of food than from the opposite extreme. As soon as the mare and foal can be separated the foal should have the run of a good pasture, as there is no food better than grass, no medicine so good as exercise, and no exercise so profitable to young animals as that which may be taken just when they feel like it.

EFFECT OF EXERCISE ON DEVELOPMENT.

I wish to call especial attention to the importance of open-air exercise as absolutely essential to a healthy, symmetrical development of bone, muscle, and the vital organs. The idea prevails to a very great extent among practical farmers that high feeding and good care will cause an otherwise good colt to grow up into an unsound, "weedy" horse; and, on the other hand, that there is nothing like "roughing it" to develop hardiness and endurance. I am of opinion that the practical results in many cases have been such as to warrant this belief. Not that there is anything bad in generous and liberal feeding, nor good in starvation and exposure; but that with the latter the colt always has pure air and abundant exercise, without which there can be no sound and healthy development. This I regard as a factor in horse-raising second only in importance to that of blood, which is purely an inherited quality, and for lack of which no after-care can ever compensate.

Abundant opportunity for exercise in the fresh, pure air, uncontaminated by stable odors, is an absolute essential to a healthy development in all young animals. It is not sufficient that the colt be *led* out at stated intervals for exercise; he needs the opportunity to romp and play, that he may extend his muscles to their utmost capacity, expand his lungs to their very depths, and send the blood coursing through every vein with fiery vigor. All this is essential to a healthy, robust development of heart and lungs, and bone and muscle; and nowhere can it be obtained in so great a degree of perfection as in the freedom of the open field. A colt that is kept in the stall and fed highly on heating grains is seldom afforded an opportunity for this health-giving exercise. Like the tender hot-house plant, he grows up deficient in stamina and vigor—a victim to his artificial surroundings, which do violence to every want of his nature. To the exhilarating race in the fields and pastures—which colts as well as boys so heartily enjoy—he is a stranger; and he grows up a stiff, clumsy brute, with only a tithe of the development of lungs and other vital organs that he might have possessed under more favorable circumstances.

This I believe to be all there is of truth in the idea that colts brought up roughly make the hardiest horses; and there is so much in it that it should attract the careful attention of men who have thousands of dollars invested in the business of breeding horses.

But while I plead for this wild freedom in behalf of the growing colt I would not lose sight of the fact that generous feeding and protection from inclement weather are also essential. I condemn *in toto* the starving process as unnecessary and hurtful. A stunted, half-starved animal will never attain to so perfect a physical development as one that has been well fed and cared for from birth. There is a definite period in life allotted to growth, and if during that period only a scanty supply of nutriment is afforded a stunted, dwarfed animal is the inevitable result, which no amount of after-care can remedy. The true policy is to promote the growth of the colt by an abundance of nutritious food, and to secure a healthy and perfect development of heart and lungs, and bone and muscle, by permitting him to romp, and race, and play at will. By following this practice all there is of good in "roughing it" will be attained, and all that is bad or dangerous in generous feeding will be avoided.

"BREAKING" THE FOAL.

Wherever it is practicable the colt should be broken to halter while yet a suckling, and the earlier in life this process is commenced the more easily will it be accomplished. He may soon be led by the side of the dam without difficulty, and when once accustomed to being guided by the halter it will be an easy matter to lead him anywhere. He may also be tied by the side of the dam as the preliminary step in teaching him to stand quietly when hitched alone. The first step in "gentling" a colt is to overcome his natural timidity by gradual approaches, and when he finds that he has no reason to fear, the work is half done. All the subsequent lessons given him, through all the various steps of breaking and training, should be based upon this plan of gradual approaches —a species of sapping and mining that will subdue the most vicious and tame the wildest colt if perseveringly followed. He should be accustomed to the bridle by means of the "bitting rig" before any attempt is made to ride him; and the mounting should always be first attempted in the stall or the lot where the colt is perfectly familiar with all the surroundings. When it is desired to break him to harness the same principle of gentleness and care to avoid giving fright should be practiced. Place portions of the harness on him at a time, and let it remain on him in his stall until he finds that it will not hurt him; then lead him out with the harness on, alone, and again by the side of another horse also in harness. Accustom him perfectly to the use of the lines, and then let him make the acquaintance of the sulky or break-cart. Push it along after him; and when he has found that it also is harmless get him between the "thills," and finally hitch him to it and drive him. It is the most convenient of all vehicles for use in breaking colts for driving, as the weight is but little and there is no danger to be apprehended from sudden turning around. Many trainers provide themselves with a stout two-wheeled vehicle, constructed like a sulky, but with very heavy "thills," so strong that the colt can not possibly break them, let what may happen. Such an arrangement is especially desirable for wild or vicious colts that have not been "gentled" when young, or for such as from improper handling have formed bad habits that must be cured.

THE VIEWS OF DR. REYNOLDS, OF LIVERPOOL.

In the introduction to Vol. II of the Shire-Horse Stud Book of Great Britain is a paper upon "Horse-Breeding" which contains so much good, sound, practical instruction, that I cannot do my readers a greater service than by supplementing what I have given on the preceding pages with so much of Dr. Reynolds' work as relates to the brood mare and the young foal, as follows:

Fillies served at two years old, and so coming into profit as reproductors at three, will rarely develop into very high class animals, and when it is considered advisable to breed from them thus early they should not be subjected to work, beyond that required to break them in, until their first foals are a couple of months old. The best age to put a mare to the horse is at three years old, so that when she is sold in the autumn of her seventh year the owner will probably have obtained two foals, the value of which, added to the earnings of the mare as a team animal, will leave her full sale price to represent the proprietor's profit. Subject to the influences previously considered, the alliance of strong young mares with aged and robust stallions is the most certain method of obtaining a yearly production of good foals. Mares that have been worked up to ten or twelve years old in towns, and acquired at that age for breeding purposes, seldom fulfill the desires of the purchaser; by the maintenance of high condition for a prolonged period they are rendered prone to sterility, and if fecundated they are apt to experience difficulties in labor. When moderately well nourished, comfortably lodged and unfatigued by excessive and long-continued labor, mares are apt to breed at all seasons of the year, thereby affording the owner an opportunity to secure the dropping of his foals at a period when the exigences of team labor are not very pressing and when a fresh and abundant supply of green food can be assured for the mutual benefit of mare and offspring. Mares which are regularly worked, or those having to seek their food in the spring from poor pastures, are much more certainly fecundated than their idle or stable-fed sisters supplied with rich and abundant provender.

The appearances of that physiological condition termed "œstrum;" "heat," "in use," etc., are usually manifested in the mare by general signs and by particular phenomena presented by the generative organs.

The intensity of the objective signs varies very much in different individuals; in some all the symptoms are evinced by inappetence, increased thirst, agitation, impatience, frequent neighing, and efforts to urinate; the vulva are swollen —the lining membrance reddened, and a white glairy discharge issues therefrom; in others no signs are recognizable by which the condition of "heat" can be inferred. Its presence is not apparent until the mare is "tried" by a stallion.

The most opportune time for a matron mare to be again served is the ninth day after foaling; for subsequent proof that she has conceived to a former service the twentieth or twenty-first day is usually selected. Many usages are still had recourse to in the endeavor to insure conception by mares that have previously shown an indisposition to be fecundated, but the barbarous customs much practiced in former years by ignorant persons for the attainment of that object are now happily becoming of less frequent occurrence.

Acting upon the knowledge that exercise has the effect of provoking the evacuation of the excreta, and also of rendering petulant females more tranquil, the Arabs gallop their mares to excess and submit them to the stallion fatigued and inclined for rest. The most novel practice in this respect is the administration of about two-thirds of a pint of vinegar to the mare immediately after service. I have no experience of this mode of treatment and I fail to see any physiological reason why it should be successful. Complaints of the infecundity of a stallion are ever frequent, and often so when the cause is entirely due to the unfit state in which the mare is presented. Unless she is served at the moment in the plenitude of heat her owner should attach no blame to the horse if the essay proves unfruitful. The abstraction of blood has in some cases been followed by successful results; but the most rational practice that can be adopted is to reduce the condition of mares refractory to conception by submitting them to a prolonged course of cooling diet, of which corn should form no constituent, and after completion of the act to leave them in a state of perfect quietude for several hours.

Sterility in the mare may be due to age or prolonged continence, especially where associated with high condition, or it may arise from abnormal conformation, or diseases of the womb, or the existence of painful wounds, or diseases in the region of the feet; it is, however, usually induced in mares prone to accumulate fat, by a superabundant supply of highly-stimulating food and the absence of sufficient work.

Medicinal treatment or surgical operations in some rare cases may cure sterility arising from a suspension of the uterine functions or abnormalities of the organ; and the operation of neurotomy has been adopted with success upon mares rendered sterile by acutely painful foot diseases. The treatment for over-plethoric mares must be that of reduction to low, or even poor condition.

With the exception that the venereal excitement usually diminishes or disappears, and the animal becomes lazy and quiet, the signs that a mare has been impregnated do not become apparent for some time, nor is the periodical reappearance of "heat" to be regarded as a conclusive evidence of non-conception. It is not impossible for œstrum to co-exist with impregnation. The inconstancy in appearance of the objective symptoms of pregnancy renders that condition but problematical (especially in mares which ordinarily show little appearance of "œstrum") until the sixth or seventh month, when the fœtal movements may usually be discerned in the flank, unless manual exploration of the uterus by vaginal examination is adopted for the purpose of ascertaining whether conception has taken place. Valuable as the operation is for determining the state of the uterus during the primary months of gestation, it should never be employed except in cases of urgent necessity, on account of the danger and possible death of the fœtus, which may be apprehended to follow its adoption with an irritable mare.

The period of gestation in the mare occupies, as a rule, from 330 to 360 days, during nearly the whole of which time it is of great importance that opportunity be afforded for a sufficiency of daily exercise, especially needful for mares which are not suckling a foal.

When intelligently organized, in regard to the different periods of gestation, ordinary farm work is exceedingly beneficial to both mare and fœtus. Throughout the whole period it is better that the labor should be continued and uniform than violent or irregular. Shafting heavy loads, especially when much backing or turning is required, should not be permitted. Toward the end of pregnancy all work necessitating unequal movements, or even excessive effort, should be discontinued, and with the appearance of the signs that parturition may be expected to take place within a week or ten days it is advisable, but not essential, that work should be entirely suspended. Pregnant mares should be stabled with due regard to security against annoyance, compression, or injury by other horses, and especially guarded against the accident of being "cast" in their stalls. Medical or surgical treatment should, so far as possible, be avoided; when absolutely necessary, the utmost possible care in its administration is required.

The food and feeding of mares in foal are of great and important interest, the science and practice whereof must be carefully studied by breeders who would be successful in maintaining their mares healthy throughout the period of gestation, and over the act of foaling, and reap the reward of stout and vigorous foals. The quantity and nutritive quality of provender supplied to a pregnant mare should be in strict accord with her individual requirements; the establishment of a just balance between food and the demands for it can be determined by an accurate perception of condition, as exemplified by the possession of vigor and evidences of efficient nutrition.

The two opposite extremes of obesity or plethora and excessive leanness or debility are to be avoided; the former predisposes to abortion and difficult labors, the latter (of the two the least evil) prejudicially influences the nutrition of the fœtus and deteriorates the subsequent secretion of milk. Grass, unaided by artificial food, is insufficient for the sustenance of breeding mares subjected to labor; to insure the yearly production of strong foals a daily allowance of corn should be continuously supplied to them; but, except in the depth of winter, or for very young or very aged mares, green food, chop and pulped roots suffice for the requirements of non-workers.

Most farmers usually keep their pregnant mares, when not suckling, on the same ration as that supplied to the other working horses. With good keepers the practice suffices to maintain adequate condition, but when the ordinary provender is of low quality the mares should receive an auxiliary allowance.

Mashes or bruised oats or barley associated with pulped roots and chopped hay or straw, moistened with linseed-cake water, are the best adapted foods for working mares in foal —so constituted they afford a substantial, at the same time a non-exciting and easily-assimilated diet. Maize is not a suitable article of diet for in-foal mares when it constitutes a chief part of their corn allowance—their newly-dropped progeny always exhibit general weakness of muscle and abnormal relaxation of the ligaments of the joints.

For mares pastured during the day, a short supply of rack or manger food given in early morning renders their digestive organs less susceptible to the possibly deleterious influences of dew-saturated grass. More than any other farm animals brood mares require to be supplied with diet of the best obtainable quality; every description of food likely to undergo rapid fermentation, or to produce indigestion, must be scrupulously avoided. Long fasts are exceedingly prejudicial, and in cases where they are unavoidable or have been occasioned through neglect small quantities of tepid water and equally diminished rations of easily digestible food should only be allowed at intervals until the hunger and thirst have been reduced to their normal standards.

Pregnant mares should not be exposed to the influences of very excessive heat nor very severe cold, nor be pastured or folded with store oxen or young horses.

Abortion is produced by any cause operating to disconnect the union of the fœtal membranes with the uterus. These causes are very various and may obtain at all periods of preg-

STALLIONS, BROOD MARES AND FOALS. 173

nancy. Predisposition to abortion is to be found in peculiar conformations of the pelvis, enlargements of the iliac bones, diseases of the womb, constitutional irritability, the influences of too stimulative diet or the reverse, wet seasons, a previous miscarriage, and all circumstances opposed to efficient nutrition and respiration.

The more direct mechanical causes are falls, blows, compressions of the abdomen, violent and spasmodic exertion. Functional disorders, severe illnesses, large draughts of cold water or eating iced grass may be considered as the most frequent physiological causes.

The symptons of abortion vary with the term of gestation at which it occurs. When it follows shortly after conception the precursory signs, as well as the fact itself, are frequently unnoticed, and the proprietor is led to believe that the mare has not been fecundated; on the other hand, when miscarriage takes place towards the end of the gestative period the premonitory symptoms are almost identical with the signs of normal parturition, but the pains of abortion invariably precede the changes in the appearance of the external organs of generation, which in normal foaling are noticeable some time before the labor pains come on. The usual signs of the fœtus being dead, and not expelled immediately afterwards, are symptoms of ill-health in the mare accompanied by a puriform and offensive bloody discharge from the vulva.

The prevention of abortion is the avoidance of all causes which may have a tendency to produce it. In advanced pregnancy when a symptom of approaching miscarriage has been manifested the greatest care in the subsequent management of the mare is necessary. She should be placed in a roomy, darkened loose box, left perfectly unmolested, and the services of an experienced veterinary surgeon immediately sought. Whenever a mare has "picked her foal" the cause should, if possible, be determined, and means adopted to prevent other pregnant mares being exposed to similar conditions. They should also be removed to a distance from the place, on account of the mysterious sympathetic influence exercised upon the organism of pregnant animals by the mere occurrence of abortion in one of their companions. The attention required by a mare after abortion materially depends upon the indications of her general health. It very frequently happens that the placental membranes are retained in the uterus; these should be removed before decomposition of their component parts is possible, and the mare should not be covered again until every appearance due to the mishap has entirely subsided.

The characteristic signs that the gestative period has been fully and naturally completed, and that parturition may be shortly expected to take place, are very pronounced and so familiar to all persons who have had any experience in the management of brood mares that they need not be enumerated.

The natural instinctive desire for shade and solitude experienced by the mare at this crisis should be indulged by placing her in a warm, roomy and well-littered loose box, so arranged that the progress she makes can be constantly ascertained without causing her annoyance by interruption. Normal parturition in the mare is very rapid; at her full time and with the fœtus naturally placed the act is generally accomplished in a short space of time and without assistance.

The sense of uneasiness created by the presence of the fully-developed fœtus determines contraction of the abdominal muscles and diaphragm, as well as the walls of the womb itself; at the same time the orifice of the latter organ becomes dilated, succeeding efforts of expulsion push the muzzle and fore feet of the fœtus further through the neck of the uterus, in which situation they may be recognized immersed in the fluids of the yet unruptured membranes. More violent pains then force the head and shoulders through the pelvis, and another last contraction expels the posterior parts and completes the act.

If the labor is prolonged and the pains are very strong, a quiet and careful examination should be made, for the purpose of ascertaining whether there is sufficient room for the fœtus to pass through the pelvic arch, and also to determine whether the foal occupies a natural position. In the first

STALLIONS, BROOD MARES AND FOALS. 175

case more time may be allowed; in the second the fœtus will be required to be adjusted. To judge accurately of either of these conditions the attendant must be an experienced man and know the exact time when interference is necessary. Very great harm is occasioned by premature and unnecessary meddling. He should make re-examinations from time to time, and if increased room is but tardily provided he must take care, by securing the parts presented, that the fœtal position does not become changed from a natural to a malpresentation through the continued and violent throes of the mare. Dilatation of the passage may be assisted by gentle and well-applied traction upon those portions of the fœtus that are naturally presented. The causes of difficult labor and the means to be adopted to overcome obstructions to delivery, with the treatment of the patient after parturition, are so numerous and belong so intrinsically to the science of veterinary surgery that they have no place here. Whenever serious obstacles to delivery exist the aid of an experienced veterinary obstetrician should be promptly sought, and no violent tractile efforts employed until his arrival; but if the membranes are ruptured, as they probably will be before it is considered necessary to obtain skilled aid, it is wise to secure with cords the head or legs of the foal when easily practicable. It sometimes happens, especially with old and debilitated mares, that the act of parturition becomes protracted from weakness alone. Such cases not only demand the administration of powerful internal stimulants, but require the employment of well-timed, gentle and firm traction upon the fœtus made to coincide with the throes of the mare; spasmodic, jerking efforts, which do not correspond with the parturient pains, in all cases do much harm and are of little or no assistance to the act.

After an easy labor strong mares require nothing but attention to their comfort and ordinary wants and protection from currents of cold air, but if the *accouchement* has been prolonged and painful a stimulant should be immediately given; debilitated mares under the last-named circumstance require frequent alcoholic stimulants, nourishing gruel and good nursing.

The fœtal envelopes, or after-birth, are usually expelled in a short time after natural labor; when retained for a day or two no danger may be apprehended, so long as the mare does not strain and her health continues unimpaired; but surgical interference for their removal becomes necessary when retained sufficiently long to render putrefaction probable.

Aged mares, having very large and pendulous abdomens, derive much comfort from a wide bandage passed several times around the body, adjusted evenly and with a view of affording support without exerting undue pressure.

After-pains continued for more than an hour are to be regarded as evidence of possibly some important derangement of the womb and requiring skilled aid. The application of a mustard and linseed poultice over the region of the loins is always consistent treatment in these cases and may be adopted at once to economize valuable time before the arrival of the veterinary surgeon.

When a mare foals in a standing position the fœtus glides down the thighs and reaches the ground unhurt; the umbilical cord is severed and dangerous hemorrhage thereby prevented. When the act is accomplished in a recumbent attitude, and the mare remains down, the cord must be divided between two ligatures previously tied around it a couple of inches apart, but if the mare rises immediately the cord will be ruptured in a safe and satisfactory manner.

Many foals are lost through want of attention at the moment of birth. When the functions of respiration are not promptly established in the new-born foal, efforts must be made to excite them by blowing violently up the muzzle and into the mouth, and by briskly rubbing the body with a wisp. If breathing is but slowly promoted a few teaspoonfuls of brandy and water, given after the first few respirations, will be of material service to invigorate the low vital powers.

As soon as the mare has recovered from the shock the maternal instinct should be encouraged by allowing her to perform the office of nurse to her progeny, which will be physically benefited thereby. If the dam refuses to dry and caress her offspring, a little flour sprinkled over the back of the latter will sometimes attract her kindly to it; should this means fail the foal must be dried with soft flannel, conducted to the teat, and assisted to obtain its first aliment.

It is sometimes necessary to protect the foal from ill-intention by the peevish dam, but after the mare has permitted the foal to suck, and has evinced maternal solicitude for its welfare by licking and caressing it, no fear need be entertained that she will subsequently injure it willfully.

All the means briefly reviewed as necessary for the preservation of the newly-born foal and comfort of the mare are to be continued for a period more or less prolonged, as their conditions and surrounding circumstances indicate. If both mare and foal are healthy, and especially if the mare has been pastured up to the time of foaling, they will be benefited by being turned to grass during fine weather in a week or so after the birth; but they must be sheltered from rain and cold, particularly at night, so long as the weather continues unfavorable.

At this early period the mare should never be permitted to graze until she has had a small allowance of sweet hay or some other nutritious dry food, nor should she be subjected to work for at least three weeks after parturition. Some mares, especially primiparous ones, do not furnish sufficient milk for the sustenance of their offspring. In these cases the mammary glands must be frequently stimulated by the foal and subsequently submitted to gentle friction, and a supply of succulent, easily-digestible food allowed. In the absence of a plentiful supply of grass, boiled barley made into a sloppy mash, with the addition of some treacle and a little salt, is a palatable, nourishing diet, tending to increase the lacteal secretion. If these means fail to excite a sufficient flow of milk the foal must be periodically suckled by a foster mare, or be artificially nourished. Should the season not admit of mares being pastured, barley mashes, pulped roots, scalded oats and hay of the best procurable quality, should be liberally supplied. A plentiful allowance of water, or, for bad milking mares, nutritious gruel is necessary.

Most mares, however, secrete a plentiful, and many a superabundant supply of milk. Such do not require, soon after foaling, a more liberal allowance of food than they previously received. The provision of rich but close herbage suffices for their general requirements In early life, too, foals are prone to contract dangerous diseases of the digestive organs, and on that account it is undesirable that they should be allowed, until several days old, to take the whole milk supply of a free-nourishing or well-fed dam. Under such circumstances the foal should not have access to the mare until part of the contents of the udder have been drawn off. After some days, when the foal has become stronger, the above-named precautions are unnecessary. A more liberal allowance of food may then be supplied, to be regulated by the demands made upon her nutritive functions by the growth of her foal and the wear and tear of labor to which she may be subjected.

In districts where the mare is not required to work until the foal is weaned grass suffices for all her requirements. The best old pastures should, however, be reserved for her use. When these cease to afford sufficient green food by reason of drouth or overstocking the deficiency must be made up by an allowance of cut artificial grasses, lucerne or clover, given with discretion.

If at any time during the period of lactation the udder becomes inflamed, hot or tense, the diet must be promptly reduced, the milk reservoir very frequently emptied, and warm fomentations adopted, to be followed by very gentle friction with soap and water (greasy substances ought not to be rubbed upon the glands, or, if used, the residuum should be carefully removed by subsequent washing). If the foal is dead, or can conveniently be weaned, a dose of physic may be administered to the mare. Under other circumstances it may be necessary to put the mare under medical treatment of less drastic character.

The usual time for weaning is when the foal has arrived at the age of five or six months, when, if the mare has reconceived, or has been or is about to be severely worked, it is for her benefit that the separation should not longer be delayed.

If the milk secretion is not excessive no danger need be

apprehended from the process of weaning, which it is desirable in all cases to effect gradually. On the contrary, the separation of the foals from free-nourishing mares must be accomplished by degrees. For some days prior to final removal of the foal the intervals of allowing it to suck must be increased in length, and the food allowance of the mare reduced in quantity and quality for a corresponding time.

If practicable, also, the mare should be more severely worked. After ultimate severance of the foal the glands must be periodically hand-drawn and a brisk purgative administered. Restricted diet, particularly in regard to fluid and succulent provender, should be enjoined until the secretion of milk is completely suspended. Mares kept only for breeding purposes, if in good condition and not enfeebled by age or other circumstances, may continue to nourish their foals for a much longer period—until, in fact, a natural weaning takes place and the milk secretion ceases. The weaning of foals from mares not subjected to labor and furnishing a full lacteal secretion must be accomplished with the exercise of all the hygienic and medicinal precautions previously indicated, and rendered especially necessary by abstinence from work.

Throughout the period of lactation, and very especially during that portion of it when the foal receives the whole of its sustenance from the dam, it is requisite for the mare to be supplied with good food calculated to furnish material for the elaboration of wholesome milk.

The first milk after parturition, called "colostrum," differs materially in composition from the subsequent secretion. It contains principles adapted to remove the mecomium (as the effete matters collected in the foal's intestines during fœtal life are technically termed); on that account it is highly necessary that the newly-born foal should be supplied with the milk from its own dam, at least until the mecomium has been expelled and the bowels have assumed their natural function.

Until the approach of the time for weaning a foal should be permitted to have access to its dam at intervals of not exceeding four hours.

It is frequently alleged that "heated milk" is extremely prejudicial to the foal. I admit there is a probability of troublesome skin disease being caused by allowing a foal to partake of the milk of a mare when she is overheated, but I think the danger of "heated milk" producing diarrhœa or "scour" is exaggerated, or rather that the evil consequences in this particular respect are as much attributable to the fact that the young animal, pressed by hunger, partakes too greedily and too plentifully, and, as a consequence, is primarily attacked with acute indigestion.

It is always better to be on the safe side and allow the mare to become cool and to bathe her distended glands with lukewarm water before the foal is admitted to her.

It is not always that a mare which secretes a copious supply of milk is a good nourisher; some, especially old mares, or those subjected to very heavy work and inefficiently fed, elaborate a fluid deficient in nutritive quality, a circumstance rendered evident by the condition of the foal, which will become wasted and probably attacked with diarrhœa.

In such cases the mare must be especially well nourished, and, in instances of extreme necessity, the foal assisted by artificial lactation; it should also, as soon as possible, be encouraged to take manger food, of which boiled beans should constitute the basis, in order that the advantage of an early weaning may be secured.

Notwithstanding the purgative effects of the colostrum, the young foal frequently suffers from constipation of the bowels, and especially so if the dam is or has been during the later periods of pregnancy fed with dry or indigestible food; certainly so if the mare has had an acute attack of dyspepsia near the end of the gestative term. Many persons establish the rule that every foal should have a dose of oil shortly after birth. The practice is generally good—none but beneficial effects are likely to result therefrom, and the life of the foal must be regarded as unsafe until free evacuation of the bowels has been effected. When preceding circumstances have rendered it probable that the foal will be constipated, the exhibition of a full dose of castor oil is imperatively indicated, and, in addition, frequent enemata of warm soap and water are recommended.

It can not be expected, nor is it desirable, that the numerous diseases incident to breeding animals of the equine species and their progeny can be even very briefly reviewed in an essay of this kind; the consideration of such a subject properly appertains to veterinary science. There is, however, one malady affecting young foals which, on account of its frequency and fatality, may be glanced at.

No disease is more prevalent among sucking animals, and few so fatal, as diarrhœa. Although less subject than calves, foals are often carried off by it within a short space of time. The causes have not been accurately determined, but the most eminent veterinarians attribute it to changes of unknown character, and brought about by unascertained causes in the composition of the milk.

Two facts relating thereto have, however, been proved, viz.: that the causes are often widely diffused; and, secondly, that their potency is increased by defective hygienic surroundings, especially unwholesome stable accommodations and overcrowding of animals. Unless curative treatment is very early adopted an unfavorable issue is almost certain, and the generally fatal nature of the disease gives little hope of cure when the symptoms have become fully developed. At the outset a full dose of castor oil ought to be given, the action of which is to be followed by repeated small doses of carbonate of iron and carbonate of soda, with laudanum and brandy, given in cold rice-meal gruel. As food bean-meal, made into the consistency of milk and given at short intervals, is extremely beneficial, and should take the place of a large proportion of the mare's milk. The diet of the mare is to be completely changed, and the foal and dam promptly removed to other quarters As curative treatment is so rarely successful, efforts must be made for preventing the disease. The provision of good, dry, clean lodgings, pure water, and the occasional administration of alkaline carbonates to the mare, the diet of which should be wholesome, and be partly composed of leguminous seeds, are the means most likely to be attended with beneficial results.

Dr. Reynolds' remarks upon brood mares lead me to speak of the effects of pasture upon mares at the time of service. It is the general opinion of those who have given close attention to this subject that mares, when *first turned to grass*, after having been kept stabled and on dry feed for a considerable period, are not so likely to get in foal as those that have been on grass for some time previous to service by the stallion; or as those that are not on grass at all. The theory is that turning mares to grass produces, for a time, a sort of general muscular relaxation, or softening, that is not favorable to conception. I have always advised that mares which had been kept stabled previous to being sent to the stallion should be kept on dry food for at least four weeks after the service. On the other hand, I have thought it best, when mares that had been kept on grass for a considerable previous period were sent for service, that they should be so kept for some time afterward. At such times I would avoid *any* material change in the food or treatment. If the mare has been kept on grass let her so remain for at least a month; if she has been kept stabled and in idleness let her remain so for a few weeks; if she has been worked continue to work her moderately. Of course these directions apply to such mares only as have not proven hitherto barren. In case a mare has been served repeatedly and has failed to conceive, a radical change in food and management may bring about the desired result.

CHAPTER III.

THE BREEDS OF HORSES.

GENERAL FEATURES.

The horse tribe, or genus equus, embraces the horse, the ass, the quagga, and the zebra. The members of these different species may be bred together for one generation only, the produce being a hybrid which does not possess the powers of reproduction—a provision of nature which effectually blocks the way to a blending of these different species into one and preserves to each its specific character.

The original habitat of the horse is not known, but it is clear that at the earliest periods known to history they existed in a wild state in various parts of Europe, Asia and Africa, and that they differed greatly in many particulars, before they were subjected to domestication and broken up into the more modern breeds. Those inhabiting hot, dry, and unproductive regions, where a sparse supply of food made frequent changes of grazing grounds a necessity essential to existence, were distinguished for spirit, activity, speed, and endurance. Of these the horses of Turkey, Persia, and later of Arabia, and also those on the African side of the Mediterranean presented the most characteristic type. Those found in low, flat regions abounding in nutritious herbage were larger, more sluggish, and less graceful. Europe, from the North Sea to the Euxine, once contained immense numbers of wild horses of this type. In the inhospitable mountain regions of Europe, Asia and Africa were always found rough-coated, hardy ponies—the most diminutive specimens of the race.

These points of divergence among horses prevailed throughout the three Grand Divisions of the Eastern Hemisphere, with many minor points of difference or peculiarities existing in various localities. The horses of Northern Africa—the Barbs especially—were very tall, with long legs, very short bodies, and possessed great speed; while those of Turkey and Persia were rather heavier-bodied, on shorter legs, and possessed greater powers of endurance. Arabia most probably obtained her horses originally from Turkey, Persia, and the regions further northward and eastward. Indeed, prior to their general domestication horses appear to have been more abundant in Eastern Central Asia than in any other part of the world. Tartary and Circassia were at a very early day famous for the immense numbers of their horses. Those of Tartary were greatly inferior in point of beauty to those of the regions further southward, but they were a hardy race. Their heads were large; ears long, wide and drooping backward; legs short and stout; muzzle and jaws fringed with long, stiff hair, or bristles; mane thick and bushy; hair long and shaggy, and some of them with hair frizzled or curly In color they were usually a brownish dun, some of them approximating a cream color. In the high mountainous regions of Northern India, near the head waters of the great rivers of that country, were found a race of very diminutive ponies. Corsica had, down to a very late period, a race of small, wild horses, vicious and untamable. Early writers describe a peculiar race of horses found in the mountains near the coast in Northern Africa called *Coomsie* by the natives. They were said to be 10 or 11 hands high, of a reddish color, with broad foreheads, short heads, wide between the eyes, muzzle small, ears wide, eyes small, hair long, and the tail covered with hair like that of the body to its extremity, but terminating in a tuft of long, black hair.

A characteristic difference between the Asiatic horses and those of Africa has been noticed by many writers, in that while in the Asiatic varieties the length of body is about equal to the height at the withers, those of Africa are much shorter, the height being considerably more than equal to the length of body. And this difference appears to have been so pronounced that Prof. Low questions whether they were not descended from species originally and radically distinct. Spain, of all European countries, appears to have drawn most largely upon Africa for her supply of horses, the Moorish conquest, perhaps, having been the primary cause of this; and here we find the horses, many centuries ago, partaking largely of the character of the African Barb.

In color these horses differed as greatly as do the modern domesticated ones. In Tartary many of them were dun, with dark manes and tails and with a dark streak along the spine and sometimes across the shoulders. Many of the horses of Asia Minor, Persia, and Syria were milk white, and these were much prized for use on grand occasions by chiefs and rulers. Near the western terminus of the Himalaya range of mountains there was a race of white horses spotted with brown. Many of the mountain ponies of other parts of Asia were piebald. A race of spotted horses abounded in Afghanistan. The large horses that originally inhabited the low, flat region that stretches across Europe from the North Sea to the Euxine were black, as were also many of the African Barbs; and black was the prevailing color of the tall, fleet Barbs of Nubia and Dongola, but these usually had white legs. Grays, bays, browns, and chestnuts abounded in Southern Asia.

Thus we see from what an infinite variety, caused originally, we may infer, by differences in climatic conditions and consequently of nutrition and habit, our domesticated horses have been derived. And we can see here why atavism should occasionally surprise us with a reversion to the curly, frizzled hair, the black dorsal streak, the rat tail, the parti-colored hair, etc., among our domesticated breeds, and what a formidable task has been the development of distinct breeds from elements so divergent.

THOROUGHBREDS.

In undertaking to write upon the breeds of horses we very naturally commence with the thoroughbred, because that is the oldest and best established of all the breeds of Europe and America. The term thoroughbred is often used in America, but seldom in England, as a synonym for well bred or purely bred; but it was originally and should now be used only as the name by which the English race horse is designated. The same horses are sometimes denominated "blood horses," from the well-established purity of their lineage.

The thoroughbred horse is peculiarly a Brit-

THE BREEDS OF HORSES. 189

A TYPE OF THE THOROUGHBRED.

ish production—the result of the characteristic love of the sports of the turf and the chase inherent in the English people. At a very early period the attention of the rulers of Great Britain was earnestly directed to the work of improving the breeds of horses of that kingdom. These horses were notoriously deficient in size, and the earliest efforts were directed toward improvement in that particular by the importation of heavy horses from Normandy, Flanders and Germany. It would be interesting to trace, step by step, these efforts, but our space will not admit of such detail. The era of improvement commenced with the conquest of the islands by the Saxons; but it was many years before there appears to have been any clearly-defined or well-settled purpose, the object at one time appearing to be an increase of size by large importations of the heavy horses of Flanders, and again, to give speed, gracefulness of motion and beauty of form, by the introduction of what is known as Oriental blood —that of the Arab, the Turk and the Barb. It is evident that from a very early period the blood of the Barb and of the Turk was held in higher esteem than that of the Arab, the latter having been regarded as undersized, and esteemed rather for beauty of form and graceful action than on account of any real superiority.

For several years preceding the reign of

Charles II horse-racing appears to have been rapidly growing into favor as an amusement and recreation among the English people; and from that time until the present contests for supremacy upon the turf have stirred the British heart as no other amusement has ever done. To the constant growth and popularity of this sport, which for more than two hundred years has been regarded as the national amusement of that country, are we indebted for persistence in a course of breeding which has given us this race of horses so pre-eminently distinguished throughout the world for speed and endurance upon the race-course; and which, on account of the great care taken in their breeding, and their consequent purity of lineage, were the first race of animals to which the term *thoroughbred* was applied.

The foundation upon which this now well-established breed was built was a promiscuous mingling of the horses of the Island of Great Britain—first with the larger races of Europe, especially of Normandy, Flanders, and Germany, and subsequently with the lighter, more agile and graceful horses of Spain, which were themselves almost identical with the Barbs on the other side of the Mediterranean. Frequent importations were also made direct from Egypt, Morocco, and Tunis. and likewise from Arabia and various parts of Turkey, until this Oriental blood to a considerable extent permeated all the horse stock of Great Britain excepting those bred especially for agricultural purposes. So thoroughly had the passion for turf sports, or horse-racing, taken possession of the English people as early as the reign of Charles II that ability to run and win in a race was even then regarded as the principal test of merit in horses, and those most successful on the turf were most highly prized for breeding purposes. From that time down to the present, embracing a period of more than two hundred years, the selection of breeding stock by English breeders of thoroughbred horses has been constantly made with this as the primary object.

With the advent of Charles II, in the last half of the seventeenth century, breeding for speed and endurance upon the race-course began to be conducted upon something like a definite plan; the records of turf performances were carefully kept, especial attention was paid to the pedigrees of horses designed for the turf, and an aristocracy of blood came to be recognized in the horses of England. This monarch sent his "master of the horse" to the Levant to procure horses with which to found a breeding stud. This purchase comprised three very famous Turkish stallions and some mares that in the equine literature of the day were called the "royal mares," and these royal mares are by

THE BREEDS OF HORSES. 193

many supposed to be the foundation of the strict thoroughbred. This is, however, only approximately correct, for it is well known that several other mares were from time to time introduced from the Orient and that the produce of many mares not descended from nor related to these royal mares have been distinguished upon the turf and recognized as thoroughbreds.

About the middle of the eighteenth century the publication of the English Racing Calendar was commenced. In this the names of all the horses that participated in the regular races were published, and in a very few years it became the custom to give also the name of the sire in each case. This publication has been continued, with very little change in form or matter, down to the present day, and the records of performances and names of performers therein contained furnished the basis for the stud book of thoroughbred horses. A collection embracing all the pedigrees of distinguished horses that could be obtained was published as early as 1786. Subsequent to this several attempts at a compilation of pedigrees from the Racing Calendar and other sources was made, but it was not until 1791 that the English Stud Book took its present form.

The standard of admission to the first volume of the Stud Book appears to have been simply creditable performance upon the turf, as shown by the Racing Calendar, it being taken for granted that no horse could be a creditable performer that was not well bred—an assumption that has never yet been found at fault. The first volume compiled upon this basis furnished the foundation for all subsequent ones; and few names have been admitted to registry that do not trace, without admixture, on both sides, to an ancestry that is recorded in the first volume or to subsequent importations of Oriental blood.

Prof. Low, in his great work upon the "Domesticated Animals of Great Britain," in commenting upon the various importations of foreign blood that went to make up the foundation of the English blood horse, says:

> The lighter horses for speed, introduced previous to the reign of James 1, were Spaniards, Barbs and Turks. But King James, on his accession to the English crown, resolved to try the Arabian, with which his reading had probably rendered him familiar. He purchased a horse of that race, imported from the east by an English merchant, Mr. Markham, for which he paid the sum, great in those days, of £500. This horse, however, in no way distinguished on the turf or for his stock, attracted little attention. The Duke of Newcastle, who afterward wrote a remarkable work on horses, took an especial dislike to this Arabian, abused him as a bony creature, good for nothing, because being trained to the course he could not run. This opinion seems to have exercised a great influence on the breeders for the turf, and it was not until after the lapse of more than a hundred years that the neglected Arabian was again resorted to. During this long period Barbs and Turks from the Levant were the

horses chiefly imported and mingled in blood with the pre-existing race.

Of the foreign horses early introduced into England, one familiarly known as the White Turk was the property of Mr. Place, the stud groom of the Lord Protector Cromwell. Another was brought by the Duke of Berwick from the siege of Budy in the reign of James II; and a third, the Byerly Turk, became the most distinguished of all the foreign horses of that period. He was the charger of Capt. Byerly in the wars of William in Ireland about the year 1689. Of the lineal descendants of this horse one was King Herod, born in 1758, bred by His Royal Highness William, Duke of Cumberland, brother of George II. This fine horse, on retiring from the turf, was employed as a stallion, and got 497 winners at our various race-courses, computed to have gained to their owners £201,505.

In the later years of Queen Anne an Arabian had been brought to England which tended to impress a new character on the English turf. This animal, the progenitor of some of the finest horses that have perhaps existed in the world, was purchased at Aleppo by a merchant, the brother of Mr. Darley of Yorkshire. He was supposed to have been of the Desert breed, although his precise lineage was not determined. He got The Devonshire, or Flying Childers, and another horse termed Bartlett's Childers, who was never trained, but who was the ancestor of Eclipse, one of the most remarkable horses of which we have any record.

The Devonshire, or Flying Childers, born in 1715, was so named from his breeder, Mr. Leonard Childers, of Carr House, near Doncaster, from whom he was purchased when young by the Duke of Devonshire. He was a chestnut horse, with four white legs. He was of noble form, of matchless courage, and the fleetest horse that had ever been upon the English turf.

Eclipse was got by Marske, a grandson of Bartlett's Childers, out of Spiletta. He was foaled in the year 1764, during the eclipse of that year, from which circumstance he took his name. He was bred by the Duke of Cumberland, and on the death of that prince was sold to Mr. Wildman, a salesman at Smithfield; and afterward he became the property of Mr. O'Kelly. Eclipse had not the grandeur of form of Flying Childers, and might have escaped notice but for the accidental trial of his stupendous powers. He was about 15.1 hands high. His shoulders were very low, oblique, and so thick above that, according to the observation of the time, a firkin of butter might have rested upon them. He stood very high behind, a conformation suited to his great power of progression. He was so thick winded as to be heard blowing at a considerable distance. In the language of honest John Lawrence: "He puffed and blowed like an otter, and galloped as wide as a barn-door." No sooner were his powers exhibited on the turf than every eye was set to scrutinize his form, and he was then admitted to possess in perfection the external characters indicative of great speed. A volume was written on his proportions by M. Saintbel, a veterinary surgeon, whose investigations showed that his figure differed greatly from the conventional form which speculative writers had assigned as the standard of perfection. He was of an indomitable temper, and his jockeys found it in vain to attempt to hold him, but contented themselves with remaining still on the saddle while he swept along, his nose almost touching the ground. His full speed was not determined, since he never met with an opponent sufficiently fleet to put it to the proof. He not only was never beaten, but he was able to distance some of the best horses of his time; and the fleetest could not keep by his side for fifty yards together.

This remarkable horse first appeared on the turf at the age of five, in 1769. In the first heat he set off of his own accord and easily gained the race, his rider pulling him in vain with all his force for the last mile. O'Kelly, observing this and being aware of his horse's powers, offered in the second heat to "place the horses," and he took heavy bets that he did so. When called upon to declare he said: "Eclipse first, the rest no place." He gained his wagers. Eclipse was first, and all the others were distanced, or, in the language of the turf, had no place. From this time Eclipse was continually on the turf and gained every race. No horse daring to contend with him he closed his career of seventeen months by walking over the Newmarket Course for the King's Plate in October 1770. During this brief period it is said that he gained £25,000 for his owner. He was then employed with prodigious profit as a stallion. He got 334 winners at our numerous race-courses, who are computed to have gained about £160,000 to their owners, besides cups and plates. He died in 1789 at the age of twenty-five.

Another horse of foreign lineage, scarcely inferior to the Darley Arabian in the fame and value of his descendants, and by many supposed to have exercised a yet more important influence on the horses of the turf, is the Godolphin Barb, who lived a short time later than the Darley Arabian, having been born about the year 1724. This splendid horse was long regarded as an Arabian, although his characters approached to those of the Barb. He was found dragging a water cart in France, and was probably one of those neglected presents of horses, frequent at that time, from the Barbary powers to the French court. He was brought to England and finally presented to Lord Godolphin, in whose stud he remained a considerable time before his value was suspected, and then only it was discovered in consequence of the excellence of one of his sons, Laih, out of Roxana, who proved to be the fleetest horse, Childers excepted, that had till then appeared on the English turf. His grandson, Matchem, was in a peculiar degree noted for the excellence of his stock. This latter horse is supposed to have yielded his owner, Mr. Fenwick, upward of £17,000 as a stallion alone. He died in 1781, having had 354 sons and daughters, all winners at our numerous race-courses, and computed to have gained to their owners £151,097.

It is the general opinion of the best-informed English turfmen that the Oriental stallions which contributed most largely to the formation of the English thoroughbred were Place's White Turk, the Byerly Turk, Lister's, or the Straddling Turk, the Darley Arabian, Curwen's Barb, Lord Carlisle's Turk, the Godolphin Arabian (a Barb), the Leeds Arabian, Honeywood's White Arabian, Combe's Grey Arabian, Bell's Grey Arabian, D'Arcy's Turk, Selaby Turk, the Ancaster Turk, Compton's Barb, the Toulouse Barb, Stanyan's Arabian, Lowther Barb, Taffolet Barb, Hutton's Grey Barb, Honeywood's Arab, Sedley Barb, and Wellesley's Arabian. Of those above mentioned Lister's Turk got Brisk and Snake, Darley Arabian got Flying Childers, Carlisle's Turk got the Bald Galloway, and Godolphin Arabian got Blank, Regulus and Cade. The "royal mares" were imported Barbs.

Of these Oriental sires it is generally admitted that the Godolphin Arabian—imported 172 years ago—is the last that has proven of any benefit to the English stock; and while this blending of the blood of the Orient with the old races of England furnished the foundation, there cannot be the slightest doubt that the care and skill of English breeders in selecting and coupling with the stoutest, best and fleetest for successive generations has been a more potent factor in the formation of the breed, as it now exists, than the Arabian and Barb blood, to which history and tradition has ascribed its superiority. Many importations of the choicest blood of the Orient have been made both to this country and England within the last half century, and yet scarcely a name among them can be found in the pedigree of a horse that has distinguished himself upon the turf. The Arabian horses possess undoubted beauty of form and grace of motion, but they are notoriously inferior in point of size to the average thoroughbred, being rarely over 14 hands high; and their produce from the best of mares have been failures both in the stud and on the race-course. In every instance in which the speed and stoutness of our thoroughbreds have been tested side by side with the Arabian the former have proven superior to their eastern competitors. Hence, recent crosses of Oriental blood, while they do not warrant exclusion from the stud book, are not looked upon with favor by the best breeders of England or America. The thoroughbred of to-day is greatly superior to his Oriental ancestor in size, speed, endurance, and every other useful quality, excepting, possibly, that of docility.

So thoroughly have our people been imbued with the idea that Arabia was the fountainhead from which all modern equine excellence has been drawn that to venture an opinion to the contrary has been equivalent, in the mind of the average horse essayist, to writing one's self down as an ignoramus upon equine history. And yet it is doubtful if ever a race of horses has been more thoroughly overrated. The greater portion of Arabia is, in point of fact, illy adapted to the rearing of horses, and prior to the days of Mahomet horses were scarcely recognized as a part of the possessions of the Arab, their riches consisting chiefly in camels, oxen, sheep, and goats. But Mahomet was an enthusiastic lover of the horse, and while he succeeded in engrafting upon so large a proportion of the inhabitants of the eastern world his own peculiar religious tenets he also imbued his followers with a great degree of his enthusiastic admiration for the horse. Indeed, kindness to and love for this noble animal was made a part of the religious duty of all true Mussulmans, and from the days of Mahomet down to the present time the Arabian has held his stud, and especially his mares, in a sort of superstitious reverence. Mahomet selected for himself a magnificent stud, and his followers to this day seek to trace the genealogy of their choicest horses to the mares that were his favorites. But their pedigrees, divested of all the high-sounding flourishes with which they are accompanied, mean but little and are altogether unreliable.

The following is a copy of one of these documents, which accompanied Hamdan, a grey stallion imported by A. Keene Richards, in 1856, as we find it recorded in Bruce's American Stud Book:

RAMADON 21, 1272.

This is to certify, That at the date of this document Messrs. Keene and Troye bought from Sheik Hammed Es. Sohiman, the son of Shalan, the grey horse, even the horse of Hammed, the son of Sohiman, who is the son of Shalan, even the sheik of the Arabs of Anayza. The said horse is a Koheylan, the son of an old Koheylan father and of an old Koheylan mother. We declare this by fortune, to which God and Mahomed, the apostle of God, are witnesses. There is no better horse, being from the side of both father and mother a blood horse. He is a Koheylan, the son of a Koheylan, and his mother is a Koheylan purer than milk. He was born and brought up in the land of Nesjd.

This is the genealogy of the said horse. God is omnipotent.

The sale was made at the land of Sophira.

[SEAL]　　HAMMED ES. SOHIMAN, *the son of Shalan.*

Witnesses:
The writer of this document, who stands in need of God.
　　　　　ARD-ALLAH, *the son of Nowphal, the lecturer.*
　　　　　MAHAMMAD, *the son of Mashial.*
　　　　　AKHBIEF, *the son of Mashaul.*
　　　　　ISH-SHE-RA-TAH, *agent of Fysal-Ish-Shalaa.*

As before remarked, Arabia was one of the latest of the Oriental countries to engage in rearing horses; and there can be no question but that the enthusiasm of the followers of the Prophet had as much to do in creating the great reputation that the Arabian horses soon thereafter attained, and which they hold to this day, as the quality of the animals themselves.

The thoroughbred having been for so many generations bred with especial reference to his capacity as a *race* horse, it is not surprising that he should have acquired peculiarities of form and temper that render him undesirable for the more sober and steady uses of every-day life.

He has been bred to *run*, and the form best adapted to speed, and the mental qualities that most certainly insure the pluck, and energy, and determination so essential to success in a hard-fought race, have been the qualities aimed at by breeders and the standard by which selections have been made. Such a course of breeding has made the thoroughbred, as a racer, rather too lithe and light in form and too nervous and excitable in temper for ordinary business uses; but in speed, endurance and resolution they surpass all other breeds, and there is scarcely a race of horses in existence but may be improved by a cross with them. This fact is almost universally recognized, and nearly all countries upon the civilized globe have for many years regarded the English thoroughbred, or "blood horse," as the basis of all substantial improvement.

Our American horses are largely permeated with the blood of the English thoroughbred. Many of the best stallions and mares of England have been imported to this country, and their influence is seen on every hand. It enters largely into the ground-work of all our trotting strains, and it is doubtful if a single great road horse or trotter has been produced in this country that did not possess a large share of this royal blood as a foundation upon which the trotting superstructure has been built.

There exists great ignorance, even among many who pass for intelligent, well-informed horsemen, as to what constitutes a thoroughbred horse. Nearly every agricultural society in the land has a class in its premium list for thoroughbred horses; and yet many of the managers of these societies have a very indefinite idea as to what is requisite to render a horse eligible in this class. Questions of this nature are referred to me almost every year for a decision as to eligibility; and many of them are of such a nature that a very slight knowledge of the subject ought to enable the officers of these societies to decide for themselves. On this account I beg pardon of the well-informed reader while I briefly recapitulate.

In the first place it should be understood that we derive the name, as well as the breed of horses to which it applies, from our British cousins across the water, as has been fully set forth in the preceding pages; and that the term, when applied to horses, is used to designate one particular breed, and that is the running horse. All our American thoroughbreds are, therefore, imported from England, or are descendants of animals so imported. A recent cross with an imported Arab or Barb, while it does not vitiate the blood nor render an animal ineligible as a thoroughbred, is not usually regarded as desirable, from the fact that the course of selection which has been practiced by the breeders of thoroughbred horses in England and America for the last hundred years has given us a race that is generally considered to be far superior to the Oriental horse of to-day in speed, size and stoutness. The compiler of the stud book for thoroughbred horses in this country has relaxed the English rule somewhat, and admits to registry animals that show an unmixed descent for five generations of pure blood; and while under this rule many animals may be admitted that are not in the strict sense of the word thoroughbreds, yet if for five generations nothing but thoroughbred sires are to be found in the pedigree the quantity of alien blood remaining must necessarily be infinitesimally small; and by usage the animal so bred is in this country ranked as a thoroughbred. The American Stud Book for thoroughbred horses, five volumes of which have been issued, is edited and published by Col. S. D. Bruce, of the *Turf, Field and Farm,* New York.

If our agricultural societies would bear in mind that *none* of our American trotters, no matter how long the pedigree, and none of our imported or native draft horses, are eligible to compete for premiums offered for thoroughbreds, they would spare themselves much trouble. No pedigree that has Rysdyk's Hambletonian, Abdallah, Morgan, Bellfounder, Hiatoga, Mambrino Chief, Royal George, Patchen or any other of our prominent trotting sires in it can belong to a thoroughbred. It may appear strange to some that it is necessary to make this statement; yet I have seen premiums awarded in the thoroughbred class to trotting stallions at both State and county fairs; and I have known some cases where imported draft horses have been entered in this class and were supposed to be eligible.

TROTTERS AND ROADSTERS.

It can scarcely yet be said that we have a distinctive breed of driving horses or roadsters. The horses used for light driving, fast trotting, etc., are largely a conglomeration of all breeds and types. Some of them approximate the French Canadian pony in form and action, while others possess most of the characteristics of the thoroughbred; but so popular have trotting races become in this country, and so universal is the fancy for fast driving horses, that at almost all our horse shows and fairs the roadster class will be found more largely represented than any other, and often more largely than all others combined. Indeed the roadster is more distinctly an American feature than any other in our equine product; and we have almost if not quite reached the time when the American trotting horse may properly be classed as a distinct breed. As the thoroughbred was the result of the inherent love of the turf and the chase so characteristic of the people of Great Britain, so the American trotting horse is the result of a fashion that has demanded the fastest and stoutest trotting horses in the world for driving on the road; and to this end we have selected and bred until our horses clearly surpass all others in this particular. Among these horses we have several recognized families of especial prominence, all more or less related, all more or less distinguished for the one quality of speed as trotters, but each possessing features that are to some extent peculiarly its own, but none of them entitled to be separately classed as a breed.

Of these we may mention the *Hambletonians*, descended on the paternal side from imported Messenger (a thoroughbred) through his son Mambrino (also a thoroughbred), and Mambrino's son Abdallah, out of a mare of unknown blood, who in turn got Rysdyk's Hambletonian, out of a mare by Bellfounder (an imported Norfolk trotter), and his second dam probably having two crosses to imported Messenger. Through Rysdyk's Hambletonian, on the paternal side, we have the Volunteers, the Edward Everetts, the Alexander's Abdallahs, the Almonts, the Messenger Durocs, the Sentinels, the Electioneers, the Happy Mediums, the Wilkeses,

THE BREEDS OF HORSES. 207

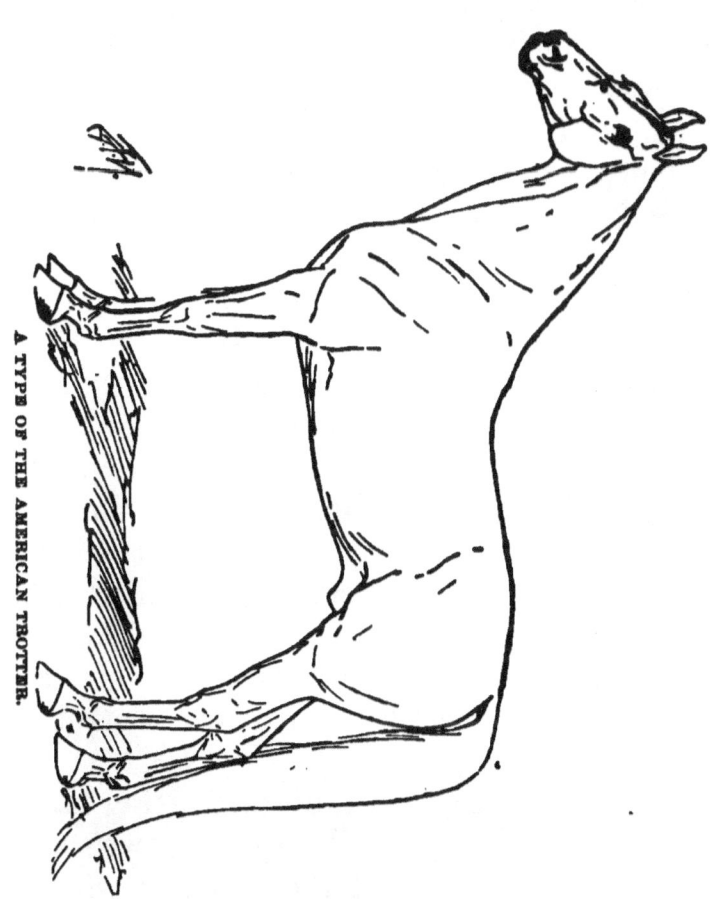

A TYPE OF THE AMERICAN TROTTER.

the Dictators, and all the various so-called Hambletonians of the present day. This celebrated horse, justly entitled to be classed as the great progenitor of the American trotter, was bred in Orange Co., N. Y., foaled in 1849, and was kept in that county until his death, which occurred March 26, 1876.

Then we have the *Mambrinos*, that take their name from Mambrino Chief, who was got by Mambrino Paymaster, a son of the Mambrino above referred to as the grandsire of Rysdyk's Hambletonian. The dam of Mambrino Chief, like the dam of Abdallah, was a mare of unknown blood. He was bred in Orange Co., N. Y., foaled in 1844, and when ten years old was taken to Kentucky, where he died in 1861. Upon the highly-bred and thoroughbred mares of that region he was very successful as a sire of fast trotters, and the mares got by him have been especially noted as producers of great trotters when coupled with other trotting strains.

The *Clays* constitute another trotting family of note. The original Henry Clay was a famous trotting stallion, foaled 1837, got by Andrew Jackson (also a famous trotter), who was a grandson of Bashaw (an imported Barb), and related to imported Messenger through the second dam of his sire, who was by that horse. The dam of Henry Clay was a great trotting mare, whose blood is unknown. From this horse we have the various families of Clays of the present day, and also the Patchens—the trotting stallion George M. Patchen, the greatest trotting stallion of his day, and the original of the name, being a grandson of the original Henry Clay.

The *Morgans* are perhaps our oldest trotting family; and if they have not produced our very fastest trotters their produce undoubtedly deserve to take the very highest rank as good-tempered, hardy and pleasant roadsters. They are descended, in the paternal line, from a horse called Justin Morgan, that was bred in Vermont, foaled 1793, and died 1821. His blood has never been positively known, although it is pretty well established that the thoroughbred predominated. From him we have the Morrills, the Fearnaughts, the Ethan Allens, the Black Hawks (not including the descendants of Long Island Black Hawk, who was by Andrew Jackson, grandson of Bashaw, above alluded to, and had none of the Morgan blood in his veins), the Daniel Lamberts, the Knoxes and the Golddusts. The popularity of this family at one time was unbounded; and no blood, excepting that of the thoroughbred, has been so generally disseminated and so highly esteemed throughout the United States. At present it is not so highly prized by those who place speed above all other qualities; but go where you will among livery-stable keepers or horse-railroad managers and ask them what type of horse they have found most profitable to use and wear out on the road, and they will almost invariably answer, "The old-fashioned Morgan."

The *Bashaws*, another popular family of trotters, are very closely related to the Clays and Patchens, having a common ancestry in Young Bashaw, who was the sire of the Andrew Jackson above referred to. Young Bashaw was by the imported Bashaw (heretofore mentioned in the pedigree of Henry Clay), his dam was by a thoroughbred sire, and his grandam was by imported Messenger. The most celebrated of the Bashaw family proper come through Long Island Black Hawk, who was by Andrew Jackson, out of a mare by Mambrino, son of Messenger. Through him we have Green's Bashaw (so well known in the west), the Mohawks, and many others of note.

The *Pilots:* The blood of the old black pacer Pilot, who was of French Canadian ancestry, has mingled kindly with our best trotting strains, and many of our very best and fastest trotters trace to him, mainly through his son Pilot Jr. (a horse owned for many years by the late R. A. Alexander, of Kentucky), out of a mare that was nearly thoroughbred. Old Copperbottom, also a Canadian pacer; Hiatoga, a horse bred in Virginia; Columbus, and Royal George, both from Canada, have all been very popular sires, and no compendium of the origin of the American trotting horse would be complete without reference to them.

In no department of stock-breeding is the influence of heredity and of patient selection with a view to the transmission and improvement of a desired quality more apparent than in the breeding of the trotting horse. Sixty years ago the American trotting horse, *as a breed*, was unthought of; and one that could trot a mile in less than three minutes was a wonderful animal! But the ability to trot fast was a desirable quality and breeders sought to perpetuate it. Animals that excelled the average of the species as trotters were selected to breed from, with a view to perpetuating and intensifying this quality; but as its possession was at that time an accident—a spontaneous variation—it was found that but few of the immediate descendants of the animals first chosen with a view to breeding fast trotters could trot faster than their remote ancestors. But when such of them as did show improvement in this direction were again selected for breeding purposes and coupled together it was found that, while there were still many failures, the proportion of the descendants that showed improvement in the trotting gait beyond the average of their ancestors was materially increased. And so by selecting from generation to generation from such families as have shown a tendency to improvement in this quality we have made great progress toward founding a breed of trotting horses.

So generally is the attention of the breeders of trotting horses directed to the "bright particular stars" that blaze out in the trotting firmament each succeeding year that we lose sight of the immense number of horses that trot in 2:30 to 2:50—a gait that twenty-five, and even fifteen, years ago was fast enough to entitle a horse to rank as a creditable performer on the turf, and in our admiration for these great performers we have failed to note the extent to which the *average* speed of the American trotter has been improved and the certainty with which trotters, possessing what a few years ago would have been classed as more than ordinary speed, are now being bred. What horseman who has reached the age of fifty years cannot remember how very rare three-minute trotters were when he was a boy! And yet what a large proportion of our Hambletonians, Clays, Bashaws, and Mambrinos now trot faster than three minutes!

The progress made by American trotters during the past twenty-five years, as demonstrated by the average speed of the animals which compete at our prominent trotting meetings, is something very often overlooked by those who do not give the subject particular attention. Year by year there have been vast accessions to the list of horses with records of 2:30 or better, and of course the influence of this constant influx of fresh speed cannot but be made manifest upon the turf. Taking the records of the oldest prominent trotting track—that of Buffalo, N. Y.—as a guide, we find the average time of all the heats trotted there during the summer meetings from 1866 to 1884, inclusive, to have been as follows:

1866	2:38½	1876	2:23
1867	2:34½	1877	2:24¼
1868	2:31¾	1878	2:21½
1869	2:29¼	1879	2:23¼
1870	2:28¾	1880	2:20
1871	2:25¾	1881	2:20¾
1872	2:26	1882	2:21¾
1873	2:26½	1883	2:21¾
1874	2:24½	1884	2:21¼
1875	2:25½		

These figures speak volumes. From 2:38½ in 1866 to 2:20 in 1880 and 2:20¾ the following year is a tremendous stride, and it will be seen that the reduction has been a steady as well as a notable one. Of course it is not every season that such flyers as Maud S. and St. Julien appear at the same meeting, as was the case at Buffalo in 1880, while the following year half a dozen of our best trotters were out at once, which accounts for the exceptionally low average for these two years; but, taking the average of the Buffalo track for the first five years of its existence, we find it to be 2:32½, while for the five years from 1880 to 1884, inclusive, it is reduced to 2:21¼.

The annual summer meeting of 1885 was omitted at Buffalo, and, beginning with that year at Cleveland, another one of our prominent trotting associations, we find the averages have been as follows:

1885	2:22¼	1889	2:21¼
1886	2:20½	1890	2:20
1887	2:20½	1891	2:19½
1888	2:20	1892	2:19¼

The averages for the last four years, as shown in the foregoing, do not fairly represent the average speed of the trained horses that participated in the trotting contests from the fact that within that period stake races for trotters two and three years old have been a prominent feature of the Cleveland meetings, and the records made by these immature trotters being included in our computation have kept the averages much above what they would otherwise have been.

While much of this increase in the average speed of our trotting horses should, in justice, be attributed to improvement in our vehicles and tracks, and to increased skill in the trainer, yet it is undeniable that by far the greater portion of it has resulted from increased capacity in our horses, bred for three, four or five generations especially with reference to this quality. It is also worthy of especial remark that over ninety-five per cent of all the horses with records of 2:25 or better, whose breeding can be traced even as far as the sire, are more or less closely related to one or more of our recognized trotting families.

The experience of the last decade has demonstrated beyond a question that by confining our selections for breeding purposes to the descendants of the well-known trotting families the probabilities of producing fast trotters are infinitely greater than by going outside; for within these families the trotting gait has been cultivated by selection and use until heredity has been made to lend its powerful aid in transmitting what was originally a spontaneous or accidental superiority; and the breeder who introduces a single cross in which the trotting gait has not become an inherent quality only adds to the probabilities of failure and postpones the day when we shall be able to breed fast trotters with certainty. We may possibly yet have something to do before we can claim to have established a breed of trotting horses, but the more closely we confine ourselves to judicious selections from the families that *trot* and *produce* trotters the more rapid will be our progress in the formation of a breed possessing a reasonable degree of uniformity in conformation and in which superiority at the trotting gait shall be an inherent and transmissible quality.

It may *possibly* become necessary to resort to crosses outside of these trotting families for improvement in some other quality; but there is no out-cross that we can make without danger to the transmission and improvement of the trotting gait. Even those of our trotters that belong to none of the recognized trotting families are almost invariably the result of selection with a view to this faculty. In almost every case of "breeding unknown" we have found that the dam was "a fast trotter." In short, the more thoroughly we investigate the course of breeding that has produced our trotting horses the more completely does it confirm the theory of breeding from animals that possess the quality we wish to perpetuate.

Those who tell us that we must infuse more of the blood of the thoroughbred into our trotting strains, because that blood is the foundation of all modern excellence in the horse, find their counterpart in those gentlemen of the old school—old fogies I had almost said—who used to be continually arguing for more of the blood of the Orient in the thoroughbred. The argument in each case is identical. The blood of the Arab and of the Barb was the foundation for the more modern thoroughbred. The Oriental horse represented the very highest type of speed and endurance; and from this source the thoroughbred derived all its original excellence. To keep up these good qualities, and to improve the English race horse, these good old gentlemen argued that we must constantly draw from the fountain-head—the source of all improvement. But, by and by, the time came when all horsemen were compelled to admit that a further infusion of this material—which constituted a most excellent foundation—was no longer needed, because the thoroughbred horse of the British Isles had become immensely superior to his Oriental ancestor. English breeding, training and selecting has done the work, and the man who now introduces a cross of the Arab or Barb in his thoroughbred stud is very justly considered blind to his own interest.

And so with breeding trotters. Granted that the endurance and vim and energy that make the great trotter come from the thoroughbred: and granted, even, that the *form* for speed at the trotting gait comes from the same source; we have selected, and trained, and bred with an especial view to adaptation to this special purpose, until we have a fixed characteristic— an inheritance of speed at the trotting gait, and an inheritance of mental quality, adapting the horse to this special use, in which the modern American trotter is as much superior to the average thoroughbred as is the best race horse that ever struck hoof upon the Epsom Downs to the average Arab of to-day.

Manifestly, the principal valuable qualities that our trotters have derived from the thoroughbred are courage and endurance. No one will claim that, as a breed, the thoroughbreds are fast trotters; and more, no one will claim that a single thoroughbred has ever excelled at that gait, judged by our standard of speed. The trotter is an American product—a creature the result of our own selection, breeding and training. What, then, can we gain by a stronger infusion of the blood of the thoroughbred? Certainly not more speed at the trotting gait, because it is not there, and cannot come from that source! We *may*, and doubtless can, in some cases get more courage and greater powers of endurance from this quarter, but beyond these two qualities I cannot conceive of a single point in which the American trotter can be improved by a fresh infusion of racing blood. It is against reason and against the experience of breeders the world over; and the man who rings the changes on "high breeding," and the "form for speed," and the "disposition to go fast," and the "foundation of all equine excellence," as arguments in favor of breeding from thoroughbreds to produce trotters, voluntarily shuts his eyes to the experience of the world in stock-breeding. The intelligent gentleman who breeds horses for the running turf selects his breeding-stock from the choicest-developed running strains—the families that can show upon their escutcheon the longest roll of mighty performers—and by pursuing this course he steadily improves his stock; and so the intelligent breeder of trotting horses will select from families in which speed at the trotting gait has become an inherent and transmissible quality.

I can see no reason why this great principle, which forms the correct basis of all good stock-breeding, should not apply to the breeding of trotting horses as well as to setter dogs. The get of a bulldog out of a setter bitch would probably possess more *courage* than a purely-bred setter, and a puppy so bred might *possibly* act well in the field; but no man accustomed to the business would back a litter so bred, in a field trial, against a litter of pure setters! And so, if it is a trotting horse we are after, it has always been my advice that the breeder should get as deeply into the trotting lines of blood as possible. The exceptional cases quoted by the advocates of the thoroughbred prove nothing. We cannot go very far as yet into any of our trotting strains of blood without running into a thoroughbred cross, or else running into obscurity. I should certainly very greatly prefer that my trotting brood mare or stallion, after showing a few crosses of Hambletonian, Pilot, Mambrino Chief, or Clay blood, should trace to a thoroughbred ancestry than to the dunghill, because in the former case we know that we are anchored upon a solid foundation of courage and endurance. But we have our trotting structure already reared to handsome proportions upon this foundation; why then should we overturn what has already been done and commence again to build on the same rock? To do so is, in my opinion, a step in the wrong direction.

This position is so self-evident—so perfectly in accord with the known laws of heredity—that I am surprised that it should be questioned by any man of ordinary intelligence. That mares with one or two trotting crosses on a thoroughbred pedigree are preferable, even for breeding trotters, to mongrels of no individual merit and no pedigree, no one in his sober senses will deny; and that mares by Hambletonian, or George Wilkes, or Mambrino Patchen, or Pilot Jr., or Mambrino Chief, or any other noted trotting sire, out of thoroughbred dams, should themselves produce great trotters when coupled with a well-bred trotting sire, as in the case of the dam of Maud S., is no surprise, and no argument whatever against my position, but confirms it. That the *next* remove from the blood of the race horse, if the remove be with choice trotting blood, will produce a still greater proportion of fast trotters, is what I assert. We want good, tried and approved trotting blood upon this foundation; and the more of this material we can put there, and the further we are pushed away from that foundation *by such material*, the better for certainty in producing fast and reliable trotting horses.

PACERS AND SADDLE HORSES.

Pacing horses have long been highly prized in all countries where horseback riding has been much practiced as a means of locomotion in the transaction of business, partly on account of the greater ease of this gait to the rider, partly because a change in the gait of the horse is a relief to one who needs must be in the saddle for a whole day at a time, and for the further reason that it has usually been considered a more speedy gait than the trot. Hence horses that can both trot and pace have long been bred in many portions of the United States. Experience has most thoroughly demonstrated the fact that the trot and pace are, to a very considerable degree, interchangeable;

and that most horses can be taught to adopt either the one gait or the other at the pleasure of the rider or driver, as an intermediate manner of progression between the walk and the gallop. Instances where horses that have shown unusual speed as pacers have been changed into speedy trotters, mainly by increasing the weight of the shoes on the fore feet, are of every-day occurrence; and trotters may with equal facility be taught the pacing gait by the use of "hobbles" so adjusted as to compel the animal to move both legs on the same side together, instead of moving the fore leg in unison with the hind leg on the opposite side, which constitutes the difference between the pace and the trot.

The success which has attended these and other methods of changing horses from one gait to the other, and the further fact that horses which show great speed as pacers so frequently descend from the well-established trotting families, has led to the generally-established belief among horse-breeders that the trotting and pacing gaits are essentially the same; or rather that the taking of the one gait or the other is more a matter of accident or training than of inheritance. I cannot subscribe to this theory myself, however, further than to admit that the form which is usually found in the fast pacer (a rather steep rump,

THE BREEDS OF HORSES.

A PACING CONFORMATION.

with high, thin withers and well-bent hock, see page 223,) is one which appears to be well adapted to great speed in trotting when once the gait has been changed by any process of training. It is undeniable, however, that the form which is usually seen in our fast trotters (see page 207) is not that of the natural pacer, for with the former we frequently find—as in the case of Maud S. and many other notable trotters—that the animal is higher at the hips than at the withers; and while I have frequently seen horses possessing this conformation trained to the pacing gait, yet they never take kindly to it, neither do they ever become fast pacers. On account of this obvious difference in form between our best trotters and best pacers I am decidedly of the opinion that when speed at either gait is especially sought for, the breeding of the two types together should not be encouraged; but rather that the breeder of trotting horses should adhere to that form which usually accompanies the highest speed at the trotting gait, and *vice versa*. Some of our well-established trotting families—notoriously some branches of the Hambletonian family—produce a large per cent of horses possessing the pacing conformation, and which pace naturally from birth; and selection from these and others possessing similar characteristics will at a very early day create a distinct breed of pacing horses.

Horseback riding, which in the early settlement of our country was of necessity extensively practiced, has of late years become a fashionable recreation, and the business of raising and training saddle horses is now a lucrative one. More attention has been paid to it hitherto in the States of Kentucky, Tennessee, Missouri, and the southern portions of Ohio, Indiana and Illinois than in any other parts of the United States, and here natural pacers are very common. The other so-called saddle gaits, as the running walk, the fox trot, the rack, and the canter, are largely the result of care and skill on the part of the trainer; although some strains of horses undoubtedly train to them more kindly than others; but the conformation which I have previously described as belonging more especially to the natural pacer, appears to train more naturally and readily than that of the trotter to the various saddle gaits, and from horses approximating this form, or a medium between the two, I would recommend the breeder and trainer of saddle horses to make his selections rather than from either of the extreme typical forms. An association has been formed for the purpose of promoting the breeding of saddle horses, and a stud book for them has been instituted with headquarters at Louisville, Ky. As foundation stock, stallions that have been especially distinguished as sires of good saddle horses have been taken, and a persistent and systematic effort to establish a breed of saddle horses is now being made. In England the trot is now the favorite saddle gait; the fox trot, the running walk, the pace and the rack, which in this country are in such high favor, are not now seen there at all under the saddle, and our "gaited saddle horses" would be a decided innovation on Rotten Row in Hyde Park, although horses that ambled or paced were very popular there a hundred years ago.

ORLOFF TROTTERS.

Although the Orloff trotters of Russia have been but sparingly introduced into this country, yet they are so frequently referred to in discussions upon horse-breeding, and especially in those pertaining to the breeding of trotting horses, that a history of the breed and a comparison of their merits with our own trotters cannot fail to be interesting. The breed takes its name from Count Alexis Orloff Tschismensky, an enthusiastic horseman of Russia, who, in 1775, imported from Arabia a grey stallion named Smetanxa, said to have been of unusual size and strength. A Danish mare was bred to this imported Arabian stallion, and the produce was a horse known as Polkan 1st. From a union of this half-blood with a Dutch mare sprang a stallion known as Bars 1st, who is generally regarded as the progenitor of the Orloff race of trotters. The fame of this quarter-blood, Bars 1st, was chiefly perpetuated through his sons Lubeznay 1st, Lebed 1st and Dobroy 1st.

It is worthy of special note that we have an almost exact parallel of the course of breeding which laid the foundation for the Orloff trotting horse in the case of the imported Barb, Grand Bashaw, a grey stallion imported to the United States from Tripoli by Mr. John C. Morgan. This horse got Young Bashaw (also grey), out of Pearl by First Consul, and he in turn got Andrew Jackson, out of a mare of unknown blood. It will be observed that the Russian trotter Bars 1st and Andrew Jackson were each three removes from their Oriental ancestry, and that in this third remove the trotting excellence first began to manifest itself. Bars 1st laid the foundation for the Orloff trotting horse, and was himself a distinguished trotter; Andrew Jackson was the most noted trotting stallion of his day, and from him are descended the Bashaw, Patchen and Clay trotters of the present time. We have no positive knowledge as to the breeding of the Danish mare, the dam of Polkan 1st, or of the Dutch mare that produced

Bars 1st, while Pearl, the dam of Young Bashaw, was a well-bred mare, she being by a thoroughbred sire, out of Fancy by imported Messenger. As to the blood of the dam of Andrew Jackson we are left to conjecture. The similarity of the foundation of these two races of trotting horses is therefore quite apparent.

Count Orloff and his successor, V. T. Shiskin, devoted themselves assiduously to the improvement of these horses, selecting their stallions exclusively from the foundation above alluded to, but resorting frequently to English and Dutch mares of known excellence; so that the Orloff trotter, like the American, is of a mixed origin, and neither the Arab, the Barb nor the English thoroughbred can claim exclusive paternity in either case. Selection and crossing, with a view to adaptation for a specific use, has accomplished the work of creating in both countries a race of trotting horses. Count Orloff was an intelligent enthusiast in the business—as all successful breeders have been—and he persistently refused to part with any of his entire horses, preferring that he alone should dictate the choice of sires to be used to perpetuate and improve the race. After his death the stud was scattered; a considerable portion of it passed into the possession of the crown, but several private studs were founded, and a stud book was instituted to aid in the work of keeping the race free from further admixture, although with the Russians, as with us, the question is not very well settled as to what constitutes the best trotting pedigree, and purity of blood is a rather vague and indefinite term when applied to the Orloff as well as to the American trotter. The Count had been an enthusiastic patron of the race course as a means of developing and testing the powers of his horses, and since his time the government has given its powerful aid to promote the same object, not only by establishing breeding studs, but by furnishing more than one-half of the prize-money that is contested for at these trotting races, which have been held regularly in that country for the last sixty years. Russian trials of speed are regulated by law, and the driver or owner who violates any of the rules which have been laid down to secure fair contests is liable to take an unceremonious trip to Siberia at government expense—a punishment that, as might be supposed, is much more effectual in suppressing fraud than is that of an edict of expulsion issued by our National Trotting Associations.

I had the pleasure, a few years ago, of meeting Mons. Jules Goujon, who has long been a resident of Moscow, and who is intimately connected with the turf sports of that country. From him I learned many interesting particulars concerning the Orloff horse and the methods of breeding, training and driving in that country. He states that—

The entries for the races are according to age qualifications, except those for horses past six years old, which are free for all. The heats are never less than three versts, and the deciding heat is at the same distance. In races of four and one-half versts the deciding heat is at three versts. Races of six and twelve versts are decided in one heat. The first prize is not given to the horse that comes in first in the race, but in the deciding heat. The number of horses entered in each race is unlimited, but they are started three at a time, and the two horses out of the entire number of starters that trot the distance in the least time, according to the watch, take part in the deciding heat. If the horse winning in the first trial comes in second in the second trial then a third heat settles the question of supremacy. Only two moneys are given. There are three tracks, of oval shape, inclosed one within the other, one for each horse. The outer is one and a half versts (one mile) long; the two others are shorter, one by twelve sagenes (eighty-four feet) and the other by twenty-three sagenes (161 feet). The first horse is started on the exterior track, in front of the stand, and the two others, in order to equalize the distance, are started in the rear, on their respective tracks, which are selected by lot.

The horses come up at a jog, each one to his place. A judge is placed beside each horse whose duty it is, by waving a bit of cloth, to notify the starter, who is in the stand, that the horse under his charge has arrived at his position. The horses are started from the stand by the stroke of a bell, which sets in motion at the same time the hands of a great dial which marks minutes and seconds. At the instant the first horse passes the winning score the judge strikes a blow which stops the first hand of the dial, and in the same way for the second horse. This automatic system gives the time of the race, by means of the clock, without error, and enables the judge, who is placed at the distance post to decide which

THE BREEDS OF HORSES. 231

of the horses are distanced, to better know the precise instant when the race is finished. A distance in Russia is thirty sagenes (210 feet) for a race of three versts, and seventy-five sagenes (525 feet) for a race at a greater distance. Only three false starts are allowed; after that number the judges can fine the driver of the horse that is responsible for the false starts, or can refuse to allow him to go the course. In case a driver does not try to win with a horse the judges may fine him, and on a repetition of the offense he is liable to visit Siberia for a couple of years—a punishment which I imagine, from what I hear, would be salutary for some of your American drivers.

A horse is allowed to make but three breaks during a heat of three versts, and the same number in the deciding heat. If he makes more he is out of the race, and so is he if he makes more than thirteen jumps in one gallop. Each horse in the race has a judge especially assigned to watch his movements, whose decision as to whether the horse makes more than three breaks or more than the permitted number of jumps in one break is without appeal; he has only to touch a button of an electric machine designating the offending horse, and a groom on horseback in front of the stand at once rushes off to notify his driver to quit the track.

For all the prizes given by the societies any one can trot, as he pleases, to a droschka (the national Russian vehicle, four-wheeled and very clumsy and heavy as compared with the sulky,) or to a sulky with two wheels and four reins. The weight of the vehicle and of the sulky is equally *ad libitum* for all the prizes given by the societies. The Government, for prizes which it gives, specifies for itself the kind of vehicle, its weight, the weight of the driver, and the distance to be trotted.

There are two seasons for racing. The summer races occur in May and June, and are trotted twice a week, on Sunday and Wednesday. They are started at 6 o'clock in the evening, the days being so long in Russia that it is light until 11 o'clock at night, and thus the heat of the day is avoided, which is an advantage for both the horses and the spectators.

In winter the races are always trotted on Sundays, and on the ice. But two horses are started at a time, and on the opposite sides of the same course, which is but one verst in length.

The droschka of which Mons. Goujon speaks, although a rather clumsy-looking vehicle to American eyes, is really a very light and easy-running road wagon, weighing only about seventy pounds. The verst is 3,500 feet in length, being a fraction less than two-thirds of a mile.

I have before me, as I write, a statement of the best time made at all distances, in Russia, each year, from 1861 to 1876, inclusive, from which it would appear that no improvement was made in the speed or endurance of the Orloff trotter during the last five years embraced in this period. The fastest time ever made for one verst was 1:40, by Poitieshnoy, in 1869, which rate of speed, if kept up for one mile, would be a very little below 2:31. This rate of speed has never been reached by any other Russian horse—the nearest approach to it being 1:42⅓. The same horse has the best record at three versts, being 5:00, equal to two miles in 5:01¾. This appears to have been an exceptional case, however, as the next best performances are three versts in 5:06 once, and 5:07 twice. The best time for four and a half versts is 7:52, equal to 7:54¼ for three miles. For seven and a half versts the best time is 13:49, equal to 13:56¾ for five miles. For thirty versts the best time is 1:08:30, equal to twenty miles in 1:08:53½, which is by over three minutes the best performance by a Russian horse at that distance. Comparing these records with those of our American trotters we find the following:

Best Russian Time.		*Best American Time.*		*Difference.*
One mile.........	2:31	One mile...........	2:04	:27
Two miles......	*5:01¼	Two miles..........	4:33¼	:27¾
Three miles......	7:52½	Three miles.........	7:21¼	:31¼
Five miles.......	13:56¾	Five miles.........	13:00	:56¾
Twenty miles....	1:08:53½	Twenty miles......	58:25	10:28½

From the foregoing the superiority of American trotters, at all distances, is very clearly shown. I do not share in the often-expressed opinion that our system of training, our tracks and our vehicles are materially better than the Russian. Thousands of American trotters have beaten the best one-mile time made in Russia; and although two-mile races are not common in this country, the exceptionally fast time of 5:01¾ for that distance made by Poitieshnoy has been beaten by nearly all of our great trotters; and I have no doubt but that we have hundreds of trotters in training to-day that are capable of beating that time by several seconds. No Orloff trotter has ever succeeded in trotting twenty miles within an hour by nearly nine

* Exceptional time—5:07¾ being the best with this single exception.

minutes, while *five* American horses have accomplished that feat. Another point of contrast, in which the American trotter shows at a great advantage over his Russian competitor, appears to be in campaigning qualities. The oldest reported Orloff winner is twelve years. Goldsmith Maid was in her prime at twenty. Pietel, the most noted Orloff campaigner, was a winner for four successive years; the Maid was a winner for thrice that length of time, while most of our great trotters have steadily improved until they were fifteen or sixteen years of age.

It is also worthy of note that while the Russian trotter appears to have attained his maximum of speed several years ago, the improvement on the part of our American horses in this respect, within the past ten years, has been truly wonderful. Certainly the showing for speed and endurance of the Orloff trotter does not compare favorably with the American, although the former undoubtedly possesses both of these qualities to a high degree. It is claimed, however, that in beauty of form the Orloff is greatly the superior of our American production; but here, again, I must be permitted to put in a demurrer; for, if the animals that I have seen may be taken as fair specimens of the breed, the facts are certainly the reverse of this statement. Our breeders will undoubtedly object to the prevailing color of the Orloffs, as upon an analysis of the winners in that country we find that fifty-five per cent are greys, twenty-four per cent blacks, fourteen per cent bays or browns, and six per cent light bays.

FRENCH COACH HORSES.

As early as 1780 the French Government began a systematic effort to improve the native horse stock of that country, especially for the cavalry service, by the introduction of Thoroughbred and Hunting stallions from England, and offering their services to the farmers at a merely nominal fee. From that time down to the present the French Government has continued its paternal supervision of the horse-breeding interests of that country, introducing from year to year Thoroughbred stallions in considerable numbers, and selecting the best of the male produce resulting from the union of the imported stallions and the French mares for use in the stud. Since about 1840, however, the introduction of Thoroughbred stallions has fallen off in that portion of France devoted especially to Coach-horse breeding, while the number of native-bred horses selected for use in the stud has proportionately increased. At times, under the supervision of the Government, the introduction of Thoroughbred sires has ceased almost entirely; and again, when those in authority have been of the opinion that the blood of the Thoroughbred could still be used to advantage, fresh importations have been made. Some of these imported stallions left a marked impress upon the horse stock of the country, notably among these being the horse Young Rattler, imported about 1820, whose produce were especially remarkable for their stylish, high-headed appearance, and high, proud-stepping action. The get of this horse were largely selected by the Government agents for breeding purposes, and to him more than to any other one of these imported sires the present Inspector-General of the Government haras, the Vicomte de la Motte-Rouge, ascribes the origin of the present so-called Coach horse of France. The foundation had been previously laid by crossing and recrossing with the Thoroughbred, but Young Rattler and the stallions of his get gave the qualities which the French people especially fancied for coaching uses. Since that period this coach-horse type has received more largely than any other, perhaps, the fostering care and patronage of the Government; and certainly very marked improvement has been effected and a considerable degree of uniformity has been secured. Much official encouragement has been given to the development of trotting speed, although this has always been held subservient to that par-

THE BREEDS OF HORSES. 237

A TYPE OF THE FRENCH COACH (DEMI-SANG).

ticular style, carriage, and form of action which has been so highly prized by the French people in horses for the carriage or coach. In some families of the breed a very creditable degree of trotting speed has been attained; and this without sacrificing the especially coach-horse characteristics. The size has been maintained by a turf law which excludes all horses under $15\frac{1}{4}$ hands high from competing for trotting prizes; and endurance has been cultivated by encouraging long-distance races—usually two miles or over—and on the turf instead of a hard, smooth track, as in the United States. These long-distance contests inevitably weed out the "soft ones," while trotting on the turf shortens the stride, increases the knee action, and necessarily quickens the step in order to attain speed, thus retaining and cultivating in their fastest trotters the peculiar knee action and step desired in the coach horse. The prevailing color is bay, but there are many chestnuts among them and blacks are occasionally seen.

When the system of breeding above alluded to was inaugurated the produce of the union of the Thoroughbred sires with the French mares were called *demi-sang* (half-blood); and notwithstanding the "breeding-up" process which has constantly been going on for over one hundred years these horses are still called *demi-sang* in France and are so classed in the prize lists for the horse shows of that country. They are also sometimes spoken of in France as Normans, from the fact that they are chiefly bred in what was formerly known as Normandy.

It is only within a recent period that French Coach horses have attracted attention at the hands of American importers and breeders; the draft horses of that country having largely monopolized the attention of American stock-raisers traveling in France. But within the past ten years the growing demand for stylish, high-stepping coach horses in America has led to the importation of French Coachers in considerable numbers. The course of breeding that has produced these horses in France is much the same as that which has created the modern Cleveland Bay of England, the blood of the Thoroughbred largely predominating in both, the chief difference being in the mares that have constituted the basis.

It must not be understood from what has been said in the foregoing that the breeding of Coach horses is carried on throughout all of France, nor that the use of Thoroughbred stallions is now discouraged by the Government. It is only in the departments of Orne, Calvados, Manche, Seine-Infeieure, and a part of Eure that the attention of the Government is especially directed to the production of Coach horses. In the departments above named there are two haras, or Government stables, one at Pin and the other at St. Lo. In other departments, as in Eure, Orne, Eure et Loir, Loir et Cher and Sarthe, attention is chiefly given to the Percheron, while the Boulonnais, the Breton and the Thoroughbred are encouraged elsewhere.

It may also be of interest to note in this connection that in addition to the stallions owned by the French Government there are two classes of stallions of various breeds owned by private individuals that may be mentioned as receiving Governmental recognition. First, *approved* stallions, which after inspection by the authorities are granted a subsidy for remaining in the country and serving mares at prices fixed by their owners. This subsidy amounts in the case of Thoroughbred stallions to from about $150 to $500 a year; Coach horses (*demi-sang*), $75 to $150 a year; and draft horses from $50 to $100 a year. The second class are *authorized* upon inspection to serve mares, but receive no subsidy. No stallions excepting those belonging to the Government, and those that are approved or authorized, are allowed to do stud duty.

CLEVELAND BAYS.

Many years ago, before railways came into general use, there existed in England a famous breed of strong carriage or coach horses known as Cleveland Bays. They were bred chiefly in the vale of Cleveland, in the East Riding of Yorkshire, and were uniformly of a bay color; hence the name Cleveland Bay. But with the advent of the railway and the improvement of the roadways in general, the demand for the strong horses of which the Cleveland Bay was the type fell off until finally it came to be regarded as practically extinct, and all English writers upon the horse with whom I am conversant, who wrote from about 1840 down to ten years ago, such as Youatt and Burn, Youatt and Spooner, Prof. Low and "Frank Forrester," have treated of the Cleveland Bay as no longer in existence as a distinct breed. "Frank Forrester" (Henry William Herbert), the most recent of these writers, in Vol. II, p. 20, of his great work, speaks as follows of the course of breeding which has rendered the Cleveland Bay extinct:

> The first gradation, when pace became a desideratum with hounds, was the stinting of the best Cleveland Bay mares to good thoroughbred horses, with a view of the progeny turning out hunters, troop-horses, or, in the last resort, stage-coach horses, or, as they were termed, machiners. The most promising of these half-bred colts were kept as stallions; and mares, of the same type, with their dams,

stinted to them produced the improved English carriage horse of fifty years ago.

The next step was the putting of the half-bred fillies, by thoroughbreds out of Cleveland Bay mares, a second time to thoroughbred stallions; their progeny to become the hunters, while themselves and their brothers were lowered into the carriage horses; and the half-bred stallions, which had been the getters of carriage horses, were degraded into the sires of the new, improved cart horse.

From this, one step more brings us to the ordinary hunter of the present day of provincial hunting countries, for light weights, and persons not willing, or able, to pay the price of thoroughbreds. These are the produce of the third and fourth crosses of thorough blood on the improved mares, descended in the third or fourth degree from the Cleveland Bay stock, and are in every way superior, able and beautiful animals, possessing speed and endurance sufficient to live with the best hounds in any country, except the very fastest, such as the Melton Mowbray, the Northamptonshire, and, perhaps, the Vale of Belvoir, where the fields are so large, the land all in grass, and the scent so fine that fox-hunting in them is in fact steeple-chasing; so that no fox can live before the hounds on a fine scenting day above half an hour, nor any horse, except a thoroughbred, live even that time *with* the hounds, having fourteen stone or upward on his back.

No sort of breeding in England is so profitable as this. The breeder is comparatively secure against anything like ultimate loss, while he has a fair chance of drawing a capital prize in the shape of a first-rate hunter or a carriage horse of superior quality; and it is to the breeding of such a class of animals that the attention of the farmers in horse-breeding counties is wholly directed at this date.

For this reason one has no more pure Cleveland Bays, the use of the stallion of that breed being entirely discontinued; large, bony, slow thoroughbreds of good form and great power, which have not succeeded on the turf, having been substituted for them, even for the getting of cart and farming-team horses; and the farmers finding it decidedly to

THE BREEDS OF HORSES. 243

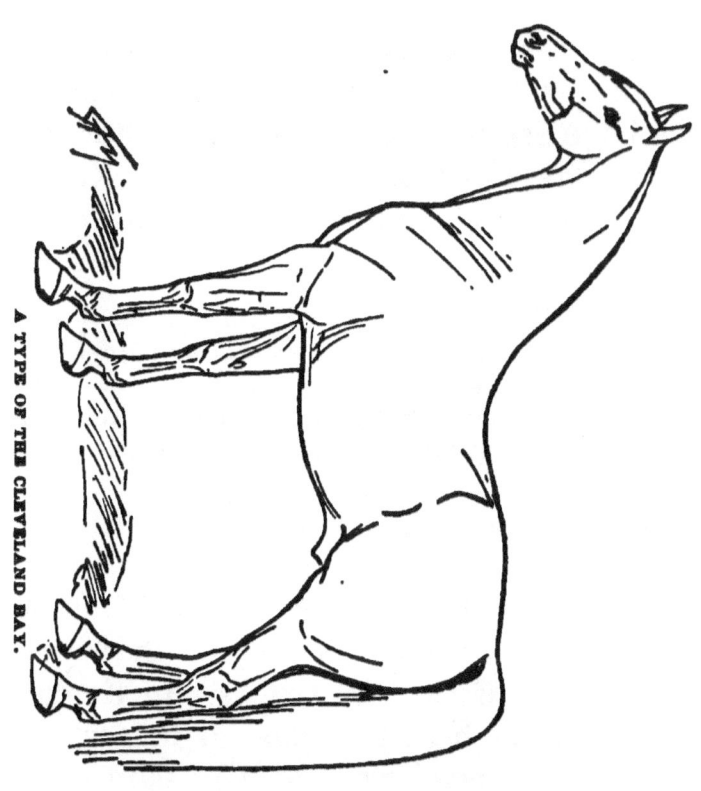

A TYPE OF THE CLEVELAND BAY.

their advantage to work large, roomy, bony, half or two-third-bred mares, out of which, when they grow old, or if by chance they meet with an accident, they may raise hunters, coach horses, or, at the worst, chargers or machiners, rather than to plow with garrons and weeds, the stock of which would be valueless and worthless except for the merest drudgery.

Within the last ten years the English agricultural press and English writers upon the horse have begun to again speak of the Cleveland Bay as a breed, but as late as Nov. 18, 1881, I find the London *Live-Stock Journal*, the only distinctively live-stock serial publication in Great Britain, stating that:

> The Cleveland that some people write about is not a Cleveland; it is only the nearest approach to what the Cleveland was like. If there is such a thing as a pure Cleveland the owner should stick to him; the breed, it is possible, may be resuscitated.

The *Mark Lane Express* of about the same date qualified a reference of the same sort by the remark, "if there be such a breed"; and Mr. Frederick Street, who as late as 1883 wrote "The History of the Shire Horse" in England, speaking of the heavier classes of horses, says: "The only distinct breeds now recognized are the Shire horse or English Cart horse, the Clydesdale and the Suffolk; the Cleveland Bay being well-nigh extinct." In January, 1884, I addressed a letter to Mr. George T. Turner, then editor of the *Mark Lane Express*, of London, asking for his opinion as to whether the Cleveland Bay still existed as a distinct breed in that country. He replied in substance that of late a demand for the old sort of Cleveland Bays had sprung up, and the breed was in a fair way to be resuscitated. He thought there was material enough left to operate on, and stated, to quote his exact words, that "the Cleveland is undoubtedly the produce of the thoroughbred horse (race horse or hunting stallion) on the North country cart mares; this was the origin of the breed, and it was created for coaching purposes. The coaches, toward the last, required faster horses, and these were superseded by the railway. So the Cleveland fell into desuetude. Now they are wanted again for fast, heavy town work. If a stud book were started we should see that material was in existence." He added that he would agitate the question in England.

A week or two later there appeared in his paper, the *Mark Lane Express*, the following:

In reply to a question from a correspondent in the United States as to the present status of the Cleveland breed of horses in this country, we are of opinion that there is material enough left, especially in Yorkshire, to form the basis of a herd book and a very profitable breeders' industry. The railway locomotive drove the old Cleveland Bay horse off the road, but the more modern type of Cleveland horse, or at all events Yorkshire-bred horses of the Cleveland stamp, with rather more of the thoroughbred stallion's influence apparent, are precisely the cattle that are to be seen in the use of railway companies for their lighter work, especially the newly-appointed omnibuses which have been started by the railway companies in London, and for which the cheaper French horses hitherto used are neither strong enough nor fast enough. It is remarkable that the railway companies, which took the old Cleveland horse's occupation away, should be among the first to give it back again in a different form; but it is plain enough to anyone who will give the necessary attention to the subject that the light van work of the new heavy omnibus work of the metropolis is bringing to London a lot of very superior and valuable horses from the northern breeding districts, which to all appearances have the old Cleveland blood for their basis, and which obtain their speed and style from the judicious use of the blood of the thoroughbred stallion.

This seems to leave no room for doubt that the Cleveland Bay of to-day has been or is being created, as was the breed when it was formerly considered a breed, by a mingling of the blood of the thoroughbred race horse with that of the large bay mares of Yorkshire. There is still much stock remaining in that region possessing the old Cleveland Bay characteristics, and it is evident that the same course of breeding which originally formed the breed may speedily restore it—if the work has not already been done—from the material remaining in that country. Whatever of this material there may yet be in existence in Yorkshire and elsewhere in England will no doubt be utilized for this purpose, and to this end the new Cleveland Stud Book, which was inaugurated in 1884, will doubtless be of great service.

HACKNEYS.

The word Hackney has long been used in England in a sense synonymous with the term roadster as used in this country; but latterly it has been adopted as the specific name of a breed of horses deservedly popular in Great Britain, and rapidly growing in favor in the United States. To write the history of the development of this breed would be to write a history of horse-breeding in Norfolk and the adjacent counties of England for the last one hundred and fifty years. But Mr. Euren, the compiler of the English Hackney Stud Book, dates the real beginning of the true English Hackney breed with the advent of the Shales or Shields horse, the "Original Shales" of the stud book, foaled about 1760. This horse was got by Blaze, a son of the famous race horse Flying Childers, and his dam is spoken of as "a strong, common mare."

The claim of the "Original Shales" to distinction rests chiefly in the fact that he was the sire of the famous horses Scot Shales and Driver, both said to have been remarkably game and fast trotters. Scot Shales is said by the historian John Lawrence to have been "the first trotting stallion of eminence of which we have any account." He was kept for service chiefly in Lincolnshire, and in 1772 was advertised as "remarkable for getting exceeding fine colts and good goers."

As to Driver, it was claimed, in the advertisements of some of his descendants, that he trotted seventeen miles in one hour. He was foaled about 1765, and his fame was perpetuated chiefly through Jenkinson's Fireaway, foaled 1780, the original of the well-known Fireaway family of Hackneys, and the sire of the famous Wroot's Pretender. Jenkinson's Fireaway must have been a great trotter, as it is said that "he trotted two miles on the Oxford Road in five minutes; and, chiefly through his son, Wroot's Pretender, exercised a potent influence upon the horse stock of Norfolk, Lincoln, Yorkshire, and the North of England generally. This horse, Wroot's Pretender, is invested with especial interest to American horsemen from the fact that he was the grandsire of imported Bellfounder, that got the Charles Kent mare, the dam of that great American progenitor of trotters Rysdyk's Hambletonian. It is alleged of Wroot's Pretender, that "when five years old he trotted sixteen miles in one hour, carrying sixteen stone;" and that he was exceedingly popular and extensively patronized in the stud is shown in the alleged fact that his serving fees for mares for the years 1803-4-5 amounted to £761 15s. 6d. (about $3,695), "exclusive of the groom's fees"—a very handsome sum, indeed, for that period. He was a black, very blood-like in appearance, and lived to a very great age. A writer in the *Sporting Magazine* for July, 1821, when this horse was thirty-three years of age, speaks of him as follows:

> He was brought last year out of the East Riding of Yorkshire by a "break-neck dealer," being "turned adrift," no one suspecting it possible for him to propagate his species any longer; but I have seen ten or twelve of his produce (yearlings) as well as foals this season, which are very promising. He is a dark brown, 15.2 hands, and it appears was bred by Christopher Rook [Wroot], Long Sutton, Lincolnshire. His first performance was in that county, when he trotted two miles in 5 min., 54 sec., with a high weight, upon green sward. I well remember his first appearance in a market town in the north. The "Johnny Raws" smiled at his worn-out, emaciated form, but the moment room was given for him to get upon his pins every other stallion that was exhibited retired into the shade in an instant. As he was rattling along, apparently at full speed, a cur dog casually crossed the road; the people imagined it would be trampled upon, but the generous animal darted over it in grand style, to the astonishment of every individual

Wroot's Pretender got Stevens' Bellfounder, the sire of imported Bellfounder (Jary's Bellfounder, 55 of the stud book). Velocity, the dam of imported Bellfounder, must have been a mare of great merit, as will be seen by the following extract from the *Norwich Mercury* of Nov. 8, 1806:

> On Wednesday se'nnight the long depending trotting match for one hour took place between that celebrated brown mare Velocity, the property of Mr. Roger Jary of Ashill, and that

fast-trotting chestnut horse Doubtful, the property of Mr. King of Wymondham, for 50 guineas, which was decided in favor of Mr. Jary's mare. The distance they trotted within the time was fifteen miles and a half, and Mr. Jary's mare had to turn round sixteen times on account of galloping, while the horse did not turn round once.

Returning to Scot Shales, it would be manifestly improper to omit some account of his famous son Hue and Cry. Of this horse John Lawrence in the *Sporting Magazine* of June, 1821, says:

I saw him several times while he was advertised as a covering stallion, upwards of twenty years. He was then fifteen or sixteen years old, perhaps 15 hands one-half high, a bright bay with some white, a good figure, and master of sixteen stone. * * * Of his performances I know nothing very particular, but that he was one of the speediest trotters of his day, whence his name, from the hue and cry he raised whilst dashing along the road with a posse of horses galloping on each side and behind him. He was a horse of rare temper and courage, a true trotter, and got good stock. He trotted the mile considerably under three minutes, carrying a high weight, and trotted the hour several times, but I am uninformed of the number of miles. When I saw him his fore feet were entirely ruined, the result of having had, some years previously, his shoes fitted whilst red hot. It is a curious circumstance that in the annals of racing no notice is to be found of trotters. I could never trace the commencement of trotting as a race, nor the notice of any trotting stallion before Shales. There seems to have been a succession of trotting stallions of the name of Shales since that period in Lincolnshire and Norfolk, the most famous districts in the world for trotters, beyond a doubt.

Through Scot Shales the Hackney breed gets another one of its most distinguished representatives, Marshland Shales (No. 435 of the stud book), whose sire was Thistleton Shales (a son of Scot Shales) and his dam by Hue and Cry, above mentioned, making him strongly inbred to the Scot Shales. This horse was a chestnut, foaled 1802, stood 14¾ hands high, and had a remarkably heavy crest, which in old age fell over considerably—a peculiarity which reappears in many of his descendants to this day. In his day he was regarded by the people of Norfolk, and the North of England generally, as the greatest trotter that the world had ever produced. In August, 1810, he "trotted a match race of over seventeen miles, carrying over twelve stone," and won in 56 minutes. He trotted many races and it is said was never beaten.

I have given the foregoing particulars (condensed mainly from Mr. Euren's Stud Book) concerning a few of the noted Norfolk trotters —the original of the more modern Hackney— of seventy-five and one hundred years ago, in order to show that as early as the beginning of the present century the horses of Norfolk and the North of England had acquired a high reputation as trotters and road horses; and while the authenticity of many of these very remarkable performances has been questioned it is clearly established that the Norfolk trotters of that period were able to trot long distances at a high rate of speed, carrying heavy weight; and that they were in high repute as "riding horses for general purposes."

In our Morgan horses of fifty years ago we had a near approach to the modern English Hackney in size, form, and gait. The typical Hackney is pre-eminently a practically useful road horse. Very compactly and strongly built, with good strong legs and feet, seldom over $15\frac{1}{4}$ hands high, short in the back, large at the girth, closely ribbed up, the trotting action short, quick and "trappy," they constitute a breed of horses peculiarly well adapted to use on the road. They have not been fancied in England for many years past as riding horses, neither has any especial effort been made to develop speed at the trotting gait, but they have been for a long time bred especially with a view to the development of a horse fit to draw any sort of rig at a quick pace on the road; and for this purpose they are considered in that country as without an equal in the whole world. They are of all colors, but bays, browns and chestnuts are more frequently seen than any other. An active demand has sprung up in the United States for these horses within the past five years and a stud-book organization has been effected, with Dr. Wm. Seward Webb of New York as Secretary.

THE BREEDS OF HORSES. 253

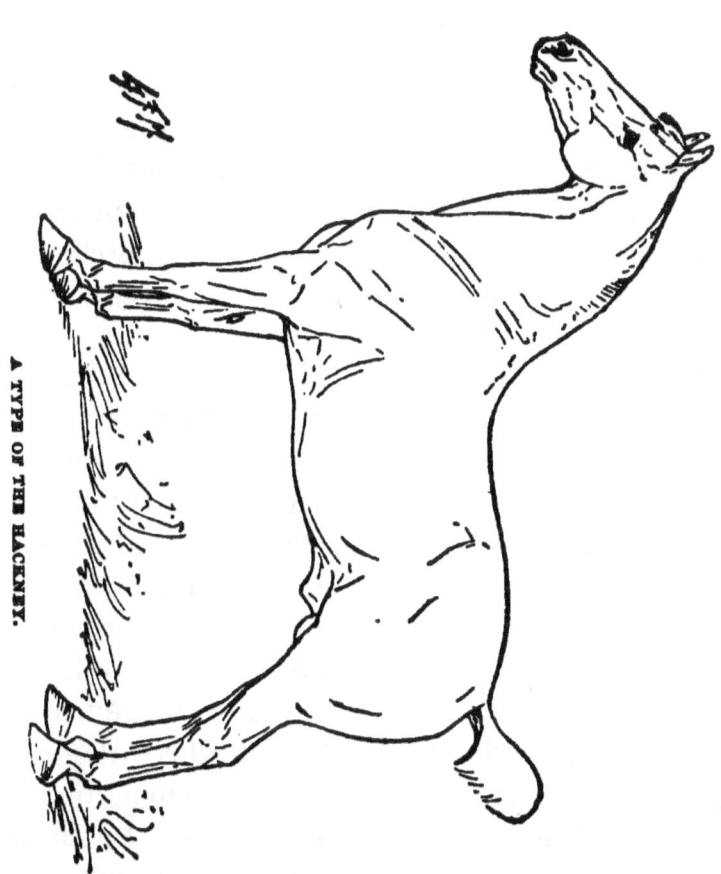

A TYPE OF THE HACKNEY.

ENGLISH SHIRE OR CART HORSES.

No point in equine history is better established than is the fact that to the regions bordering on the Western coast of Europe, once known as Normandy and Flanders, the world is indebted for the basis of its various breeds of draft horses. Flanders especially was famed, away back in the middle ages, for its famous breed of Black horses; and this race appears to have been the prevailing one throughout tne north of ancient Gaul and of Germany, from the mouth of the Rhine eastward, and Prof. Low thinks "inhabited in the wild state the vast region of marsh and forest which stretched all through Europe, eastward, to the Euxine sea." It was from this source that the rulers of Great Britain drew in large numbers for the purpose of increasing the size of the horses of the Island. How or when this breed originated is a subject upon which history throws no light; but as early as the eleventh century they were largely imported into England, and royal edicts and regulations were repeatedly issued for the purpose of encouraging the use of the large stallions of this breed. King John imported at one time 100 choice stallions from Flanders, Edward II followed in the same course, and it would seem that in the time of Henry VIII these Flemish horses were inseparably associated in the British mind with the idea of immense size and massive proportions, for we are told that when King Henry first saw the Princess Anne of Cleves, a large, coarsely-formed woman, who was to be his fourth spouse, he expressed his opinion of her by the ejaculation: "Egad, she is like a great Flanders mare!"

It is not my purpose to follow up, step by step, the several importations that were made, from time to time, of these heavy horses from Germany, Holland and Flanders, nor to recount the various stages of development which resulted in the formation of what is now known as the Shire horse or English Cart horse. One of the early Earls of Huntingdon is mentioned by Prof. Low as having been especially active in his efforts to improve the British breeds of heavy horses; and Robert Bakewell, who first taught the world the great principles of good stock-breeding, brought his great genius and skill to bear upon the same object. He went himself to Holland, where he selected several mares which he brought back with him to England; and by pursuing the same methods of careful selection, mating and feeding by which he had achieved such distinguished success with other kinds of stock, he showed the English people how to form a breed of draft horses which has since become famous the world over. Other breeders followed his example, and as late as the beginning of the present century importations of both stallions and mares from Flanders were by no means uncommon.

At this time the black color was still a characteristic and distinguishing feature of the heavy horses of England, as it was of the parent stock from across the channel. They were of immense size, with great strength, but were heavy, dull and sluggish in temperament, and slow and awkward in motion. Prof. Low, writing of these horses in his "Domesticated Animals of the British Islands," says:

> The modern English Black horse retains the general characteristics of the pre-existing race, but greatly modified. His color is usually a sooty black, with frequently a white lozenge-shaped mark on the forehead; and he has very generally one or more of the feet and part of the legs, and not unfrequently the muzzle, white. His body is massive, compact and round; his limbs are stout, his chest is enormously broad, and his neck and back are short. His mane is thick and somewhat frizzled, and his legs below the knee and hock are hairy down to the heels. His whole aspect conveys the idea of great physical power without corresponding action. The main defects of his conformation and temperament are his too great bulk of body and want of action and mettle. For a pull with a heavy weight he is admirable; but he steps out short, and is slow in all his motions.
>
> These powerful horses are in extensive demand, not only in the midland counties, where they are reared, but over all the south of England, for the labors of the field, and for wagon and heavy carriages of all kinds. They are everywhere to be seen, moving at a slow pace, in the numerous heavy wagons by which merchandise is conveyed inland, and in great numbers in all the larger cities and seaport towns, where they are used for transport of heavy goods at wharves, for the carriage of coal, timber, building materials, and for

a thousand purposes. In London, where the largest and finest are in demand for the carts of brewers, the wagons of coal merchants, and other uses, the stranger sees with admiration the vast number of enormous carriages in endless motion through the crowded streets, drawn by teams of the largest horses in the world; and, doubtless, there is something noble in the aspect of these huge creatures, yoked in lines, and obedient to the voice amidst all the tumult of a great city; but examination shows that there is an excessive waste of power, both in the unnecessary bulk of the animals and in the manner in which their services are performed. They are usually attached in lines, which causes them to pull with sudden jerks and with unequal force; and, in turning the corners of narrow streets and lanes it is often seen that the entire weight of the enormous carriage is thrown, for a time, upon the shaft horse. It is contended by many that extreme weight and bulk of body are necessary for these horses to enable them to resist the jolting and sudden obstacles encountered on the rough pavement which they never leave; but, in truth, it is habit and a species of pride which lead the owners of wagons to prefer the largest and most showy horses to those of moderate size and more useful action; for experience cannot but show that it is muscular force and not the *vis inertiæ* of great weight of body which best enables a horse to overcome continued obstacles. The mere gratification of taste, however, in the employment of these splendid horses would scarcely require a passing censure were it not that this gratification exercises a really hurtful influence in the breeding districts, causing attention to be directed to size and appearance rather than to useful properties, and tending to perpetuate that unnecessary bulk of body which constitutes so great a defect in the breed. Nor is this influence unimportant in degree; for it is to be observed that the demand for horses of the largest class is not confined to the capital, but extends to all the numerous cities and populous towns where drays and wagons are in use. When animals of the largest size are in demand, and the highest prices are paid for them, it becomes the interest of breeders to employ large stallions and use every means to favor the development of size in individuals. In the counties of Lincoln and Cambridge, whence the great London drays are chiefly supplied, a breeder measures his success by the stature of the individuals which he is able to rear. At the age of two and one-half years the colts are often seventeen hands high. They are bought at this age by graziers near the capital and used in the light work of the plow until four years old, when they are fit for the services to which they are destined, and disposed of at high prices.

In 1879 a society was organized in England for the purpose of preparing and publishing a stud book of the Shire or Cart horse of England, and in February, 1880, the first volume of the work, which has since grown to fourteen volumes, was issued. In an introduction to this first volume by R. S. Reynolds, M. R. C. V. S., it is stated that—

> The draft horse of the present day undoubtedly, and unfortunately, is one of mixed and impure breed; there exist few, if any, whose genealogy on both dam's and sire's side can be traced for even four generations. The assumption of an admixture of extrinsic blood is made more evident by comparison of the conformation and color of the existing race with the Shire horse of seventy years ago. Authorities upon horse-breeding forty or fifty years since were ceaseless in their objections to the slow, ponderous movement of the draft horses of their day, and strongly urged the necessity for crossing them with animals of more slender build, in order to attain increased activity and quicker pace. A large section of the horse-working community is now suffering from a too extended application of this crossing, possibly because breeders did not pursue an intelligent and systematic course in the selection of suitable animals for the attainment of their intended object, leaving too much to fortuitous circumstances, and probably attaching too much importance to activity, which, if attained at the expense of

deterioration in strength, becomes a defect for the purposes of town work.

For the business of commercial centers like Liverpool, for instance, where the team work is subordinate to the dock, warehouse and railway regulations, rapidity of movement is found to be a very secondary desideratum to the possession of individual strength. Under these conditions a team (two) of dray horses must be fully capable of working a net load of five tons, the task of shafting which it is obvious no lightly-built animal can accomplish satisfactorily.

A written description of a high-class Shire stallion of sixty years ago may, for the purpose of comparison, possess considerable interest to breeders of the present time. Such a sketch can, of course, but very imperfectly convey to the reader's mind an idea of the conformation of one of these old sires, but it may possibly afford a framework whereon his imagination can build those features which a literary representation fails to make clear.

With very few exceptions (and those exceptions chestnut), black, dark brown, and grey are the only colors met with in the descriptions of draft stallions living in the first quarter of the present century. To account for this limitation two reasons may be advanced: first, fashion in color may have been considered a very important element in the selection of a sire; second, the light browns, bays, chestnuts, and roans of the present day are probably due to extensive infusions of light-horse blood.

Whichever of the two reasons is accepted as the correct one, inquiry among old horsemen leaves no room for doubt that black, brown, and grey were by far the most common colors of draft horses. It is further ascertained that black predominated over the two other colors, so much so that the eastern counties horse was known and described as the "Black Lincolnshire horse"; also that the highly-esteemed brood mares of Derbyshire were chiefly of that color. The color of the black horse was not remarkable for intensity, but partook more of a very dark slaty hue, some few specimens of which are now occasionally seen in Lincolnshire. In the majority of cases these black horses were marked to a very considerable extent with white upon the legs and face. In Derbyshire the white facial markings often gave rise to the names of horses; for instance, the numerous "Blazes" were undoubtedly so called from the possession of a blaze face; other appellations, as "Ball," "Bald horse," "Balled-faced horse," more rarely met with, possibly implied a greater suffusion with white than the title "Blaze."

In Staffordshire the prevailing color appears to have been brown; as early as 1806 horses are described as descendants of the "old brown Staffordshire breed." Grey horses appear to have been more common in counties south of Derbyshire and Staffordshire, but it is probable that the coats of many of the so-called black horses had interspersed therein a considerable sprinkling of white hairs, and that they were occasionally described as greys; there is one instance, about forty years ago, of an Oxfordshire horse being sometimes described as a black and at another period a grey.

The head was large in all its dimensions, well placed on the neck by strong, broad and deep attachment; the forehead and face wide, expressive and intelligent; a side view of the jaws and muzzle represented those parts to be remarkable for depth; the ears were small and carried slightly outward the eyes somewhat small, not prominent, but generally mild and moderately intelligent in expression; the nostrils and mouth large, firm and well closed; the neck was long, arched and remarkable for its depth, and for the strength of its insertion *between* the shoulder-blades, not as it is now frequently seen, badly placed, by having the appearance of being fused, as it were, *upon* the front edge of the blade bones, a conformation affording insufficient room for the collar, and therefore one most defective for the purposes of heavy draft. The shoulders were massive, muscular, upright, low and thick at the withers, thrown well outward beyond the insertion of the neck by the front ribs being properly arched. The fore arm was long, strong and muscular; the knee broad and flat in all its aspects; the fore and hind cannons short and thick, frequently measuring upward of twelve inches in circumference, covered with coarse skin and having a "beefy" appearance and touch, more marked in

THE BREEDS OF HORSES. 261

advanced age than in youth. The pastern bones of the fore leg were very short, strong and upright, those of the hind leg being much more obliquely placed. The feet, as a rule, especially the fore ones, were large, flat, weak at the heels, and invested with horn of somewhat soft and spongy texture. Thighs narrow, being insufficiently clothed with muscle on their inner aspects to prevent the appearance of what is vulgarly but characteristically termed "split up." The hocks were of rather defective formation, but showing little predisposition to disease, generally too short, too round, and not sharply defined; for these reasons it may be inferred that the hind action was limited and comparatively wanting in elasticity. The general contour of the hind legs was considerably bent, the hocks being thrown backward and the feet forward. The breast wide and full of muscle, indicative of great strength rather than quick movement; the back longer, narrower and "dipping" rather too much behind the withers. The heart-ribs were well arched, but not very deep; the hinder ones were also rounded, but short, the last one placed too far forward, giving to the body an appearance of undue length and "lightness." The croup bent at considerable angle, denoting what would now be considered want of quality. The dock strong and thick, with powerful broad attachment to the trunk.

The *tout ensemble* of the stallion exhibited grand development of the fore-hand; which rendered the appearance of the hind parts very mean by comparison—a conformation, however, that a moment's reflection will show to be in perfect accord with natural ordination; from mankind downward in the scale of mammalian creation, the entire male is deficient in that development of the posterior parts so notable in the perfect female of each species, and for apparent reasons.

The growth of hair upon these old stallions was remarkably luxuriant, that of the mane and tail being abundant, strong in texture, glossy, and very often several feet in length. The cannons, fetlocks, and coronets, both fore and hind, were garnished with a profusion of coarse, long hair, distinctive of the Cart horse breed. The silky growth in corresponding situations of the present day has probably become thus modified from the admixture of extrinsic blood, from local influences, from altered methods in the system of rearing and managing young stock, or from a combination of two or all these causes.

It is perhaps worthy of observation that there were, and still remain, some specimens of three apparently distinct types of draft horses exemplified by differences in the local distribution of long hair:

1st. Horses having the upper lip garnished with a long, thick mustache, considered at one time a distinguishing characteristic of the Lincolnshire horse. The color of these appendages is always black, white, or a mixture of the two, and invariably corresponds with the hue of the skin from which they spring.

2d. Horses having the lips, muzzle and eyelids destitute of hair. The skin in these situations, being either entirely bald or covered with exceedingly fine down, is almost invariably flesh-colored, sometimes marked with small dark spots and blotches. Specimens of this type may possibly have originated the appellations "bald horse" and "balled-faced horse."

3d. Horses having a long tuft of hair growing from the front of each knee, and rarer examples having also a similar growth (quite distinct from the ordinary hair of the back of the cannons) from the hind part of the hock, just below its point. Animals of this type are now seldom seen. In my experience they are more frequently met with in Wales than in the English shires, though no reason can be assigned why that is so. It is found that these peculiar hirsute growths invariably accompany a luxuriant development of long hair in its ordinary situations, and generally a more than ordinary strength of bone below the knees and hocks. Sex does not appear to exert any influence in determining the special characteristics of any of the three types, stallions, mares and geldings being equally prone to inherit these peculiarities from progenitors similarly possessed.

These horses have long been extensively bred in Leicestershire, Staffordshire, Derbyshire,

THE BREEDS OF HORSES. 263

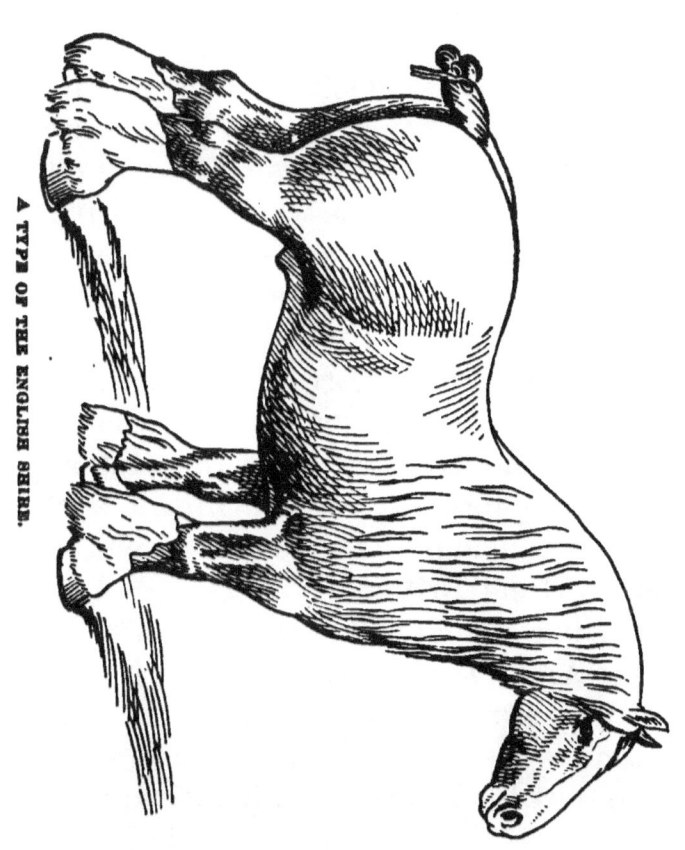

A TYPE OF THE ENGLISH SHIRE.

Oxfordshire, Lancashire, Yorkshire, Cheshire, Nottingham, Northampton, Lincolnshire, and Cambridgeshire; the last two counties named perhaps producing the most thoroughly characteristic and representative animals of the breed.

There has been a decided tendency among breeders of Shire horses for twenty years past to breed more for quality than size, and consequently somewhat of the rugged massiveness which formerly characterized the breed has disappeared, making the typical Shire horse of to-day much more active, alert, and spirited, and with considerable more "finish" and "style" in his appearance than his progenitors of forty years ago. Our illustration is an exact reproduction by photograph from life of a Shire stallion of considerable note as a recent prize-winner in Great Britain.

The importation of this great breed of heavy horses to America was not pushed with as much energy nor carried on to anything like so great an extent as the merits of the breed would have justified until within a comparatively recent period. Occasional importations of one or two animals at widely different periods were made, but within the past twelve years they have been imported in considerable numbers. They have grown rapidly in popularity in the great agricultural States of the Mississippi Valley, and a stud book for the breed has been established, of which three volumes have been issued. Chas. Burgess of Wenona, Ill., is Secretary of the Association having the work in charge.

CLYDESDALES.

To the casual observer the difference in appearance between the Clydesdale and the Shire horse is not especially noticeable. They certainly possess many features in common, and to give a history of the Clydesdale breed would simply be to recapitulate much of what has been written in the preceding pages concerning the origin of the draft breeds of England, for they have been evolved from the same original stock and by substantially the same course of selection and breeding. We have the same origin for both breeds in the great Black horse breed of Flanders. We hear of them first in Lanarkshire, when William, Earl of Douglas (one of the ancestors of the Duke of Hamilton, who in later years became so famous as a breeder of Clydesdales), obtained a special edict of "safe conduct" from King Edward to take "ten grooms and ten large horses from certain places in Scotland to certain places in Teviotdale in the King's dominions." This safe conduct was issued July 1, 1352, and is the earliest positive mention we have of great horses in Scotland. The editor of the Clydesdale Stud Book, commenting on this document, says:

Unfortunately it does not say where the horses came from; but as Baliol held the Douglas estates it would appear as though they were to be taken from Lanarkshire into Teviotdale, then in possession of the English. Douglas' quarrel with his kinsman, William of Douglas, the Knight of Liddesdale, whom he slew, taking possession of his estates; his rupture with King Edward of England, and his turning of Baliol out of the ancestral estates of the Douglas family in Liddesdale, Annandale and Clydesdale, leave little room for doubt that if large horses did not exist in Lanarkshire previous to this date, as the extensive trade done with Flanders by the Scottish merchants lead us to believe they did, some, if not all, of the black stallions found their way to Douglas Castle, in the Upper Ward of Lanarkshire.*

Scotch authorities generally concur in naming the Upper Ward of Lanarkshire as the place where the Clydesdale breed was first brought to any considerable degree of perfection, and in the "Retrospective Volume" of the Clydesdale Stud Book we read that:

Some time between 1715 and 1720, John Paterson, of Lochlyoch, on the estate and in the parish of Carmichael, grandson of one John Paterson, who died at Lochlyoch in 1682, went to England and brought from thence a Flemish stallion, which is said to have so greatly improved the breed in the Upper Ward as to have made them noted all over Scotland. The Lochlyoch mares were famous in the Upper Ward during the latter half of the last and the first two decades of the present century; and a Mrs. Paterson, of Lochlyoch, mother of the present tenant of Drumalbin, now ninety-seven years of age, still has recollection of a noted black mare from which many of the best stock in the Upper Ward are descended. The family tradition is strongly supported by the fact that the Patersons were in the habit of noting down important agricultural items from a very early period; and

---

* Clydesdale Stud Book, Vol. II, p. xvi.

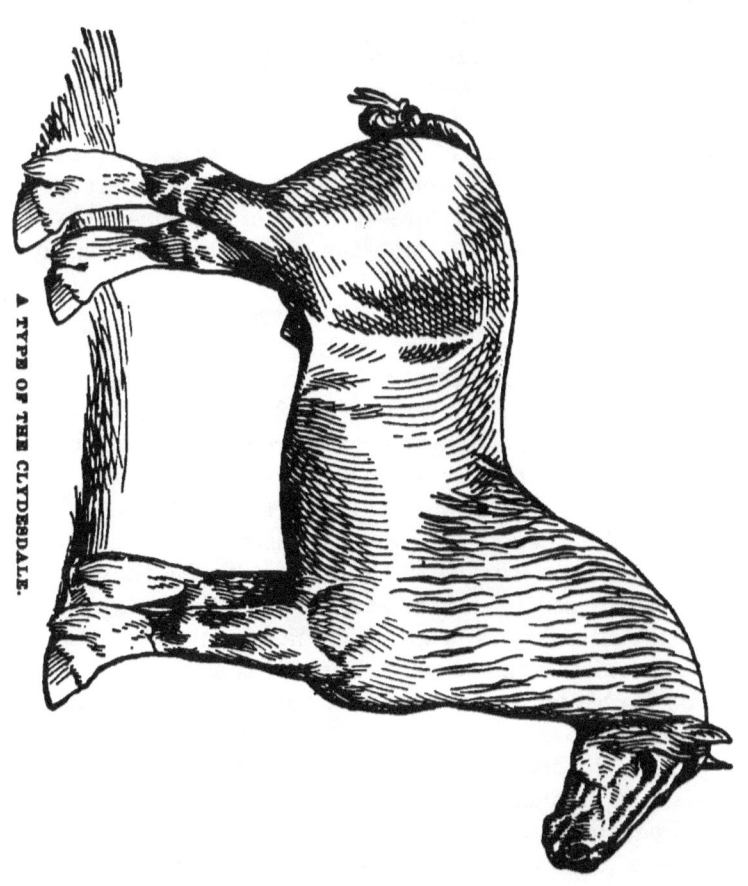

A TYPE OF THE CLYDESDALE.

the present representative of the family, Mr. Paterson of Drumalbin, has in his possession a family tree of all the descendants of that John Paterson who died in 1682. In the year 1836, in reference to a day's plowing given to one of the Patersons on leaving Lochlyoch for Drumalbin, the following remarks appeared in an Edinburgh newspaper, from which it will be seen that their claim to being the founders of the breed was then recognized. After descanting on the merits of the family and kindred topics, the writer proceeds: "And it may be here worthy of remark, that it was a brother of Mr. Paterson's grandfather who brought the notable stallion from England to Lanarkshire—the sire of the famous Clydesdale breed of horses of which the county has been so long and justly proud."

What were the distinguishing features of the native breed previous to the introduction of the Flemish horse, about 1715, cannot now be definitely determined, but there can be little doubt that they were mostly of English origin, and of a mixed character. The old drove road from Scotland to England crosses the Clyde at Hyndford Bridge, and leads across the hills by Carmichael and Crawfordjohn—the very center of the then horse-breeding district; and the intercourse which the farmers would thus have with their neighbors from the south, and the amount of traffic done by packhorses, would doubtless allow of many opportunities for selecting animals calculated to improve the breed.

The Lochlyoch mares were generally browns and blacks, with white faces and a little white on their legs; they had grey hairs in their tails, occasional grey hairs over their bodies, and invariably a white spot on their belly, this latter being recognized as a mark of distinct purity of blood. The mares died out at Lochlyoch about thirty years ago.

The Lochlyoch stock having been long noted in the Upper Ward and largely drawn upon by breeders, there is no doubt that to them, or, more correctly, to the black horse of 1715, the Clydesdale horse owes its present distinctive character.*

There can be no question as to the fact that

---

*Clydesdale Stud Book, Vol. I, p. xvii.

there was an almost constant mingling of the blood of the Shire or Cart horse of England with that of the Clydesdale of Scotland, and that at the present day the differences between the two breeds are so very slight that many intelligent breeders of both England and Scotland have urged, and continue to urge, that they should be classed as a single breed, and that but one stud book should be maintained for them. It is a well-known fact that the "English cross" can be clearly traced in the pedigrees of some of the most successful up to the time of the establishment of the Clydesdale Stud Book (1877) of the comparatively recent prize-winners and sires of Scotland. In 1877 the Clydesdale Society of Great Britain and Ireland was formed, and the compilation of the Clydesdale Stud Book was at once begun. The work has been vigorously followed up until fifteen volumes have been issued. Since the publication of this stud book was begun (1877), and also that of the Shire Horse Stud Book (1880) the lines have been more closely drawn, and crossing between the heavy horses of England and Scotland has not been regarded with favor. Hence the draft horses of the two countries are gradually assuming a more distinct type, as I have endeavored to show in the typical illustrations given.

Further interesting information concerning

the early history of Clydesdale breeding in Scotland I quote from the introduction to Vol. II of the Clydesdale Stud Book, as follows:

From the articles in a large and handsome work on our "National Breeds of Animals," published under the auspices of the Highland and Agricultural Society, with beautiful illustrations by Howe, it would appear that the Upper Ward farmers brought several animals from England which bred well. Thus in an account of Meg, which won first prize at the Highland and Agricultural Society's Show at Glasgow, in 1828, it was said that she was by a grandson of Young Britain, by James Thompson's (of Broomfield, Glasgow) Britain, a grandson of Blaze, a horse belonging to Mr. Scott, of Brownhill, Carstairs, Lanark, which, as mentioned in the history to the Retrospective Volume, won the first prize at a show held in the Grassmarket, Edinburgh, in 1785. Blaze, which traveled in the Lothians and Berwickshire, is described as a beautiful jet black, his legs silvery white to the knees and hocks, and a broad white stripe or blaze down the face. In a letter from Mr. French, of Burnhouses, who, at the request of the editor of the volume, waited upon Mr. Scott, then eighty-nine years of age, the sire of Blaze is said to have been an English draft horse. This may possibly have been the case; but from the description given of the heavy black horses of England of that period it is not likely to have been one of them, but more likely a Cleveland, if not one of the light-legged pack horses used in Yorkshire and other parts of England at the commencement of the present century. The dam of Young Briton is also reported to have been a Derbyshire mare. Meg, which is a brown with white markings—the same color as her dam—is a stylish, upstanding, lengthy mare, with an exceedingly neat head and clean legs; in fact, she is what would nowadays almost be described by west-country dealers as "gyp." A portrait is also given in the work of a noted horse, Young Clydesdale, a stallion of considerable reputation at the time in the Lothians and Berwick. He is represented in plow harness, with collar and "breeching," a costume now rarely seen on a stallion.

Like Meg, he seems to possess a thoroughbred look about the head, in which is set a very full, vigorous eye, has a shoulder well sloped, and an apparently clean fore leg, with a slight fringe. His fault on the portrait, which, it has to be remarked, is drawn from life, is want of muscular development in the hind quarters and thighs. There is a total absence, as in the case of Meg, of superfluous hair, the pastern-joints and foot being clearly defined. In color Young Clydesdale was a jet black, with white markings. He is said to have descended from Blaze, the colors of the most successful progeny of which seem to have been blacks and greys—colors now not in favor, the latter being, as regards entire colts, very unfashionable. This is, no doubt, owing to the action of the Highland and Agricultural Society in restricting their competition to black-bays and brown-bays, and Mr. Frame's practice of castrating all grey colts.

Probably the directors thought grey an unsuitable color at the time for horses for agricultural purposes. As the ban is now removed in competition, and as grey horses look particularly stylish in street lorries, little objection can be taken to them. Gray horses, it may be remarked, are of a different original stock to either blacks or bays. Campbell Smith, in his work, being of the opinion that they are part of the original grey or white stock of the Euxine, and that they are always of higher stature than the bays, which are from Africa, the Teutonic word *bayard*, from which, in his opinion, the word bay is derived, signifying "a horse." It is worthy of notice that the latter word is never used to denote colors of animals other than horses. The greys are always, too, it will be observed, strong, handsome horses, and in days when the color was more fashionable among breeders were preferred as cavalry chargers; hence those magnificent horses of the Scots Greys which evoked the admiration of Napoleon I at Waterloo. That the breed was distinct in descent, till mixed within the past 150 years or so, may be noted from the fact that you rarely, if ever, get a grey unless the sire or dam is grey, while the fact that you can get a brown from a grey or with a grey stallion shows that the strain has gradually been overpowered by the denser blood of the blacks and browns.

It has been remarked that the Clydesdale has been improved as regards size and strength during the past thirty or forty years, or since the period when Young Clydesdale's type was fashionable. A good deal of this is due to the admixture of blood from the south, which has, however, been done at the risk of losing ancient important characteristics of activity and quality. Those breeders who have worked in this direction have generally, however, kept the Clydesdale type in view, and no doubt many of the animals brought back were crosses from the Scotch horses or mares which the south-country buyers purchased from time to time at the Scottish fairs, but the pedigrees of which unfortunately could not be traced. The breed, therefore, has not been so much improved as some writers would try to make out, and at Kilburn Show the merest tyro in horses could distinguish in their classes the Clydesdales from the more ponderous but less active draft horses of the English shires.

It is well known that the Clydesdale owes its quality and other good characteristics to the pasture; sluggishness and coarse, greasy legs being the characteristics of animals reared on low-lying lands with moist pastures; while on dry hill or mixed sandy lands, the grass of which contains plenty of lime, active animals, with sound, clean legs and healthy, durable hoofs, are bred and grazed to advantage. * * * Indeed, to the rich sand-mixed lands of Kintyre, the healthy herbage which covers the thin soils of the Galloways, and the nourishing blades of grass which cover the lime-containing hills of Lanarkshire, the Clydesdale of the present day greatly owes his activity and quality—characteristics which have always rendered him superior in the eyes of the foreigner when viewed alongside his more massive market competitor in the south, reared on the "wershy" herbage of the fens.

Modern Clydesdales are of all colors, bays, browns, and blacks predominating, although there are some greys and chestnuts, while white markings on face, feet, and legs are quite com-

THE BREEDS OF HORSES. 273

mon with all the colors. They have been extensively imported into the United States and Canada, and have exercised a very powerful influence upon the horse stock of our country. No other breed of draft horses, saving the Percheron, has been so extensively introduced, and between these two breeds the contest for popular favor has been waged upon very nearly equal terms for several years past. The question of color has always been a strong point in favor of the Clydesdales with American breeders as against their French rivals, the latter being usually grey, while with the former dark colors are the prevailing ones.

The Clydesdale Society of America was organized in 1877. The first volume of the American Clydesdale Stud Book was issued in 1882, and six volumes of the work have been printed. Col. Chas. F. Mills of Springfield, Ill., has been Secretary of the Society from its organization, and has done a valuable service to the Clydesdale interest in America by compiling the records of the early importations and preparing for publication the volumes of the stud book that have been issued.

PERCHERONS.

The Percheron is an ancient French breed, originally famed for its capacity for rapid locomotion with a heavy load, and especially adapted to drawing the heavy diligences or post-coaches used in France before the days of the railway and locomotive and has long been the most popular of all draft breeds with the people of France. Tradition had always attributed to the Percheron—confessedly among the most active and powerful of the heavy breeds of the European continent—an Oriental origin; but it was not until the researches recently made in the compilation of pedigrees for the first volume of the Percheron Stud Book of France that the extent to which the blood of the Orient had entered into the formation of the Percheron race was fully realized. What the Darley Arabian was to the English thoroughbred, and the Grey Arabian Smetanxa to the Orloff, the Grey Arabian Gallipoli appears to have been to the Percheron horse of France. Diligent and persistent inquiry in the family records and traditions of the best breeders of La Perche has enabled the compiler of the Percheron Stud Book of France to trace definitely a large proportion of the most noted Percheron horses of modern times to this Arabian sire, that was imported about 1820. In fact, this Oriental blood, wherever introduced, in all nations and all climates, has been a powerful factor in effecting improvement in the equine race.

There is every reason to believe that this

THE BREEDS OF HORSES.

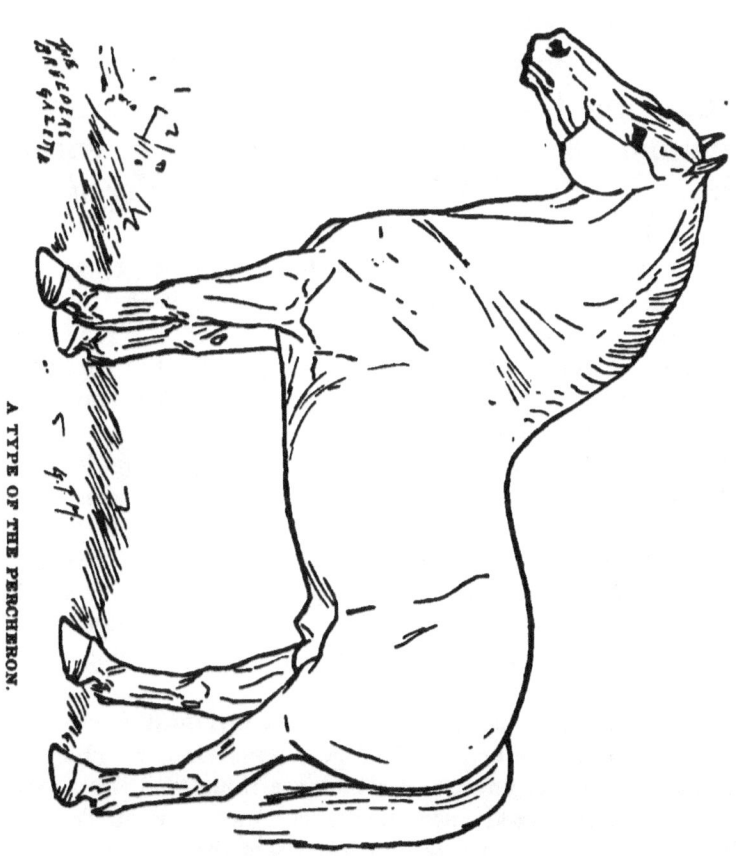

A TYPE OF THE PERCHERON.

breed, like the draft breeds of England and Scotland, derived its size originally from the large Black horse breed of Flanders; but from the fact that grey has for many generations been the prevailing color it is evident that some very powerful agency has been at work, modifying the type until it has but little in common with this old parent stock except size. In Vol. I of the American Percheron Stud Book it is stated that:

The little of history that can be found touching this breed definitely points to an eastern origin. Some French authorities date its beginning as far back as 732, when France was invaded by the Saracens, 300,000 strong, under the command of the famous chief Abdérame. The utter defeat and overthrow of this barbarian host by the French, under Charles Martel, on the plains between Poitiers and Tours, left the fine Arab and Barb steeds upon which many of the invaders were mounted in the hands of the victors; and these horses, crossed upon the large, strong, native mares of that region, if they did not form the starting point for the breed which, since that time, has become so famous, undoubtedly had much to do with creating the foundation upon which it was ultimately built.

Another large infusion of the same Oriental blood took place upon the return of the Crusaders, who brought with them many of the finest of Arabian stallions; and these were also extensively used upon the already excellent stock of La Perche, and served to stamp upon them the form and other distinctive marks of the Arab to a still greater degree than they already possessed. The infusion of fresh Arabian and Andalusian blood was kept up for many years at irregular intervals; the Lord of Montdoubleau, Geoffroy IV, Rotrou, Count of Mallart, Count of La Perche, Count Roger of Bellesmer, and many others of the nobility, having been distinguished for the importations made by them and the interest which they took in the subject of breeding horses; and as late as about 1820 we find that two famous Arabian stallions, Godolphin and Gallipoli, both grey, were imported and extensively used under the direction of the government. * * *

Aside from the history and traditions of the country the Percheron horse himself furnishes unmistakable evidence, in his form, disposition, color, and general characteristics, that he is closely allied to the Arab. These characteristics have been materially modified, it is true, and the size has been greatly increased; but, in the hands of the excellent horsemen of La Perche, and under the careful and fostering supervision of the government, which exercised a direct control over the selection of sires, he seems to have retained many of the excellent qualities of his Oriental ancestry; and this, added to the greatly increased size which had been attained, made the horses of La Perche many years ago the wonder of the world for their specialty of rapid draft—their ability to move a heavy load at a rapid gait.

It was this acknowledged superiority of the Percheron horse in the diligences, post-coaches, and omnibuses of France that first caused the attention of the outside world to be directed to them. It was not simply as draft or cart horses that they were distinguished; on the contrary, had they possessed no excellence beyond this they would scarcely have attracted any attention; for other countries possessed horses that, for the purposes of heavy draft alone, were certainly their equals, if not their superiors; but it was in that happy combination of size and form which gave them activity, quickness of motion, strength, and endurance that they were found to excel the horses of all other countries. * * * But, with the introduction of railroads, the use of the post-coach and diligence was practically abandoned; and as this was the speciality for which the Percherons we have described had been bred, so, with the new order of things, came a demand for horses of larger type (greater weight, a heavier bone, and more substance were required), and since that time the improvement of the Percheron in this direction has especially engrossed the attention of the French breeder. * * *

As the immense draft horses of the North (Flemish) were closely allied to, if not identical with, the large breed that prevailed in Normandy and La Perche prior to the modifications produced by the introduction of the blood of the Arabian and the Barb, heretofore alluded to, it was very natural that, when the Percheron breeders found it desirable to increase the size of their horses, their eyes should be turned toward this kindred race, from which other countries had already drawn so heavily for the same purpose. Accordingly we find that mares in large numbers were taken from these northern departments, and from Belgium, under the various names of Belgians, Boulonnais, mares of Picardy, etc., and were bred to the stallions of La Perche. Stallions from the same countries were also extensively introduced, under various names, and of slightly differing types; but, notwithstanding the multiplicity of names arising from the different departments in which they had been bred, and the slight variation in form that existed, they were, after all, nothing more nor less than the Flanders draft horse—the same blood that had already exercised so potent an influence upon the horse stock of Great Britain.

The new infusion of this ancient kindred blood has been so general throughout the entire district which was once the home of the Percheron horse, that it is now difficult to find a pure Percheron as they were bred in that region fifty years ago. The old type that once made these horses so famous has been sacrificed to the demands of commerce for greater size, and for many years past it has been the chief aim of the Percheron breeder to produce a horse that should comply with this demand, without sacrificing the activity, hardiness and docility for which the ancient Percheron race was famed.

Subject to the change above alluded to, the Percheron is extensively bred in the departments of Eure, Orne, Eure et Loir, Loir et Cher, and Sarthe; and they have also found their way further north and toward the sea coast in the departments of Seine-Inférieure and Calvados, embracing almost the entire ancient province of Normandy; but nowhere are they found so purely bred, and so nearly allied to the original Percheron type, as in the five departments first above mentioned—their original home. In that part of Normandy lying along the coast, especially north of the Seine River, the Flemish element seems to have made its influence more strongly felt, and there the horses possess more of the Flemish and less of the Percheron characteristics than those bred farther south, in the heart of La Perche, which will account for the diversity in the character of the horses brought to this country by our importers. Those who have purchased near the coast, or north of the river Seine, have usually obtained horses that leaned strongly toward the Flemish type. They are larger, coarser and more sluggish, with less energy, endurance and action, than those bred in Eure et Loir and the adjacent departments. They are better adapted to heavy draft purposes than their lighter, but more hardy, active and stylish relations of the interior, frequently weighing from 1,700 to 2,000 lbs. in high flesh, and producing larger horses when crossed upon our common stock.

In the report which I made to the Department of Agriculture, in 1883, of my observations on the live stock of Europe, I spoke of the Percheron as follows:

I went first to the sales stables of Paris, fortified with what knowledge I had been able previously to obtain upon the subject, beginning with that of M. Vidal, a noted horse-dealer of Paris, who has undoubtedly sold more stallions to American importers than all the other horse-dealers of Paris combined. In reply to my question he said: "Fully ninety per cent of the horses that I buy to sell to Americans, for stallions, come from beyond Chartres, in the Perche; the others are picked up here and there, wherever we can find one good enough for the market; but we sell them all as Percherons." The other dealers all told substantially the same story. After spending a few days in Paris, talking with horsemen and gathering what information I could, I determined to see the Percheron breeding district for myself. All authorities agreed in pointing out Nogent-le-Rotrou, situated about one hundred miles southwest from Paris, in the ancient Province of La Perche, as the heart of the Percheron breeding country. * * * On the day of my arrival at Nogent-le-Rotrou a large number of Percheron breeders had met to consult upon the propriety of establishing a Percheron Stud Book, in order to preserve the purity of the race and to protect themselves from unscrupulous dealers in Paris and elsewhere. I was much interested in the discussion which took place. The gentlemen present represented the principal breeders for some twenty or thirty miles around, and I was told that they owned at least one hundred stallions that had been kept for service this season. I questioned many of them. Among others, the statement of Mr. Ernest Perriot, one of the most noted of the breeders present, is a fair sample of what all had to say. He is a very intelligent gentleman, and has sold many horses to American buyers. I should judge him to be about fifty years of age. His statement was in substance as follows: "I have been breeding horses right here all my life, and my father and grandfather were in the same business before me. We never breed or sell any other than pure Percherons. We have usually kept six or seven stallions each year for service. They travel around the country, serving mares owned by the farmers at about twenty-five francs each. We keep an eye on these mares, know where the best ones are, and when the foals are weaned we buy many of the best ones each year and keep them until we can sell them at a fair profit. I am sure there has been nothing but recognized pure Percheron stallions used in our stud since the time of my grandfather, and nothing else has been used in this whole Percheron region within my knowledge. There is a tradition that about the time my grandfather engaged in the business some Boulonnais blood was introduced into this country for the purpose of increasing the size of the Percherons, but certainly there has been none since about fifty years ago. The true Percherons will now average as large or larger than the Boulonnais. Neither Mr. Dunham, Mr. Dillon, nor any other American importer, has ever bought any Norman horses here. We don't have any such horses. You can see plenty of Normans in Paris; they are small horses, mostly bays, and are used in the cabs and carriages. They are generally half-bloods, got by English thoroughbred sires, and some of them are out of Percheron dams, and they are usually called Anglo-Normans."

The same statements, substantially, in regard to purity of race and the name, were obtained from all the breeders interviewed, notably Auguste Tacheau (Province of Sarthe), Pierre Sagot (Province of Eure et Loir) and Celestin Caget (Province of Orne). In fact, so far as I could learn, it was almost an insult to ask one of the breeders present if he bred or sold any other than Percheron horses, and they spurned the term "Norman" with contempt. * * * It was an agreeable surprise to me to learn that so much pains has been taken by these Percheron breeders to preserve the purity of the race. I had often heard it asserted, even by some importers, that nobody knew anything about it; that the Percherons were mongrels, and that no man in France could give the pedigree of his horse. I found, on the contrary, that, while they have not paid much attention to preserving the maternal genealogy, many of the sires can easily be traced six or eight generations.

Many draft horses have been imported from France to the United States, and most of them have been of the Percheron breed; but owing to the fact that nearly all of our early importers were ignorant of the French language very few of them were able to obtain much information concerning the French breeds or the methods of breeding prevailing in that country; and they were largely at the mercy of the horse dealers of Paris, Havre, Rouen, Dieppe and other cities. Consequently very indefinite, and, in many cases, positively erroneous ideas were entertained by them, and great confusion resulted. Some importers brought what they called Percherons, others brought Normans, some brought Percheron-Normans, and still others brought Norman-Percherons, but there were very few who claim to have imported Boulonnais, although many of the latter were brought over by the earlier importers. This confusion and lack of information resulted finally in much angry controversy, incited chiefly by rivalries among interested parties.

The first importations of draft horses from France that attracted anything like general attention in this country were those brought to Union and Pickaway counties, Ohio, in 1851, and these were, by their importers, simply called French horses. Another importation to the same region followed in 1856, and yet another in 1857; and they were also known only as French horses. In 1865 J. H. Klippart, secretary of the Ohio Board of Agriculture, went to Europe, and these horses having become very popular in his State, he made their origin and history an especial object of study while in France. On his return he submitted a report to the Ohio State Board, in which he gave an exhaustive account of the horses of France, and stated that our so-called French horses were Percherons. In 1853 Col. Charles Carroll, of Baltimore, Md., imported from France a stallion which he called a Percheron. In 1866 Mr. S. W. Ficklin, of Charlottesville, Va., made an importation of these horses, and he also brought with him the use of the name Percheron. The Hon. William T. Walters, of Baltimore, Md., spent several years during and just after the close of our late war, in France, and while there he became so enamored of the Percherons that, returning in 1868, he brought with him quite a number of horses, which he called Percherons in this country. He also caused to be translated and published an interesting work entitled the "Percheron Horse," written by Du Huys, Master of the Horse to Louis Napoleon. This book, together with the writings of Mr. Klippart and Mr. Walters, and the usage of the importers before named, served to fix the appellation of Percheron quite firmly upon these horses throughout the middle and eastern States, so far as they were known. Twelve years prior to the first Ohio importation mentioned above Mr. Edward Harris had imported four horses from France which he called Normans. These horses were considerably smaller than the Percheron importations of a later date, and, although they were extensively noticed in the newspapers of that day, they failed to attract public attention to any considerable degree.

In the autumn of 1854 Louis Napoleon, one

of the two French horses imported to Ohio in 1851, was taken to Illinois, and in 1858 was sold to E. Dillon & Co. of Normal. This horse soon attained great notoriety, the Messrs. Dillon showing him and his get at many State and County fairs as Norman horses; and this name soon became quite generally applied to them in Illinois and the adjoining States. From 1868 down to the present time the importations of these horses have been very numerous, and importers and breeders have used various names by which to designate them; some calling them Percherons, some Normans, and others combining the two names, some placing the Percheron first and others beginning with the Norman.

But a better understanding of the subject has resulted in ending these controversies; it having become generally understood in this country that France, like Great Britain, has several more or less distinct breeds of draft horses, to each of which a separate and distinctive name is attached, and each having a separate locality in France wherein it was mainly bred, as is the case with the various breeds of England and Scotland. The organization of the Société Hippique Percheronne of France in July, 1883, and the consequent publication of a stud book in that country for the Percheron breed, has done much to enlighten the people of this country upon the subject, and still further light was shed and the situation rendered more intelligible to those who really cared to know the facts, by the publication, at about the same period, of a stud book for the Boulonnais breed.

The organization of the Percheron Society of France and the publication of a stud book for the breed in that country has already done much toward preserving its purity; and if it shall continue to be honestly and carefully managed, as I have every reason to think it has been up to this time, it will afford a guarantee as to purity of lineage which was sadly lacking in the early days of the introduction of the breed into this country. Most of the horses bought by the early American importers from dealers in the large cities of France have doubtless possessed a good share of Percheron blood, but there was then no means of ascertaining the facts. Our importers had to rely solely upon their own eyes and the integrity of French horse-dealers; and the dealers of Paris, Rouen, Dieppe, and Havre were no more reliable and scrupulous than the average horse-dealer in other parts of the world. Those who went direct to the district which was once known as La Perche, now comprised in the Departments of Eure et Loir, Loir et Cher, and Sarthe, where Percheron horses have for generations been bred in their purity, and where the fame of the Percheron race is still guarded as a priceless treasure, have doubtless usually obtained Percheron horses. But the Société Hippique Percheronne and the other stud-book organizations of France now furnish a directory of blood which few honest importers will care to ignore, and the result cannot fail to add to the popularity of the Percheron breed in both France and America.

It will not be out of place in this connection to mention the fact that the American Percheron Stud Book, of which four volumes have now been issued, was the first stud book for any breed of draft horses ever published in the world, the society under the auspices of which it is published having been organized in February, 1876, and the first volume of its stud book appearing in September of the same year. The present Secretary of the American Percheron Association and editor of its stud book is S. D. Thompson of 722 W. Monroe street, Chicago.

BOULONNAIS.

This is another French draft breed, and next to the Percheron, which it closely resembles in many features, is the most highly esteemed and most generally disseminated of the draft breeds in that country. Its home is in the region of Boulogne-sur-Mer in the department of Pas de Calais, in the localities known as High Boulonnais, Low Boulonnais, and Calaisis, but it is

THE BREEDS OF HORSES. 287

also found in the districts of Bethune and St. Omer, and somewhat through the departments of Oise, Aisne, Eure et Loir and Seine Inférieure. For more than a century its existence as a distinct breed has been recognized, and its characteristic features well defined. It differs from the, to us better known, Percheron, in that it is more thoroughly and exclusively a horse for heavy draft—especially fitted for a heavy load at a slow pace. They have heavier quarters, shorter heads, thicker necks, with shorter, bushier mane than the Percheron, but with correspondingly lighter bodies. The prevailing colors are grey, bay and roan, the grey perhaps preponderating. A very considerable number of horses of this breed have been imported into the United States under some of the many *aliases* mentioned in connection with the Percheron breed on the preceding pages, but more latterly perhaps simply as French draft horses. But as they now have a distinct stud book of their own in France there is no necessity for further confusion, and certainly the breed has enough of merit in and of itself to render any attempt at concealment of its identity positively foolish.

OTHER FRENCH DRAFT BREEDS.

The other well-defined and generally recognized French draft breeds are the *Breton* breed, smaller than the Percheron, and bred chiefly in the department of Cotes du Nord and around Le Conquet. The most thoroughly characteristic representatives of the breed, it is said, are to be found in the canton of Léon. They are usually grey, but bays and roans are sometimes found. The *Ardennais* breed is also a small draft breed found in the districts of Rethel and Vauquiers, in the department of Ardennais. Thé *Poitevin* breed bears a close resemblance to the Boulonnais, except that they are usually bay in color. They are very heavy boned and the mares of this breed are highly prized for raising mules.

There is a stud book published in the United States called the French Draft Stud Book— formerly called the Norman Stud Book—of which six volumes, under the two names, have been issued. C. E. Stubbs of Fairfield, Ia., is Secretary of the Society having this publication in charge. In this stud book horses of any of the French draft breeds, or crosses between them, may be registered.

THE SUFFOLK PUNCH.

The *Suffolk Punch* of England is especially classed as an agricultural horse in that country, and is bred chiefly in the county from which it takes its name. They are uniformly of a chestnut or sorrel color, not so large as the Shire

THE BREEDS OF HORSES.

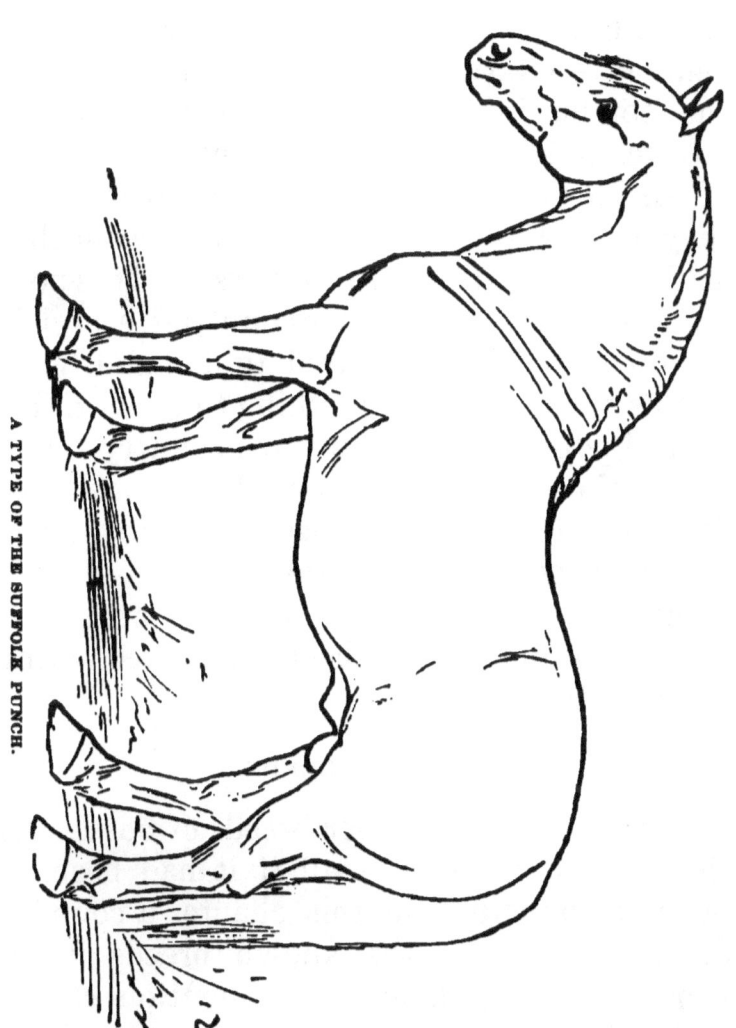

A TYPE OF THE SUFFOLK PUNCH.

horses or Clydesdales, but compactly built, round-bodied, long-backed, short-legged horses, rather light-boned for their weight, and with the general reputation of being rather defective in the feet, but in this respect greatly improved of late years. This is perhaps the best-established of all the heavy breeds of Great Britain, but they are not so universally popular even there as the Clydesdale and Shire horses. It is possible that the fact that other countries, especially our own, have not appeared to demand horses of this type has had something to do with their lack of popularity in their own country. Very few of them have been brought to the United States, and such as have been imported appear to have attracted but little attention. A stud book has been instituted for this breed, and several volumes have been published within the past ten years.

OTHER BREEDS.

There are several other breeds of horses that should be noticed in detail if it had been my purpose to include in this chapter a complete description of all the known breeds in the world. Among them I may mention chiefly:

The *Belgian Draft* breed, very heavy bodied, thick-set, short-quartered, short-legged, compact draft horses of various colors, with a good deal of spirit but rather sluggish in action.

Although several of them have been brought into the United States—chiefly into Illinois and Indiana—they do not appear to have grown much in popular favor in competition with the British and French draft breeds.

German or *Oldenburg Coach* horses have also been introduced to some extent within the past four or five years. They possess many features in common with the French and English Coach breeds, and like them are largely made up of crosses from the Thoroughbred, which they resemble to a greater or less degree in proportion as the blood of the Thoroughbred has entered into their ancestry.

Shetland Ponies, too well known to need any description in a work of this nature, take their name from the Shetland Islands, where they originated, doubtless through the effect of the bleak climate and scanty subsistence to which the original specimens of the race have been for ages subjected upon these islands. They are also bred in considerable numbers in the North of Scotland. There are other comparatively diminutive races, as the Welsh or Exmoor ponies, the Norwegian ponies, and others of Europe and Asia, as mentioned in the beginning of this chapter, but a more specific description of each and all of them would be more interesting to the student of natural history than to the practical American breeder.

The *Mustangs*, or wild horses, that were found upon the plains of Texas and New Mexico, and elsewhere on our own continent, are a tough, hardy, and usually ill-tempered race of small horses, remarkably agile and sure-footed, and have descended from the original Spanish stock brought to Mexico by the Spaniards in their early efforts at the conquest of that country. The Indian ponies, formerly so common in our Western Territories, have undoubtedly the same origin, and many of them, especially those that have been bred in the higher latitudes, approximate very closely the form and size of the Shetland pony. The hardiness and powers of endurance of many of these horses are simply marvelous; but these valuable qualities are largely neutralized by ill-temper and lack of size. Thoroughbred sires, as well as stallions of the various draft breeds, have been used upon these Mustang mares with excellent results in most cases. When tamed and broken they are especially adapted for use in herding cattle upon the great ranches of our Western plains, and for this purpose the genuine Mustang is the chief reliance of the herdsman.

CHAPTER IV.

DISEASES PECULIAR TO BREEDING STOCK.

PART I.

The following extracts from articles prepared at my request, by Prof. James Law, of Cornell University, for publication, at various times, under my direction, treat especially of matters to which this chapter is devoted and will, I am sure, be found highly interesting and valuable to my readers:

HYGIENE OF THE EYE.*

"As ye sow so shall ye reap," is as true of the propagation of animals as of the propagation of grain or weeds. In the case of sightless or partially blind horses it is especially true. In whatever country or district we find blind mares and stallions used for breeding, there we find a large proportion of even the young horses with faulty eyes. In whatever country, on the other hand, we find all horses with impaired eyesight rejected for breeding purposes, there we find the number of blind horses steadily decreasing. This depends not alone on the fact that "like produces like," but upon this additional one, that the greater part of the blindness in horses depends on a specific disease which is as surely hereditary as gout or rheumatism. This is the too familiar "moon blindness," or recurring inflammation of the eyes. Formerly this was very prevalent in England, but the sys-

---

* *The Breeder's Gazette*, Vol. I, p. 508.

tematic rejection of the diseased animals as breeders has greatly reduced the number of blind horses in later years. In America there is still a very wide margin for improvement. The blind stallion and the blind mare should be alike discarded, and it is well to avoid the progeny of horses that have suffered from this recurring ophthalmia, even though their own eyes may still be apparently sound.

Among the indications that an animal has suffered from the disease are the following; A slight bluish opacity around the margin of the transparent cornea; a sunken appearance of the eye, which seems smaller than natural; the existence of an angular interruption in the regular curve of the upper eyelid about one-third from its inner end; and a tendency to shy from imperfect sight. If in addition to this there is a loss of the clear luster of the iris (around the pupil), and an undue feeling of tension and resistance when the eyeball is pressed through the lid, or if there is a cataract, the evidence becomes the more conclusive. A cataract is recognized by a whitish opaque spot behind the pupil. It is best seen when the horse is led toward the stable door, so that the light may fall on the eyes from above and in front, while the interior of the stable forms a dark background. In bad cases the entire pupil is filled up by the opaque spot and the horse becomes blind on that side. An animal showing such features, or one which suffers at intervals from swelling or watering of the eyes, should never be used for breeding.

Nearsightedness is another quality which is derived from parents, and which is especially dangerous, by causing the horse to shy. It is further manifested in most cases by a peculiar bulging appearance of the eye, by reason of an extra convexity of the cornea.

The foals of horses that have suffered from moon-blindness are not all equally subject to its attacks. Much of the difference depends on the varying activity of the disease in the parent at the time of conception or during the period of pregnancy. A case strongly illustrative of this may be noted: A mare not predisposed to recurring ophthalmia, had a burdock entangled in the forelock so as to be directly

DISEASES PECULIAR TO BREEDING STOCK. 295

upon the eye, which was thus kept inflamed and running for a length of time during the course of pregnancy. The progeny—a filly—had the eye on the same side defective and represented by a small, opaque black mass. The dam recovered and afterward bore colts with sound eyes, as did also the one-eyed filly in due course of time. This but expresses a general law—that the disorder which is active and causes suffering at the time of reproduction is most likely to tell injuriously on the progeny. When, therefore, all the progeny inherit a constitutional predisposition to moon-blindness those which are begotten or born during a period of active disease and suffering on the part of one or both parents are most likely to become permanently blind. Another dominating cause of moon-blindness is the occurring in the predisposed animal of debility or weakness from any influence. It may be safely assumed that whatever undermines the general health or lowers the hardy vigor of such predisposed animals tends to bring on the disease. Thus coarse, fibrous, or innutritious fodder often acts in this way. An exciting, over-stimulating diet acts in the same way. An animal that keeps sound on a diet of oats or barley may fall a victim if fed on Indian corn. Overwork or the combination of hard work and a diet insufficient to repair the excessive waste is equally injurious. Debilitating diseases of all kinds are equally liable to superinduce the malady. An attack of influenza, a chronic indigestion, or the presence of worms in the stomach or bowels, may be the immediate cause of moon-blindness, one without which the hereditary tendency might have remained latent. Some causes, however, deserve more special attention because of their general operation or more wide-reaching effects.

It is notorious that certain countries and districts suffer more from recurring ophthalmia than others. In a general way it is the more moist and relaxing that furnish the most victims. The West of England and the whole of Ireland furnish more subjects of ophthalmia than does the dry eastern coast of Great Britain. The damp, marshy and cloudy region to the north of the Pyrenees suffers badly, while in the dry, clear atmosphere of Catalonia, to the south of these mountains, the disease is almost unknown. So notorious is this that dealers are in the habit of buying in Southern France, at a low price, horses that have had but one attack of ophthalmia and of transporting them to Catalonia where, as a rule, they escape any further seizure.

The effect of a damp, sunless, relaxing climate, however, is productive of a heavy, lymphatic stamp of horse, which is always more predisposed to affections of this kind than the horses of fine fiber and nervous temperament. In this respect the North American continent should be more favorable to the horse than the moister climate of England, being an approximation toward the climate of Syria and North Africa, the cradle of all that is excellent in horse flesh; yet even in the United States a low, marshy, damp, and cloudy region is to be avoided when it is wanted to develop the highest speed or the greatest vigor and endurance. Places and climates that prove most favorable for the raising of meat-producing animals are most likely to deteriorate the horse by developing a loose, open texture of bone, a bulky but soft, flabby muscle, and an undue tendency to sluggishness and fattening. The lymphatic temperament thus indicated is that which especially predisposes to ophthalmia, and if such young animals are retained in such a climate they are particularly liable to suffer.

Close stables are hurtful in various ways. The relaxing effect of the stable upon the young horse is always marked; but this is especially so when, as in dealers' stables, the air is kept extra hot to produce a *fine coat*. The damp rising from the lungs and skin of the animals and from the dung and urine is especially injurious because of its relaxing effects, but still more so because of the active decomposition which it maintains in the organic matter floating in the air or lodged on the walls, floors and woodwork. The effect of this is seen in the great predominance of diseases of the air passages in young horses that have been recently stabled; and upon animals predisposed to ophthalmia the same disturbing influence tends similarly to the development of that affection. Apart from the debility and fever which this change brings about it will be observed that the air of the

DISEASES PECULIAR TO BREEDING STOCK. 297

stable repeats on a small scale the damp, hot, cloudy, relaxing climate which we have seen to be the most favorable to the development of the disease we are dealing with.

For breeding and growing horses, therefore, it is all-important to secure dry, airy, roomy stables and to keep these clean and sweet. A naturally porous or well-drained soil, a sunny exposure and a sufficiency of ventilating orifices above and below, so disposed as not to create cold draughts, are points of especial value.

Stables should be so constructed as to avoid darkness on the one hand and a full glare of sunshine striking the eyes on the other. Darkness is usually associated with uncleanliness, damp and close air; but apart from these it is injurious in hindering the proper development of red blood globules which are so essential to sound and vigorous health. It further tends to weaken the eyes and to expose them to suffering and inflammation when suddenly taken out into the full glare of sunshine. When the sunlight is reflected from snow, from white walls, or from the white dust of a limestone soil it becomes increasingly injurious. It is well to have a stable well lighted but the sunlight should be made to enter behind or to one side, and not to fall directly on the eyes of the animal.

How common an occurrence is the presence of hay seed or chaff in the eyes of animals. Nothing can conduce more to the development of a latent predisposition to ophthalmia. The sensibility of the eye is adapted to its situation which is protected by the margins of the orbit against solid objects of large size while it is especially liable to be invaded by fine particles of sand, dust, etc. A smooth marble or finger may be made to touch the eyeball without great suffering, while a grain of sand or ashes produces exquisite torture. To avoid these smaller and more hurtful bodies hay racks should be made no higher than the ordinary manger and if filled from above it should be through a closely-boarded chute so that neither seed nor dust may readily drop into the eyes.

The above remarks are equally applicable to the dust of the highway in summer. With breeding animals especially it is dangerous to drive in the cloud of dust raised by a leading wagon, but how much more so if the horse is hereditarily predisposed to ophthalmia. In the same way we should guard the horse against the cinders flying into open railway cars, from the dust of a threshing machine blowing upon the horses engaged in driving it, the dust of a harrow driven in the same direction as the wind, the smoke of burning rubbish, etc.

In addition to the bad effects of insufficient, faulty, or too stimulating food, already referred to, it is well to note that the consumption of too much sugar is liable to induce disease of the eye. This is especially likely to result from a too exclusive diet of sorghum, or from the large admixture of molasses with the food. It may, indeed, be questioned whether the notoriously evil effects of a diet of Indian corn on the eyes is not partly due to the abundance of starch in its composition and to the conversion of that starch into sugar in the system.

THE EYE AS AFFECTED BY THE TEETH.*

The process of teething is calculated to rouse into activity a latent predisposition to disease of the eye in horses. The rapid progress of teething in the horse and the completion of the process at an early age determines much vascular and nervous excitement about the head, and the weakest point in many cases being the eyes these are too often the parts to suffer. To illustrate the influence of teething it need only be said that at three years old the horse acquires eight new grinding teeth and four front ones. A year later he acquires eight additional grinders, four front teeth and four tushes. It is small wonder that at these ages the gums and soft pad of the upper jaw swell; that the horse refuses his food, or eats with little appetite; that he drops morsels half chewed, and that he appears at times sluggish, dull and feverish. Nor is it surprising that at this age the progeny of horses that have suffered from recurring ophthalmia themselves show symptoms of the same disease. It is this tendency to diseases of the eyes during the eruption of the permanent

---

* *The Breeder's Gazette*, Vol. I, p. 536.

teeth which has drawn horsemen's attention to the *wolf teeth* as the supposed cause of the evil. The wolf teeth, however, come up with the first set of molars, and are therefore in the mouth during the whole of early life and until the adjacent teeth—the front upper grinders -are shed. Whenever, therefore, a young horse suffers from diseased eyes the owner or attendant opens the mouth and finding wolf teeth concludes that these are the cause of the trouble. The wolf tooth is imbedded not more than half an inch in its socket, while the adjacent grinders, and even the front nippers, extend into the bone for about two inches. These other teeth are, therefore, far more likely to produce irritation than are the wolf teeth, and, as a matter of fact, the congestion of the palate, familiarly known as *lampas*, occurs close behind the front teeth and not near the wolf teeth. In the shedding of the back grinders, too, it is not at all uncommon to have so much irritation caused that it extends to the throat and causes sore throat and cough. But around the insignificant wolf teeth it is rare to find any irritation at all, and that only when they deviate from their true direction. The temporary recovery from sore eyes after the extraction of the wolf teeth is just what would have happened had the teeth been left in place, and proves only that the disease appears and disappears alternately.

The excitement attendant on teething is natural, yet it is well to check this when it threatens to become severe or to rouse sympathetic inflammation of the eyes. If costiveness appears during the process the substitution for a portion of the diet of soft mashes of wheat-bran, of fresh, succulent grass, of roots, apples, or silage will prove beneficial. If these are not available or are ineffective one or two ounces of Glauber's salts may be given daily in the feed. If the old teeth do not fall early and spontaneously, but remain entangled on the crowns of the new ones after the latter have cut the gums, they should be removed; if the gums become red, swollen and tender, a slight scarifying of the surface so as to let a little blood will usually relieve; and if new teeth, and especially the tushes, produce tension and pain by their pressure before cutting the gums, their eruption should be assisted by a deep incision with the lancet down to the hard tooth substance.

UMBILICAL HERNIA IN YOUNG FOALS.*

This condition is usually very easy to recognize. A pouched or pyriform swelling appears in the median line of the abdomen, immediately below the navel, which on manipulation is felt to contain movable contents which glide readily on each other and can be easily returned into the abdominal cavity by pressure. Then in the center of the navel can be felt an opening of variable size, which may admit one, two, or four fingers. On relaxing the pressure the sack fills up again more or less promptly and fully. When manipulating their contents, and during their return, there will usually be felt, and even heard, some gurgling from the admixture of liquids and gases in the contained intestine.

It is needless to mention here more than one mode of treatment that should serve every purpose in the very young, in which the tissues of the navel are still embryonic cells, and the opening, therefore, easily closed. Procure a piece of sole leather from four to six inches square to apply upon the navel after the mass of the intestines has been passed back into the belly. To each corner of the leather pad attach an elastic band and bring the same upward around the body, tying them over the spine. Pass a band around the lower part of the neck to act as a collar. From the lower part of this collar carry an elastic band between the four legs and attach it to the anterior border of the leather pad. From the same collar, on each side of the shoulder, carry an elastic band back on the side of the chest and tie it successively to the two elastic bands which encircle the body. The essential point is that all of the bands should be elastic, so that they yield and accommodate themselves to the movements of the abdomen in breathing and of the body in all its varied motion. If a similar bandage is applied with *inelastic* bands drawn tight enough to keep the pad in contact with the umbilicus in all the breathing movements it is liable to cause

---

* *The Breeder's Gazette*, Vol. 1, p. 281.

severe and even fatal straining. As an accessory to the pad and elastic bands may be applied on the umbilicus a liberal amount of melted pitch, or pitch and wax, which will bind the band and skin and still further secure against any descent of the hernia. If by these means the bowels can be prevented from descending through the opening the walls of that opening will speedily contract and become fibrous and the possibility of future protrusion will be obviated.

In cases of longer standing—in colts, for example, of several months old—the embryonic cellular tissue around the navel has already been developed into fibrous material, so that the contraction and closure is not so speedy, and in such cases it may be desirable, when the hernia is small, to leave it to nature—at least until the colt is one or two years old. In such cases a spontaneous cure often ensues; but the opening is rarely so completely effaced, nor so strongly closed, as when effected by bandage immediately after birth.

The explanation of the spontaneous recovery is this: The lower part of the abdomen in the adult horse is occupied by the large intestines to the utter exclusion of the small. In the young foal these are scarcely larger than the small intestines and easily protrude through any natural or artificial orifice. As the foal grows, however, and subsists more and more on coarse and solid food, the large intestines gain in size, and in mature life they vary from four to twelve inches in diameter at different points. The blind gut, which is one of the largest, lies obliquely across above the navel, and by its great bulk forms an internal pad, which most effectually shuts off the small intestines from this region.

"SCOURS" OR DIARRHŒA IN COLTS.

In all young animals there is a certain amount of secretions from the liver, pancreas, stomach and bowels prior to birth, and when the new being comes into the world these products are accumulated in the form of firm, tenacious masses, in the last gut. At first the bowels are torpid, and the stiff, tenacious contents, or *meconium*, obstructs all progress. The natural laxative, which nature has furnished to clear away this product, is the milk first secreted, and when abundant this usually serves every purpose. But from various causes this milk may be deficient in amount or altered in quality and may fail to produce free evacuation of the bowels. Then follow costiveness, impaction of the bowels with the waste products of the digestion of milk, decomposition of these products, impairment or alteration of the secretions of the whole digestive apparatus, and, finally, irritation, excessive watery secretion, unnaturally active movements of the bowels, perhaps even inflammation, and, of course, scouring. For this condition, which is a very common one, the preventive is to watch the foal closely for the first twenty-four hours, and if the bowels are not freely moved to give a dose of three ounces of castor or olive oil with a teaspoonful of laudanum.

In the young the liver is relatively far larger and more active than in the adult. As might be expected, it is at the same time more liable to disorder. In many cases of indigestion in young foals the extreme fœtor of the discharges, the coated appearance of the tongue, and the yellowness of the membranes of the eyes and nose, testify to the existence of this derangement. In such cases after the operation of the oil much good may often be derived from one grain of calomel and twelve grains of chalk intimately mixed and repeated two or three times a day.

Anything that affects the general health of the mare is liable to modify the milk. When mares are used in harness during lactation it occasionally happens that a fretful animal becomes so fevered that the quality of the milk is materially altered, and the foal, coming to her hungry, gorges itself with what acts like a veritable poison, inducing indigestion, with skin eruptions or diarrhœa. So it is with other unhealthy conditions of the mother. In all febrile, wasting, or disordered states, the milk is more or less altered, and every such alteration is a threat to the sound digestion of the foal and may prove a proximate cause of scouring. With some it is a common practice after the mare has been excited by work to keep the foal apart until all the milk found in the bag has been drawn off, since they justly conclude that what is secreted later, when the period of ex-

DISEASES PECULIAR TO BREEDING STOCK. 303

citement is past, will prove more wholesome. In the same manner we ought to correct, as far as possible, any alteration of health on the part of the dam.

We know that the relative amount of water and solids in the milk is greatly affected by the nature of the food. A suckling animal in good health has a richer and more concentrated milk when fed on dry hay, and especially with a liberal supply of grain. Now the very richness of this milk may unduly stimulate the digestive organs of the young animal, and any such undue stimulation borders on disease. A slight congestion of the stomach or a temporary suspension of its secretions may lead to the formation of larger masses of curd, which are difficult to dissolve and lie but as permanent irritants in the abused organ. Although the best course is to prevent the formation of these, it is often needful to treat them, and perhaps nothing will serve our purpose better than a dose of castor oil, as above advised, to be repeated in three days; and in the interval two table-spoonfuls of a solution of rennet in wine, repeated morning, noon and night of each day. To prevent recurrence of the indigestion the rennet may be continued for some time, and the mare should be allowed an abundance of water, not too cold, and one or two soft mashes daily. The rennet solution may be prepared by taking one-eighth of the fourth stomach of a calf and steeping in a pint of wine. Water may be substituted for wine if a sufficient amount of salt or a few drops of carbolic acid are added to prevent putrefactive change.

For the suckling mare grass is unquestionably the natural food. Left to nature she brings forth her young at the period when pastures are luxuriant, and on this diet her milk is abundant and good, but not too rich nor concentrated; and yet even green food is not always most conducive to the health of mare and foal. Occasionally in early spring the fresh grass is so rank and its growth so rapid that it contains an excess of water; and even its constituent organic elements appear to differ from those of a less rapid growth, and the result is acute indigestion and violent diarrhœa. This, which shows itself primarily in the mare, may be propagated in the foal as well by the morbid products secreted in the milk. Nothing is more certain than that very many chemical agents introduced into the system of the mother pass out largely by the milk. It is an old practice to give a dose of salts or other purgative to the mother, with the view of acting on the bowels of the offspring. Poisons, too, taken into the system of the mother, will often pass out in the milk and affect the more susceptible offspring rather than the less impressible nurse. Hence it is that green food that has been grown under unusual conditions, fodder that has been spoiled in harvesting, impure waters with an excess of decomposing organic matter, and mineral waters containing laxative salts, may appear to act even more severely on the sucking animal than on its dam through which these were derived. The notice of these things is, perhaps, sufficiently suggestive to lead to their correction when they are found to exist. It need only be stated that green food which is actively irritant when used alone will often prove harmless when employed in connection with grain or other dry food; but occasionally this will fail, and each case must be judged by its own results.

Confinement in close buildings is inimical to mare and foal alike. In both it induces a relaxed, weakened condition, which lays the system open to health-disturbing causes. The effect on the mare impairs the quality of the milk, and this in its turn reacts on the foal, which, thus placed between two fires, is doubly liable to suffer. But close confinement is too often associated with impure air and filthy surroundings, and nothing can well be more hurtful to health than this unhygienic combination. After foaling, as before, mares should have the means of taking free exercise, and if in early spring they can not do this in the pasture each ought to have the run of a yard connected with a dry, comfortable shed, where she and her foal may use and develop their locomotive organs and strengthen their constitutions.

Perhaps nothing is more hurtful to the young than a cold, damp bed. Suddenly transferred from a warm medium to the cold of early spring, it is of no small importance that the young animal should be protected against the excess of cold which comes of damp and evaporation, or even freezing.

DISEASES PECULIAR TO BREEDING STOCK.

The sympathy between the skin and the bowels is of the most intimate kind, and in earliest youth, when the susceptibility of the bowels is so great, the chilling of the surface often leads to disastrous congestions of the bowels and fatal scouring.

Similar to the above is exposure to cold rain storms. A passing shower may do no harm, even if cold; but a prolonged exposure to rain, with a low temperature, is terribly trying to the system of the new-born foal, and often leads to disorders of the digestive organs, with persistent and fatal diarrhœa.

Only two more conditions may be referred to, and both are connected with a more advanced period of colthood than are those already mentioned. When the foal begins to feed he may suffer from all those conditions of the food that prove noxious through the milk of the mother. A feed, for example, of a too stimulating grain, or of a too rank and aqueous grass, of fodder that has been badly harvested and rendered musty or bleached and fibrous, of grain or hay that has been altered by ergot or smut, and of roots and tubers that have been frosted or diseased—these and others may at times give rise to irritation in the as yet comparatively inhabituated stomach, and scouring is a not distant consequence.

The second evil result of faulty food and water is the presence of worms in the intestines. All the round worms of the intestines of the horse can live in water and moist earth, or in fresh vegetation, in their early and immature condition. Thus they are liable to be taken in continually with the food and water, and developing in the intestines they lay eggs almost without limit as to numbers, to be hatched and sped on the same noxious course. Hence it is that in pastures that have been grazed by horses year after year, and with drinking ponds and shallow wells into which the washings of the surface can find their way, the colts are particularly liable to worms; and diarrhœa from this cause is by no means infrequent. In such a case there is the general unthrifty appearance of the wormy animal, and the rubbed, frizzled appearance of the hair at the root of the tail which bespeaks the itching of the anus. The most marked symptom, however, is the presence of the worms in the durg, and these can usually be found if carefully sought for. In such a case it is well to give a dose of physic to clear away the mucus in which the vermin live; and if this is associated with a vermifuge the majority of the parasites may be expelled at once. Six table-spoonfuls of castor oil, with two or three tea-spoonfuls of oil of turpentine, according to the size of the foal, should be well shaken together and given as one dose. After this has operated twenty grains of powdered sulphate of iron and ten grains of santonin may be given daily for a week, when the dose of oil and turpentine may be repeated, which will usually clear away all the parasites that remain in the bowels.

In conclusion, a caution is needed against a too common method of treating diarrhœa from the outset with opium and astringents with the view of cutting short the discharge. As a rule scouring is but an indication of the presence in the stomach or bowels of some cause of irritation, and all attempts to quiet the irritation by opium or astringents serve but to imprison the cause of trouble and thus prolong its irritant action. The soundest policy in all such cases is to expel the disturber with a bland laxative like castor oil, guarding its action, if need be, by a little laudanum or other soothing agent; and only later, when the irritant has been expelled, to check the discharge and shelter and protect the irritated bowels by weak solutions of gum arabic, of slippery-elm, or by well-boiled linseed tea or starch. But even then these must be used in moderation lest they should produce a secondary constipation, which will prove even more hurtful than the diarrhœa. A good prescription for this stage, and which may be repeated once, twice, or thrice a day, as may be necessary, is eight grains of kino, one ounce tincture of cinnamon, one-half drachm of gum arabic, and two drachms of chalk. To sucking animals this may be given along with the preparation of rennet, and should only be continued so long as the bowels are loose and irritable.

STRANGLES OR DISTEMPER.

However strangles may be produced, or whatever accessory causes may favor its development, there can be no doubt

DISEASES PECULIAR TO BREEDING STOCK. 307

that once in existence it can be propagated by contagion. We frequently see all the young horses on a number of adjacent farms suffering at once from this malady, while a farm entirely surrounded by these, but which has had no direct equine communication with them, maintains a clean bill of health. But let one of the sick colts be introduced into the latter, and speedily all the horses unprotected by any antecedent attack present the unequivocal symptoms of strangles. Lastly, in many different cases the malady has been conveyed from horse to horse by inoculation, thus attesting in the most undoubted manner the presence of contagion. We are the more particular in enforcing this fact of contagion that most English authors deny its existence, and thus blind their readers to a most important measure of precaution. In many seasons the affection assumes a uniformly mild and regular form, and passing promptly through all its stages, is invariably followed by a satisfactory recovery. In other seasons it shows the greatest tendency to an irregular course—to a tardy and imperfect maturation of the swellings, to inflammation and abscess in unwonted situations, and to secondary formations of matter in distant and vital organs, with most injurious or fatal results. If we conclude that the disease is in the air, or in the system only, as English authors assert, we may well decide that we can do little to hinder its appearance in the more fatal seasons, or to favor it in the safer and milder ones. If, however, we recognize the truth that the disease may be to a great extent prevented by seclusion and disinfection, while its development can be secured by exposure to contagion, we can protect our studs in the less favorable outbreaks, and even pass them through the malady in the milder ones, thus saving many lives and many more cases of roaring, thick wind, chronic coughs, and other affections of the air passages.

Strangles is usually preceded by a period of incubation, manifested by a staring coat, loss of condition, dullness and languor, with perspiration and fatigue under slight exertion. These are followed by rise of the body temperature, heat and clamminess of the mouth, redness of the eyes and interior of the nose, and a watery distillation from both, driveling of saliva from the mouth, accelerated breathing and pulse, costiveness, scanty, high-colored urine, and increased thirst. Now the characteristic swellings appear in front of the throat and between the two branches of the lower jaw. This is a uniformly rounded swelling, hot and tender, firm and resistant in the center, but softer, more doughy and pitting on pressure on the surface and around the margins. After two or three days, in the regular cases, the center of the swelling softens and fluctuates from contained pus, and a few days later still it bursts, discharging an abundant white, creamy matter, and speedily heals up, this being accompanied by a restoration to vigorous health.

Sometimes the swelling is situated in the throat and may press inward on the pharynx, preventing swallowing and causing a rejection of water and food by the nose. In other cases it presses on the larynx, shutting off the air from the lungs and causing the most difficult, stertorous breathing, or even proving fatal by suffocation. At other times the swelling beneath the lower jaw is replaced, or supplemented, by similar swellings in distant parts of the body, but mainly in the groups of the lymphatic glands, in the neck, shoulder, groin, chest, abdomen, or elsewhere. In these cases the danger is always greatly enhanced, but it will be proportionate to the vitality of the organs in which the inflammation and suppuration supervenes. In some instances the swelling first appears in its natural situation under the jaw, but fails to come to a head, remaining hard and indolent for an indefinite length of time. In all such cases the strength is much run down and there is a great tendency to the formation of matter in important internal organs, and especially in the brain, with fatal results. In such cases, too, there is a great tendency to enormous dropsical and bloody effusions in the head and limbs as the result of debility and a very depraved condition of the blood.

Suggestion has already been made of the great importance of guarding against exposure to contagion, to change of locality, or to any of the exciting causes of the disease, when that shows any tendency to assume an irregular or fatal form in a district. Disinfectants even may be used in the stables, such as fumes of burning sulphur diluted so as to be breathed without irritation, or the exhalations from shallow basins of carbolic acid and alcohol. We may add the further precaution not to expose to cold, wet, nor exhaustion during convalescence from this affection, as many cases of irregular course and untoward results have occurred from the lack of just such care.

In the treatment of the affection much more reliance is to be placed on sound hygienic measures than on medication. The patients should be fed liberally on scalded or boiled grain, or wheat-bran, and if this can be given from a nose-bag it will soothe and relieve the air passages and greatly hasten the formation of matter and recovery. This should be done at least twice a day. No less important is the continuous application of warmth and moisture to the swelling between the jaws. This may be accomplished by persistent fomentation with warm water, by the application of a poultice in a bag of thin cotton, or, better and more conveniently, by enveloping the head in a sheet, with holes cut for the ears and eyes, and laced down the middle of the face, and inserting a large wet sponge so that it may lie in contact with the swelling. This can be kept saturated with warm water by pouring a little into it occasionally. When the matter approaches the surface, and appears to be separated from the finger by a thin layer of skin only, it should be freely opened with a sharp knife. The fomentations may be kept up until the surrounding hardness has entirely disappeared. The swellings in unwonted situations should be similarly treated, so as to seek a discharge of the matter externally. The formations in internal organs are too often fatal because of the vital importance of the structures involved.

This is a malady through which most horses pass once in their lives. In this respect it resembles measles, scarlatina and other eruptive fevers of children. Precisely what are the conditions which lead to its development it may be difficult to state in so many words, but there can be no doubt that among the many predisposing causes change of locality holds a very high place. Horses moved from one county or State to another, from a hilly to a flat region, or the reverse, from inland to the seaside, or from the country to the town, are those in which the disease is most apt to be developed. So strong indeed is this influence of altered climate that a second and even a third attack may be determined in the same animal by extensive change of residence. In horses, on the other hand, kept continuously in the same locality, a second attack is very rare.

DISEASES PECULIAR TO BREEDING STOCK.

PART II.

Prepared expressly for this work by Dr. N. H. Paaren, for many years State Veterinarian of Illinois.

THE STALLION—EXTERNAL INJURIES.

The accidents and ailments to which the stallion may be said to be especially liable are comparatively few. Among the external injuries to which he is exposed are those he may receive while he is about to serve the mare; such as bruises, lacerations, sprains, injuries of the sexual organs, etc., and which may be caused by the mare's resistance, from want of proper assistance of the keeper, or by the too great eagerness and impatience of the stallion himself. Among the requirements to his early restoration to service, as well as to successful treatment when injured in this manner, is total abstinence from sexual intercourse. Minor wounds or slight hemorrhage may be treated with frequent applications of cold water or mild astringent lotions. Considerable bleeding, consequent upon more extensive lacerations, may require the use of hot iron or ligatures, and that the wounds be closed by stitching or by strings of sticking-plaster. Where inflammatory action exists, besides internal sedative remedies (aconite, fifteen to twenty drops, repeated hourly until six or eight doses have been given) use locally either

DISEASES PECULIAR TO BREEDING STOCK. 311

cold or warm applications; and when œdemic or dropsical swelling exists apply warm aromatic decoctions, frequently renewing the same, and exercise the animal several times daily. Extensive or persistent dropsical swelling of either the sheath or the penis may be relieved by longitudinal free lancing and continued warm bathing. In cases of profuse suppuration apply astringent lotions (alum, sulphate of zinc, or acetate of lead; strength, one to twelve of water). Fistulas should be slit open to give free escape to matter and facilitate applications of remedies (nitrate of silver) to destroy false membrane; thereafter, zinc ointment, carbolized cosmoline, etc.

INFLAMMATION OF THE PENIS.

It is evidenced by pain, heat, swelling, more or less inability to extend or retract the organ, painful urinating, a straddling gait, more or less depression of spirit and loss of appetite. Most frequently caused by kicks from the mare, injury by hairs of the mare's tail obstructing free entrance to the vagina, etc. After cleansing the penis and the sheath with warm water and soap apply zinc or lead ointment, or if much swelling prevails use frequent bathing with hayseed tea or decoction of other aromatics with vinegar. In case of abscess formation, besides frequent attention to cleanliness use injections of solutions of sulphate of zinc or sulphate of copper (from one to two drachms to a half-pint of water). If the stallion is unable to retract or retain the penis within the sheath it will be necessary to support the member in a horizontal position by means of a broad linen bandage or sling fastened over the loins. The diet should be loosening and spare.

INFLAMMATION OF THE TESTICLES.

This is evidenced by a stiff, straddling gait, or more or less lameness; swelling and pain of one or both testicles, including the testicular cord; total loss of spirit and ability to service, and which latter condition, in severe cases, may become permanent on account of structural disorganization of the testicles. Treatment should be conducted as indicated in the previous case. The testicles should be supported by the use of a suspensorium. Scarification must never be employed in enlargement of the testicles, except in the case of abscess formation. Chronic enlargement or induration should be counteracted by the use of weak mercurial ointment, to which may later be added a small proportion (one to twenty-four) of iodine; but this latter should never be used while local pain or inflammation remains.

CANCER OF THE PENIS AND THE SHEATH.

This condition is generally mistaken for warts, on account of some similarity of appearance. It is generally located at the edges or inside of the sheath and at extremity or spongy body of the penis. In appearance it is a tumor of varying size, with a granulated or sprouting surface, of a dirty red color, the edges of which bleed on slight provocation, and from which a fetid ichor is discharged The skin and underlying tissue surrounding these tumors are generally more or less thickened and knotty. When located near the course of the urethra there may be more or less difficulty in urinating. There is a possibility of this disease being transmitted by the genital parts of the stallion to the mare, and *vice versa*. The best course of treatment consists in the entire disintegration of the tumor by aid of the red-hot iron and the subsequent application of ordinary healing remedies. There is a kind of tumor affecting the genital organs, which is of a non-contagious nature, called sarcoma, and which may be removed by the same means.

PROLAPSE, OR PARALYSIS OF THE PENIS.

Prolapse may exist without a paralytic condition of the organ, or it may be due to paralysis, affecting posterior parts of the body. Prolapse, with or without co-existing paralysis, may be caused by various local injuries of a mechanical nature, and it may co-exist with or be due to inflammation of the penis, to rheumatism, etc. Depending upon possible complications of a more general or extensive nature, the condition may be either of temporary duration, amenable to treatment, or it may result in permanently disqualifying the animal for stud service. One of the first requirements to successful treatment consists in the use of a suspensorium or loin bandage. To the dorsum and sides of the penis apply tincture of iodine or turpentine, once daily, by light penciling of the parts, and internally administer spinal stimulants, such as nux vomica (fifteen grains to a scruple, twice daily) with valeriana (one ounce of the powdered root).

SCROTAL HERNIA.

The descent of a portion of the intestines, through the inguinal canal, into the scrotum or bag which contains the testicles, is sometimes met with in entire males of all ages. It may be congenital, or acquired soon after birth, or at any time in after-life, from a variety of causes, such as violent efforts, jumping, kicking, violent throwing or rolling during attacks of colic or bloating, too frequent and excited copulation, violent exertions in pulling heavy loads, especially uphill, etc. Sometimes the descent of intestine into the scrotum is not due to any of the causes named, but may occur from a relaxed condition of the abdominal muscles or a too spacious inguinal canal (abdominal ring). In young colts scrotal hernia does not always manifest itself by sudden or violent symptoms; in fact the animal may, to all appearance, suffer no inconvenience; but as there will always be danger of strangulation, with its sequels of inflammation of the bowels, gangrene of the incarcerated portion and death of the animal, such cases should be attended to as soon as they are discovered, both in young and old. Whenever colic occurs in stallions a careful examination of the contents of the scrotum should never be omitted. It will be evident to any thinking man that, in a case where violent symptoms of colic are induced by strangulation of a portion of intestine in the scrotum, the administration of medicines, instead of remedying the case, may only tend to hasten a fatal termination. The cause of the symptoms, being of a mechanical origin and nature, can be remedied only by mechanical means, aided by proper medicinal adjuncts. In young colts, when no untoward symptoms exist in connection with scrotal hernia, the return of the intestinal contents of the scrotum may be effected by taxis; that is, by laying the animal on its back, raising the hinder part of the body from the ground as far as possible, and by gentle manipulation of the scrotal contents cause their return to the abdominal cavity. The animal should then be laid on its side and allowed to rise as quietly as possible. A return of intestine into the scrotum may not occur again; but should it happen more than twice it will be best to castrate the animal without unnecessary delay, the removal of the testicles being done by the so-called covered operation. It would be highly improper and dangerous to castrate such an animal in the usual manner by opening the tunica vaginalis (so-called striffing or white sack), which is in direct connection with the abdominal cavity. Scrotal hernia in older animals should be treated in a similar manner; that is, the animal should be made resistless by the proper administration of anæsthetics, probably the least dangerous of which is the following combination, which is almost invariably used by myself in all animals, viz.: one part of alcohol, two parts of chloroform, and three parts of sulphuric ether, administered by saturating a sponge, which should then be held close to (not against) the lower nostril, while a towel or small blanket is laid loosely over the sponge and half of the head. Both nostrils should never be covered by the sponge. When entirely under the influence of the anæsthetic the animal should be laid on its back; sacks filled with oats or packed with hay should be placed under the crupper and loins to raise that part of the body from the ground; equilibrium of the body being maintained by strong bands holding the four limbs; the oiled hand and arm inserted through the rectum; and by manipulation of the intestines, simultaneously with judicious manipulation of the contents of the scrotum, the intestinal contents of the latter may be entirely returned to the abdominal cavity. Should, however, these efforts prove unsuccessful, nothing remains but to resort to a surgical operation, the particulars of which I omit describing, as such an operation could be successfully performed only by a veterinary expert. Should the contents of the scrotum be successfully returned, without surgical operation, it would be

DISEASES PECULIAR TO BREEDING STOCK. 315

prudent to castrate the stallion by the covered method, to avoid future similar occurrence. Many a fine stallion, supposed to be affected with spasmodic colic, undoubtedly suffers the most excruciating pains of strangulated scrotal hernia and dies in the hands of unsuspecting owners or attendants with the real cause of suffering and death undiscovered, for which reason I have discussed this subject at length.

WATERBAG, SO-CALLED.

This condition may exist as a simple dropsical (œdematous) infiltration of the connective tissue of the scrotum, and as one of the sequels of influenza or other internal diseases. Water or serum, contained in the scrotal sac, together with the testicles, may be the result of local injury or abdominal dropsy. In old stallions this condition may, and does often, co-exist with degeneration or chronic diseases of the testicles. It is also met with in young, weakly colts, as a result of general debility. Simple dropsical infiltration may be treated locally by stimulating applications, and internally by the administration of diuretics, succeeded with tonics, liberal keep and proper daily exercise. Accumulation of water in the scrotal cavity may be returned to the abdomen by placing the animal on its back and raising the hinder quarters; and the absorption and elimination of the fluid may then be accomplished by the administration of laxative or diuretic remedies, succeeded with tonics, liberal keep and exercise. When the aqueous accumulation in the scrotum is due to, and co-exists with degeneration or enlargement of one or both testicles, castration may be resorted to.

EXCESSIVE VENERY (*Satyriasis*).

A condition in which excessive sexual excitement occurs at frequent intervals, even almost uninterruptedly, may exist in both sexes. In the stallion ejaculation of semen may occur during the paroxysm of erection and excitement, or just before sexual connection. The condition manifests itself mainly when the stallion is kept within the sight or smell of mares, or in the same stable; seldom when he is kept absolutely secluded. It may be a consequence of idleness, together with a want of sexual intercourse, and especially when the animal is kept on very rich and stimulating food; otherwise, a constitutional predisposition to excessive virility may exist. The evil may be remedied by seclusion, more frequent sexual intercourse, work, less nutritious food, the administration of occasional laxatives; also by the use of bromide of potassium in two-drachm doses; or camphor with nitrate of potassium, respectively one and two-drachm doses. Castration as a last resort.

NON-EMISSION OF SEMEN, OR "PROUDNESS," SO-CALLED.

The question is frequently asked: "What causes a stallion to dismount proud?" or "What can be done for a 'proud' stallion?" This condition is a variety of sterility in which sexual intercourse is not finished with an ejaculation of semen, either because that fluid does not enter the urethra, or because its forcible expulsion is prevented by some obstacle in the course of the urethra. Non-emission may be congenital or acquired, and permanent or temporary. It may be, and probably most frequently is, the result of either masturbation or over-taxation of the sexual organs. Dr. Howe says on this subject: "The power of erection remains intact, but the patient exerts himself in vain to produce an orgasm. This condition may continue a few weeks, disappear and then return. It is by no means a permanent condition, but it may lead to permanent sterility and impotence. Some writers say that it is due to spasm of the orifices of the ejaculatory duct, which prevents the passage of seminal fluid into the urethra; others, that it is due to a lack of secretion in the various glands. This latter view, however, is not tenable, because such patients are subject to nocturnal pollutions as a result of lascivious dreams. It is more than probable that there is a temporary paralysis of sensation existing in the prostatic portion of the urethra, in the ducts, and perhaps in the vesicles. This lack of sensation prevents the reflex muscular action necessary for the propulsion of the semen."

This latter view coincides with my opinion, stated above, as to the most frequent causes of this condition in stallions,

DISEASES PECULIAR TO BREEDING STOCK. 317

namely: sexual abuse or over-taxation; and the treatment which I have generally recommended, and which has been most successful, has had for its object to restore the sexual powers to their normal condition by remedies which tone up the system at large and excite the reflex activity of the genito-spinal center. Thus the following combination may be used twice or thrice daily during one week, viz.: Half an ounce each of tincture of iron and Fowler's solution of arsenic, and two drachms of tincture of nux vomica, given in half a pint of flaxseed tea or water sweetened with molasses. During the following week may be given, twice or thrice daily, half an ounce of fluid extract of damiana and one ounce of tincture of valeriana, in half a pint of sweetened water. Meanwhile, frequent bathing with cold water should be applied along the urethra, from the anus downward; and the stallion should be withheld from service during at least one month.

SEXUAL SLUGGISHNESS.

Among the causes of sexual indifference in the presence of the opposite sex in heat may be mentioned too long continued abstinence or sexual restraint, over-taxation of the male sexual organs, abnormal condition of these, other internal diseases, insufficient or innutritious food, general debility, obesity, etc. Treatment consists in the removal or avoidance of the causes; when indicated, nutritive and stimulating food, liberty out-doors with mares. To force sexual activity by stimulating or irritating nostrums does not generally prove permanently successful.

SPERMATORRHŒA.

This is a condition in which the semen is discharged without friction of the male organ. It is one of the consequences of masturbation, and may also result from debility of sexual organs from over-taxation of these. Treatment consists in the prevention or avoidance of the causes, isolation, frequent cold applications locally, and the administration internally of tonic and astringent remedies, such as iron, sulphate of zinc or sulphate of copper, in one-drachm doses,

VESICULAR ERUPTIONS ON THE PENIS.

Phlyctenoid vesicular eruptions on the penis are sometimes met with in stallions, and are by some regarded as a non-malignant species of chancre. It is a pellucid vesicle containing a serous fluid, which sometimes also occurs in young stallions that never have been used for service. The vesicles, after bursting, leave small ulcers, which readily heal when cleanliness of the parts is attended to. Otherwise they may become more or less aggravated and incapacitate the animal for service. During the eruption of the vesicles more or less local pain and inflammation exists. An animal thus affected should not be used for service. Treatment consists in frequent bathing, first with a solution of one part of Goulard's extract and ten parts of water. When inflammation has subsided use frequent applications of a solution of alum in water, and cleanse the parts with soap and water. In aggravated or protracted cases use frequent bathing with a solution of one part of chloride of lime in twelve to fifteen parts of cold water. Internal remedies are generally not necessary.

FOUL SHEATH.

Accumulation of sebaceous matter, cuticular desquammation and other deposits within the cavity or folds of the sheath often cause considerable local irritation and consequently more or less swelling of the sheath. This latter condition may also be due to accumulation of serum in the areolar or subcellular tissue, in consequence of local or general debility, or from some constitutional cause; and the swelling of the sheath, from whatever cause, may exist to such an extent as to impede the extension or protrusion of the penis, and cause the animal to acquire the habit of discharging the urine within the sheath. The irritation already existing within thus becomes aggravated; decomposition of the accumulated greasy substances is thereby enhanced and putrescence and fetor ensue. During summer this may attract flies, which "blow" the parts and cause accumulation of myriads of maggots within the sheath. Continued irritation may produce more or less local inflam-

DISEASES PECULIAR TO BREEDING STOCK. 319

mation and ulceration, and ultimately impair the general condition of the horse. When soap is used in cleansing the parts they should be rinsed with clean water thereafter. Oil or greasy substances should never be applied after cleansing, as is frequently done, for these substances are apt to decompose and cause renewed irritation. If the parts were for some time daily cleansed and then bathed with a solution of chlorinated lime, in the proportion of two ounces to a quart of cold water, gradual improvement and a subsequently permanent healthy condition would be likely to result. The use of this solution would also prevent the appearance of maggots. The horse's general condition should be improved by liberal keep, the administration of tonic remedies internally, and if he is used for work, by lessening or discontinuing the same for a sufficient length of time.

MASTURBATION.

It occurs to me that I should not close my remarks on the most common ailments to which the stallion is subject without referring to an evil with which I presume all of my readers are familiar. In fact, the subject of masturbation, or self-abuse, is one of considerable interest and importance, not only to horsemen, but to all breeders of live stock. It is a remarkable fact that our literature on live-stock matters almost entirely ignores the subject. There certainly cannot be any impropriety in discussing this matter in a work entirely devoted to the interest of breeding, especially when we consider the often serious results of the practice and the inconvenience and trouble it often causes during the season of training, or when, for other reasons, the stallion is withheld from service. I remember several instances where the result upon the health and usefulness of stallions was of so serious a nature that castration was resorted to as the only effective remedy. The too frequent practice of masturbation by, and its evil effects upon, the little stallion King Phillip, with a record of 2:21, was the reason given for castrating him.

There are various causes of this habit. "Idleness begets vice" is an adage applicable to a great extent in the case of self-abuse in the males of our domestic animals. many of which, especially the better-bred and more valuable ones, are fed on stimulating food and kept idle most of their time. But besides idleness and restraint of sexual intercourse, there are other causes of the habit, among which may be mentioned special generic disturbances and excessive generic potency, and which are more frequently met with in the bull than in the stallion.

When masturbation is practiced frequently organic disease of the testicles may result; also, weakness of the loins, loss of power of propulsion, loss of flesh, and general emaciation; spermatorrhœa, as well as so-called clap, besides impotence, may supervene, and these so much the sooner if the animal is kept on low diet with the idea of thus lowering his sexual excitement.

The subject of prevention is of course one of great importance. If the animal practices masturbation by the aid of his own body or limbs it is next to impossible to prevent the same. Chastisements are of no use, and shame is out of the question. Among the remedial measures are unrestrained liberty outdoors, but which, especially with the stallion, is not generally practicable; also moderate work in the field or on the road, and regular but moderate use in the stud or herd. The main object is to prevent the exercise of the habit, if possible, but no means have been devised by which this can always be done successfully, especially when the habit has been long indulged in. The means adopted in human practice cannot very well be carried out with the same result. Among these we may, however, mention occasional blistering of the prepuce, or ringing it with silver wire, somewhat similar to ringing of the nose of swine. While the habit, by these or similar means, and by constant watching, or by applying a straight-jacket during the night, may prove successful in the human family, such stringent measures cannot be effectually applied in the case of animals, as the chances are that when the restrictions or applications are omitted, or after awhile, the animal will return to its old habits. Internal remedies, such as bromide of potassium, continued for some time, reduces sexual desire and potency,

DISEASES PECULIAR TO BREEDING STOCK. 321

but it is also apt to produce great weakness and emaciation, and could not be continued for any length of time without danger. Faradization of the spine has in some instances been used with benefit against self-abuse, but this is also likely to be of only temporary benefit; and, so far as I know, there is no sure cure for the evil. In inveterate cases, where the effects of masturbation have extended so far that the animal refuses to notice the opposite sex in heat, nothing remains but to castrate him and thus preserve his usefulness for other purposes.

CRYPTORCHIDS ("RIDGLINGS," SO-CALLED).

In common parlance the appellation of ridgling is given to a stallion in which either one or both testicles have failed to descend into the scrotum. In the cases where one testicle has descended the animal may serve the purposes of a sire and prove as fertile as if both testicles had descended. But the testicle or testicles that fail to descend into the scrotum, and are retained in the abdomen or the groin, are generally small and undeveloped, and now and then atrophied through fibrous or fatty degeneration. As a result of these malpositions or morbid changes, cryptorchids have generally been considered to be absolutely sterile, although they were known to have strong sexual desires and enjoy the capacity for copulation and ejaculation. While as a rule the ejaculated fluid is devoid of the fecundating germs, termed spermatozoæ, exceptional instances have occurred where such males have proved fertile, and where consequently the fluid must have contained spermatozoæ.

THE BROOD MARE—BARRENNESS.

A mare should not be considered barren because she does not get in foal, even after repeated service by one certain stallion, for it often occurs that a change of stallion proves effective. The causes of barrenness in mares are numerous, and among the most frequent are a phlegmatic temperament, or the reverse; excessive sexual excitement; also, reduced vitality, due to poverty of constitution, overwork, innutritious food; or the reverse condition, that of obesity; too great sexual excitement and violent efforts in the approaching stallion, especially if he is large and powerful while the mare is young and this her first experience; or the reverse, when the mare is small, old, overworked, in poor condition and low-spirited. Among causes of a mechanical nature may be mentioned obliteration or stricture of the vagina; supersensitiveness, with spasmodic closure of the vagina; vaginal or uterine tumors; engorgement or induration of the neck of the womb; obliteration or great narrowing of the canal of the neck of the womb, or its closure by glutinous exudation; occlusion of the fallopian tubes (which connect the womb with the ovaries); morbid or abnormal condition of the ovaries. All morbid discharges, due to retention of a portion or all of the after-birth, or to catarrh or leucorrhœa (so-called whites), effectively prevent pregnancy. I coincide with the opinion of experienced breeders, that pasturage upon red clover is among the fertile causes of barrenness in mares; and I believe that impotence in mares in this case is due to the honey contained in the flowers, this opinion being based upon the fact that a continued consumption of pure honey will produce impotence in both sexes of mankind. Nymphomania is also a cause of barrenness.

Many of the conditions named above are of a permanent character; others are amenable to treatment, and may be successfully avoided, remedied or removed. Thus, too great excitability of the mare may be overcome by starving her during twenty-four hours (not withholding drinking water), and driving her till she begins to tire just before service. The removal of tumors should be effected by surgical means; closure of the neck of the womb may be overcome by digital manipulation, which is best effected during heat. When due to supersensitiveness, or spasmodic contraction, a sponge, saturated with fluid extract of belladonna, may be inserted in the vagina and brought in contact with the neck of the womb, and remain inserted during an hour before service, when it should be removed, the parts cleansed with warm water, and the stallion admitted. The cases of barrenness which are most likely to yield to treatment are those where signs of heat occur at regular intervals, as here the cause is

DISEASES PECULIAR TO BREEDING STOCK. 323

generally of a mechanical nature. But when the animal never shows any sign of heat the prospects of its appearance are very unfavorable. Sexual energy may be restored in mares that have been overworked, or are in a poor condition from want of proper nutrition, by a reversal to freedom from work and liberal keep upon nutritious and stimulating food. In phlegmatic mares, or such where sexual sluggishness or indifference exists, if not due to obesity, they should be fed on rich and stimulating food, often changed, occasionally steamed or cooked, among which may be mixed a handful of hempseeds twice daily. By way of experiment, fluid extract of damiana may be tried in half-ounce doses, together with tincture of cantharides in half-ounce doses, mixed with half a pint of flaxseed tea, and such a dose given twice or thrice daily during a week, and repeated with intervals of one week for a term of three weeks; meanwhile letting the mare once or twice weekly come near the stallion, or be placed near him in the stable. The medicines may be bought at wholesale price by buying a pound or pint of each; otherwise the experiment will be too costly.

NYMPHOMANIA.

Excessive venery exists in the female as well as in the male, and is evidenced by an insatiable desire for sexual intercourse, the mare appearing to be almost constantly in heat. This condition has several causes for its existence, among which may be mentioned undue irritation or congestion of the ovaries, the fallopian tubes, or the womb, which causes the secretion of a peculiar irritating fluid. Scrofulous affections of the generative organs, or tuberculosis, especially of the body of the womb and its divergences, are known to be frequent causes of nymphomania. The state of the generative organs, under the last-named causes, is such as to render conception impossible; while at the same time the irritation induced by the morbid secretions continually induces an excessive and unnatural sexual desire. Under the existence of any of these conditions gestation could not exist, neither could conception be accomplished. A mare affected with nymphomania is a continual disturber of the peace and quiet in the stable, and often dangerous while in harness. When this condition has existed only a short time, conception may be brought about by spare keep, loosening food and laxative medicines. Two drachms each of camphor and saltpetre, given morning and evening during a week, often allays the excitement and irritation, when the stallion should be admitted; but it is totally useless to admit the stallion while the excitement of nymphomania exists. In some exceptional instances the amputation of the clitoris has proved successful. In old offenders the last remedy is spaying, and with that the nuisance is abated; but the operation is often dangerous to the life of the mare.

TUMORS WITHIN THE VAGINA AND UTERUS.

These may occur of various kinds and sizes, and frequently have a narrow neck. Their presence may be productive of slimy or bloody discharges of more or less offensive odor. When numerous or large they may cause prolapse of the vagina, difficult urinating, more or less frequent straining, and may hinder or obstruct copulation. Their successful removal, by twisting, ligation, dissection, or by means of the ecraseur, will of course depend upon their location, their shape, form of basis or attachment, etc.

LEUCORRHŒA, OR SO-CALLED WHITES.

This consists of a more or less copious slimy or purulent discharge, originating in the vagina or in the womb, and may be acute or chronic. Among its causes may be mentioned exposure to cold after foaling, other acute or chronic diseases, such as influenza, glanders, etc., or the presence of polypus, melanotic or other kinds of tumors within the vagina or uterus, the existence of recto-vaginal fistula, cancer of the womb, atrophy of the womb, etc. Depending upon the cause, the treatment should be either local or general. If the animal is in poor condition, treatment should be assisted by liberal keep on nutritious food. Among internal remedies may be mentioned juniper berries, savin, ergot, resin, common turpentine, muriatic acid, oak bark, of which the following formula may serve as an example: Take half an ounce of

DISEASES PECULIAR TO BREEDING STOCK. 325

common turpentine, twenty drops of muriatic acid, two drachms of powdered ginger, and ten ounces of decoction of oak bark. Give such a dose once a day during a week. In cases where the discharge is very profuse sugar of lead and oil of turpentine may be used, as follows: Take one drachm of sugar of lead, dissolve it in a sufficient quantity of warm water, add thereto two drachms of oil of turpentine, previously beaten into an emulsion with one yolk of egg; shake this mixture well together with half a pint of flaxseed tea, and give such a dose morning and evening during a week. The local treatment should be conducted as follows: By inserting the hand it may be ascertained whether the discharge proceeds from the womb, which is likely to be the case if the cervix or neck of the womb is wide open. In this case injection of warm water should be made into this organ by means of a long, flexible catheter, with a view of washing out the contents; after which, by the same means, make injections twice or thrice daily of tar water, clear lime water, or a solution of sulphate of zinc (half an ounce to each pint of water). A change of remedy often hastens the cure of such cases; wherefore, a solution of sugar of lead (two drachms to each pint of water) may be used every second week. The contents of the womb should, as far as possible, be withdrawn before the remedies are injected. In case the disease is confined to the vagina the cleansing and application of medicine may be done by the use of an ordinary syringe that will hold at least half a pint. For uterine application the capacity of the syringe should be from a pint to a quart. If the morbid discharge from the genital parts is due to the presence of polypi, or any other kind of tumors, of course the internal as well as local treatment above suggested will be useless, as a permanent cure under such circumstances would wholly depend upon whether these tumors were removable or not.

COLT FOUNDER, SO-CALLED.

Laminitis, or so-called founder, after foaling, is generally more troublesome or dangerous than the same disease occurring at other times and from other causes. It is sometimes complicated with metritis, or inflammation of the womb, or some other excitant malady, which should be ascertained, and treatment of such complications directed according to their nature. (See "Inflammation of the Womb.") Among the causes of colt founder is a plethoric condition, resulting from improper diet and regimen during the last months of pregnancy. Mares subjected to moderate work and light, nutritious diet, are seldom affected with this malady, while those kept idle and fed largely on corn or rich food are more commonly affected. In some instances breeders are known to have given their brood mares large and nutritious mashes, with the intention of promoting a large flow of milk. When such a diet is combined with total inactivity, as is common, with a mistaken view of avoiding abortion, a state of plethora is readily induced, which has a great tendency to the development of local inflammations, and among these the so-called colt founder. The treatment should, from the beginning of the evil, be like that adopted for the same disease generally, but more energetic, both locally and internally. Saline laxatives (a pound of Epsom or Glauber's salts, etc.), succeeded with sedatives (aconite, fifteen to twenty-drop doses, not exceeding six doses, at intervals of two hours); and poultices applied to the feet, after the shoes have been removed and the edge of the hoof has been pared down, leaving the sole and the frog intact, so that the bearing of the animal's weight comes most upon the central part of the foot. Not the least effective remedy is that of allowing the colt to suck, and, if necessary, additional stripping of the udder, with a view of promoting increased secretion of the mammary glands. In some cases, with acute inflammation and high fever, no milk is secreted; nevertheless the sucking should never be omitted. The return of milk generally indicates a successful issue. A mare subject to such affection should not be bred so as to have her colt too early in the year; for if she could be turned out on a good pasture before foaling the trouble would most likely be entirely avoided. She must not be fed so as to become plethoric or fat. Give good oats, occasional soft mashes, with bran and flaxseed-meal, say at least once a week, and

DISEASES PECULIAR TO BREEDING STOCK. 327

avoid corn during the last six weeks. Keep constantly some common salt placed within reach, in a separate small trough, and do not mix it among the food. The quantity consumed may safely be left to the animal's instinct, but access to good drinking water at least thrice daily should be given. When too early for grass, a roomy, well-littered box-stall, or comfortable, closed shed, should be allowed during the last two months of pregnancy. Give gentle exercise daily, or liberty out-doors during daytime when the weather is moderate and dry. Accidents from company with other horses, by kicking, etc., may be avoided by providing a small inclosed dry yard adjacent to her shed or box-stall.

ŒDEMA DURING PREGNANCY.

During the latter part of the period of gestation the mare is subject to dropsical swelling, especially of the udder and along the under surface of the chest and abdomen. Such local accumulations, and consequent more or less stiffness, generally disappear after foaling; but sometimes they are apt to become quite extensive, and may call for treatment. Such mares should never be kept tied up in a stall, but should be given the same facilities and liberty as recommended in the preceding paragraph, with access to common salt, as stated. Friction by hand-rubbing or a stiff brush, and the application of highwine or spirits of camphor, are among the remedies employed in such cases. Laxative remedies, as well as remedies to excite the kidneys to action, are not safe to employ during the latter part of gestation, as they are apt to produce abortion. Vegetable tonics, such as powdered gentian root, may be given among food once or twice a day during a few days to a week, in four to six-drachm doses.

SUPERIMPREGNATION.

According to its nature, superimpregnation is divided into two forms, technically termed superfœtation and superfœcundation. Cases of the first form occur after one or more sexual connections during the period of one and the same heat, and the consequence is the production of twins or triplets. The second form appears after coital connection during the time of any subsequent period of evolution or heat; and though there may, in such a case, be two or more fœtuses developing within the uterus at the same time, they cannot be regarded as twins or triplets, because their natural term of gestation terminates unequally, the difference depending upon the length of time that passed between the two different acts of conception; and, besides, if no accidental or detrimental influences should occur during the original term of gestation they would be born of two entirely independent acts of parturition. Superimpregnation, in its two forms, may occur after sexual connection with one or with several males. The difference in time between the two acts of parturition, in cases of superfœcundation, in recorded cases, has been from two to six months.

HEAT DURING PREGNANCY.

As a rule, when conception has taken place, the regular periods of heat terminate, and do not reappear until after parturition. But there are exceptions to this rule, and these are due to the fact that during gestation an ovule may mature, and, as a consequence, heat will appear. This may happen in all species of animals and during any period of gestation. If during such heat sexual intercourse should happen, conception may take place again, constituting superfœcundation.

LACERATION OF THE RECTUM.

Occasionally reports have come to hand concerning cases where, during the service of the stallion, the rectum became lacerated. These reports invariably contained statements of a fatal termination. While laceration of the rectum may happen during the normal performance of coition, it is, however, more likely to occur when, as sometimes happens, the penis enters the rectum instead of the vagina. Laceration of the rectum during coition may be considered as incurable and generally causes death of the mare.

ABORTION.

The causes of abortion are numerous. Among these may be mentioned colic, violent external injuries, violent exertions, heroic medicines, musty food, rancid oil-cake, rich and stimulating food in liberal quantities, impure water, etc.; also, disease of the fœtus and its enveloping membranes, and a predisposition after previous abortion. Abortion does not always occur immediately, but frequently after several weeks of preparation; and treatment to prevent abortion is useless after the act has commenced. When it is known that an animal has received an injury, or an exciting cause has been in operation that might produce abortion, some preventive treatment may be adopted, such as small doses of camphor (a scruple to half a drachm) with opium (one scruple) twice or thrice daily during one to three days; or half-drachm doses of powdered sulphate of iron; this latter mixed among food twice a day for a few days, not to exceed a week.

DIFFICULT PARTURITION.

As before stated the mare should, towards the time of foaling, be placed in comfortable, roomy quarters by herself. She should not be interfered with when foaling, unless there should appear to be unnatural presentation, unusual length of time or other difficulty; and when assistance appears to be necessary preparations should be made to facilitate the same. All stable implements, loose troughs and buckets should be removed, and clean bedding should be furnished. A bucket of warm water and sponge, and oil to lubricate the hand and arm before insertion, should be at hand, as well as a few flat and pliable light ropes, and such obstetrical instruments as may be required. A few strong hands, that may be necessary for assistance, should also be present. The mare should be haltered and held by an assistant. The hand and arm should be oiled, for the purpose of first emptying the rectum of possible contents, as should also the urinary bladder, by gentle compression or by the aid of a catheter. The hand and arm should then be washed, and it should be remembered that if finger rings are worn they should be removed before the hand is introduced into the genital parts; and if the finger-nails are long they should be shortened.

The complications or unnatural presentations are very various; but a few of the most common will be considered here, as the more complicated cases will require skilled veterinary assistance. The usual and proper presentation of the foal is with both fore legs first, and next, resting upon these, the head will appear. In such a case help is not called for, unless the colt be a very large one, or the mare small with a narrow pelvis, when a little assistance may be carefully given by gently drawing upon the legs after the head is well forward. But if there should appear only one fore leg, or one or both hind legs, or the head is presented without the legs, assistance should be rendered without delay. It is generally necessary in such cases to return the foal, but this should be done only between the throes of the mare, and with care not to injure the foal.

At other times the head will be found to be bent downward, with the occipit or top pressing firmly against the brim of the pelvis, and the feet only presented to our view. Here our object must be to pass the fœtus back until we can grasp the head, and should we be able to reach it, we will find a very convenient spot in the cavities of the orbits to place a finger and thumb, when, by a little exertion, the head may be brought into its proper place.

One of the most common forms of irregular presentation is the one in which both fore feet appear, with the head doubled back or to one side. Before returning the foal a flat or pliable rope should be fastened to each of the fore legs above the fetlocks. Pressure should then be made against the breast of the foal, and usually the head will then come into line, if the foal is pushed far enough in. The ropes on the feet are applied to secure them in case they should slip into a wrong position, and actual pulling, if any should become necessary after the foal is brought into position, should never be done by these ropes, but by the feet and the head, and not between the labor pains, but only when the mare herself helps.

Should the head be presented without the fore legs a slip-noose of soft cord should be applied around the lower jaw. The head should then be pushed inward as far as possible, and the feet, one by one, drawn forward into position and secured with soft rope, as above stated. The head should

DISEASES PECULIAR TO BREEDING STOCK. 331

then, by aid of the hand and partly by the rope, be secured and placed upon the fore legs, when gentle traction, not by the ropes, should be proceeded with as in the foregoing case. It will be useless to attempt to bring the foal forth with the head alone protruding, nor should the attempt be made, as the life of the colt will thus be endangered.

Again, we meet with what are termed breech presentations, where the tail only presents itself to our view, and the hind legs are doubled under the body; and these will be found to offer an insuperable obstacle to natural expulsion. The hand must be introduced, so as to fasten cords around each leg above the hocks, after which the fœtus must be passed as far back into the uterus as possible, to enable us to bring forward the feet, when the birth may be easily accomplished.

In the case where only one fore leg is presented, the other one extending inward, and the head pressed against the pelvic bone, the soft cord should be applied around the protruding leg; then the hand, armed with a soft slip-noose, should secure this around the lower jaw, after which pressure should be made against the breast and the foal pushed in so far as to allow the head to be placed in position by an assistant gently pulling on the rope attached around the jaw. Then the other fore leg is to be secured and brought forward, whereupon moderate traction may be made upon both legs and the head, but not by the ropes. If the expulsive pains of the mare are strong the tightly impacted state of the head will offer considerable difficulty in manipulation.

One of the most dreaded of all other cases is where the animal has been neglected and the fœtus is discovered to have been dead several hours. Putrefactive fermentation will be found to have taken place, an immense quantity of gas has diffused itself in the cellular tissue, and the fœtus has attained twice its natural size. The safest and almost only method to adopt in such cases will be to dissect the fœtus away; for although it may present itself in a natural position, we should not be warranted in having recourse to any means to endeavor to excite the uterus to contract upon its contents, as we invariably find that great prostration of strength and extreme debility have been produced by the frequent and powerful efforts of the animal to expel the fœtus.

There are various other unnatural presentations and causes in operation to prevent the natural process of parturition, as, for instance, dropsy or from the urachus being impervious, when the whole of the urine secreted by the young animal during the fœtal life would collect in its bladder and thus cause an immense enlargement of its abdomen; or, the fœtus may partake of the form of a *lusus naturæ*, where we have a redundancy or multiplicity of natural parts, as of two heads and one body, or *vice versa*, etc. A hard and unyielding (rigid) state of the neck of the uterus will also prevent labor. Should it proceed from spasmodic contraction of that part, as is sometimes the case, constant pressure by the hand will often relieve it and thus cause it to dilate; but if we cannot dilate it in this way the best method is to carefully divide it with a bistoury. Tumors in the vagina also are great obstacles to the passage of the fœtus, and it is frequently found necessary to dissect them away before delivery can be effected.

In all cases where we have preternatural presentation our object must be to endeavor to bring it as near to a natural one as possible. Whenever turning or altering the position of the young one must be had recourse to, it should be done, if possible, before the uterus has firmly contracted itself around the body or its contents; for it is always a circumstance which renders the operation infinitely more difficult and dangerous and not infrequently impracticable. The skilled veterinarian when called to attend in protracted cases very often finds the uterus strongly contracted around its contents and the operation so replete with difficulty and danger, both to the mother and the young, that he cannot hope for the preservation of them both, and perhaps turning has become impracticable. Some other expedient must then be resorted to and the young one destroyed to save the life of the mother. If the fœtus cannot be extracted by moderate force recourse must be had to embryotomy or removal by dismemberment, beheading, disemboweling, etc.

It will be useless to describe the more difficult presentations, as they will require for their safe delivery, where such is possible, a variety of instruments and appliances, with which, and their proper use, the breeder cannot be expected to be familiar. In all difficult cases the farmer or breeder will find it to his advantage to send without delay for a properly educated veterinary surgeon, who alone is capable, from his knowledge of the anatomy of the genital organs, of rendering efficient assistance in complicated and difficult cases. But it is to be regretted that the scarcity of this class of men is so great, wherefore much suffering and considerable loss must unavoidably be sustained.

LACERATION OF THE PERINÆUM.

To a mare to which such an accident has happened the queer name of a "gill-flirt" is vulgarly applied. The injury consists in a laceration of the membrane between the anus and the genital organs, caused by difficult parturition, especially in cases where the foal is very large and the labor pains excessively strong. Treatment by way of uniting the parts by sutures generally proves unsuccessful unless instituted immediately after the accident. When the laceration has not included the anal sphincter a partial healing sometimes occurs with surgical assistance. The condition does not unfit a mare for future breeding; but special care is required at the time of service to so direct the stallion (who should stand on higher ground than the mare if she is large) that the vagina proper, and not the rectum, be entered; that is, if the entire extent of the perinæum, including the anal sphincter, be lacerated. In this latter event there is also the unpleasant feature of the dung passing from the rectum into the vagina, making the voiding of the same to some extent difficult and more or less incomplete and offensive.

To the foregoing pages of this chapter by Dr. Paaren I may very properly add the following:

MANGE.

In cases where colts are troubled with mange a very prominent and extensive horse-breeder of my acquaintance has long made use of the following remedy with uniform good results: Take one gallon of linseed oil, one-half pound sulphur reduced to a fine powder, one-half pound common gunpowder, also powdered fine; mix thoroughly and apply to every part of the animal with a brush. Let it remain on three days, then wash off and renew for another three days, and so on until a cure is effected.

LICE ON COLTS.

For this troublesome pest the following is the remedy mainly relied upon by Dr. A. J. Murray: Take an ounce of common smoking tobacco and put into a gallon of water. Put this on the stove so as to make an infusion of it, as if one were making tea, and when this preparation has cooled sufficiently wash the animal's body with it and the lice will disappear. It sometimes happens that parts of the body are not wet with this infusion, so that some of the lice escape. When this happens the application of the tobacco must be repeated.

For the same trouble, Prof. Joseph Hughes of the Chicago Veterinary Medical College prescribes the following: Rub the infested parts thoroughly with a mixture of one part of kerosene and three of lard.

Dr. Paaren's prescription in such cases is as follows: Dissolve six drachms of borax in two quarts of warm water, and when cold add thereto two and one-half pints of acetic acid. Apply this solution twice weekly by means of a stiff brush.

CHAPTER V.

DISEASES OF THE GENERATIVE ORGANS.

[Prepared by Dr. James Law, F. R. C. V. S., Professor of Veterinary Science, etc., in Cornell University, for the report on "Diseases of the Horse," published by the United States Department of Agriculture. Reprinted by permission of the Chief of the Bureau of Animal Industry.]

CONGESTION AND INFLAMMATION OF THE TESTICLES—
ORCHITIS.

In the prime of life, in vigorous health, and on stimulating food stallions are subject to congestion of the testicles, which become swollen, hot, and tender, but without any active inflammation. A reduction of the grain in the feed, the administration of one or two ounces of Glauber salts daily in the food, and the bathing of the affected organs daily with tepid water or alum water will usually restore them to a healthy condition.

When the factors producing congestion are extraordinarily potent, when there has been frequent copulation and heavy grain feeding, when the weather is warm and the animal has had little exercise, and when the proximity of other horses or mares excite the generative instinct without gratification, this congestion may grow to actual inflammation. Among the other causes of orchitis are blows and penetrating wounds implicating the testicles, abrasions of the scrotum by a chain or rope passing inside the thigh, contusions and frictions on the gland under rapid paces or heavy draught, compressions of the blood-vessels of the spermatic cord by the inguinal ring under the same circumstances, and finally sympathetic disturbance in cases of disease of the kidneys, bladder, or urethra. Stimulants of the generative functions, like rue, savin, tansy, cantharides, and damiana, may also be accessory causes of congestion and inflammation. Finally, certain specific diseases like *mal du coit*, glanders, and tuberculosis, localized in the testicles, will cause inflammation. Apart from actual wounds of the parts the symptoms of orchitis are swelling, heat, and tenderness of the testicles, straddling with the hind legs alike in standing and walking, stiffness and dragging of the hind limbs or of the limb on the affected side, arching of the loins, abdominal pain, manifested by glancing back at the flank, with more or less fever, elevated body temperature, accelerated pulse and breathing, inappetence, and dullness. In bad cases the scanty urine may be reddish and the swelling may extend to the skin and envelopes of the testicle, which may become thickened and doughy, pitting on pressure. The swelling may be so much greater in the convoluted excretory duct along the upper border of the testicle as to suggest the presence of a second stone. Even in the more violent attacks the intense suffering abates somewhat on the second or third day. If it lasts longer it is likely to give rise to the formation of matter (abscess). In exceptional cases the testicle is struck with gangrene or death. Improvement may go on slowly to complete recovery, or the malady may subside into a subacute and chronic form with induration. Matter (abscess) may be recognized by the presence of a soft spot, where pressure with two fingers will detect fluctuation from one to the other. When there is liquid exudation into the scrotum, or sack, fluctuation may also be felt, but the liquid can be made out to be around the testicle and can be pressed up into the abdomen through the inguinal canal. When abscess occurs in the cord the matter may escape into the scrotal sack and cavity of the abdomen and pyæmia may follow.

Treatment consists in perfect rest and quietude, the administration of a purgative (one to one and one-half pounds of Glauber's salts) and the local application of an astringent

DISEASES OF THE GENERATIVE ORGANS. 337

lotion (acetate of lead two drachms, extract of belladonna two drachms, and water one quart) upon soft rags or cotton wool, kept in contact with the part by a suspensory bandage. This bandage, of great value for support, may be made nearly triangular and tied to a girth around the loins and to the upper part of the same surcingle by two bands carried backward and upward between the thighs. In severe cases scarifications one-fourth inch deep serve to relieve vascular tension. When abscess is threatened its formation may be favored by warm fomentations or poultices, and on the occurrence of fluctuation the knife may be employed to give free escape to the pus. The resulting cavity may be injected daily with a weak carbolic-acid lotion, or salol may be introduced. The same agents may be used on a gland threatened with gangrene, but its prompt removal by castration is to be preferred, antiseptics being applied freely to the resulting cavity.

SARCOCELE.

This is an enlarged and indurated condition of the gland resulting from chronic inflammation, though it is often associated with a specific deposit like glanders. In this condition the natural structure of the gland has given place to embryonal tissue (small, round cells, with a few fibrous bundles), and its restoration to health is very improbable. Apart from active inflammation, it may increase very slowly. The diseased testicle is enlarged, firm, non-elastic and comparatively insensible. The skin of the scrotum is tense, and it may be œdematous (pitting on pressure), as are the deeper envelopes and spermatic cord. If liquid is present in the sack the symptoms are masked somewhat. As it increases it causes an awkward, straddling, dragging movement of the hind limbs, or lameness on the affected side. The spermatic cord often increases at the same time with the testicle, and the inguinal ring being thereby stretched and enlarged a portion of intestine may escape into the sack, complicating the disease with hernia.

The only rational and effective treatment is castration, and even this may not succeed when the disease is specific (glanders, tuberculosis).

HYDROCELE—DROPSY OF THE SCROTUM.

This may be merely an accompaniment of dropsy of the abdomen, the cavity of which is continuous with that of the scrotum in horses. It may be the result, however, of local disease in the testicle, spermatic cord, or walls of the sack.

The *symptoms* are enlargement of the scrotum and fluctuation under the fingers, the testicle being recognized as floating in water. By pressure the liquid is forced in a slow stream and with a perceptible thrill into the abdomen. Sometimes the cord, or the scrotum, are thickened and pit on pressure.

Treatment may be the same as for ascites, yet when the effusion has resulted from inflammation of the testicle or cord, astringent applications (chalk and vinegar) may be applied to these. Then if the liquid is not reabsorbed under diuretics and tonics it may be drawn off through the nozzle of a hypodermic syringe which has been first passed through carbolic acid. In geldings it is best to dissect out the sacks.

VARICOCELE.

This is an enlargement of the venous network of the spermatic cord and gives rise to general thickening of the cord from the testicle up to the ring. The same astringent dressings may be tried as in hydrocele, and this failing castration may be resorted to.

ABNORMAL NUMBER OF TESTICLES.

Sometimes one or both testicles are wanting; in most such cases, however, they are merely partially developed and retained in the inguinal canal or the abdomen (cryptorchid). In rare cases there may be a third testicle, the animal becoming to this extent a double monster. Teeth, hair and other indications of a second fœtus have likewise been found in the testicle, or scrotum.

DEGENERATION OF THE TESTICLES.

The testicles may become the seat of fibrous, calcareous, fatty, cartilaginous, or cystic degeneration, for all of which the appropriate treatment is castration. They also become the seat of cancer, glanders, or tuberculosis, and castration is requisite, though with less hope of arresting the disease. Finally they may become infested with cystic tapeworms, or the armed round worm (*sclerostomum equinum*).

WARTS ON THE PENIS.

These are best removed by seizing them between the thumb and forefinger and twisting them off. Or they may be cut off with scissors and the roots cauterized with nitrate of silver.

DEGENERATION OF PENIS—PAPILLOMA, EPITHELIOMA.

The penis of the horse is subject to great cauliflower-like growths on its free end, which extend back into the substance of the organ, obstruct the passage of urine, and cause very fetid discharges. The only resort is to cut them off, together with whatever portion of the penis has become diseased and indurated. The operation, which should be performed by a veterinary surgeon, consists in cutting through the organ from its upper to its lower aspect, twisting or tying the two dorsal arteries and leaving the urethra longer by half an inch to one inch than the adjacent structures.

EXTRAVASATION OF BLOOD IN THE PENIS.

As the result of kicks, blows, or of forcible striking of the yard on the thighs of the mare which it has failed to enter, the penis may become the seat of effusion of blood from one or more ruptured blood vessels. This gives rise to a more or less extensive swelling on one or both sides, followed by some heat and inflammation, and on recovery a serious curving of the organ. The treatment in the early stages may be the application of lotions of alum or other astringents to limit the amount of effusion and favor absorption. The penis should be suspended in a sling.

PARALYSIS OF THE PENIS.

This results from blows and other injuries, and also in some cases from too frequent and exhausting service. The yard hangs from the sheath, flaccid, pendulous and often cold. The passage of urine occurs with lessened force, and especially without the final jets. In cases of local injury the inflammation should first be subdued by astringent and emollient lotions, and in all cases the system should be invigorated by nourishing diet, while thirty-grain doses of nux vomica are given twice a day. Finally, a weak current of electricity sent through the penis from just beneath the anus to the free portion of the yard, continued for ten or fifteen minutes and repeated daily, may prove successful.

SELF-ABUSE—MASTURBATION.

Some stallions acquire this vicious habit, stimulating the sexual instinct to the discharge of semen by rubbing the penis against the belly or between the fore limbs. The only remedy is a mechanical one, the fixing of a net under the penis in such fashion as will prevent the extension of the penis or so prick the organ as to compel the animal to desist through pain.

MAL DU COIT—DOURINE.

This is propagated, like syphilis, by the act of copulation and affects stallions and mares. It has been long known in Northern Africa, Arabia and Continental Europe. It was imported into Illinois in 1882 in a Percheron horse.

From one to ten days after copulation, or in stallions it may be after some weeks, there is irritation, swelling, and a livid redness of the external organs of generation, sometimes followed by the eruption of small blisters, one-fifth of an inch across, on the penis, the vulva, clitoris and vagina, and the subsequent rupture of these vesicles and the formation of ulcers or small open sores. Vesicles have not been noticed in this disease in the dry climate of Illinois. In the mare there is frequent contraction of the vulva, urination, and the discharge of a watery and later a thick viscid liquid of a whitish, yellowish, or reddish color, which collects on and soils the tail. The swelling of the vulva increases and decreases alternately, affecting one part more than another and giving a distorted appearance to the opening. The affection of the skin leads to the appearance of circular white spots, which may remain distinct or coalesce into extensive patches which persist for months. This with the soiled tail, red, swollen, puckered and distorted vulva, and an increasing weakness and paralysis of the hind limbs, serve to characterize the affection. The mare rarely breeds, but will take the male and thus propagate the disease. The disease winds up with great emaciation and stupidity, and death in four months to two years. In horses which serve few mares there may be only swelling of the sheath for a year, but with frequent copulation the progress is more rapid. The penis may be enlarged, shrunken, or distorted; the testicles are unusually pendant and may be enlarged or wasted and flabby; the skin, as in the mare, shows white spots and patches. Later the penis becomes partially paralyzed and hangs out of the sheath; swelling of the adjacent lymphatic glands (in the groin) and even of distant ones, and of the skin, appear, and the hind limbs become weak and unsteady. In some instances the glands under the jaw swell and a discharge flows from the nose as in glanders. In other cases the itching of the skin leads to gnawing and extensive sores. Weakness, emaciation and stupidity increase until death, in fatal cases, yet the sexual desire does not seem to fail. A stallion without sense to eat except when food was put into his mouth would still neigh and seek to follow mares. In mild cases an apparent recovery may ensue, and through such animals the disease is propagated to new localities to be roused into activity and extension under the stimulus of service. The diseased nerve centers are the seat of cryptogamic growths. (Thannhoffer.)

Treatment of the malady has proved eminently unsatisfactory. It belongs to the purely contagious diseases and should be stamped out by the remorseless slaughter or castration of every horse or mare that has had sexual congress with a diseased animal. A provision for Government indemnity for the animals so destroyed or castrated and a severe penalty for putting any such animal to breeding would serve as effectual accessory resorts.

CASTRATION OF STALLIONS.

This is usually done at one year old, but may be accomplished at a few weeks old at the expense of an imperfect development of the fore parts. The simplicity and safety of the operation are greatest in the young. The delay till two, three or four years old will secure a better development and carriage of the fore parts. The essential part of castration is the safe removal or destruction of the testicle and the arrest or prevention of bleeding from the spermatic artery found in the anterior part of the cord. Into the many methods of accomplishing this limited space forbids us to enter here, so that the method most commonly adopted, castration by clamps, will alone be noticed. The animal having been thrown on his left side and the right hind foot drawn up on the shoulder, the exposed scrotum, penis and sheath are washed with soap and water, any concretion of scrum being carefully removed from the bilocular cavity in the end of the penis. The left spermatic cord, just above the testicle, is now seized in the left hand, so as to render the skin tense over the stone, and the right hand, armed with the knife, makes an incision from before backward, about three-fourths of an inch from and parallel to the median line between the thighs, deep enough to expose the testicle and long enough to allow that organ to start out through the skin. At the moment of making this incision the left hand must grasp the cord very firmly, otherwise the sudden retraction of the testicle by the cremaster muscle may draw it out of the hand and upward through the canal and even into the abdomen. In a few seconds, when the struggle and retraction have ceased, the knife is inserted through the cord, between its anterior and posterior portions, and the latter, the one which the muscle retracts, is cut completely through. The testicle will now hang limp and there is no longer any tendency to retraction. It should be pulled down until it will no longer hang loose below the wound and the clamps applied around the still attached portion of the cord, close up to the skin. The clamps, which may be made of any tough wood, are grooved along the center of the surfaces opposed to each other, thereby fulfilling two important indications, (*a*) enabling the clamps to hold more securely and (*b*) providing for the application of an antiseptic to the cord. For this purpose a drachm of sulphate of copper may be mixed with an ounce of lard and pressed into the groove in the face of each clamp. In applying the clamp over the cord it should be drawn so close with pincers as to press out all blood from the compressed cord and destroy its vitality, and the cord applied upon the compressing clamps should be so hard-twined that it will not stretch later and slacken the hold. When the clamp has been fixed the testicle is cut off one-half to one inch below it, and the clamp may be left thus for twenty-four hours; then, by cutting the cord around one end of the clamp the latter may be opened and the stump liberated without any danger of bleeding. Should the stump hang out of the wound it should be pushed inside with the finger and left there. The wound should begin to discharge white matter on the second day in hot weather, or the third in cold, and from that time a good recovery may be expected.

CONDITIONS FAVORABLE TO SUCCESSFUL CASTRATION.

The young horse suffers less from castration than the old and very rarely perishes. Good health in the subject is all important. Castration should never be attempted during the prevalence of strangles, influenza, catarrhal fever, contagious pleurisy, bronchitis, pneumonia, purpura hæmorrhagica, or other specific disease, nor on subjects that have been kept in close, illy ventilated, filthy buildings, where the system is liable to have been charged with putrid bacteria or other products. Warm weather is to be preferred to cold, but the fly-time should be avoided or the flies kept at a distance by the application of a watery solution of tar, carbolic acid or camphor to the wound.

CASTRATION OF CRYPTORCHIDS (RIDGELINGS).

This is the removal of a testicle or testicles that have failed to descend into the scrotum, but have been detained in the inguinal canal or inside the abdomen. The manipulation requires an accurate anatomical knowledge of the parts, and special skill, experience, and manual dexterity, and cannot be made clear to the unprofessional mind in a short notice. It consists, however, in the discovery and removal of the missing gland by exploring through the natural channel (the inguinal canal), or, in case it is absent, through the inguinal ring or through an artificial opening made in front and above that channel between the abdominal muscles and the strong fascia on the inner side of the thigh (Poupart's ligament). Whatever method is used the skin, hands, and instruments should be rendered aseptic with a solution of murcuric chloride, 1 part; water, 2,000 parts (a carbolic-acid lotion for the instruments), and the spermatic cord is best torn through by the ecraseur. In many such cases, too, it is desirable to sew up the external wound and keep the animal still to favor healing of the wound by adhesion.

PAIN AFTER CASTRATION.

Some horses are pained and very restless for some hours after castration, and this may extend to cramps of the bowels and violent colic. This is best kept in check by carefully rubbing the patient dry when he rises from the operation and then leading him in hand for some time. If the pain still persists a dose of laudanum (one ounce for an adult) may be given.

BLEEDING AFTER CASTRATION.

Bleeding from the wound in the scrotum and from the little artery in the posterior portion of the spermatic cord always occurs, and in warm weather may appear to be quite free. It scarcely ever lasts, however, over fifteen minutes and is easily checked by dashing cold water against the parts.

Bleeding from the spermatic artery in the anterior part of the cord may be dangerous when due precaution has not been taken to prevent it. In such cases the stump of the cord should be sought for and the artery twisted with artery forceps or tied with a silk thread. If the stump cannot be found pledgets of tow wet with tincture of muriate of iron may be stuffed into the canal to favor the formation of clot and the closure of the artery.

STRANGULATED SPERMATIC CORD.

If in castration the cord is left too long, so as to hang out of the wound, the skin wound in contracting grasps and strangles it, preventing the free return of blood and causing a steadily advancing swelling. In addition the cord becomes adherent to the lips of the wound in the skin, whence it de-

DISEASES OF THE GENERATIVE ORGANS. 345

rives an increased supply of blood and is thereby stimulated to more rapid swelling. The subject walks stiffly, with straddling gait, loses appetite, and has a rapid pulse and high fever. Examination of the wound discloses the partial closure of the skin wound and the protrusion from its lips of the end of the cord—red, tense, and varying in size from a hazelnut upward. If there is no material swelling and little protrusion the wound may be enlarged with the knife and the end of the cord broken loose from any connection with the skin and pushed up inside. If the swelling is larger the mass constitutes a tumor and must be removed. (See below.)

SWELLING OF THE SHEATH, PENIS, AND ABDOMEN.

This occurs in certain unhealthy states of the system in unhealthy seasons, as the result of operating without cleansing the sheath and penis, or of keeping the subject in a filthy, impure building, as the result of infecting the wound by hands or instruments bearing septic bacteria, or as the result of premature closure of the wound and imprisonment of matter.

Pure air and cleanliness of groin and wound are to be secured. Antiseptics, like the mercuric chloride lotion (1 part to 2,000), are to be applied to the parts; the wound, if closed, is to be opened anew, any accumulated matter or blood washed out, and the antiseptic liquid freely applied. The most tense or dependent parts of the swelling in sheath or penis, or beneath the belly, should be pricked at intervals of three or four inches and to a depth of half an inch and antiseptics freely used to the surface. Fomentations with warm water may also be used to favor oozing from the incisions and to encourage the formation of white matter in the original wounds, which must not be allowed to close again at once. A free, cream-like discharge implies a healthy action in the sore, and is the precursor of recovery.

PHYMOSIS AND PARAPHYMOSIS.

In cases of swelling, as above, the penis may be imprisoned within the sheath (phymosis) or protruded and swollen so that it cannot be retracted into it (paraphymosis). In these cases the treatment indicated above, and especially the scarifications, will prove a useful preliminary resort. The use of astringent lotions is always desirable, and in case of the protruded penis the application of an elastic or simple linen bandage, so as to press out the blood and accumulated fluid, will enable the operator to return it.

TUMORS ON THE SPERMATIC CORD.

These are due to rough handling or dragging upon the cord in castration, to strangulation of unduly long cords in the external wound, to adhesion of the end of the cord to the skin, to inflammation of the cord succeeding exposure to cold or wet, or to the presence of septic or irritant matters. These tumors give rise to a stiff, straddling gait, and may be felt as hard masses in the groin connected above with the cord. They may continue to grow slowly for many years until they reach a weight of fifteen to twenty pounds and contract adhesions to all surrounding parts. If disconnected from the skin and inguinal canal they may be removed in the same manner as the testicle, while if larger and firmly adherent to the skin and surrounding parts generally they must be carefully dissected from the parts, the arteries being tied as they are reached and the cord finally torn through with an ecraseur. When the cord has become swollen and indurated up into the abdomen such removal is impossible, though a partial destruction of the mass may still be attempted by passing white-hot pointed irons upward toward the inguinal ring in the center of the thickened and indurated cord.

CASTRATION OF THE MARE.

Castration is a much more dangerous operation in the mare than in the females of other domesticated quadrupeds, and should never be resorted to except in animals that become unmanageable on the recurrence of heat and that will not breed, or that are utterly unsuited to breeding. Formerly the operation was extensively practiced in Europe, the incision being made through the flank and a large proportion of the subjects perishing. By operating through the vagina the risk can be largely obviated, as the danger of unhealthy inflammation in the wound is greatly lessened. The animal should be fixed in a trevis, with each foot fixed to a post and a sling placed under the body, or, better, it may be thrown and put under chloroform. The manual operation demands special professional knowledge and skill, but it consists essentially in making an opening through the roof of the vagina just above the neck of the womb, then following with the hand each horn of the womb until the ovary on that side is reached and grasped between the lips of the forceps and twisted off. It might be torn off by an ecraseur especially constructed for the purpose. The straining that follows the operation may be checked by ounce doses of laudanum, and any risk of protrusion of the bowels may be obviated by applying the truss advised to prevent eversion of the womb. To further prevent the pressure of the abdominal contents against the vaginal wound the mare should be tied short and high for twenty-four or forty-eight hours, after which I have found it best to remove the truss and allow the privilege of lying down. Another important point is to give bran mashes and other laxative diet only, and in moderate quantity, for a fortnight, and to unload the rectum by copious injections of warm water in case it should threaten to become impacted.

STERILITY.

Sterility may be in the male or in the female. If due to the stallion, then all the mares put to him remain barren; if due to the mare, she alone fails to conceive.

In the stallion sterility may be due to the following causes: (a) Imperfect development of the testicles, as in cases in which they are retained within the abdomen; (b) inflammation of the testicles, resulting in induration; (c) fatty degeneration of the testicles in stallions liberally fed on starchy food and not sufficiently exercised; (d) fatty degeneration of the excretory ducts of the testicles (*vasa deferentia*); (e) inflammation or ulceration of these ducts; (f) inflammation or ulceration of the mucous membrane covering the penis; (g) injuries to the penis from blows (often causing paralysis; (h) warty growths on the end of the penis; (i) tumors of other kinds (largely pigmentary) affecting the testicles or penis; (*j*) nervous diseases which abolish the sexual appetite or that control over the muscles which is essential to the act of coition; (*k*) azoturia with resulting weakness or paralysis of the muscles of the loins or the front of the thigh (above the stifle); (*l*) ossification (anchylosis) of the joints of the back or loins, which renders the animal unable to rear or mount; (*m*) spavins, ringbones, or other painful affections of the hind limbs, the pain of which in mounting causes the animal to suddenly stop short in the act. In the first three of these only (*a*, *b* and *c*) is there real sterility in the sense of the non-development or imperfect development of the male vivifying element (spermatozoa). In the other examples the secretion may be perfect in kind and amount, but as copulation is prevented it cannot reach and impregnate the ovum.

In the mare barrenness is equally due to a variety of causes. In a number of breeding studs the proportion of sterile mares has varied from 20 to 40 per cent. It may be due to: (*a*) Imperfect development of the ovary and non-maturation of ova; (*b*) cystic or other tumors of the ovary; (*c*) fatty degeneration of the ovary in very obese, pampered mares; (*d*) fatty degeneration of the excretory tubes of the ovaries (fallopian tubes); (*e*) catarrh of the womb, with muco-purulent discharge; (*f*) irritable condition of the womb, with profuse secretion, straining, and ejection of the semen; (*g*) nervous irritability, leading to the same expulsion of the male element; (*h*) high condition (plethora) with profuse secretion and excitement; (*i*) low condition with imperfect maturation of the ova and lack of sexual desire; (*j*) poor feeding, overwork and chronic debilitating diseases, as leading to the condition just named; (*k*) closure of the neck of the womb, temporarily by spasm or permanently by inflammation and induration; (*l*) closure of the entrance to the vagina through imperforate hymen, a rare though not unknown condition in the mare; (*m*) acquired indisposition to breed, seen in old, hard-worked mares, which are first put to the stallion when aged; (*n*) change of climate has repeatedly been followed by barrenness; (*o*)

DISEASES OF THE GENERATIVE ORGANS. 349

hybridity, which in male and female alike usually entails sterility.

The *treatment* of the majority of these conditions will be found dealt with in other parts of this work, so that it is only necessary here to name them as causes. Some, however, must be specially referred to in this place. Stallions with undescended testicles are beyond the reach of medicine and should be castrated and devoted to other uses. Indurated testicles may sometimes be remedied in the early stages by smearing with a weak iodine ointment daily for a length of time and at the same time invigorating the system by liberal feeding and judicious work. Fatty degeneration is best met by an albuminoid diet (wheat bran, cotton-seed meal, rape cake) and constant, well-regulated work. Saccharine, starchy and fatty food (potatoes, wheat, corn, etc.) are to be specially avoided. In the mare one diseased and irritable ovary should be removed to do away with the resulting excitability of the remainder of the generative organs. An irritable womb, with frequent straining and the ejection of a profuse secretion, may sometimes be corrected by a restricted diet and full but well-regulated work. Even fatigue will act beneficially in some such cases; hence the practice of the Arab riding his mare to exhaustion just before service The perspiration in such a case, like the action of a purgative or the abstraction of blood just before service, benefits by rendering the blood vessels less full, by lessening secretion in the womb and elsewhere, and thus counteracting the tendency to the ejection and loss of semen. If these means are ineffectual a full dose of camphor (two drachms) or of salacin may at times assist. Low condition and anæmia demands just the opposite kind of treatment—rich, nourishing, albuminoid food, bitter tonics (gentian), sunshine, gentle exercise, liberal grooming and supporting treatment generally are here in order. Spasmodic closure of the neck of the womb is common and is easily remedied in the mare by dilatation with the fingers.

The hand, smeared with belladonna ointment and with the fingers drawn into the form of a cone, is introduced through the vagina until the projecting, rounded neck of the womb is felt at its anterior end. This is opened by the careful insertion of one finger at a time until the fingers have been passed through the constricted neck into the open cavity of the womb. The introduction is made with a gentle, rotary motion, and all precipitate violence is avoided, as abrasion, laceration or other cause of irritation is likely to interfere with the retention of the semen and with impregnation. If the neck of the womb is rigid and unyielding from the induration which follows inflammation—a rare condition in the mare, though common in the cow—more force will be requisite, and it may even be needful to incise the neck to the depth of one-sixth of an inch in four or more opposite directions prior to forcible dilatation. The incision may be made with a probe-pointed knife, and should be done by a professional man if possible. The subsequent dilatation may be best effected by the slow expansion of sponge or seaweed tents inserted into the narrow canal. In such cases it is best to let the wounds of the neck heal before putting to horse. An imperforate hymen may be freely incised in a crucial manner until the passage will admit the human hand. An ordinary knife may be used for this purpose, and after the operation the stallion may be admitted at once or only after the wounds have healed.

INDICATIONS OF PREGNANCY.

As the mere fact of service by the stallion does not insure pregnancy it is important that the result should be determined, to save the mare from unnecessary and dangerous work or medication when actually in foal, and to obviate wasteful and needless precautions when she is not.

The cessation and non-recurrence of the symptoms of heat (horsing) is a most significant though not infallible sign of conception. If the sexual excitement speedily subsides and the mare persistently refuses the stallion for a month she is probably pregnant. In very exceptional cases a mare will accept a second or third service after weeks or months, though pregnant, and some mares will refuse the horse persistently, though conception has not taken place, and this in spite of warm weather, good condition of the mare, and lib-

DISEASES OF THE GENERATIVE ORGANS. 351

eral feeding. The recurrence of heat in the pregnant mare is most likely to take place in hot weather. If heat merely persists an undue length of time after service, or if it reappears shortly after, in warm weather and in a comparatively idle mare on good feeding, it is less significant, while the persistent absence of heat under such conditions may be usually accepted as proof of conception.

An unwonted gentleness and docility on the part of a previously irritable or vicious mare, and supervening on service, is an excellent indication of pregnancy, the generative instinct which caused the excitement having been satisfied.

An increase of fat, with softness and flabbiness of muscle, a loss of energy, indisposition for active work, a manifestation of laziness, indeed, and of fatigue early and easily induced, when preceded by service, will usually imply conception.

Enlargement of the abdomen, especially in its lower third, with slight falling in beneath the loins and hollowness of the back, are significant symptoms, though they may be entirely absent. Swelling and firmness of the udder, with the smoothing out of its wrinkles, is a suggestive sign, even though it appears only at intervals during gestation.

A steady increase in weight (one and one-half pounds daily) about the fourth or fifth month is a useful indication of pregnancy. So is a swollen and red or bluish-red appearance of the vaginal mucous membrane.

From the seventh or eighth month onward the foal may be felt by the hand (palm or knuckles) pressed into the abdomen in front of the left stifle. The sudden push displaces the foal toward the opposite side of the womb and as it floats back its hard body is felt to strike against the hand. If the pressure is maintained the movements of the live foal are felt, and especially in the morning and after a drink of cold water, or during feeding. A drink of cold water will often stimulate the fœtus to movements that may be seen by the eye, but an excess of iced water may prove injurious, even to the causing of abortion. Cold water dashed on the belly has a similar effect on the fœtus and equally endangers abortion.

Examination of the uterus with the oiled hand introduced

into the rectum is still more satisfactory, and if cautiously conducted no more dangerous. The rectum must be first emptied and then the hand carried forward until it reaches the front edge of the pelvic bones below, and pressed downward to ascertain the size and outline of the womb. In tne unimpregnated state the vagina and womb can be felt as a single rounded tube, dividing in front to two smaller tubes (the horns of the womb). In the pregnant mare not only the body of the womb is enlarged but still more so one of the horns (right or left), and on compression the latter is found to contain a hard, nodular body, floating in a liquid, which in the latter half of gestation may be stimulated by gentle pressure to manifest spontaneous movements. By this method the presence of the fœtus may be determined as early as the third month. If the complete natural outline of the virgin womb cannot be made out careful examination should always be made on the right and left side for the enlarged horn and its living contents. Should there still be difficulty the mare should be placed on an inclined plane, with her hind parts lowest, and two assistants, standing on opposite sides of the body, should raise the lower part of the abdomen by a sheet passed beneath it. Finally the ear or stethoscope applied on the wall of the abdomen in front of the stifle may detect the beating of the fœtal heart (125 per minute) and a blowing sound (the uterine sough), much less rapid and corresponding to the number of the pulse of the dam. It is heard most satisfactorily after the sixth or eighth month and in the absence of active rumbling of the bowels of the dam.

DURATION OF PREGNANCY.

Mares usually go about eleven months with young, though first pregnancies often last a year. Foals have lived when born at the three-hundredth day, so with others carried till the four-hundredth day. With the longer pregnancies there is a greater probability of male offspring.

HYGIENE OF THE PREGNANT MARE.

The pregnant mare should not be exposed to teasing by a young and ardent stallion, nor should she be overworked or fatigued, particularly under the saddle or on uneven ground.

DISEASES OF THE GENERATIVE ORGANS. 353

Yet exercise is beneficial to both mother and offspring, and in the absence of moderate work the breeding mare should be kept in a lot where she can take exercise at will.

The food should be liberal but not fattening, oats, bran, sound hay, and other foods rich in the principles which form flesh and bone being especially indicated. All aliments that tend to indigestion are to be especially avoided. Thus rank, aqueous, rapidly-grown grass and other green food, partially ripe rye grass, millet, Hungarian grass, vetches, peas, beans, or maize are objectionable, as is over-ripe, fibrous, innutritious hay, or that which has been injured and rendered musty by wet, or that which is infested with smut or ergot. Food that tends to costiveness should be avoided. Water given often, and at a temperature considerably above freezing, will avoid the dangers of indigestions and abortions which result from taking too much ice-cold water at one time. Very cold or frozen food is objectionable in the same sense. Severe surgical operations and medicines that act violently on the womb, bowels or kidneys are to be avoided as being liable to cause abortion. Constipation should be corrected if possible by bran mashes, carrots or beets, seconded by exercise, and if a medicinal laxative is required it should be olive oil or other equally bland agent.

The stall of the pregnant mare should not be too narrow so as to cramp her when lying down or to entail violent efforts in getting up, and it should not slope too much from the front backward as this throws the weight of the uterus back on the pelvis and endangers protrusions and even abortion. Violent mental impressions are to be avoided, for though the majority of mares are not affected thereby, yet a certain number are so profoundly impressed that peculiarities and distortions are entailed on the offspring. Hence there is wisdom shown in banishing parti-colored or objectionably tinted animals and those that show deformities or faulty conformation. Hence, too, the importance of preventing prolonged acute suffering by the pregnant mare, as certain troubles of the eyes, feet, and joints in the foals have been clearly traced to the concentration of the mother's mind on corresponding injured organs in herself. Sire and dam alike tend to reproduce their personal defects which predispose to disease, but the dam is far more likely to perpetuate the evil in her progeny which was carried while she was personally enduring severe suffering caused by such defects. Hence an active bone spavin or ringbone, causing lameness, is more objectionable than that in which the inflammation and lameness have both passed, and an active ophthalmia is more to be feared than even an old cataract. For this reason all active diseases in the breeding mare should be soothed and abated at as early a moment as possible.

EXTRA-UTERINE GESTATION.

It is rare in the domestic animals to find the fœtus developed elsewhere than in the womb. The exceptional forms are those in which the sperm of the male, making its way through the womb and Fallopian tubes, impregnates the ovum prior to its escape, and in which the now vitalized and growing ovum, by reason of its gradually increasing size, becomes imprisoned and fails to escape into the womb. The arrest of the ovum may be in the substance of the ovary itself (ovarian pregnancy), in the Fallopian tube (tubal pregnancy), or when by its continuous enlargement it has ruptured its envelopes so that it escapes into the cavity of the abdomen it may become attached to any part of the serous membrane and draw its nourishment directly from that (abdominal pregnancy). In all such cases there is an increase and enlargement of the capillary blood-vessels at the point to which the embryo has attached itself so as to furnish the needful nutriment for the growing offspring.

All appreciable symptoms are absent unless from the death of the fœtus or its interference with normal functions general disorder and indications of parturition supervene. If these occur later than the natural time for parturition they are the more significant. There may be general malaise, loss of appetite, elevated temperature, accelerated pulse, with or without distinct labor pains. Examination with the oiled hand in the rectum will reveal the womb of the natural unimpregnated size and shape and with both horns of one size. Further exploration may detect an elastic mass apart

DISEASES OF THE GENERATIVE ORGANS. 355

from the womb and in the interior of which may be felt the characteristic solid body of the fœtus. If the latter is still alive and can be stimulated to move the evidence is even more perfect. The fœtus may die and be carried for years, its soft structures becoming absorbed so as to leave only the bones, or by pressure it may form a fistulous opening through the vagina or rectum. In the latter cases the best course is to favor the expulsion of the foal and to wash out the resulting cavity with a solution of carbolic acid one part to water fifty parts. This may be repeated daily. Where there is no spontaneous opening it is injudicious to interfere, as the danger from the retention of the fœtus is less than that from septic fermentations in the enormous fœtal sack when that has been opened to the air.

MOLES—ANIDIAN MONSTERS.

These are evidently products of conception in which the impregnated ovum has failed to develop naturally and presents only a chaotic mass of skin, hair, bones, muscles, etc., attached to the inner surface of the womb by an umbilical cord which is itself often shriveled and wasted. They are usually accompanied by a well-developed fœtus, so that the mole may be looked upon as a twin which has undergone arrest and vitiation of development. They are expelled by the ordinary process of parturition, and usually, at the same time, with the normally developed offspring.

CYSTIC DISEASE OF THE WALLS OF THE WOMB— VESICULAR MOLE.

This condition appears to be due to hypertrophy (enlargement) of the villi on the inner surface of the womb, which become greatly increased in number and hollowed out internally into a series of cysts or pouches containing liquid. Unlike the true mole, therefore, they appear to be disease of the maternal structure of the womb rather than of the product of conception. Rodet, in a case of this kind which had produced active labor pains, quieted the disorder with anodynes and secured a recovery. Where this is not available attempts may be made to remove the mass with the ecraseur or otherwise, following this up with antiseptic injections, as advised under the last heading.

DROPSY OF THE WOMB.

This appears as a result of some disease of the walls of the womb, but has been frequently observed after sexual congress, and has therefore been confounded with pregnancy. The symptoms are those of pregnancy, but without any movements of the fœtus and without the detection of any solid body in the womb when examined with the oiled hand in the rectum. At the end of four or eight months there are signs of parturition or of frequent straining to pass urine, and after a time the liquid is discharged clear and watery, or muddy, thick and fetid. The hand introduced into the womb can detect neither fœtus nor fœtal membrane. If the neck of the womb closes the liquid may accumulate a second time, or even a third, if no means are taken to correct the tendency. The best resort is to remove any diseased product that may be found attached to the walls of the womb and to inject it daily with a warm solution of carbolic acid two drachms, chloride of zinc one-half drachm, water, one quart. A course of bitter tonics, gentian two drachms, sulphate of iron two drachms, daily, should be given, and a nutritious, easily digested and slightly laxative diet allowed.

DROPSY OF THE AMNIOS.

This differs from simple dropsy of the womb in that the fluid collects in the inner of the two water bags (that in which the foal floats) and not in the otherwise void cavity of the womb. This affection can occur only in the pregnant animal, while dropsy of the womb occurs in the unimpregnated. The blood of the pregnant mare contains an excess of water and a smaller proportion of albumen and red globules, and when this is still further aggravated by poor feeding and other unhygienic conditions there is developed the tendency to liquid transudation from the vessels and dropsy. As the watery condition of the blood increases with advancing pregnancy, so dropsy of the amnios is a disease of the last four or five months of gestation. The abdomen is large

DISEASES OF THE GENERATIVE ORGANS. 357

and pendulous and the swelling fluctuates under pressure, though the solid body of the fœtus can still be felt to strike against the hand pressed into the swelling. If the hand is introduced into the vagina the wound is found to be tense and round, with the projecting rounded neck effaced, while the hand in the rectum will detect the rounded swollen mass of the womb so firm and tense that the body of the fœtus cannot be felt within it. The mare moves weakly and unsteadily on its limbs, having difficulty in supporting the great weight, and in bad cases there may be loss of appetite, stocking (dropsy) of the hind limbs, difficult breathing, and colicky pains. The tension may lead to abortion, or a slow, laborious parturition may occur at the usual time.

Treatment consists in relieving the tension and accumulation by puncturing the fœtal membrane with a canula and trocar introduced through the neck of the womb and the withdrawal of the trocar so as to leave the canula *in situ*. Or the membranes may be punctured with the finger and the excess of liquid allowed to escape. This may bring on abortion, or the wound may close and gestation continue to the full term. A course of tonics (gentian root two drachms, sulphate of iron two drachms, daily) will do much to fortify the system and counteract further excessive effusion.

DROPSY OF THE LIMBS, PERINÆUM, AND ABDOMEN.

The disposition to dropsy often shows itself in the hind and even in the fore limbs, around and beneath the vulva (perinæum) and beneath the abdomen and chest. The affected parts are swollen and pit on pressure, but are not especially tender and subside more or less perfectly under exercise, hand-rubbing and bandages. In obstinate cases rubbing with the following liniment may be resorted to: Compound tincture of iodine, two ounces; tannic acid, one-half drachm; water, ten ounces. It does not last over a day or two after parturition.

CRAMPS OF THE HIND LIMBS.

The pressure of the distended womb on the nerves and blood-vessels of the pelvis besides conducing to dropsy occasionally causes cramps of the hind limbs. The limb is raised without flexing the joints, the front of the hoof being directed toward the ground, or the spasms occurring intermittently the foot is kicked violently against the ground several times in rapid succession. The muscles are felt to be firm and rigid. The cramps may be promptly relieved by active rubbing or by walking the animal about, and it does not reappear after parturition.

CONSTIPATION.

This may result from compression by the gravid womb and is best corrected by a graduated allowance of boiled flaxseed.

PARALYSIS.

The pressure on the nerves of the pelvis is liable to cause paralysis of the hind limbs, or in the mare of the nerve of sight. These are obstinate until after parturition, when they recover spontaneously or under a course of nux vomica and (locally) stimulating liniments.

PROLONGED RETENTION OF THE FŒTUS (FOAL).

In the mare, though far less frequently than in the cow, parturition may not be completed at term, and the foal may continue to be carried in the womb for a number of months, to the serious or even fatal injury of the mare. Hamon records one case in which the mare died after carrying the fœtus for seventeen months, and Caillier a similar result after it had been carried twenty-two months. In these cases the fœtus retained its natural form, but in one reported by Gohier the bones only were left in the womb amid a mass of apparently purulent matter.

The *cause* may be any effective obstruction to the act of parturition, such as lack of contractile power in the womb, unduly strong (inflammatory) adhesions between the womb and the fœtal membranes, wrong presentation of the fœtus, contracted pelvis (from fracture, or disease of the bones), or disease and induration of the neck of the womb.

The mere prolongation of gestation does not necessarily entail the death of the foal; hence the latter has been born alive at the four-hundredth day. Even when the foal has

DISEASES OF THE GENERATIVE ORGANS. 359

perished putrefaction does not set in unless the membranes (water bags) have been ruptured and septic bacteria have been admitted to the interior of the womb. In the latter case a fetid decomposition advances rapidly and the mare usually perishes from poisoning with the putrid matters absorbed.

At the natural period of parturition preparations are apparently made for that act. The vulva swells and discharges much mucus, the udder enlarges, the belly becomes more pendant, and the animal strains more or less. No progress is made, however; there is not even opening of the neck of the womb, and after a time the symptoms subside. The mare usually refuses the male, yet there are exceptions to this rule. If the neck of the womb has been opened and putrefying changes have set in in its contents the mare loses appetite and condition, pines, discharges an offensive matter from the generative passages, and dies of inflammation of the womb and putrid infection. In other cases there is a slow wearing out of the strength and the mare finally dies of exhaustion.

The treatment is such as will facilitate the expulsion of the foetus and its membranes and the subsequent washing out of the womb with disinfectants. So long as the mouth of the womb is closed time should be allowed for its natural dilatation, but if this does not come about after a day or two of straining the opening may be smeared with extract of belladonna, and the oiled hand, with the fingers and thumb drawn into the form of a cone, may be inserted by slow oscillating movements into the interior of the womb. The water bags may now be ruptured, any malpresentation rectified (see "Difficult Parturition") and delivery effected. After removal of the membranes wash out the womb first with tepid water and then with a solution of two ounces of borax in half a gallon of water.

This injection may have to be repeated if a discharge sets in. The same course may be pursued even after prolonged retention. If the soft parts of the foetus have been absorbed and the bones only left these must be carefully sought for and removed, and subsequent daily injections will be required for some time. In such cases, too, a course of iron tonics (sulphate of iron, two drachms daily) will be highly beneficial in restoring health and vigor.

ABORTION.

Abortion is, strictly speaking, the expulsion of the impregnated ovum at any period from the date of impregnation until the foal can survive out of the womb. If the foal is advanced enough to live it is *premature parturition*, and in the mare this may occur as early as the tenth month (three-hundredth day).

The mare may abort by reason of almost any cause that very profoundly disturbs the system. Hence very violent inflammations of important internal organs (bowels, kidneys, bladder, lungs) may induce abortion. Profuse diarrhœa, whether occurring from the reckless use of purgatives, the consumption of irritants in the food, or a simple indigestion, is an effective cause. No less so is acute indigestion with evolution of gas in the intestines (bloating). The presence of stone in the kidneys, ureters, bladder, or urethra may induce so much sympathetic disorder in the womb as to induce abortion. In exceptional cases wherein mares come in heat during gestation service by the stallion may cause abortion. Blows or pressure on the abdomen, rapid driving or riding of the pregnant mare, especially if she is soft and out of condition from idleness; the brutal use of the spur or whip, and the jolting and straining of travel by rail or boat are prolific causes. Bleeding the pregnant mare, a painful surgical operation, and the throwing and constraint resorted to for an operation are other causes. Traveling on heavy, muddy roads, slips and falls on ice, and jumping must be added. The stimulation of the abdominal organs by a full drink of iced water may precipitate a miscarriage, as may exposure to a cold rain-storm or a very cold night after a warm day. Irritant poisons that act on the urinary or generative organs, such as Spanish flies, rue, savin, tansy, cotton-root bark, ergot of rye or other grasses, the smut of maize and other grain, and various fungi in musty fodder are additional causes. Frosted food, indigestible food, and above all green succulent

DISEASES OF THE GENERATIVE ORGANS. 361

vegetables in a frozen state have proved effective factors, and filthy, stagnant water is dangerous. Low condition in the dam and plethora have in opposite ways caused abortion, and hot relaxing stables and lack of exercise strongly conduce to it. The exhaustion of the sire by too frequent service, entailing debility of the offspring and disease of the fœtus or of its envelopes, must be recognized as a further cause.

The symptoms vary mainly according as the abortion is early or late in pregnancy. In the first month or two of pregnancy the mare may miscarry without observable symptoms and the fact only appear by her coming in heat. If more closely observed a small clot of blood may be found behind her, in which a careful search reveals the rudiments of the foal. If the occurrence is somewhat later in gestation there will be some general disturbance, inappetence, neighing, and straining, and the small body of the fœtus is expelled enveloped in its membranes. Abortions during the later stages of pregnancy are attended with greater constitutional disturbance and the process resembles normal parturition, with the aggravation that more effort and straining is requisite to force the fœtus through the comparatively undilatable mouth of the womb. There is the swelling of the vulva, with mucus or even bloody discharge; the abdomen droops, the flanks fall in, the udder fills, the mare looks at her flanks, paws with the fore feet and kicks with the hind, switches the tail, moves around uneasily, lies down and rises, strains, and, as in natural foaling, expels first mucus and blood, then the waters, and finally the fœtus. This may occupy an hour or two, or it may be prolonged for a day or more, the symptoms subsiding for a time, only to reappear with renewed energy. If there is malpresentation of the fœtus it will hinder progress until rectified, as in difficult parturition. Abortion may also be followed by the same accidents, as flooding, retention of the placenta and leucorrhæa.

The most important object in an impending abortion is to recognize it at as early a stage as possible, so that it may be if possible cut short and prevented. Any general indefinable illness in a pregnant mare should lead to a close examination of the vulva as regards swelling, vascularity of its mucous membrane and profuse mucous secretion, and above all any streak or staining of blood; also the condition of the udder, if that is congested and swollen. Any such indication, with colicky pains, straining, however little, and active movement of the fœtus or entire absence of movement, are suggestive symptoms and should be duly counteracted.

The changes in the vulva and udder, with a soiled and bloody condition of the tail, may suggest an abortion already accomplished, and the examination with the hand in the vagina may detect the mouth of the womb soft and dilatable and the interior of the organ slightly filled with a bloody liquid.

Treatment should be preventive if possible, and would embrace the avoidance of all causes mentioned, and particularly of such as may seem to be particularly operative in the particular case. Where abortions have already occurred in a stud, the especial cause in the matter of food, water, exposure to injuries, overwork, lack of exercise, etc., may often be identified and removed. A most important point is to avoid all causes of constipation, diarrhœa, indigestion, bloating, violent purgatives, diuretics or other potent medicines, painful operations and slippery roads, unless well frosted.

When abortion is imminent the mare should be placed alone in a roomy, dark, quiet stall, and have the straining checked by some sedative. Laudanum is usually at hand and may be given in doses of one or two ounces, according to size, and repeated after two or three hours, and even daily if necessary. Chloroform or chloral hydrate, three drachms, may be substituted if more convenient. These should be given in a pint or quart of water to avoid burning the mouth and throat. Or viburnum prunifolium, one ounce, may be given and repeated if necessary to prevent straining.

When all measures fail and miscarriage proceeds, all that can be done is to assist in the removal of the fœtus and its membranes as in ordinary parturition. As in the case of retention of the fœtus, it may be necessary after delivery to employ antiseptic injections into the womb to counteract

DISEASES OF THE GENERATIVE ORGANS. 363

putrid fermentation. This, however, is less requisite in the mare than in the cow, in which the prevalent contagious abortion must be counteracted by the persistent local use of antiseptics. After abortion a careful hygiene is demanded, especially in the matter of pure air and easily digestible food. The mare should not be served again for a month or longer, and in no case until after all discharge from the vulva has ceased.

SYMPTOMS OF PARTURITION.

As the period of parturition approaches the swelling of the udder bespeaks the coming event, the engorgement in exceptional cases extending forward on the lower surface of the abdomen and even into the hind limbs. For about a week a serous fluid oozes from the teat and concretes as a yellow, wax-like mass around its orifice. About twenty-four hours before the birth this gives place to a whitish, milky liquid, which falls upon and mats the hairs on the inner sides of the legs. Another symptom is enlargement of the vulva, with redness of its lining membrane and the escape of glairy mucus. The belly droops, the flanks fall in, and the loins may even become depressed. Finally the mare becomes uneasy, stops feeding, looks anxious, whisks her tail, and may lie down and rise again. In many mares this is not repeated, but the mare remains down; violent contractions of the abdominal muscles ensue; after two or three pains the waterbags appear and burst, followed by the fore feet of the foal, with the nose between the knees, and by a few more throes the fœtus is expelled. In other cases the act is accomplished standing. The whole act may not occupy more than five or ten minutes. This, together with the disposition of the mare to avoid observation, renders the act one that is rarely seen by the attendants

The navel string, which connects the foal to the membranes, is ruptured when the fœtus falls to the ground, or when the mare rises, if she has been down, and the membranes are expelled a few minutes later.

NATURAL PRESENTATION.

When there is a single foal the common and desirable presentation is with the fore feet first, the nose between the knees, and with the front of the hoofs and knees and the forehead directed upward toward the anus, tail and croup. (Plate IX, Fig. 1.) In this way the natural curvature of the body of the fœtus corresponds to the curve of the womb and genital passages, and particularly of the bony pelvis, and the foal passes with much greater ease than if it were placed with its back downward toward the udder. When there is a twin birth the second foal usually comes with its hind feet first, and the backs of the legs, the points of the hocks and the tail and croup are turned upward toward the anus and tail of the mare. (Plate IX, Fig. 2.) In this way, even with a posterior presentation, the curvature of the body of the foal still corresponds to that of the passages, and its expulsion may be quite as easy as in anterior presentation. Any presentation aside from these two may be said to be abnormal and will be considered under "Difficult Parturition."

DIFFICULT PARTURITION.

With natural presentation this is a rare occurrence. The great length of the fore limbs and face entail in the anterior presentation the formation of a long cone, which dilates and glides through the passages with comparative ease. Even with the hind feet first a similar conical form is presented and the process is rendered easy and quick. Difficulty and danger arise mainly from the act being brought on prematurely before the passages are sufficiently dilated, from narrowing of the pelvic bones or other mechanical obstruction in the passages, from monstrous distortions or duplications in the fœtus, or from the turning back of one of the members so that the elongated conical or wedge-shaped outline is done away with. But prompt as is the normal parturition in the mare, difficult and delayed parturitions are surrounded by special dangers and require unusual precautions and skill. From the proclivity of the mare to unhealthy inflammations of the peritoneum and other abdominal organs, penetrating wounds of the womb or vagina are liable to prove fatal. The

DISEASES OF THE GENERATIVE ORGANS. 365

contractions of the womb and abdominal walls are so powerful as to exhaust and benumb the arm of the assistant and to endanger penetrating wounds of the genital organs. By reason of the looser connection of the fœtal membranes with the womb, as compared with those of ruminants, the violent throes early detach these membranes throughout their whole extent, and the foal, being thus separated from the mother and thrown on its own resources, dies at an early stage of any protracted parturition. The foal rarely survives four hours after the onset of parturient throes. From the great length of the limbs and neck of the foal it is extremely difficult to secure and bring up limb or head which has been turned back when it should have been presented. When assistance must be rendered the operator should don a thick woolen undershirt with the sleeves cut out at the shoulders. This protects the body and leaves the whole arm free for manipulation. Before inserting the arm it should be smeared with lard. This protects the skin against septic infection and favors the introduction of the hand and arm. The hand should be inserted with the thumb and fingers drawn together like a cone. Whether standing or lying the mare should be turned with head down hill and hind parts raised as much as possible. The contents of the abdomen gravitating forward leave much more room for manipulation. Whatever part of the foal is presented (head, foot) should be secured with a cord and running noose before it is pushed back to search for the other missing parts. Even if a missing part is reached no attempt should be made to bring it up during a labor pain. Pinching the back will sometimes check the pains and allow the operator to secure and bring up the missing member. In intractable cases a large dose of chloral hydrate (one ounce in a quart of water) or the inhalation of chloroform and air (equal proportions) to insensibility may secure a respite, during which the missing members may be replaced. If the *waters* have been discharged and the mucus dried up the genital passages and the body of the fœtus should be lubricated with lard or oil before any attempt at extraction is made. When the missing member has been brought up into position, and presentation has been rendered natural, traction on the fœtus must be made only during a labor pain. If a mare is inclined to kick it may be necessary to apply hobbles to protect the operator.

PREMATURE LABOR PAINS.

These may be brought on by any violent exertion, use under the saddle, or in heavy draft, or in rapid paces, or in travel by rail or sea, blows, kicks, crushing by other animals in a doorway or gate. Excessive action of purgative or diuretic agents, or of agents that irritate the bowels or kidneys, like arsenic, Paris green, all caustic salts and acids, and acrid and narcotico-acrid vegetables, are equally injurious. Finally the ingestion of agents that stimulate the action of the gravid womb (ergot of rye or of other grasses, smut, various fungi of fodders, rue, savin, cotton-root, etc.) may bring on labor pains prematurely.

Besides the knowledge that parturition is not yet due, there will be less enlargement, redness and swelling of the vulva, less mucous discharge, less filling of the udder, and less appearances of wax and probably none of milk from the ends of the teats. The oiled hand introduced into the vulva will not enter with the ease usual at full term, and the neck of the womb will be felt not only closed, but with its projecting papillæ, through which it is perforated, not yet flattened down and effaced, as at full term. The symptoms are indeed those of threatened abortion, but at such an advanced stage of gestation as is compatible with the survival of the offspring.

The *treatment* consists in the separation of the mare from all other animals in a quiet, dark, secluded place, and the free use of anti-spasmodics and anodynes. Opium in drachm doses every two hours, or laudanum in ounce doses at similar intervals, will often suffice. When the more urgent symptoms have subsided these doses may be repeated thrice a day till all excitement passes off or until the passages have become relaxed and prepared for parturition. Viburnum prunifolium, in ounce doses, may be added if necessary. Should parturition become inevitable it may be favored and any necessary assistance furnished.

DISEASES OF THE GENERATIVE ORGANS. 367

DIFFICULT PARTURITION FROM NARROW PELVIS.

A disproportion between the fœtus got by a large stallion and the pelvis of a small dam is a serious obstacle to parturition sometimes seen in the mare. This is not the rule, however, as the foal up to birth usually accommodates itself to the size of the dam, as illustrated in the successful crossing of Percheron stallions on mustang mares. If the disproportion is too great the only resort is embryotomy.

FRACTURED HIP-BONES.

More commonly the obstruction comes from distortion and narrowing of the pelvis as the result of fractures. (Plate XIV, Fig. 2.) Fractures at any point of the lateral wall or floor of the pelvis are repaired with the formation of an extensive bony deposit bulging into the passage of the pelvis. The displacement of the ends of the broken bone is another cause of constriction, and between the two conditions the passage of the fœtus may be rendered impossible without embryotomy. Fracture of the sacrum (the continuation of the backbone forming the croup) leads to the depression of the posterior part of that bone in the roof of the pelvis and the narrowing of the passage from above downward by a bony ridge presenting its sharp edge forward.

In all cases in which there has been injury to the bones of the pelvis the obvious precaution is to withhold the mare from breeding and to use her for work only.

If a mare with a pelvis thus narrowed has got in foal inadvertently abortion may be induced in the early months of gestation by slowly introducing the oiled finger through the neck of the womb and following this by the other fingers until the whole hand has been introduced. Then the waterbags may be broken and with the escape of the liquid the womb will contract on the solid fœtus and labor pains will ensue. The fœtus being small it will pass easily.

TUMORS IN THE VAGINA AND PELVIS.

Tumors of various kinds may form in the vagina or elsewhere within the pelvis, and when large enough will obstruct or prevent the passage of the fœtus. Gray mares, which are so subject to black pigment tumors (*melanosis*) on the tail, anus, and vulva, are the most likely to suffer from this. Still more rarely the wall of the vagina becomes relaxed, and being pressed by a mass of intestines will protrude through the lips of the vulva as a hernial sac, containing a part of the bowels. Where a tumor is small it may only retard and not absolutely prevent parturition. A hernial protrusion of the wall of the vagina may be pressed back and emptied so that the body of the fœtus engaging in the passage may find no further obstacle. When a tumor is too large to allow delivery the only resort is to remove it, but before proceeding it must be clearly made out that the obstruction is a mass of diseased tissue, and not a sac containing intestines. If the tumor hangs by a neck it can usually be most safely removed by the ecraseur, the chain being passed around the pedicle and gradually tightened until that is torn through.

HERNIA OF THE WOMB.

The rupture of the musculo-fibrous floor of the belly and the escape of the gravid womb into a sac formed by the peritoneum and skin hanging towards the ground is described by all veterinary obstetricians, yet it is very rarely seen in the mare. The form of the fœtus can be felt through the walls of the sac, so that it is easy to recognize the condition. Its cause is usually external violence, though it may start from an umbilical hernia. When the period of parturition arrives the first effort should be to return the fœtus within the proper abdominal cavity, and this can sometimes be accomplished with the aid of a stout blanket gradually tightened around the belly. This failing, the mare may be placed on her side or back and gravitation brought to the aid of manipulation in securing the return. Even after the hernia has been reduced the relaxed state of the womb and abdominal walls may serve to hinder parturition, in which case the oiled hand must be introduced through the vagina, the fœtus brought into position, and traction coincident with the labor pains employed to secure delivery.

TWISTING OF THE NECK OF THE WOMB.

This condition is very uncommon in the mare, though occasionally seen in the cow, owing to the greater laxity of the broad ligaments of the womb in that animal. It consists in a revolution of the womb on its own axis, so that its right or left side will be turned upward (quarter'revolution), or the lower surface may be turned upward and the upper surface downward (half revolution). The effect is to throw the narrow neck of the womb into a series of spiral folds, turning in the direction in which the womb has revolved, closing the neck and rendering distention and dilatation impossible.

The period and pains of parturition arrive, but in spite of continued efforts no progress is made, neither water-bags nor liquids appearing. The oiled hand introduced into the closed neck of the womb will readily detect the spiral direction of the folds on its inner surface.

The method of relief which I have successfully adopted in the cow may be equally happy in the mare. The dam is placed (with her head up-hill) on her right side if the upper folds of the spiral turn toward the right, and on her left side if they turn toward the left; and the oiled hand is introduced through the neck of the womb and a limb or other part of the body of the foetus is seized and pressed against the wall of the womb, while two or three assistants turn the animal over her back toward the other side. The object is to keep the womb stationary while the animal is rolling. If success attends the effort the constriction around the arm is suddenly relaxed, the spiral folds are effaced, and the water-bags and foetus press forward into the passage. If the first attempt does not succeed it may be repeated again and again until success crowns the effort. Among my occasional causes of failure have been the prior death and decomposition of the foetus, with the extrication of gas and overdistention of the womb, and the supervention of inflammation and inflammatory exudation around the neck of the womb, which hinders untwisting. The first of these conditions occurs early in the horse from the detachment of the foetal membranes from the wall of the womb, and as the mare is more subject to fatal peritonitis than the cow it may be concluded that both these sources of failure are more probable in the equine subject.

When the case is intractable, though the hand may be easily introduced, the instrument shown in Plate VIII, Fig. 7, may be used. Each hole at the small end of the instrument has passed through it a stout cord with a running noose, to be passed around two feet or other portion of the fœtus which it may be possible to reach. The cords are then drawn tight and fixed around the handle of the instrument; then by using the cross-handle as a lever the fœtus and womb may be rotated in a direction opposite to that causing the obstruction. During this process the hand must be introduced to feel when the twist has been undone. This method may be supplemented, if necessary, by rolling the mare as described above.

EFFUSION OF BLOOD IN THE VAGINAL WALLS.

This is common as a result of difficult parturition, but it may occur from local injury before that act and may seriously interfere with it. This condition is easily recognized by the soft, doughy swelling so characteristic of blood clots, and by the dark-red color of the mucous membrane. I have laid open such swellings with the knife as late as ten days before parturition, evacuated the clots, and dressed the wound daily with an astringent lotion (sulphate of zinc one drachm, carbolic acid one drachm, water one quart). A similar resort might be had, if necessary, during parturition.

CALCULUS (STONE) AND TUMOR IN THE BLADDER.

The pressure upon the bladder containing a stone or a tumor may prove so painful that the mare will voluntarily suppress the labor pains. Examination of the bladder with the finger introduced through the urethra will detect the offending agent. A stone should be extracted with forceps (see "Lithotomy"). The large papillary tumors which I have met with in the mare's bladder have been invariably delicate in texture and could be removed piecemeal by forceps. Fortunately mares affected in this way rarely breed.

PLATE VIII.

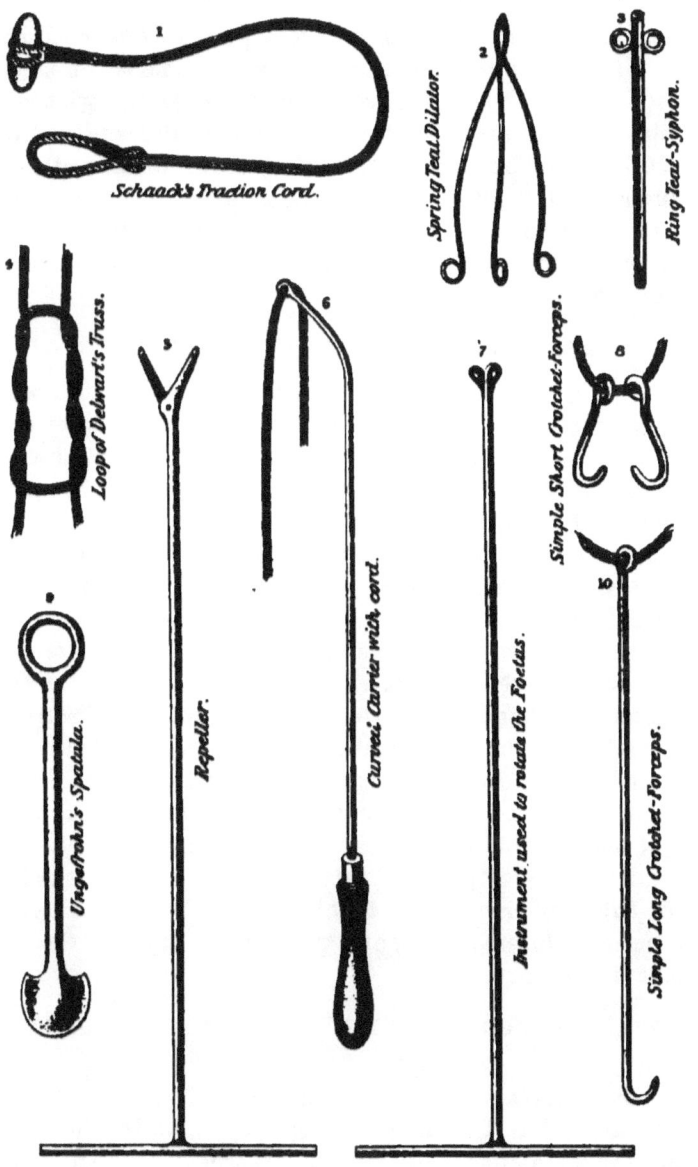

INSTRUMENTS USED IN DIFFICULT LABOR.

IMPACTION OF THE RECTUM WITH FÆCES.

In some animals, with more or less paralysis or weakness of the tail and rectum, the rectum may become so impacted with solid fæces that the mare is unable to discharge them, and the accumulation both by reason of the mechanical obstruction and the pain caused by pressure upon it will impel the animal to cut short all labor pains. The rounded swelling surrounding the anus will at once suggest the condition, when the obstruction may be removed by the well-oiled or soaped hand.

SPASM OF THE NECK OF THE WOMB.

This occurs in the mare of specially excitable temperament, or under particular causes of irritation, local or general. Labor pains, though continuing for some time, produce no dilatation of the neck of the womb, which will be found firmly closed so as to admit but one or two fingers, and this, although the projection at the mouth of the womb may have been entirely effaced, so that a simple round opening is left with rigid margins.

The simplest *treatment* consists in smearing this part with solid extract of belladonna, and after an interval inserting the hand with fingers and thumb drawn into the form of a cone, rupturing the membranes and bringing the fœtus into position for extraction, as advised under "Prolonged Retention of the Fœtus." Another mode is to insert through the neck of the womb an ovoid caoutchouc bag, empty, and furnished with an elastic tube twelve feet long. Carry the free end of this tube upward to a height of eight, ten or twelve feet, insert a filler into it, and proceed to distend the bag with tepid or warm water.

FIBROUS BANDS CONSTRICTING OR CROSSING THE NECK OF THE WOMB.

These occurring as the result of disease have been several times observed in the mare. They may exist in the cavity of the abdomen and compress and obstruct the neck of the womb, or they may extend from side to side of the vagina across and just behind the neck of the womb. In the latter

PLATE IX

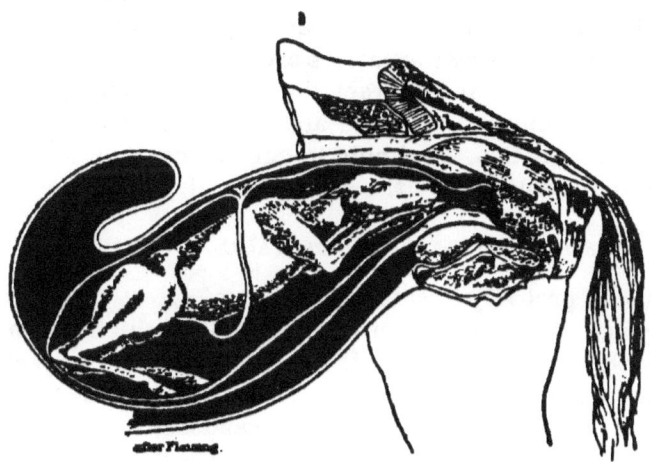

Vertebro-Sacral presentation.

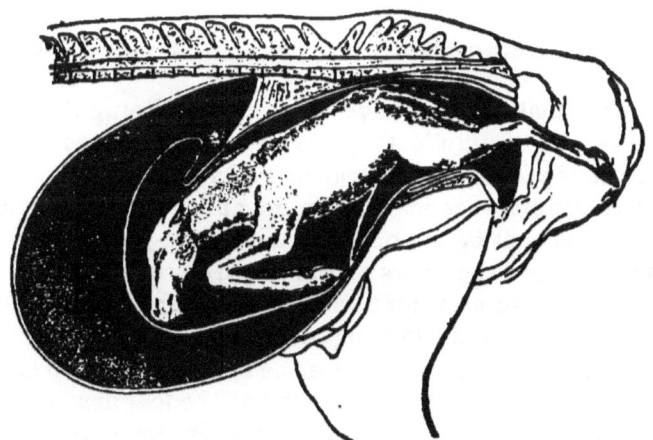

Lumbo-Sacral presentation.

NORMAL PRESENTATIONS.

position they may be felt and quickly remedied by cutting them across. In the abdomen they can only be reached by incision, and two alternatives are presented: (1) To perform embryotomy and extract the fœtus piecemeal; and (2) to make an incision into the abdomen and extract by the Cæsarian operation, or simply to cut the constricting band and attempt delivery by the usual channel.

FIBROUS CONSTRICTION OF VAGINA OR VULVA.

This is probably always the result of direct mechanical injury and the formation of rigid cicatrices which fail to dilate with the remainder of the passages at the approach of parturition. The presentation of the fœtus in the natural way and the occurrence of successive and active labor pains without any favorable result will direct attention to the rigid and unyielding cicatrices, which may be incised at one, two or more points to a depth of half an inch or more, after which the natural expulsive efforts will usually prove effective. The resulting wounds may be washed frequently with a solution of one part of carbolic acid to 50 parts of water, or of 1 part of mercuric chloride to 500 parts of water.

FŒTUS ADHERENT TO THE WALLS OF THE WOMB.

In inflammation of the mucous membrane lining the cavity of the womb and implicating the fœtal membranes the resulting embryonic tissue sometimes establishes a medium of direct continuity between the womb and fœtal membranes; the blood vessels of the one communicate freely with those of the other and the fibers of the one are prolonged into the other. This causes retention of the membranes after birth and a special risk of bleeding from the womb and of septic poisoning. In exceptional cases the adhesion is more extensive and binds a portion of the body of the foal firmly to the womb. In such cases it has repeatedly been found impossible to extract the foal until such adhesions were broken down. If they can be reached with the hand and recognized they may be torn through with the fingers or with a blunt hook, after which delivery may be attempted with hope of success.

PLATE I.

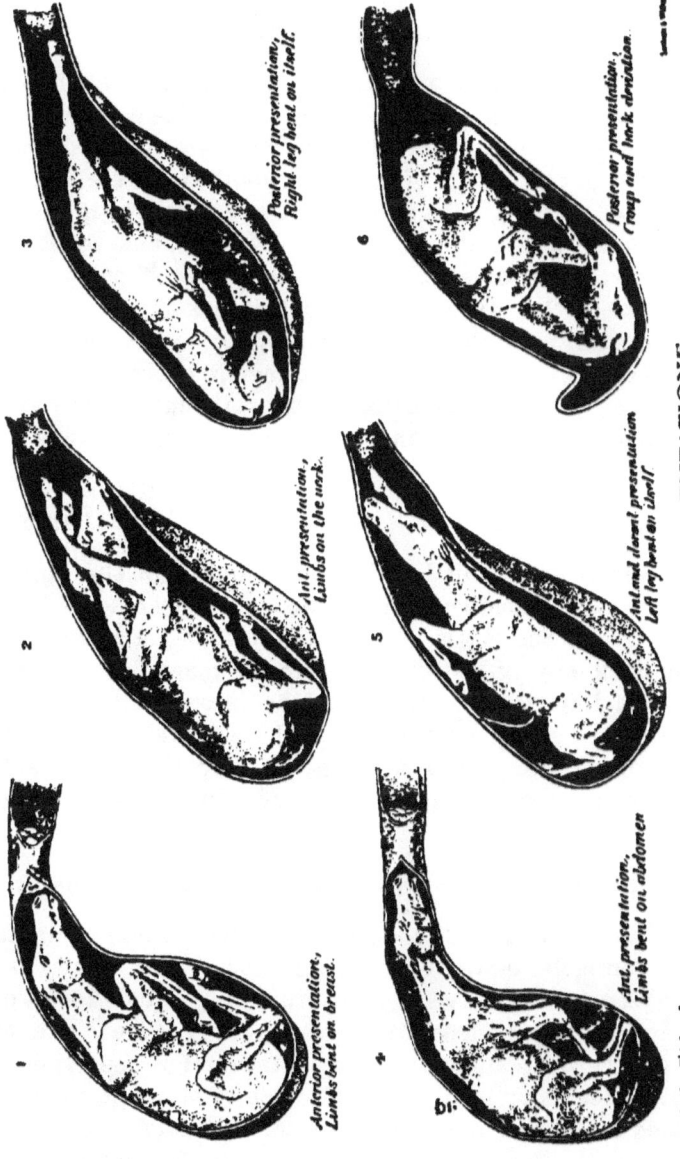

1. Anterior presentation; Limbs bent on breast.
2. Ant. presentation; Limbs on the neck.
3. Posterior presentation; Right leg bent on itself.
4. Ant. presentation; Limbs bent on abdomen.
5. Ant. and dorsal presentation; Left leg bent on itself.
6. Posterior presentation; Croup and back deviation.

ABNORMAL PRESENTATIONS.

EXCESSIVE SIZE OF THE FŒTUS.

It would seem that a small mare may usually be safely bred to a large stallion, yet this is not always the case, and when the small size is an individual rather than a racial characteristic or the result of extreme youth the rule cannot be expected to hold. There is always great danger in breeding the young, small, and undeveloped female, and the dwarfed representative of a larger breed, as the offspring tend to partake of the large race characteristics and to show them even prior to birth. When impregnation has occurred in the very young or in the dwarfed female there are two alternatives—to induce abortion or to wait until there are attempts at parturition and to extract by embryotomy if impracticable otherwise.

CONSTRICTION OF A MEMBER BY THE NAVEL STRING.

In man and animals alike the winding of the umbilical cord round a member of the fœtus sometimes leads to the amputation of the latter. It is also known to get wound around the neck or a limb at birth, but in the mare this does not seriously impede parturition, as the loosely attached membranes are easily separated from the womb and no strangulation or retarding occurs. The foal may, however, die from the cessation of the placental circulation unless it is speedily delivered.

WATER IN THE HEAD (HYDROCEPHALUS) OF THE FOAL.

This consists in the excessive accumulation of liquid in the ventricles of the brain so that the cranial cavity is enlarged and constitutes a great projecting rounded mass occupying the space from the eyes upward. (See Plate XIV, Fig. 3.) With an anterior presentation (fore feet and nose) this presents an insuperable obstacle to progress, as the diseased cranium is too large to enter the pelvis at the same time with the fore arms. With a posterior presentation (hind feet) all goes well until the body and shoulders have passed out, when progress is suddenly arrested by the great bulk of the head. In the first case the oiled hand intro-

PLATE XI.

1

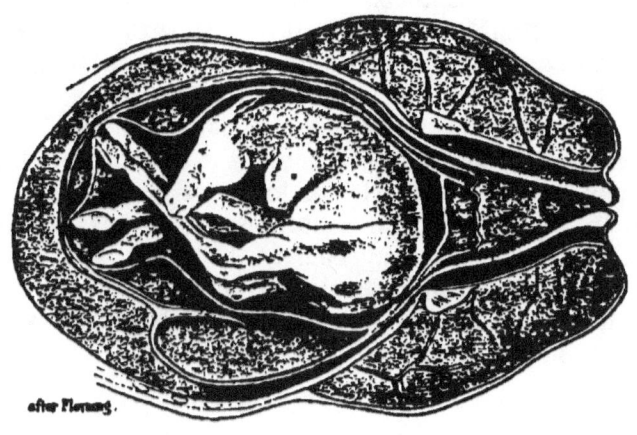

after Fleming.

Transverse presentation-Upper view.

2

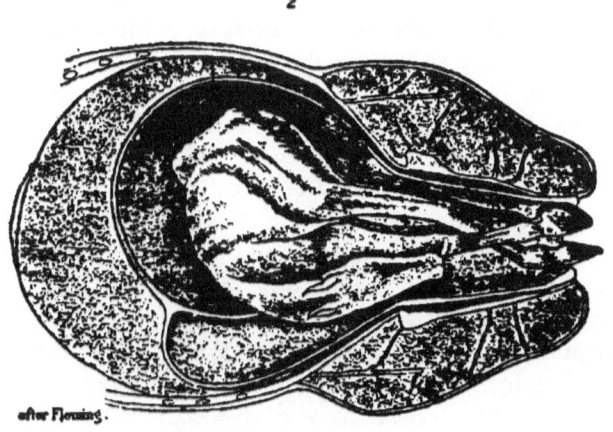

after Fleming.

Sterno-abdominal presentation-Head and Feet engaged.

Haines, after Fleming.

ABNORMAL PRESENTATIONS.

duced along the face detects the enormous size of the head, which may be diminished by puncturing it with a knife or trocar and canula in the median line, evacuating the water and pressing in the thin bony walls. With a posterior presentation the same course must be followed; the hand passed along the neck will detect the cranial swelling, which may be punctured with a knife or trocar. Oftentimes with an anterior presentation the great size of the head leads to its displacement backward and thus the fore limbs alone engage in the passages. Here the first object is to seek and bring up the missing head and then puncture it as above suggested.

DROPSY OF THE ABDOMEN IN THE FOAL—ASCITES.

The accumulation of liquid in the abdominal cavity of the fœtus is less frequent, but when present it may arrest parturition as completely as will hydrocephalus. With an anterior presentation the foal may pass as far as the shoulders, but behind this all efforts fail to secure a further advance. With a posterior presentation the hind legs as far as the thighs may be expelled, but at this point all progress ceases. In either case the oiled hand passed inward by the side of the foal will detect the enormous distention of the abdomen and its soft, fluctuating contents. The only course is to puncture the cavity and evacuate the liquid. With the anterior presentation this may be done with a long trocar and canula, introduced through the chest and diaphragm; or with a knife an incision may be made between the first two ribs and the lungs and heart cut or torn out, when the diaphragm will be felt projecting strongly forward and may be easily punctured. Should there not be room to introduce the hand through the chest the oiled hand may be passed along beneath the breast bone and the abdomen punctured. With a posterior presentation the abdomen must be punctured in the same way, the hand, armed with a knife protected in its palm, being passed along the side of the flank or between the hind limbs. It should be added that moderate dropsy of the abdomen is not incompatible with natural delivery, the liquid being at first crowded back into the

PLATE XII.

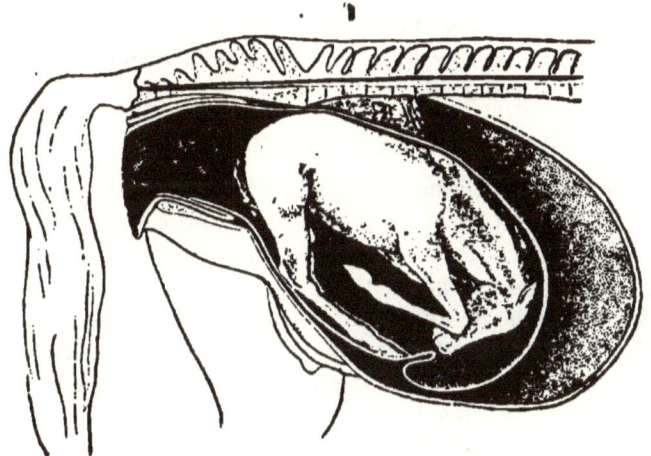

Thigh and croup presentation.

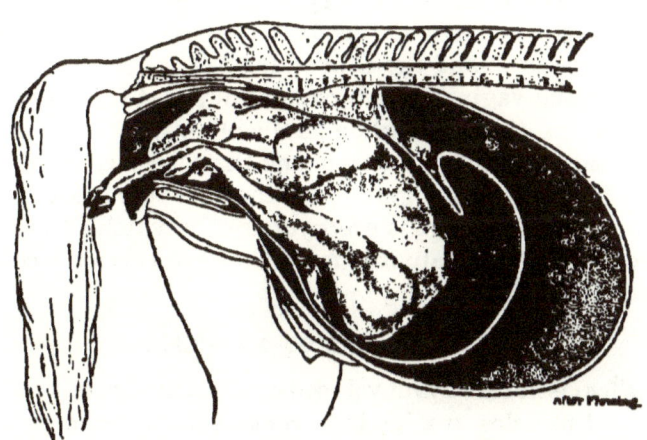

Anterior presentation. Hind limb deviation.

ABNORMAL PRESENTATIONS.

portion of the belly still engaged in the womb and passing slowly from that into the advanced portion as soon as that has cleared the narrow passage of the pelvis and passed out where it can expand.

GENERAL DROPSY OF THE FŒTUS.

In this case the tissues generally are distended with liquid and the skin is found at all points tense and rounded and pitting on pressure with the fingers. In some such cases delivery may be effected after the skin has been punctured at narrow intervals to allow the escape of the fluid and then liberally smeared with fresh lard. More commonly, however, it cannot be reached at all points to be so punctured, nor sufficiently reduced to be extracted whole, and resort must be had to embryotomy.

SWELLING OF THE FŒTUS WITH GAS—EMPHYSEMA.

This has been described as occurring in a living fœtus, but I have only met with it in the dead and decomposing foal after futile efforts have been made for several days to effect delivery. These cases are very difficult ones, as the foal is inflated to such an extent that it is impossible to advance it into the passages, and the skin of the fœtus and the walls of the womb and vagina have become so dry that it is impracticable to cause the one to glide on the other. The hair comes off any part that may be seized, and the case is rendered the more offensive and dangerous by the very feted liquids and gases. The only resort is embryotomy, by which I have succeeded in saving a valuable mare that had carried a colt in this condition for four days.

CONTRACTIONS OF MUSCLES.

The foal is not always developed symmetrically, but certain groups of muscles are liable to remain short or to shorten because of persistent spasmodic contraction, so that even the bones become distorted and twisted. This is most common in the neck. The bones of this part and even of the face are drawn to one side and shortened, the head being held firmly to the flank and the jaws being twisted to the right or left.

PLATE XIII

1

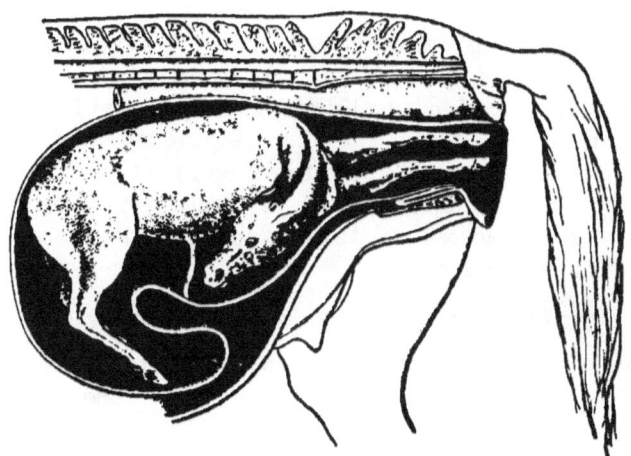

Anterior presentation. Head turned on side.

2

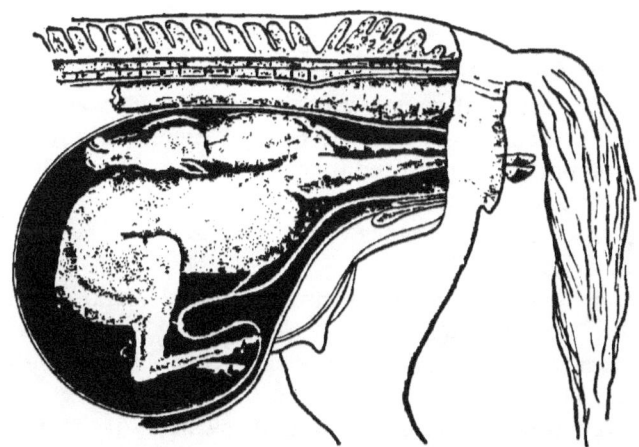

Anterior presentation. Head turned on back.

ABNORMAL PRESENTATIONS.

In other cases the flexor muscles of the fore limbs are contracted so that these members are strongly bent at the knee. In neither of these cases can the distorted part be extended and straightened, so that body or limbs must necessarily present double and natural delivery is rendered impossible. The bent neck may sometimes be straightened after the muscles have been cut on the side to which it is turned, and the bent limbs after the tendons on the back of the shank-bone have been cut across. Failing to accomplish this, the next resort is to embryotomy.

TUMORS OF THE FŒTUS—INCLOSED OVUM.

Tumors or diseased growths may form on any part of the foal, internal or external, and by their size impede or hinder parturition. In some cases what appears as a tumor is an imprisoned and undeveloped ovum which has grafted itself on the fœtus. These are usually sacculated and may contain skin, hair, muscle, bone, and other natural tissues. The only course to be pursued in such cases is to excise the tumor, or, if this is not feasible, to perform embryotomy.

MONSTROSITIES.

Monstrosity in the foal is an occasional cause of difficult parturition, especially such monsters as show excessive development of some part of the body, a displacement or distortion of parts, or a redundancy of parts, as in double monsters. Monsters may be divided into—

(1) Monsters with absence of parts—absence of head, limb, or other organ.

(2) Monsters with some part abnormally small—dwarfed head, limb, trunk, etc.

(3) Monsters through unnatural division of parts—cleft head, trunk, limbs, etc.

(4) Monsters through absence of natural divisions—absence of mouth, nose, eyes, anus, confluent digits, etc.

(5) Monsters through fusion of parts—one central eye, one nasal opening, etc.

(6) Monsters through abnormal position or form of parts—curved spine, face, limb, etc.

PLATE XV.

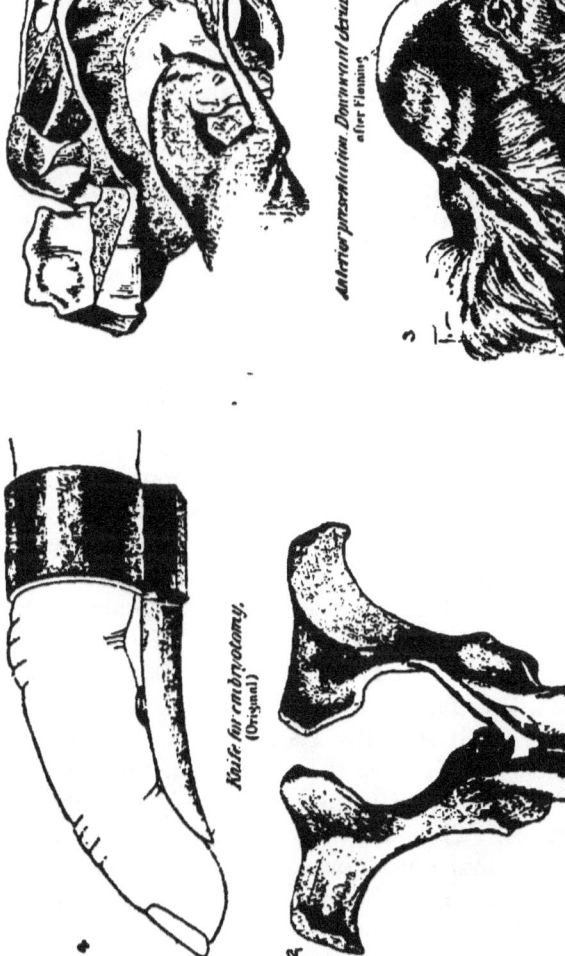

1. *Anterior presentation. Downward deviation of the head,* after Fleming.
2. *Deformed pelvis,* after Fleming.
3. *Hydrocephalic head of colt,* after Fleming.
4. *Knife for embryotomy,* (Original).

Anterior Presentations: VARIOUS CAUSES OF DIFFICULT LABOR.

(7) Monsters through excess of formation—enormous head, supernumerary digits, etc.

(8) Monsters through imperfect differentiation of sexual organs—hermaphrodites.

(9) Double monsters—double-headed, double-bodied, extra limbs, etc.

The *causes* of monstrosities appear to be very varied. Some monstrosities, like extra digits, absence of horns or tails, etc., run in families and are produced almost as certainly as color or form. Others are associated with too close breeding, the powers of symmetrical development being interfered with, just as in other cases a sexual incompatibility is developed, near relatives failing to breed with each other. Mere arrest of development of a part may arise from accidental disease of the embryo; hence vital organs are left out, or portions of organs, like the dividing walls of the heart, are omitted. Sometimes an older fœtus is inclosed in the body of another, each having started independently from a separate ovum, but the one having become embedded in the semi-fluid mass of the other and having developed there simultaneously with it, but not so largely nor perfectly. In many cases of redundance of parts the extra part or member has manifestly developed from the same ovum and nutrient center with the normal member to which it remains adherent, just as a new tail will grow out in a newt when the former has been cut off. In the early embryo, with its great powers of development, this factor can operate to far greater purpose than in the adult animal. Its influence is seen in the fact pointed out by St. Hilaire that such redundant parts are nearly always connected with the corresponding portions in the normal fœtus. Thus superfluous legs or digits are attached to the normal ones, double heads or tails are connected to a common neck or rump, and double bodies are attached to each other by corresponding points, navel to navel, breast to breast, back to back. All this suggests the development of extra parts from the same primary layer of the impregnated and developing ovum. The effect of disturbing conditions in giving such wrong directions to the developmental forces is well shown in the experiments of St.

DISEASES OF THE GENERATIVE ORGANS. 385

Hilaire and Valentine in varnishing, shaking, and otherwise breaking up the natural connections in eggs, and thereby determining the formation of monstrosities at will. So, in the mammal, blows and other injuries that detach the fœtal membranes from the walls of the womb or that modify their circulation by inducing inflammation are at times followed by the development of a monster. The excitement, mental and physical, attendant on fright occasionally acts in a similar way, acting probably through the same channels.

The monstrous forms likely to interfere with parturition are such as from contracted or twisted limbs or spine must be presented double; where supernumerary limbs, head, or body must approach the passages with the natural ones; where a head or other member has attained to an unnatural size; where the body of one fœtus has become inclosed in or attached to another, etc.

Extraction is sometimes possible by straightening the members and securing such a presentation as will reduce the presenting mass to its smallest and most wedge-like dimensions. To effect this it may be needful to cut the flexor tendons of bent limbs or the muscles on the side of a twisted neck or body; and one or more of the manipulations necessary to secure and bring up a missing member may be required. In most cases of monstrosity by excess, however, it is needful to remove the superfluous parts, in which case the general principles employed for embryotomy must be followed. The Cæsarian section, by which the fœtus is extracted through an incision in the walls of the abdomen and womb, is inadmissible, as it practically entails the sacrifice of the mare, which should never be done for the sake of a monster. (See "Embryotomy.")

ENTRANCE OF TWINS INTO THE PASSAGE AT ONCE.

Twins are rare in the mare, and still more rare is the impaction of both at once into the pelvis. The condition would be easily recognized by the fact that two fore limbs and two hind would occupy the passage at once, the front of the hoofs of the fore feet being turned upward and those of the hind feet downward. If both belonged to one foal they would be turned in the same direction. Once recognized, the condition is easily remedied by passing a rope with a running noose round each foot of the foal that is farthest advanced or that promises to be most easily extracted, and to push the members of the other fœtus back into the depth of the womb. As soon as the one fœtus is fully engaged in the passage it will hold its place and its delivery will proceed in the natural way.

TABLE OF WRONG PRESENTATIONS.

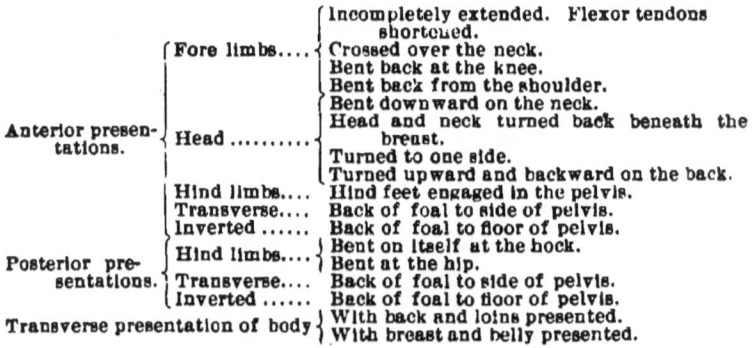

FORE LIMBS IMCOMPLETELY EXTENDED.

In cases of this kind not only are the back tendons behind the knee and shank-bone unduly short, but the sinew extending from the front of the shoulder-blade over the front of the elbow and down to the head of the shank-bone is also shortened. The result is that the fore limb is bent at the knee and the elbow is also rigidly bent. The condition obstructs parturition by the feet becoming pressed against the floor of the pelvis or by the elbow pressing on its anterior brim. Relief is to be obtained by forcible extension. A rope with a running noose is passed around each fetlock and a repeller (see Plate VIII), planted in the breast is pressed in a direction upward and backward while active traction is made on the ropes. If the feet are not thereby raised from the floor of the pelvis the palm of the hand may be placed beneath them to protect the mucous membrane until they have advanced sufficiently to obviate this danger. In the absence of a repeller a smooth rounded fork-handle may be employed. If the shortening is too great to allow of the extension of the limbs in this way the tense tendons may be cut across behind the shank-bone and in front of the elbow, and the limb will be easily straightened out. This is most easily done with an embryotomy knife furnished with a ring for the middle finger, so that the blade may be protected in the palm of the hand. (See Plate XIV, Fig. 4.)

ONE FORE LIMB CROSSED OVER THE BACK OF THE NECK.

With the long fore limbs of the foal this readily occurs and the resulting increase in thickness, both at the head and shoulder, offers a serious obstacle to progress. (See Plate X. Fig. 2.) The hand introduced into the passage detects the head and one fore foot, and further back on the same side of the head the second foot, from which the limb may be traced obliquely across the back of the neck.

If parturition continues to make progress the displaced foot may bruise and lacerate the vagina. By seizing the limb above the fetlock it may be easily pushed over the head to the proper side, when parturition will proceed normally.

FORE LIMB BENT AT THE KNEE.

The nose and one fore foot present, and on examination the knee of the missing fore limb is found farther back. (Plate X, Fig. 1.) First place a noose each on the presenting pastern and lower jaw, and push back the body of the fœtus with a repeller, while the operator seizing the shank of the bent limb extends it so as to press back the knee and bring forward the fetlock and foot. As progress is made little by little the hand is slid down from the region of the knee to the fetlock, and finally that is secured and brought up into the passage, when parturition will proceed without hindrance. If both fore limbs are bent back the head must be noosed and the limbs brought up as above, one after the other. It is usually best to employ the left hand for the right fore limb and the right hand for the left fore limb.

FORE LIMB TURNED BACK FROM THE SHOULDER.

In this case, on exploration by the side of the head and presenting limb, the shoulder only can be reached at first.

(Plate X, Fig. 4.) By noosing the head and presenting fore limb these may be drawn forward into the pelvis, and the oiled hand being carried along the shoulder in the direction of the missing limb is enabled to reach and seize the forearm just below the elbow. The body is now pushed back by the assistants pressing on the head and presenting limb or on a repeller planted in the breast until the knee can be brought up into the pelvis, after which the procedure is the same as described in the last paragraph.

HEAD BENT DOWN BETWEEN THE FORE LIMBS.

This may be so that the poll or nape of the neck with the ears can be felt far back between the fore limbs, or so that only the upper border of the neck can be reached, head and neck being bent back beneath the body. With the head only bent on the neck, noose the two presenting limbs, then introduce the hand between them until the nose can be seized in the palm of the hand. Next have the assistants push back the presenting limbs, while the nose is strongly lifted upward over the brim of the pelvis. This accomplished it assumes the natural position and parturition is easy.

When both head and neck are bent downward it may be impossible to reach the nose. If, however, the labor has only commenced, the limbs may be drawn upon until the operator can reach the ear, by dragging on which the head may be so far advanced that the fingers may reach the orbit; traction upon this while the limbs are being pushed back may bring the head up so that it bends on the neck only, and the further procedure will be as described in the last paragraph.

If the labor has been long in progress and the fœtus is jammed into the pelvis, the womb emptied of the waters and firmly contracted on its solid contents, the case is incomparably more difficult. The mare may be chloroformed and turned on her back with hind parts elevated, and the womb may be injected with sweet oil. Then, if the ear can be reached, the correction of the mal-presentation may be attempted as above described. Should this fail one or more

DISEASES OF THE GENERATIVE ORGANS. 389

sharp hooks may be inserted in the neck as near the head as can be reached, and ropes attached to these may be dragged on, while the body of the foal is pushed back by the fore limbs or by a repeller. Such repulsion should be made in a direction obliquely upward toward the loins of the mother so as to rotate the fœtus in such a way as to bring the head up. As this is accomplished a hold should be secured nearer and nearer to the nose, with hand or hook, until the head can be straightened out on the neck.

All means failing, it becomes necessary to remove the fore limbs (embryotomy) so as to make more space for bringing up the head. If even then this cannot be accomplished it may be possible to push the body backward and upward with the repeller until the hind limbs are brought to the passage, when they may be noosed and delivery effected with the posterior presentation.

HEAD TURNED BACK ON THE SHOULDER.

In this case the fore feet present, and the oiled hand passed along the forearms in search of the missing head finds the side of the neck turned to one side, the head being perhaps entirely out of reach. (Plate XIII, Fig. 1.) To bring forward the head it may be desirable to lay the mare on the opposite side to that to which the head is turned, and even to give chloroform or ether. Then the feet being noosed, the body of the fœtus is pushed by the hand or repeller forward and to the side opposite to that occupied by the head until the head comes within reach, near the entrance of the pelvis. If such displacement of the fœtus is difficult it may be facilitated by a free use of oil or lard. When the nose can be seized it can be brought into the passage as when the head is turned down. If it cannot be reached the orbit may be availed of to draw the head forward until the nose can be seized or the lower jaw noosed. In very difficult cases a rope may be passed around the neck by the hand, or with the aid of a curved carrier (Plate VII), and traction may be made upon this while the body is being rotated to the other side. In the same way, in bad cases, a hook may be fixed in the orbit or even between the bones of the lower jaw to assist in bringing the head up into position. Should all fail, the amputation of the fore limbs may be resorted to as advised under the last heading.

HEAD TURNED UPWARD ON THE BACK.

This differs from the last mal-presentation only in the direction of the head, which has to be sought above rather than at one side, and is to be secured and brought forward in a similar manner. (Plate XIII, Fig. 2.) If a rope can be passed around the neck it will prove most effectual, as it naturally slides nearer to the head as the neck is straightened and ends by bringing the head within easy reach.

HIND FEET ENGAGED IN THE PELVIS.

In this case fore limbs and head present naturally, but the hind limbs bent forward from the hip and the loins arched allow the hind feet also to enter the passages, and the farther labor advances the more firmly does the body of the foal become wedged into the pelvis. (Plate XII, Fig. 2.) The condition is to be recognized by introducing the oiled hand along the belly of the fœtus, when the hind feet will be felt advancing. An attempt should at once be made to push them back, one after the other, over the brim of the pelvis. Failing in this, the mare may be turned on her back, head, down hill, and the attempt renewed. If it is possible to introduce a straight rope carrier, a noose passed through this may be put on the fetlock and the repulsion thereby made more effective. In case of continued failure the anterior presenting part of the body may be skinned and cut off as far back toward the pelvis as possible (see "Embryotomy"); then nooses are placed on the hind fetlocks and traction is made upon these while the quarters are pushed back into the womb. Then the remaining portion is brought away by the posterior presentation.

ANTERIOR PRESENTATION WITH BACK TURNED TO ONE SIDE.

The greatest diameter of the axis of the foal, like that of the pelvic passages, is from above downward, and when the fœtus enters the pelvis with this greatest diameter engaged transversely or in the narrow diameter of the pelvis parturition is rendered difficult or impossible. In such a case the pasterns and head may be noosed and the passages and engaged portion of the foal freely lubricated with lard, the limbs may be crossed over each other and the head, and a movement of rotation effected in the foetus until its face and back are turned up toward the croup of the mother; then parturition becomes natural.

BACK OF THE FOAL TURNED TO THE FLOOR OF THE PELVIS.

In a roomy mare this is not an insuperable obstacle to parturition, yet it may seriously impede it by reason of the curvature of the body of the foal being opposite to that of the passages and the head and withers being liable to arrest against the border of the pelvis. Lubrication of the passage with lard and traction of the limbs and head will usually suffice with or without the turning of the mare on her back. In obstinate cases two other resorts are open: (1) to turn the foal, pushing back the fore parts and bringing up the hind so as to make a posterior presentation, and (2) the amputation of the fore limbs, after which extraction will usually be easy.

HIND PRESENTATION WITH LEG BENT AT HOCK.

In this form the quarters of the foal with the hind legs bent up beneath them present, but cannot advance through the pelvis by reason of their bulk. (Plate X, Fig. 3.) The oiled hand introduced can recognize the outline of the buttocks, with the tail and anus in the center and the sharp points of the hocks beneath. First pass a rope around each limb at the hock, then with hand or repeller push the buttocks backward and upward until the feet can be brought up into the passages. The great length of the shank and pastern in the foal is a serious obstacle to this, and in all cases the foot should be protected in the palm of the hand while being brought up over the brim of the pelvis. Otherwise the womb may be torn. When the pains are too violent and constant to allow effective manipulation some respite may be obtained by the use of chloroform or morphia, and by turning the mare on her back, but too often the operator fails and the foal must be sacrificed. Two courses are still open: first, to cut through the cords behind and above the hock and extend the upper part of the limb, leaving the hock bent, and extract in this way, and, second, to amputate the hind limbs at the hip joint and remove them separately, after which the body may be extracted.

HIND PRESENTATION WITH LEGS BENT FORWARD FROM THE HIP.

This is merely an aggravated form of the presentation last described. (Plate XII, Fig. 1). If the mare is roomy a rope may be passed around each thigh and the body pushed upward and forward, so as to bring the hocks and heels upward. If this can be accomplished, nooses are placed on the limb farther and farther down until the fetlock is reached and brought into position. If failure is met with, then amputation at the hips is the *dernier ressort.*

HIND PRESENTATIONS WITH THE BACK TURNED SIDEWAYS OR DOWNWARD.

These are the counterparts of similar anterior presentations and are to be managed in the same way.

PRESENTATION OF THE BACK.

This is rare, yet not unknown, the foal being bent upon itself with the back, recognizable by its sharp row of spines, presented at the entrance of the pelvis, and the head and all four feet turned back into the womb. (Plate XI, Fig. 1.) The body of the fœtus may be extended across the opening transversely so that the head corresponds to one side (right or left), or it may be vertical with the head above or below.

In any such position the object should be to push the body of the fœtus forward and upward or to one side, as may best promise to bring up the fore or hind extremities, and bring the latter into the passage so as to constitute a normal anterior or posterior presentation. This turning of the fœtus may be favored by a given position of the mother, by the free use of oil or lard on the surface of the fœtus, and by the use of a propeller.

DISEASES OF THE GENERATIVE ORGANS. 393

PRESENTATION OF BREAST AND ABDOMEN.

This is the reverse of the back presentation, the foal being extended across in front of the pelvic opening, but with the belly turned toward the passages and with all four feet engaged in the passage. (Plate XI, Fig. 2) The most promising course is to secure the hind feet with nooses and then push the fore feet forward into the womb. As soon as the fore feet are pushed forward clear of the brim of the pelvis traction is made on the hind feet so as to bring the thighs into the passage and prevent the re-entrance of the fore limbs. If it prove difficult to push back the fore limbs a noose may be passed around the fetlock of each and the cord drawn through the eye of a rope carrier, by means of which the members may be easily pushed back.

EMBRYOTOMY.

This consists in the dissection of the foetus so as to reduce its bulk and allow of its exit through the pelvis. The indications for its adoption have been furnished in the foregoing pages. The operation will vary in different cases according to the necessity for the removal of one or more parts in order to secure the requisite reduction in size. Thus it may be needful to remove head and neck, one fore limb or both, one hind limb or both, to remove different parts of the trunk, or to remove superfluous (monstrous) parts. Some of the simplest operations of embryotomy (incision of the head in hydrocephalus, incision of the belly in dropsy) have already been described. It remains to notice the more difficult procedures which can be best undertaken by the skilled anatomist.

Amputation of the fore limbs.—This may usually be begun on the fetlock of the limb projecting from the vulva. An embryotomy knife is desirable. This knife consists of a blade with a sharp, slightly hooked point, and one or two rings in the back of the blade large enough to fit on the middle finger, while the blade is protected in the palm of the hand. (See Plate XIV, Fig. 4.) Another form has the blade inserted in a mortise in the handle from which it is pushed out by a movable button when wanted. First place a noose around the fetlock of the limb to be amputated, cut the skin circularly entirely around the fetlock, then make an incision on the inner side of the limb from the fetlock up to the breast bone. Next dissect the skin from the limb, from the fetlock up to the breast bone on the inner side, and as far up on the shoulder-blade as possible on the outer side. Finally, cut through the muscles attaching the limb to the breast bone and employ strong traction on the limb so as to drag out the whole limb, shoulder-blade included. The muscles around the upper part of the shoulder-blade are easily torn through and need not be cut, even if that were possible. In no case should the fore limb be removed unless the shoulder-blade is taken with it, as that furnishes the greatest obstruction to delivery, above all when it is no longer advanced by the extension of the fore limb but is pressed back so as to increase the already thickest posterior portion of the chest. The preservation of the skin from the whole limb is advantageous in various ways; it is easier to cut it circularly at the fetlock than at the shoulder; it covers the hand and knife in making the needful incisions, thus acting as a protection to the womb; and it affords a means of traction on the body after the limb has been removed. In dissecting the skin from the limb the knife is not needful at all points; much of it may be stripped off with the fingers or knuckles, or by a blunt iron spud pushed up inside the hide, which is meanwhile held tense to render the spud effective.

Amputation of the head.—This is easy when both fore limbs are turned back and the head alone has made its exit in part. It is more difficult when the head is still retained in the passages or womb, as in double-headed monsters. The head is secured by a hook in the lower jaw, or in the orbit, or by a halter, and the skin is divided circularly around the lower part of the face or at the front of the ears, according to the amount of head protruding. Then an incision is made backward along the line of the throat and the skin dissected from the neck as far back as possible. Then the muscles and other soft parts of the neck are cut across and the bodies of two vertebræ (neck bones) are severed by cutting completely

DISEASES OF THE GENERATIVE ORGANS. 395

across the cartilage of the joint. The bulging of the ends of the bones will serve to indicate the seat of the joint. The head and detached portion of the neck may now be removed by steady pulling. If there is still an obstacle the knife may be again used to sever any obstinate connections. In the case of a double-headed monster the whole of the second neck must be removed with the head. When the head has been detached a rope should be passed through the eye-holes, or through an artificial opening in the skin, and tied firmly around the skin, to be employed as a means of traction when the missing limbs or the second head have been brought up into position.

Amputation of the hind limb.—This may be required when there are extra hind limbs, or when the hind limbs are bent forward at hock or hip joint. In the former condition the procedure resembles that for removal of a fore limb, but requires more anatomical knowledge. Having noosed the pastern, a circular incision is made through the skin around the fetlock and a longitudinal one from that up to the groin, and the skin is dissected from the limb as high up as can be reached, over the croup if possible. Then cut through the muscles around the hip joint and, if possible, the two interarticular ligaments of the joint (pubio-femoral and round), and extract the limb by strong dragging.

In case the limb is bent forward at the hock a rope is passed around that and pulled so as to bring the point of the hock between the lips of the vulva. The hamstring and the lateral ligaments of the hock are now cut through and the limbs extended by a rope tied round the lower end of the long bone above (tibia). In case it is still needful to remove the upper part of the limb the further procedure is the same as described in the last paragraph.

In case the limb is turned forward from the hip and the fœtus so wedged into the passage that turning is impossible the case is very difficult. I have repeatedly succeeded by cutting in on the hip joint and disarticulating it, then dissecting the muscles back from the upper end of the thighbone. A noose was placed around the neck of the bone and pulled on forcibly, while any unduly resisting structures were cut with the knife.

Cartwright recommends to make free incisions round the hip joints and tear through the muscles when they cannot be cut; then with cords round the pelvic bones and hooks inserted in the openings in the floor of the pelvis to drag out the pelvic bones; then put cords around the heads of the thigh-bones and extract them; then remove the intestines; and finally, by means of the loose, detached skin, draw out the body with the remainder of the hind limbs bent forward beneath it.

Reuff cuts his way into the pelvis of the foal, and with a knife separates the pelvic bones from the loins, then skinning the quarter draws out these pelvic bones by means of ropes and hooks, and along with them the hind limbs.

The hind limbs having been removed by one or the other of these procedures the loose skin detached from the pelvis is used as a means of traction and delivery is effected. If it has been a monstrosity with extra hind limbs it may be possible to bring these up into the passage and utilize them for traction.

Removal of the abdominal viscera.—In case where the belly is unduly large, from decomposition, tumors, or otherwise, it may be needful to lay it open with the knife and cut or tear out the contents.

Removal of the thoracic viscera.—To diminish the bulk of the chest it has been found advisable to cut out the breastbone, remove the heart and lungs, and allow the ribs to collapse with the lower free ends overlapping each other.

Dissection of the trunk.—In case it becomes necessary to remove other portions of the trunk the general rule should be followed of preserving the skin so that all manipulations can be made inside this as a protector, that it may remain available as a means of exercising traction on the remaining parts of the body and as a covering to protect the vaginal walls against injuries from bones while such part is passing.

FLOODING—BLEEDING FROM THE WOMB.

This is rare in the mare, but not unknown, in connection with a failure of the womb to contract on itself after parturition, or with eversion of the womb (casting the withers) and congestion or laceration. If the blood accumulates in the flaccid womb the condition may only be suspected by reason of the rapidly advancing weakness, swaying, unsteady gait, hanging head, paleness of the eyes and other muccus membranes, and weak, small, failing pulse. The hand introduced into the womb detects the presence of the blood partly clotted. If the blood escapes by the vulva the condition is evident.

Treatment consists in evacuating the womb of its blood clots, giving a large dose of powdered ergot of rye, and in the application of cold water or ice to the loins and external generative organs. Besides this a sponge impregnated with a strong solution of alum, or still better with tincture of muriate of iron, may be introduced into the womb and squeezed so as to bring the liquid in contact with the walls generally.

EVERSION OF THE WOMB.

If the womb fails to contract after difficult parturition the after-pains will sometimes lead to the fundus passing into the body of the organ and passing through that and the vagina until the whole inverted organ appears externally and hangs down on the thighs. The result is rapid engorgement and swelling of the organ, impaction of the rectum with fæces, and distention of the bladder with urine, all of which conditions seriously interfere with the return of the mass. In returning the womb the standing is preferable to the recumbent position, as the abdomen is more pendant and there is less obstruction to the return. It may, however, be necessary to put hobbles on the hind limbs to prevent the mare from kicking. A clean sheet should be held beneath the womb and all fi.th, straw and foreign bodies washed from its surface. Then with a broad, elastic (india-rubber) band, or in default of that a long strip of calico four or five inches wide, wind the womb as tightly as possible, beginning at its most dependent part (the extremity of the horn). This serves two good ends. It squeezes out into the general circulation the enormous mass of blood which engorged and enlarged the organ and furnishes a strong protective covering for the now delicate friable organ, through which it may be safely manipulated without danger of laceration. The next step may be the pressure on the general mass while those portions next the vulva are gradually pushed in with the hands; or the extreme lowest point (the end of the horn) may be turned within itself and pushed forward into the vagina by the closed fist, the return being assisted by manipulations by the other hand, and even by those of assistants. By either mode the manipulations may be made with almost perfect safety so long as the organ is closely wrapped in the bandage. Once a portion has been introduced into the vagina the rest will usually follow with increasing ease, and the operation should be completed with the hand and arm extended the full length within the womb and moved from point to point so as to straighten out all parts of the organ and insure that no portion still remains inverted within another portion. Should any such partial inversion be left it will give rise to straining, under the force of which it will gradually increase until the whole mass will be protruded as before. The next step is to apply a truss as an effectual mechanical barrier to further escape of the womb through the vulva. The simplest is made with two inch ropes, each about eighteen feet long. These are each doubled and interwoven at the bend, as seen in Plate VIII, Fig. 4. The ring formed by the interlacing of the two ropes is adjusted around the vulva, the two ends of the one rope are carried up on the right and left of the tail and along the spine, being wound round each other in their course, and are finally tied to the upper part of the collar encircling the neck. The remaining two ends, belonging to the other rope, are carried downward and forward between the thighs and thence forward and upward on the sides of the belly and chest to be attached to the right and left sides of the collar. These ropes are drawn tightly enough to keep closely applied to the opening without chafing, and will fit still more securely when the mare raises her back to strain. It is desirable to tie the mare short so that she may be unable to lie down for a day or two, and she should be kept in a stall with the hind parts higher than the fore. Violent straining may be checked by full doses of opium (one-half drachm), and any costiveness or diarrhea should be obviated by a suitable laxative or binding diet.

DISEASES OF THE GENERATIVE ORGANS. 399

In some mares the contractions are too violent to allow of the return of the womb, and full doses of opium (one-half drachm), laudanum (two ounces), or chloral hydrate (one ounce) may be demanded, or the mare must be rendered insensible by ether or chloroform.

RUPTURE OR LACERATION OF THE WOMB.

This may occur from the feet of the foal during parturition or from ill-directed efforts to assist, but it is especially liable to take place in the everted, congested and friable organ. The resultant dangers are bleeding from the wound, escape of the bowels through the opening and their fatal injury by the mare's feet or otherwise, and peritonitis from the extension of inflammation from the wound and from the poisonous action of the septic liquids of the womb escaping into the abdominal cavity. The first object is to close the wound, but unless in eversion of the womb this is practically impossible. In the last-named condition the wound must be carefully and accurately sewed up before the womb is returned. After its return the womb must be injected daily with an antiseptic solution (borax one-half ounce or carbolic acid three drachms to a quart of tepid water). If inflammation threatens the abdomen may be bathed continuously with hot water by means of a heavy woolen rag, and large doses of opium (one-half drachm) may be given twice or thrice daily.

RUPTURES OF THE VAGINA.

These are attended by dangers similar to those belonging to rupture of the womb, and in addition by the risk of protrusion of the bladder, which appears through the lips of the vulva as a red pyriform mass. Sometimes such lacerations extend downward into the bladder, and in others upward into the terminal gut (rectum). In still other cases the anus is torn so that it forms one common orifice with the vulva.

Too often such cases prove fatal, or at least a recovery is not attained, and urine or fæces or both escape freely into the vagina. The simple laceration of the anus is easily sewed up, but the ends of the muscular fibers do not reunite and the control over the lower bowel is never fully reacquired. The successful stitching up of the wound communicating with the bladder or the rectum, requires unusual skill and care, and though I have ·succeeded in a case of the latter kind I cannot advise the attempt by unprofessional persons.

INFLAMMATION OF THE WOMB AND PERITONEUM.

These may result from injuries sustained by the womb during or after parturition, from exposure to cold or wet, or from the irritant action of putrid products within the womb. Under the inflammation the womb remains dilated and flaccid and decomposition of its secretions almost always occurs, so that the inflammation tends to assume a putrid character and general septic infection is likely to occur.

The *symptoms* are ushered in by shivering, staring coat, small rapid pulse, elevated temperature, accelerated breathing, inappetence, with arched back, stiff movement of the body, looking back at the flanks, and uneasy motions of the hind limbs, discharge from the vulva of a liquid at first watery, reddish, or yellowish, and later it may be whitish or glairy, and fetid or not in different cases. Tenderness of the abdomen shown on pressure is especially characteristic of cases affecting the peritoneum or lining of the belly, and is more marked lower down. If the animal survives the inflammation tends to become chronic and is attended by a whitish muco-purulent discharge. If on the contrary it proves fatal death is preceded by extreme prostration and weakness from the general septic poisoning.

In *treatment* the first thing to be sought is the removal of all offensive and irritant matters from the womb through a caoutchouc tube introduced into the womb and into which a funnel is fitted. Warm water should be passed until it comes away clear. To insure that all of the womb has been washed out the oiled hand may be introduced to carry the end of the tube into the two horns successively. When the offensive contents have been thus removed the womb should be injected with a quart of water holding in solution one-half ounce permanganate of potash, or in the absence of the latter two teaspoonfuls of carbolic acid. Repeat twice

DISEASES OF THE GENERATIVE ORGANS. 401

daily. Fomentation of the abdomen or the application of a warm flaxseed poultice may greatly relieve. Acetanilid, in doses of half an ounce, repeated twice or thrice a day, or sulphate of quinia in doses of one-third ounce, may be employed to reduce the fever. If the great prostration indicates septic poisoning large doses (one-half ounce) bisulphite of soda or salicylate of soda may be resorted to.

LEUCORRHŒA.

This is a white, glutinous, chronic discharge, the result of a continued sub-acute inflammation of the mucous membrane of the womb. Like the discharge of acute inflammation it contains many forms of bacteria, by some of which it is manifestly inoculable on the penis of the stallion, producing ulcers and a specific gonorrhœal discharge.

Treatment may consist in the internal use of tonics (sulphate of iron three drachms daily), and the washing out of the womb, as described under the last heading, followed by an astringent antiseptic injection (carbolic acid two teaspoonfuls, tannic acid one-half drachm, water one quart). This may be repeated two or three times a day.

LAMINITIS, OR FOUNDER, FOLLOWING PARTURITION.

This sometimes follows on inflammation of the womb, as it frequently does on disorder of the stomach. Its symptoms agree with those of the common form of founder and treatment need not differ.

DISEASES OF THE UDDER AND TEATS—CONGESTION AND INFLAMMATION OF THE UDDER.

This is comparatively rare in the mare, though in some cases the udder becomes painfully engorged before parturition and a doughy swelling, pitting on pressure, extends forward on the lower surface of the abdomen. When this goes on to active inflammation one or both of the glands become enlarged, hot, tense, and painful; the milk is dried up or replaced by a watery or reddish serous fluid, which at times becomes fetid; the animal walks lame, loses appetite, and shows general disorder and fever. The condition may end in recovery, in abscess, induration, or gangrene, and in some cases may lay the foundation for a tumor of the gland.

The *treatment* is simple so long as there is only congestion. Active rubbing with lard or oil, or better, camphorated oil, and the frequent drawing off of the milk, by the foal or with the hand, will usually bring about a rapid improvement. When active inflammation is present fomentation with warm water may be kept up for an hour and followed by the application of the camphorated oil, to which has been added some carbonate of soda and extract of belladonna. A dose of laxative medicine (four drachms Barbadoes aloes) will be of service in reducing fever and one-half ounce saltpeter daily will serve a similar end. In case the milk coagulates in the udder and cannot be withdrawn, or when the liquid becomes fetid, a solution of twenty grains carbonate of soda and ten drops carbolic acid dissolved in an ounce of water should be injected into the teat. In doing this it must be noted that the mare has three separate ducts opening on the summit of each teat and each must be carefully injected. To draw off the fetid product it may be needful to use a small milking tube, or spring teat-dilator designed by the writer (Plate VIII, Figs. 2 and 3). When pus forms and points externally, and cannot find a free escape by the teat, the spot where it fluctuates must be opened freely with the knife and the cavity injected daily with the carbolic-acid lotion. When the gland becomes hard and indolent it may be rubbed daily with iodine ointment one part, vaseline six parts.

TUMORS OF THE UDDER.

As the result of inflammation of the udder it may become the seat of an indurated diseased growth, which may go on growing and seriously interfere with the movement of the hind limbs. If such swellings will not give way in their early stages to treatment by iodine the only resort is to cut them out with a knife. As the gland is often implicated and has to be removed such mares cannot in the future suckle their colts, and therefore should not be bred.

SORE TEATS, SCABS, CRACKS, WARTS.

By the act of sucking, especially in cold weather, the teats are subject to abrasions, cracks, and scabs, and as the result of such irritation, or independently, warts sometimes grow and prove troublesome. The warts should be clipped off with sharp scissors and their roots burned with a solid pencil of lunar caustic. This is best done before parturition to secure healing before suckling begins. For sore teats use an ointment of vaseline one ounce, balsam of tolu five grains, and sulphate of zinc five grains.

CHAPTER VI.

DENTITION OF HORSES.

By the kind permission of Prof. Brown of London, Chief Veterinary Adviser of the British Privy Council, I am permitted to republish the following on the "Dentition of Horses," the same being a part of a series of articles originally contributed by him for the "Journal of the Royal Agricultural Society of Great Britain":

At birth the foal has the two central temporary incisors somewhat laterally placed, in consequence of the jaw not being wide enough to accommodate them both in front. The teeth are nearly covered with the gum, and only a small portion of the upper anterior edge is to be seen free from the membrane. In some cases the extreme corners of the lateral incisors are to be detected in outline under the gum. The three temporary molars are usually entirely covered with gum at the time of birth. This state of the mouth is shown in Fig. 1, which was taken on the morning of its birth from a cart colt foaled at the Royal Agricultural College Farm.

By the end of the second week after birth the central incisors will be fairly in the mouth, and in six or eight weeks the lateral teeth and also the temporary molars are well up. In Fig. 2 the state of the incisor teeth at two months old is shown. The central incisors at this age have the surfaces very slightly worn, and the cavity or infundibulum is not

DENTITION OF HORSES. 405

surrounded by a line of worn structure; only the anterior edges of the teeth have yet been subject to attrition. In the lateral incisors the wear is confined to a small portion of the anterior edge which is nearest to the central teeth. These appearances are indicated in Fig. 4.

Between two and six months old the central and lateral incisors increase in size with the growth of the animal. At six months old the mouth has a very neat and compact appearance. The centrals and laterals are well developed, and their anterior edges are worn level. The posterior edges

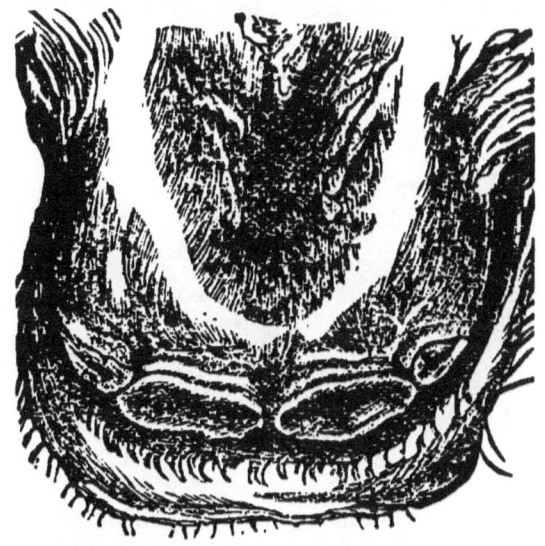

FIG. 1.—INCISORS OF FOAL AT BIRTH.

are, however, still rather below the anterior, and the table, therefore, is not perfectly formed. Fig. 3 was taken from the mouth of a cart colt at the age of six months.

Soon after seven months indications of the cutting of the corner teeth may often be seen, and in many instances the points of the teeth will be observed pricking through the gum. At nine months old the colt will have the corner incisors in the mouth with their extreme anterior edges in apposition, leaving a triangular space, which is seen most perfectly on a side view when the lips are slightly separated.

At this period the fourth molar, which is a permanent tooth from the first, begins to protrude through the gum, and by the time of the completion of the first year it is level with the temporary molars; but its surface is not worn, and the recent appearance of the tooth is most important as evidence of the age of one year.

Fig. 4 shows the shell-like character of the corner teeth and the state of the tables of the other incisors in the yearling colt; and it may be remarked that the appearances correspond with those of the teeth of the five-year-old horse, the chief difference being that in the yearling the teeth are temporary, and in the five-year-old permanent organs.

FIG. 2.—INCISORS OF FOAL AT TWO MONTHS.

A practical horseman would perhaps feel amused at the idea of the possibility of a yearling being taken for a five-year-old, or a two-year-old for a six: but in the case of rough forest ponies, in which the aspect of colthood is quickly lost, such mistakes have occurred, and it is therefore not out of place to suggest that care should be taken to discriminate between the temporary incisors, and if necessary to refer to the molar teeth in order to avoid such embarrassing blunders.

Under ordinary circumstances it will be more frequently necessary to distinguish between a yearling and a two-year-old than between one-year-old and five, and it fortunately

DENTITION OF HORSES. 407

happens that at the age of two years another molar, the fifth in situation, is in the mouth, and may be at once distinguished by its recent appearance. Soon after eighteen months the fifth molar begins to protrude through the gum, and by the termination of the second year is level with the other molars, so that any doubt which may remain after an inspection of the incisors may be settled by reference to the condition of the molars.

Figs. 5 and 6 are of foal's molar teeth at one year and at two years. It will be observed in Fig. 5 that the surfaces of four molars are worn level, while points of the new tooth,

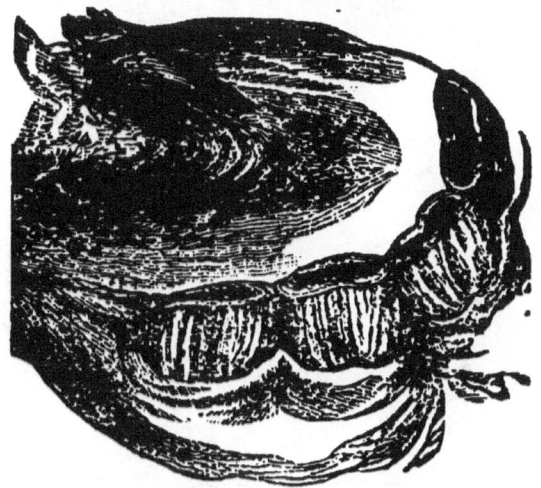

FIG. 3.—INCISORS OF FOAL AT SIX MONTHS.

the fifth in position, are rounded, excepting a small portion at the inner side of the tooth, which shows the effects of attrition, but only to a slight extent.

The incisor teeth at two years of age have their tables perfectly formed as a rule; but in some instances the corner teeth, although they have lost their shell-like character, still have a portion of their posterior edge untouched, as shown in the illustration of the mouth of a two-year-old filly (Fig. 7).

Between two and three years of age the central temporary incisors of the horse are changed for permanent teeth, and the different phases of the change are sufficiently well defined to assist the examiner in deciding whether the animal is two years off or coming three years.

At two years off, or two years and a quarter, there will be evident signs of the shedding of the upper central incisors. The gum at the necks of the teeth is somewhat sunken, and the color is rather deeper than in other parts. Very soon a red line appears in this position, and it is evident that one or both of the temporary teeth are only held in their places

FIG. 4.—INCISORS OF FOAL AT ONE YEAR.

by a small portion of the fang which has not yet been absorbed. At two years and a half the permanent teeth will generally be in the mouth. Perhaps one temporary central incisor may yet remain; but even in that case the state of the permanent teeth will be sufficient evidence of the animal's age.

The mouth of the horse at two years and a half has a very characteristic appearance, especially when viewed in the front by separating the lips. The four permanent central incisors are seen in position about half-grown, with deep cavities or infundibula extending across each tooth, present-

DENTITION OF HORSES. 409

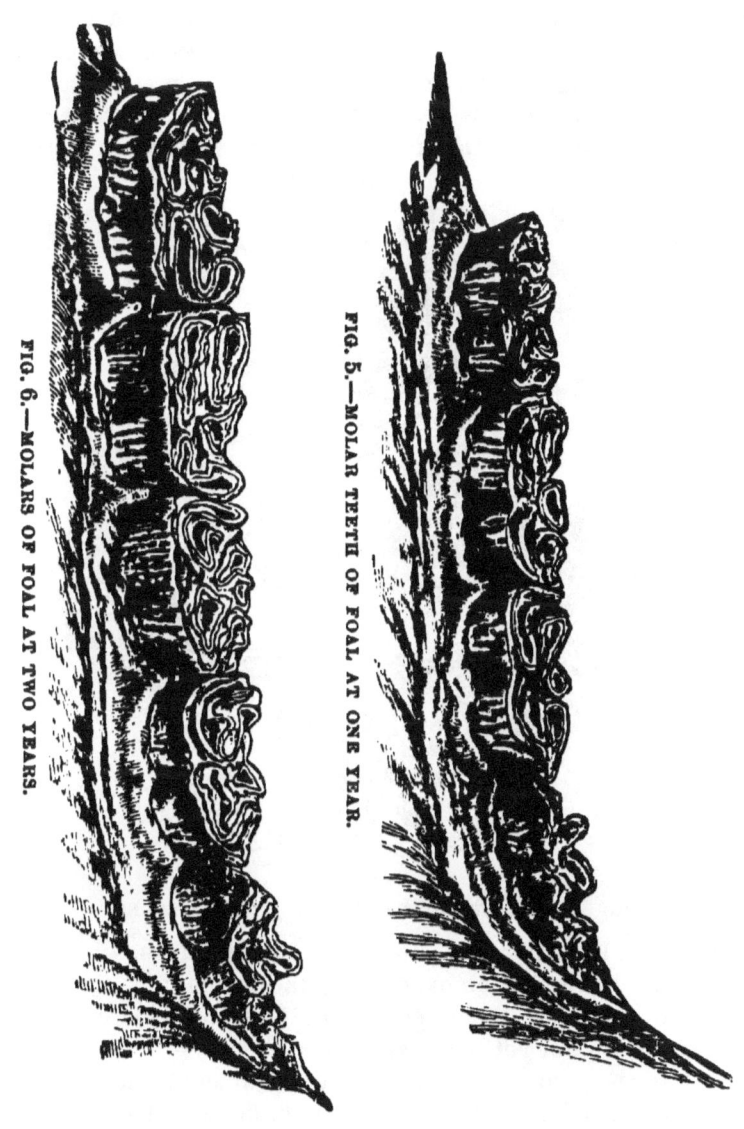

FIG. 5.—MOLAR TEETH OF FOAL AT ONE YEAR.

FIG. 6.—MOLARS OF FOAL AT TWO YEARS.

ing a striking contrast to the worn temporary teeth on each side of them. The new permanent teeth at this age are not more than half-way up, and there is consequently a considerable space between the upper and lower teeth when the temporary teeth are in apposition.

When the horse has reached the age of two years and nine months the four permanent incisors will be in actual

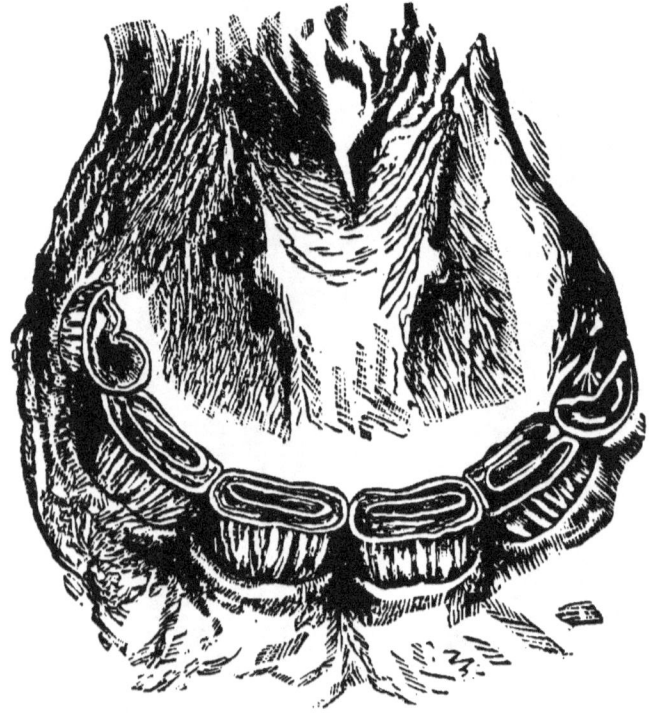

FIG. 7.—INCISORS OF CART FILLY AT TWO YEARS.

contact, at least in regard to their anterior edges, when the mouth is closed; but on examining the tables it is apparent that no wear has taken place, and the posterior edges of the teeth are not yet level with the anterior.

At three years old the central permanent incisors are fully developed and the anterior edges show a narrow line of worn surface. The posterior edges are level with the anterior, but are not worn to the same extent.

These appearances are shown in Fig. 8, which was taken from the mouth of a colt at the completion of the third year.

During the development of the central permanent incisors in the course of the third year an important change is going on in the first and second molars, the fangs of which are gradually absorbed as the permanent teeth push their way up underneath them.

FIG. 8.—INCISORS OF HORSE AT THREE YEARS.

At two years and a half old one or two of the permanent molars may be in the mouth. Sometimes the second in position is cut before the first, and a careful examination will show that the crowns of the first and second temporary molars which yet remain are only retained in their position by a slight attachment to the gum, and very little force is required to dislodge them.

412 A TREATISE ON HORSE-BREEDING.

From the completion of the third year to the termination of the fourth year the changes which have been described in reference to the central incisors and the first and second molars occur in the lateral incisors and the third and sixth molars.

At three years off the same condition of the gum which

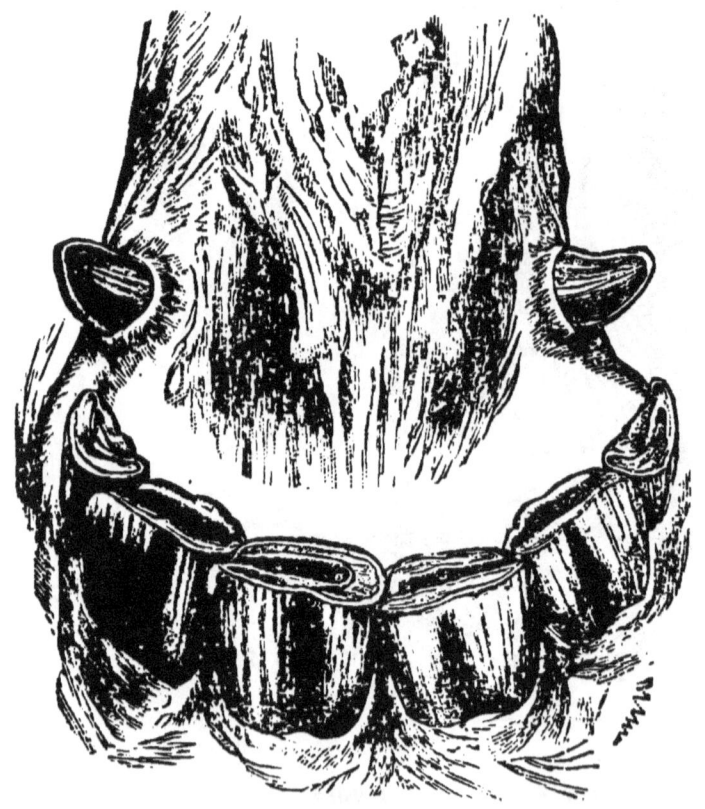

FIG. 9.—INCISORS OF HORSE AT FOUR YEARS.

was described in respect of the upper central temporary incisors now appears at the necks of the lower lateral temporary incisors. At three years and a half some or perhaps all four of the permanent lateral incisors are in the mouth, and soon afterward the third and sixth permanent molars are cut.

At four years old the horse has the lateral permanent incisors in apposition, and the fourth and sixth molars are level, or nearly level, with the other teeth.

The tusks of the horse are often through the gums at four years of age, but they are not usually fully developed before five years, and occasionally they are not well up before five years and a half. As a means of judging the age these teeth are of little importance.

Fig. 9 represents the state of the incisor teeth on the completion of the fourth year. Remarkably well-developed tusks were an exceptional feature in the mouth of the animal from which the illustration was taken; in other respects the teeth present the appearances which are ordinarily observed at the age of four years.

The only milk-teeth now remaining are the four corner incisors, which are much worn and quite different from the broad, permanent teeth, with which they are not likely to be confounded. In the lateral incisors the wear has affected the anterior edge of the tooth, and the cavity extends completely across the table, which is therefore not fully formed. In the central incisors there is a line of worn surface quite round the central cavity, and the table may be properly described as fully formed.

Incidentally it may be remarked that between the commencement and completion of the fourth year the dental changes include the cutting of four permanent incisors, two in each four tusks, and eight molars—two on each side of both jaws, making sixteen teeth, which are all advancing at the same time.

Between four years and five the corner temporary incisors are removed and the permanent teeth occupy their places. Indications of the change are seen at four years off in the upper corner incisors, and in a few months the temporary teeth are displaced and the permanent organs are in the mouth, but their edges do not meet until the fifth year is completed, and even then the contact is limited to the anterior part, and a triangular space similar to that which can be seen between the upper and lower corner teeth in the mouth of the yearling may be recognized when the lips are separated at the side of the mouth. The shell-like character of the corner permanent teeth is the special indication of five years old.

Fig. 10 shows the condition of the incisors in the mouth of a five-year-old. It is evident that the corner permanent

FIG 10.—INCISORS OF HORSE AT FIVE YEARS.

incisors show but slight indication of wear on the completion of the fifth year, only the anterior edge exhibiting the effects of attrition. The tables of the lateral incisors are fully formed by the central cavity being surrounded by a line of worn surface. In the central incisors the cavity has become extremely shallow.

With the development of the permanent incisors the permanent dentition of the horse is completed.

From the completion of permanent dentition the evidence of age is to be obtained by the inspection of the tables of the incisor teeth in regard to their form, the extent and depth of the central cavity and the shape of the central enamel.

At six years old the horse's age is judged chiefly by the amount of wear which the corner teeth have sustained, although there are other marks which are worthy of notice. The corner teeth have lost their shell-like character, and a line of worn surface surrounds the central cavity, excepting a small point where the corners touch the lateral incisors. The line of wear is broader at the anterior than at the posterior edge, and the cavity is still of considerable depth. In the lateral incisors the cavity (or mark) is shallow and much smaller than that of the corner incisors. The figure described by the central enamel is approaching an oval. The cavity in the central incisor is almost worn out but its boundaries are distinctly marked by the central enamel which surrounds it, forming an elliptical figure which extends almost across the tooth in the direction of its long diameter, and is nearer to the posterior than to the anterior edge.

The tusks are usually well developed, but their points are not worn, and the hollows on their inner surfaces are well defined.

All these characters are shown in Fig. 11 of the lower incisors of a six-year-old horse.

At seven years old the tables of the corner teeth are perfectly formed and the cavity in each tooth is very shallow. The central enamel, however, is well defined and forms an elliptical figure, which is nearer to the posterior than to the anterior edge of the tooth. In the lateral incisors the central enamel forms a figure which is nearer to the oval than to the elliptical, and the mark, which is very shallow, does not extend so far across the table of the tooth as it does at six years old. These teeth are also deeper from front to back than they were at six years.

The central incisors at seven years old have their sides elongated, so that the table approaches the figure of a triangle. The mark is very close to the posterior edge of the tooth, and the central enamel forms an oval with flattened

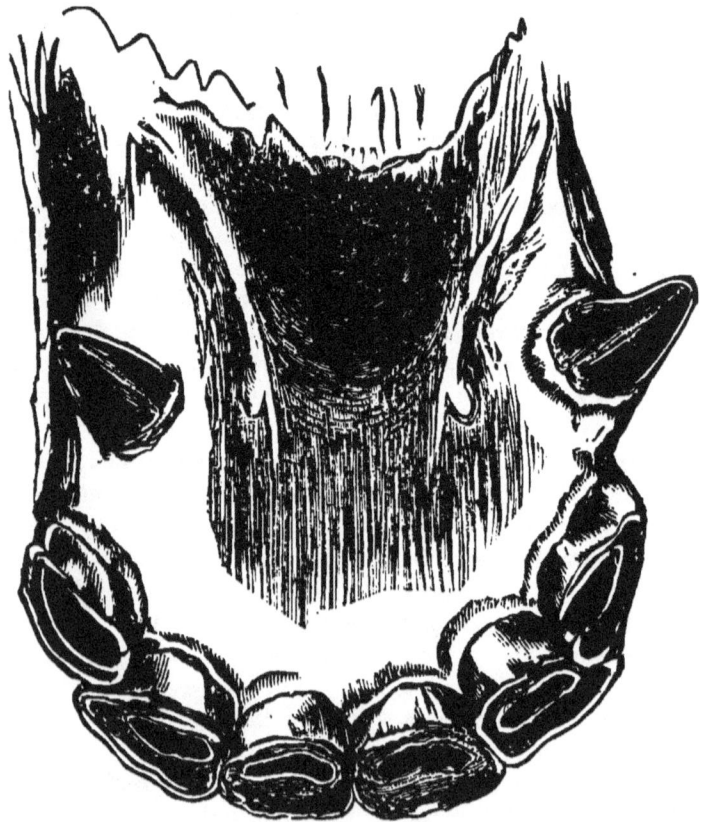

FIG. 11.—INCISORS OF HORSE AT SIX YEARS.

sides in place of the elliptical figure, which is shown in the drawing of the six-year-old mouth. The tusks are somewhat blunted at the point.

In the eight-year-old mouth the form of the tables of the incisors and the shape of the central enamel in the central incisor afford tolerably satisfactory indications of the age.

The central teeth are more distinctly triangular than they were at seven years; the central enamel in these teeth is also triangular in figure. All the tables of the incisors are worn as level as the different degrees of density of the various structures will permit. The cavities are either very shallow or quite obliterated by being filled up, although the central of the tooth tissues in each tooth is perfectly well defined.

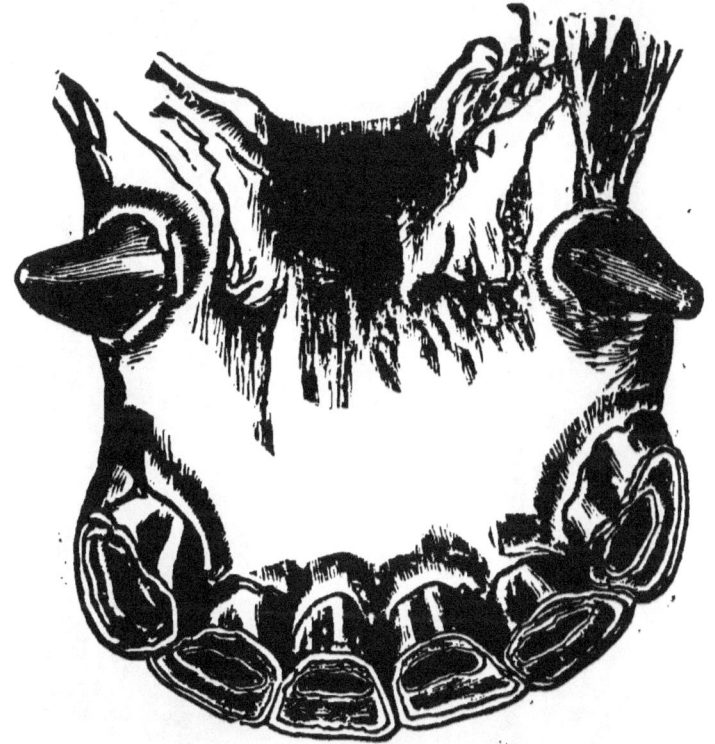

FIG. 12.—INCISORS OF HORSE AT SEVEN YEARS.

The gum of the corner incisors at eight years has lost its circular form and become square. The tusks are more blunted at the tops than in the seven-year-old mouth.

Fig. 13 shows the condition of the molar teeth soon after two years and a half. A permanent tooth, the first in position, is seen occupying the place of the temporary molar, which has fallen, and the second permanent tooth is pushing its way up under the second temporary molar, which is only

FIG. 13.—MOLARS OF HORSE AT TWO YEARS AND SEVEN MONTHS.

FIG. 17.—MOLARS OF HORSE AT THREE YEARS AND EIGHT MONTHS.

held in its place by small portions of the fangs which have not yet been absorbed. The fifth molar, which was up at two years old, is fully developed and is quite clear from the angle of the jaw. At three years old the first and second permanent molars are well up, and the top and bottom teeth are in contact when the mouth is closed, but the teeth are distinguished by the recent appearance which they present

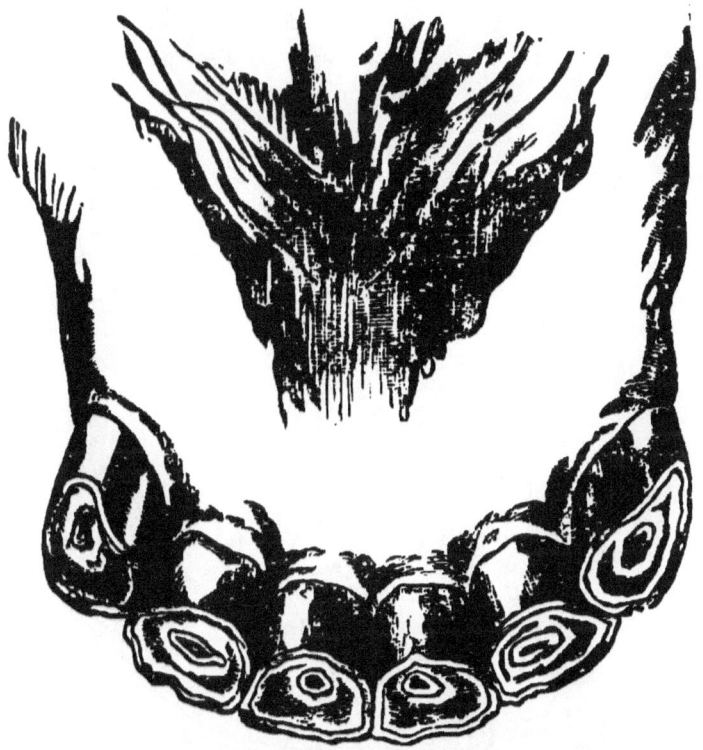

FIG. 14 —INCISORS OF MARE (SOLACE) AT TEN YEARS.

in comparison with the worn surfaces of the teeth immediately behind them. Fig. 17 shows the molar teeth of a horse at three years and eight months, when the fourth and sixth permanent molars are cut. No difficulty would be experienced in distinguishing the recent molars in the illustration. The first and second and the fourth and fifth molars show considerable wear, while the new teeth present rounded points on their surfaces and are not nearly level with the other teeth. One or two of the most projecting points of the sixth molar show the effects of attrition, but these teeth at the age of three years and a half have their posterior points close to the angle of the jaw and still covered with the gum. At four years old the fourth and sixth molars are level, or

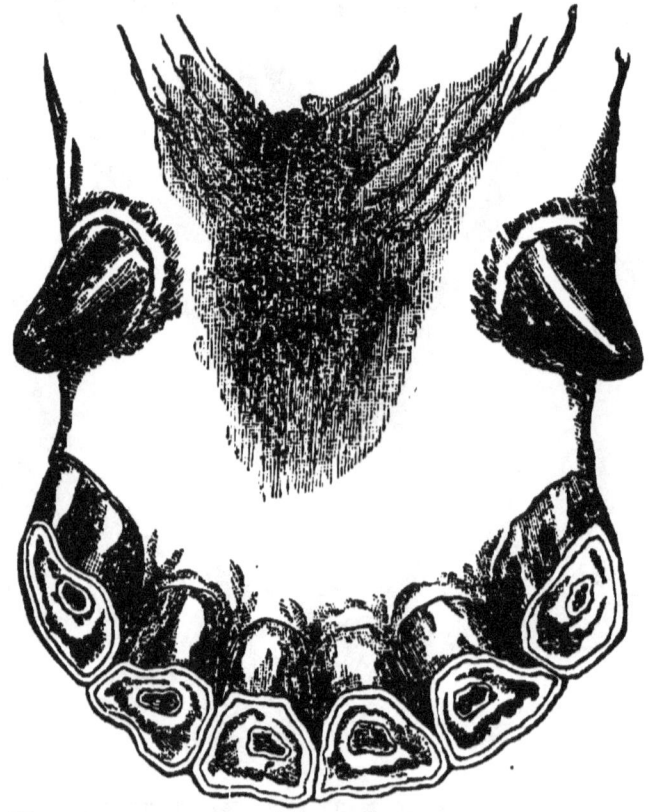

FIG. 15.—INCISORS OF HORSE (PEEP-O'-DAY BOY) AT EIGHT YEARS.

nearly level, with the other teeth. Between the commencement and completion of the fourth year the remaining eight molars are cut, two on each side of both jaws.

[Figs. 13 and 17, of molar teeth, could not be arranged in their due course.]

On comparing the tables of the teeth with those of the mare Solace (Fig. 14) at the age of ten years, it will be seen

DENTITION OF HORSES. 421

that there are certain important differences. The central incisors have quite lost the "mark," which is only represented by a dot. The central enamel in the remaining incisors forms a much smaller figure than in the ten-year-old teeth. The corner teeth have become more oval in form and only a trace of the central enamel can be seen.

From eight to ten years old the changes occasioned by the wear to which the teeth have been subjected are not sufficiently regular to enable the examiner to speak positively as to the exact age, but during this period the cavity in each

FIG. 16.—INCISORS OF HORSE (LOTHARIO) AT TWELVE YEARS.

lower central incisor is worn out and only a small circle of enamel in the tables of the central incisors remains to indicate its position. In the corner teeth at ten years old the central enamel has become round, or nearly so, as shown in the accompanying drawing (Fig. 14) of the mouth of Solace, a steeple-chase mare foaled in 1842. The teeth are depicted exactly as they appeared in the summer of 1852, and fairly represent the characters of the ten-year-old mouth.

In Fig. 15 the appearance of the eight-year-old mouth is shown. The drawing was copied from the mouth of Peep o'-Day Boy in 1852. The horse was foaled in 1844.

At twelve years old the teeth are longer from the receding of the gums, and are also narrower in consequence of having been worn toward the fang, which decreases in width from the neck of the tooth to its termination. The tusks are blunted, especially those of the upper jaw, and a quantity of tartar often surrounds those in the lower jaw. The incisors at this age project almost in a straight line from the jaws, and in some mouths a line drawn transversely across the tables of the teeth will cut the centers of all of them excepting those of the corner teeth.

Fig. 16 represents the teeth of the Thoroughbred horse Lothario, foaled in 1840, as they appeared in 1852.

After twelve or fourteen years of age the evidence which is afforded by the teeth is not definite enough to justify a positive opinion as to the animal's age.

INDEX.

Abortion. 158, 172, 328, 360.
Accidental variations, 28.
    transmissible, 31.
Adaptation to changed conditions, 19.
    to locality, 20.
Africa, the horses of, 185.
Age, effect of, upon stallions, 126.
    for castration, 140.
    indicated by the teeth, 404.
    quality of get not affected by, 127.
    suitable for breeding, 168.
Altitude, effect of, 26.
American Thoroughbreds, 202.
Arabian horses, 20, 185.
Ardennais horses, 288.
Asiatic horses, 186.
Assistance in parturition, 174, 363.
Atavism, 19, 36.
Attention to foal at birth, 176.
Average period of gestation, 155, 352.
Aversion to mare, how remedied, 121.

Bakewell's Holland importation, 256.
    skill as a breeder, 14.
Barbs, 185.
Barrenness, causes of, 144, 321, 347.
Barrier for trying mares, 119.
Bashaws, 210.
Belgians, 290.
Bellfounder's dam, 249.
Black Dorsal streak, the, 186.
Black horses of Flanders, 254.
Black Lincolnshire horses, 256.
Bleeding mares before service, 147, 169.
Blindness transmissible, 103, 293.
Boulonnais horses, 286.
Bowels of the foal, 130, 301.
Breaking the colt, 166.
Breed, definition of, 39.
Breeding draft horses, 96.
    for sex, 82.
    from unsound stock, 95.
    general principles of, 11.
Breeding in-and-in, 44.
    contradiction of, explained, 52.
    Darwin on, 51.
    effect of on hardiness, 56.
    Galton on, 47.
    Herbert Spencer's views on, 50, 53.
    how far it may be practiced, 53.
    tendency of, 46, 55.
    when not dangerous, 53.
Breeding stock, selection of, 91.
    trotting horses, 205.
Breeds formed by selection, 40.

Breeds, how formed, 38.
    modified by locality, 20.
    modified by temperature, 18.
    of horses, 184.
Breton horses, 287.
Bridle for unruly stallion, 117.
Brood mares, 143, 167, 302.
    abortion, 158, 172, 328, 360.
    at time of foaling, 176.
    colt-founder, 325.
    confinement of, 304.
    difficult parturition, 329.
    diseases and accidents of, 321, 346.
    drying the milk, 162, 178.
    effect of general health on milk, 302.
    exercise for, 152.
    food to produce milk, 159, 302.
    heat during pregnancy, 119, 328.
    laceration of the perinæum, 333.
    laceration of the rectum, 328.
    leucorrhœa or whites, 324.
    nymphomania, 323.
    œdema of pregnancy, 377.
    productive period of, 151, 169.
    superimpregnation, 327.
    stallions and foals, 88.
    tumors of the vagina, 324.
    working, 162, 167, 170.
Buffalo trotting course, 213.

Canadian horses, climatic effect on, 16.
Cancer of the penis and sheath, 312.
Cart horses, English, 254.
Castration, effect of, 138.
    effect of on development, 139.
    when it should be performed, 140, 341.
Causes of abortion, 158, 172, 328, 360.
Causes of barrenness, 144, 347.
Central Asia, the horses of, 185.
Changed conditions, adaptaton to, 19.
Change of climate, effect of, 15.
    effect on generative organs, 81.
Circassia, horses of, 185.
Clays, 208.
Cleopatra, in-breeding illustrated by, 46.
Cleveland Bays, 241.
    stud book, 246.
    type of the (illustration), 243.
Climate, effect of on the eye, 293.
    effect of on the generative organs, 81.
    influence of, 15, 20.

(423)

424　INDEX.

Climatic influences, Prof. Low on, 24.
Clydesdales, 265.
　and Shire horses blended, 269.
　stud book, American, 273.
　stud book, Scotch, 269.
　type of the (illustration), 267.
Coach horses, French, 235.
　how to breed them, 99.
Color influenced by imagination, 78.
　markings from fright, 78.
　of Clydesdales, 272.
　of Percherons, 276.
　of Shires, 260.
　transmitted, 103.
Colostrum, or first milk, 179.
Colt-founder, 325.
Colts, accidents and diseases of, 293.
　attention to at birth, 176.
　diarrhœa, or scours, in, 183, 301.
　effect of exercise on development of, 163.
　gentling the, 165.
　lice on, 334.
　mange, 334.
　teaching to eat, 160.
　the weaning of, 161.
　umbilical hernia, 300.
　worms in the intestines of, 305.
Condition of stallion for the stud, 104.
Constipation of the bowels, 180.
Controlling the sex, 82.
Controlling the stallion when in use, 114.
Coomsie horses, 186.
Coupe horses, how to breed, 99.
Courage of stallions, 139.
Cows' milk for foals, 160.
Crosses, top most important, 60.
　violent, effect of, 48.
Cross-fertilization, 28.
Crossing and in-breeding, 44.
Cryptorchids or ridgelings, 321, 343.
Curly or frizzled horses, 186.

Dam and sire, relative size of, 62.
Danger from kicking mare, 116.
　from overfeeding, 110.
Darkness injurious to the eye, 297.
Darley Arabian, 197.
Darwin, Chas. F., on in-breeding, 51.
　on reversion, 18.
Defects transmitted, 95.
Dentition of horses, 404.
Development affected by exercise, 163.
　by food and climate, 15.
　by castration, 138.
Diarrhœa in foals, 130, 301.
Difficult parturition, 175, 329, 364.
Diseased tendencies transmitted, 144.
Diseases peculiar to breeding stock, 293, 310, 335.
　of brood mares. (See brood mares, diseases of.)
　of stallions. (See stallions, diseases of.)
Distemper, or strangles, 306.
Dongola, the horses of, 188.
Draft horse, qualities of a good, 96.
Drugs and medicines for a stallion condemned, 104.
Drying off the brood mare, 162.

Dun horses of Tartary, 187.
Dwarf breeds produced by climate, 15.

Eclipse, 195.
Effect of age on fertility of stallion, 126.
　of age on quality of the get, 127.
　of castration on stallion, 138.
　of change of climate on breeds, 15, 20.
　of change of climate on generative organs, 81.
　of climate on the eye, 296.
　of exercise on development, 164.
　of first impregnation, 66.
　of imagination on color, 78.
　of overfeeding, 108, 113.
　of pasture upon breeding mares, 182.
　of teething on the eye, 296.
English Shire and Cart horses, 254.
Eruptions on the penis, 318.
Evacuation of bowels of foal, 180.
Excessive feeding dangerous, 108, 113.
Excessive venery, 315.
Exercise for brood mares, 152.
Exercising the stallion, 106.
Extent of hereditary influence, 34.
External injuries to stallions, 310.
Eye, hygiene of the, 293.
　the, as affected by the teeth, 298.

Family, value of, 13.
Feeding the stallion, 104.
　the young foal, 160.
　to increase flow of milk, 159, 174.
　to produce weight, 108.
Feet and legs, 94.
Fertility affected by in-breeding, 48.
　by condition of, 126.
　by violent crosses, 48.
Fighting between stallions, 141.
Fillies, when old enough to breed, 167.
First impregnation, influence of, 66.
　may be ignored, 76.
　Prof. Law on, 67.
First milk, or colostrum, 179.
Flanders, black horses of, 254.
Flemish blood in Clydesdales, 265.
　in Shire horses, 254.
Flemish horses, 254.
Flying Childers, 196.
Foaling, period of, 154.
　rest after, 158.
　signs of, 156.
Foals, 363.
　attention to at birth, 176, 180.
　cow's milk for, 160.
　diarrhœa, or scours, 130, 301.
　effect of milk on stomach of, 302.
　feeding young, 160.
　following the dams, 159.
　hernia, or rupture, 300.
　per cent of to mares served, 123, 129.
　strangles, or distemper, 306.
　weaning, 162.
　worms in intestines, 305.
Food for mares while suckling, 159, 302.
　for the stallion, 105.
　for young foals, 160, 303.
Formation of breeds, 38.

INDEX. 425

Foul sheath, 318.
French Coach horses, 235.
　draft breeds, 287.
　type of the (illustration), 237.
French Government subsidies, 240.
Frizzled or curly horses, 186.

Galloping mares before service, 169.
Galton, Francis, on in-breeding, 47.
General characteristics of horses, 184.
General management of stallions, 104.
General principles of breeding, 11.
Generative organs affected by change of climate, 81.
Gentling the foal, 166.
German Coach horses, 291.
Gestation, period of, 154.
Godolphin Arabian, 198.
Good pedigree, what is a, 60.
Grass, effect of on breeding mares, 182.
Grease, or scratches, in stallions, 112.

Hackneys, 247.
　type of the (illustration), 253.
Hambletonians, 206.
Hambletonian (Rysdyk's), number of mares served by, 124.
Hardiness of thoroughbreds, 57.
Headstrong stallion, bridle for, 115.
Heat during pregnancy, 119, 168, 328.
Heat, or œstrum, of mares, 119, 168, 328.
Herbert, H. W., on Cleveland Bays, 241.
Hereditary influence, extent of, 34.
　how far it may be depended on, 36.
　qualities, transmission of, 12.
Hernia, umbilical, 300.
　scrotal, 313.
High feeding dangerous, 110.
Hobbles, to prevent kicking, 117.
Holland, importations from, 256.
Horse-breeding statistics, 124, 128, 133.
Horses, adaptation to locality, 21.
　for farmers, 101.
　modified by climate, 21.
　that will sell, 101.
　the breeds of, 184.
　types in general, 184.
Hue and Cry, 250.
Humidity, the effect of, 23.
Hygiene of the eye, 293.

Imagination, effect of on color, 78.
Impregnation, causes of failure of, 14, 321, 347.
　influence of first, 66.
　may be ignored, 76.
In-breeding, 44.
　as illustrated in the Ptolemys, 46.
　contradictions of, explained, 52.
　Darwin on, 51.
　effect of on hardiness, 56.
　Galton on, 47.
　Herbert Spencer on, 50, 53.
　how far it may be practiced, 53.
　tendency of, 46, 55.
　when not dangerous, 58.
Increase in speed of trotters, 212.
Increasing flow of milk, 152, 159, 302.

India, Northern, horses of, 185.
Indian ponies, 292.
Individual quality, transmission of, 31.
Inheritance in the human family, 12.
Inherited blindness, 295.
Infirmities transmitted, 92.
Inflammation of the penis, 311, 345.
　testicles, 311, 335.
Inflamed udder, 178.
Influence of first impregnation, 66.
　of the dam, 143.
Iniquities of fathers visited upon the children, 12.
Injuries, external, to the stallion, 310.
Intestines, worms in the, 305.

Jacks fighting with stallions, 141.

Kicking by mares, how to prevent, 117.

Laceration of the perinæum, 333, 399.
　of the rectum, 338.
Lanarkshire, horses of, 265.
Lassoing stallions, 141.
Law, Prof. James on diseases of breeding stock in general, 293.
　barrenness, 145, 347.
　diarrhœa, or scours, in colts, 301.
　eye, the, as affected by the teeth, 298.
　eye, hygiene of the, 293.
　hernia, umbilical, in foals, 300.
　are, diseases of the, 346.
　anidian monsters—moles, 355.
　barrenness, causes of, 145, 347.
　bleeding from the womb, 396.
　castration of the, 346.
　constipation, 358.
　cramps of the limbs, 357.
　difficult parturition, 364.
　embryotomy, 393.
　extra-uterine gestation, 354.
　first impregnation, influence of, 67.
　flooding, 396.
　fœtus, prolonged retention of the, 358.
　gestation, extra-uterine, 354.
　labor pains, premature, 366.
　laminitis, or founder, 401.
　leucorrhœa, or whites, 401.
　moles—anidian monsters, 355.
　natural presentation, 363.
　parturition, difficult, 364.
　parturition, symptoms of, 363.
　paralysis, 358.
　peritoneum, inflammation of the, 400.
　pregnant, hygiene of the, 352.
　pregnancy, duration of, 350.
　pregnancy, indications of, 350.
　premature labor pains, 366.
　presentation, natural, 363.
　presentations, wrong, 386.
　retention of the fœtus, prolonged, 358.
　sterility, causes of, 145, 347.
　teats and udder, diseases of the, 401.
　vagina, rupture of the, 399.

INDEX.

Law, Prof. James, on diseases of breeding stock in general—mare—whites, or leucorrhœa, 401.
  womb, bleeding from the, 396.
  womb, casting or expulsion of the, 396.
  womb, diseases of the, 355.
  womb, eversion of the, 396.
  womb, inflammation of the, 400.
  womb, rupture of the, 399.
  wrong presentations, 386.
  stallion, diseases of the, 335.
  abdomen, swelling of the, 345.
  barrenness, causes of, 347.
  castration of the, 341.
  castration, bleeding after, 344.
  castration, pains after, 344.
  cryptorchids, castration of, 343.
  dourine, 340.
  mal du coit, 340.
  masturbation, 340.
  orchitis, 335.
  penis, paralysis of the, 339.
  penis, swelling of the, 345.
  penis, warts on the, 339.
  phymosis and paraphymosis. 345.
  ridgelings, castration of, 343.
  sarcocele, 337.
  sheath, swelling of the, 345.
  spermatic cord, strangulated, 344.
  spermatic cord, tumors on the, 346.
  sterility, causes of, 347.
  swelling of the abdomen, 345.
  swelling of the sheath, 345.
  testicles, abnormal number of, 338.
  testicles, degeneration of the, 338.
  testicles, inflammation of the 335.
  tumors on the spermatic cord, 346
  varicocele, 338.
Legs and feet, 135.
Leucorrhœa, or whites, 324, 401.
Lice on colts, 324.
Lighting the stable, 297.
Limits of service of stallion, 121.
Live foals, percentage of to mares served, 123, 129.
Live-Stock Journal (London) on Cleveland Bays, 244.
Low, Prof. David, on climatic influences, 24.
  on draft horses, 257.
  on thoroughbreds, 194.

Mahomet, influence of on horse-breeding in Arabia, 200.
Male should be larger than female, 62.
Malformations, 329, 364.
Mambrinos, 208.
Management of the stallion, 104.
Mange on colts, 334.
Mares, abortion in, 158, 172, 328, 360.
  aversion to by stallion, 121.
  attention to at foaling, 154. 176.
  diseases of. (See brood mares.)
  feeding while suckling, 159, 174.
  how to prevent from kicking, 117.

Mares, influence of on progeny, 143.
  means to insure impregnation, 167.
  number to be served, 121.
  suckling, food for, 159, 174.
  when in heat, 118.
  when should be bred, 118.
  when should be tried, 118.
  working when in foal, 153, 158, 172.
Markings from imagination, 78.
Mark Lane Express on Clevelands, 244.
Masturbation, 319, 340.
Milk affecting the foal, 302.
  effects of first, 179.
  for colts, 160.
  effect of on general health, 302.
  heated, effect of, 178, 302.
  increasing the flow of, 159.
Moon-blindness, 294.
Morgans, 209.
Mustangs, 292.

Nearsightedness, 294.
Ninth day after foaling best for breeding again, 118.
Non-emission of semen, or "proudness," 316.
Northern Europe, the horses of, 185.
Nostrums injurious, 107.
Nubian horses, 188.
Number of mares to be served, 121.
Nymphomania, 323.

Œdema of pregnancy, 327.
Œstrum, or heat, 118. 167.
Oil-meal for colts, 160
Oldenburg Coach horses, 291.
Old work or road mares not desirable, 154, 167.
Opening mouth of womb, 148.
Ophthalmia, 294.
Oriental sires, influence of on thoroughbreds, 198.
Orloff trotters, 226.
  and American trotters compared, 233.
  trotting rules, 230.
Ovaries, diseased, 149.
Overfeeding and lack of exercise, 112.
  dangers from, 110.

Paaren, Dr. N. H., on abortion, 328.
  barrenness in mares, 321.
  cancer of the penis and sheath, 312.
  colt-founder, 325.
  cryptorchids, or ridgelings, 321.
  difficult parturition, 329.
  excessive venery, 315.
  external injuries to the stallion, 310
  foul sheath, 318.
  heat during pregnancy, 328.
  inflammation of the penis, 311.
  inflammation of the testicles. 311.
  laceration of the perinæum, 333.
  laceration of the rectum, 328.
  leucorrhœa, or whites, 324.
  lice on colts, 334.
  masturbation, 319.
  non-emission, or "proudness," 316.
  nymphomania, 323.
  œdema during pregnancy, 327.

INDEX. 427

Paaren, Dr. N. H., on paralysis of the penis, 312.
  prolapse of penis, 312.
  scrotal hernia, 313.
  sexual sluggishness, 317.
  spermatorrhœa, 317.
  superimpregnation, 327.
  tumors of the vagina, 324.
  vesicular eruptions of penis, 318.
  waterbag, so-called, 315.
Pacers, 221.
  type of the (illustration), 223.
Paralysis of the penis, 312.
Parturition, difficult, 329, 364.
  signs of, 156, 174, 363.
Pasture, effect of on brood mares, 182.
Per cent of foals to mares served, 128, 129.
Persian horses, 185.
Pedigree in the human family, 12.
  tests of, 61.
  value of, 59.
Percherons, 273.
  type of the (illustration), 275.
Penis, inflammation of the, 311.
  cancer of the, 312.
  paralysis of the, 312.
Percheron-Norman controversy, 282.
Percheron Stud Book, American, 286.
  French, 285.
Perinæum, laceration of, 333.
Periodic ophthalmia, 294.
Perriot, Ernest, on Percherons, 280.
Pilots, 210.
Poitevins, 288.
Ponies, 185, 187.
Pregnancy, heat during, 119, 168, 328.
  signs of, 169, 350.
Pretender, Wroot's, 248.
Principles of breeding, 11.
Productive period in brood mares, 151, 169.
Prolapse of the penis, 312.
Ptolemys, an illustration from the, 47.
Puerperal fever, caused by overfeeding, 145.
Pure air essential, 164.

Quality of mare's milk, 179.
  of get not affected by age of sire, 127.

Rectum, laceration of, 328.
Relative size of sire and dam, 62.
Remarkable productiveness, 151.
Reversion to original type, 18, 31.
Reynolds, Dr. R. S., on English draft horses, 259.
  views of, 167.
Ridgelings, 321, 343.
Roadsters and trotters, 205.
Roughing it, effect of on colts, 163.
Rupture at the navel, 300.
  of the scrotum, 313.
Russian trotters, 226.
  trotting rules, 230.

Saddle horses, 221.
Scours, or diarrhœa, 130, 301.
Scrotal hernia, 313.
Selection of breeding stock, 91.

Season, fitting the stallion for the, 104.
  stallion after the close of, 135.
Service of mare, managing the stallion at, 116.
Sex, controlling the, 82.
Sexual sluggishness, 317
Shales horse, the, 247.
Sheath, foul, 318.
  cancer of the, 312.
Shetland ponies, 291.
  produced by climatic influences, 15.
Shire and Clydesdale blended, 269.
Shire horses, English, 254.
  type of the (illustration), 263.
Shire Horse Stud Book, 259.
Signs of approaching parturition, 156, 174, 363.
Signs of heat, or œstrum, 167.
  pregnancy, 169, 350.
Size of sire and dam, relative, 62.
Skimmed milk for colts, 160.
Sluggishness, sexual, 317.
Soundness, importance of, 89.
Spain, the horses of, 187.
Speed of American trotters, 213.
Spencer, Herbert, on in-breeding, 50, 53.
Spermatorrhœa, 317.
Sports, 28.
Spotted horses, 187.
Stables, how they should be lighted, 297.
Stable management of the stallion, 108.
Stallions, accidents and diseases of, 310–335.
  cancer of the penis and sheath, 312.
  cryptorchids, or ridgelings, 321, 343.
  dourine, 340.
  excessive venery, 315.
  external injuries to, 310.
  foul sheath, 318, 345.
  inflammation of the penis, 311, 345.
  inflammation of the testicles, 311, 335.
  mal du coit, 340.
  masturbation, 319, 340.
  non-emission, or "proudness," 316.
  paralysis of the penis, 312, 339.
  sarcocele, 337.
  scrotal hernia, 313.
  sexual sluggishness, 317.
  spermatic cord, tumors on the, 346.
  spermatorrhœa, 319.
  sterility, causes of, 347.
  varicocele, 338.
  vesicular eruption of the penis, 318.
  waterbag, so-called, 315.
Stallions, brood mares and foals, 83.
Stallions, controlling, when in use, 114.
  aversion of to mare, how remedied, 121.
  bridle for described, 114.
  condition for the stud, 104.
  danger from overfeeding, 110.
  effect of castration on, 138.
  effect of age, 126.
  exercise for, 106.
  fighting, 141.

Stallions, management of, 104.
   management of the, after season closes, 135.
   nostrums not good for, 104.
   number of mares to be served by, 121.
   should not be drugged, 104.
   stalls for, 108.
   superior to mares and geldings in courage, 138.
   sureness of not affected by number of mares served, 121.
   teaching to mount, 114.
Starving process condemned, 165.
Statistics of breeding, 133.
Sterility, causes of, 145, 347.
Strangles, or distemper, 306.
Suffolk Punch, 288.
   type of the (illustration), 289.
Sugar, effect of on the eye, 298.
Superimpregnation, 327.
Sure stallion, what is a, 132.

Tartary, the horses of, 185.
Teaching the foal to drink, 160.
Teasing by the stallion, 119.
Teeth, effect of on the eye, 298.
   age indicated by, 404.
Testicles, inflammation of the, 311.
Theories of sex production, 82.
Thoroughbreds, 188.
   hardiness of, 57.
   in America, 202.
   type of the (illustration), 189.
Time of foaling, 154.
Trotters and roadsters, 205.

Trotters, Orloff, 233.
Trotter, type of the (illustration), 207.
Trotting blood, foundation for, 215.
Trying mares, 118.
Tufted-tailed horses, 186.
Tumors, vaginal and uterine, 324.
Turkey, horses of, 185.
Turner, G. T., on Cleveland Bays, 244.

Udder, inflamed, 178, 401.
   the, as a sign of parturition, 156.
Umbilical hernia, 300.
Unnatural presentation, 386.
Uterine tumors, 324.

Vaginal and uterine tumors, 324.
Variations, accidental, 28, 29.
Value of pedigree, 59.
Venery, excessive, 315.
Violent crosses, effect of, 44.

Waterbag in stallions, 315.
Weaning the foal, 162.
White horses of Persia and Syria, 187.
Wild horses, various types of, 184.
Wolf teeth, 299.
Womb, closure of the, 148.
   sympathetic excitement of, 150.
Working brood mares, 162, 167, 170.
   stallions, 106.
Worms in the intestines, 305.
Wroot's Pretender, 248.

Young mares should not be bred, 177.
   stallions, number of mares to be served by, 122.

www.ingramcontent.com/pod-product-compliance
Lightning Source LLC
Chambersburg PA
CBHW051736300426
44115CB00007B/584